TRAITOR'S ODYSSEY

TRAITOR'S ODYSSEY

The Untold Story of Martha Dodd and a Strange Saga of Soviet Espionage

BRENDAN McNALLY

ICON

To Absent Friends

Published in the UK in 2024 by
Icon Books Ltd, Omnibus Business Centre,
39–41 North Road, London N7 9DP
email: info@iconbooks.com
www.iconbooks.com

ISBN: 978-183773-032-2
eBook: 978-183773-074-2

Typeset by SJmagic DESIGN SERVICES, India

Printed and bound in the UK

CONTENTS

PREFACE

I first learned about Martha Dodd during the summer of 1992. I was living in Prague and writing for one of the two 'American' newspapers which had popped up following the end of communist rule two-and-a-half years earlier. I had gone there because, for some reason, covering the Pentagon for industry newsletters was suddenly no longer fun or, for that matter, going anywhere. I knew if I was ever going to fulfill my dream of working abroad as a 'foreign correspondent', I'd either have to do it now or go and do what most of the people I'd worked with had already done and go into public relations. So I went.

It was in July or August, during what the Czechs call 'Cucumber Season', when absolutely nothing was going on. Everyone in Prague was at their summer houses, tending their gardens and sitting around their campfires at night, drinking wine, roasting sausages and singing songs. It oddly didn't matter that Czechoslovakia, their nation, was at that moment being split apart. It didn't matter because it was summer and everybody was on holiday. But the newspaper wasn't on holiday and neither was I, at least not if I intended to eat during the following month. I needed to find some stories to report.

The *Prague Post* had its offices one block off of Wenceslas Square in a run-down, five-storey building, which was now headquarters for what remained of the Communist Party. Being now just a shadow of its former self, the Party had vacant office space they were willing to rent out to anybody with dollars or deutschmarks. We had a corridor with windows on one side looking out onto the courtyard.

At the end was a large room used by the editors and advertising people. One door up from it was a small room with windows that looked out onto the side of a building, a bank of computers taking up half the wall, where it met with a bank of eight-foot wooden cabinets, half with bookshelves and drawers and where everyone kept their coats and bags. Occupying the center of the room was a rectangular wooden table with six chairs and a single red plastic telephone. This was where the freelancers worked.

At any given moment during the day, there'd be five or six of us sitting around the table with the red phone and one of the translators, taking turns calling different ministries and offices, hoping the translator could connect us and line up interviews for stories we were working on. On rare occasions, the person on the other end might directly answer questions the translator posed, but usually they'd want us to come to their offices and talk with them over coffee. This was, after all, Central Europe.

The freelancers would get their story ideas either by listening to the translators read out relevant articles they'd picked from Czech newspapers, which happened each morning at nine, or by combing the papers themselves and looking for interesting items and then getting them translated for us. If something sounded promising, we'd copy down the particulars, run it by the editor and then go to the big table with the red plastic telephone, wait our turn and try our luck. To call the process Darwinian would be an understatement. Most freelancers were gone after a day or a week. But some developed a feel for it and stayed on.

The translators were mostly kids; students or just out, and mostly, but not always from Prague. Running them was Dora Slaba, an old lady with a British accent who spoke many languages and was the head of research at the *Prague Post*. Not everyone liked Dora. Some said she was two-faced and backhanded and unfairly played favorites among the reporters, canning translators whenever she felt like it. One whom Dora fired told me afterwards he was sure Dora was StB. He might have been right. He'd grown up in Canada and said he'd learned to spot them at his dad's printing plant back in Toronto, which was staffed entirely by emigres. There was a saying I'd heard a couple of the older Press Club-types say: 'Never trust anyone who speaks English,' and there was a certain amount of truth to it. Me, I could never figure any of it out, but Dora was always nice to me, maybe because she enjoyed the questions I would throw at her. She also liked the Chinese girl from Harvard and the kid from Philadelphia who was also a busker on Charles Bridge.

That morning in question, Petra was the translator at the table. Petra had dyed-black hair and was a skate punk. Her father, it later turned out, was in the Communist Party Central Committee. But that morning Petra was my only means to get an interview. I explained that the guy I needed to talk to was with the Agricultural Chamber, the professional organisation of farmers. I held the phone and carefully punched in the number, then listened to it ring. When someone on the other end picked up, I said 'moment, prosim' and handed the phone to Petra, who then rattled off something to the guy on the other end, then paused as she listened to what he had to say. Then, putting her hand over the mouthpiece, she told me he'd said that if I wanted to come over to his office at two, he could talk to me for twenty minutes, but that I'd need a translator since he didn't speak English. Petra indicated she could do it for me, so I was all set. I got up from the table and let someone else take my chair, as I went to find the business editor.

Noon came and Petra went off to lunch. By 1.45, she still hadn't returned. I mentioned it to Dora. She looked at the clock and asked where the interview was. When I told her between Wenceslas and Vodickova, four minutes away on foot, Dora decided she'd do it. So we went.

The head of the Agricultural Chamber said he didn't know where Czech agriculture was heading, but he knew what the key issues and the challenges were. Dora translated as he spoke and I scribbled everything down as best I could. When it was over and we'd said goodbye and were making our way back to the office, I knew I had most of what I needed for a story. It would not be anything special, but it would feed me and keep me in beer for a while.

As we crossed Wenceslas, I noticed a McDonald's had just opened a few doors up from the bottom of the square. There was even a fenced-off area set up with outside tables. Feeling expansive, I asked Dora if she'd let me buy her a Big Mac. I could tell the idea amused her on a number of levels. Still, she hesitated. 'Come on,

Dora,' I said. 'Let's live a little!' Dora shook her head, rolled her eyes and gave a what-the-hell shrug.

I ordered us both Big Mac meals, and as we carried our trays outside, Dora commented that her two grandchildren had been badgering her to take them to the McDonald's on Vodickova, which, coincidentally, had opened on the same day I'd arrived. As we sat down at one of the outside tables, Dora observed, half-sarcastically, that it was 'just like a café on a Parisian boulevard'. With that in mind, she was suddenly in no hurry to eat up and go quickly back to the office. Instead, we spent nearly an hour there at our rickety table, leisurely chatting over our trays of empty food wrappers. Dora asked me what it was like being an industry reporter at the Pentagon, saying that it all sounded very exciting. It wasn't, I told her, and explained how my time had mainly been spent reporting 'programmatics', like the Navy's UYS-2 Enhanced Modular Signal Processor, and the SQQ-89 sonar and a dozen other new systems that all depended on the UYS-2 to work. As I expected, her eyes glazed over, so I changed the subject and asked, innocuously, how she'd come by her British accent. Was she English or Czech?

Dora explained that she wasn't a Czech at all, but a Jew from what had once been called the Sudetenland and that her first language was German. In her hometown of Usti nad Labem, besides her family and the tiny handful of Jews living there, everyone else was a Nazi. She was six when the Nazis came in and took over. Because her father had a business partner in London, her family were able to flee to England, where they ended up spending the war. Dora loved their time in England, stayed afterward and might have stayed permanently, had it not been for the Communist coup in Czechoslovakia in February 1948: Dora's mother, who had gone socialist, declared they must return to Czechoslovakia and be part of the revolution. So they went back. It was a big mistake. Their home was blown up and flattened along with everything else in Usti. Everyone they'd ever known there, Jew or Nazi, was gone – dead or expelled. They found the revolution that was taking place extremely unappealing. People didn't like them for being both German and Jewish. They tried to go back to England, but found they couldn't. They were stuck.

They settled in Prague; her parents found jobs and somewhere to live. Dora and her sister went to school, took crash courses in

Czech and became fluent. By the time she got into university, she was already working part-time doing announcing and other voice-work for Radio Prague's English-language service. Then it became full-time. She did that for fifteen years, from the early 1950s until the mid to late 1960s. Even though the job paid the same as everyone else's, it came with numerous benefits, so by all standards, she was doing a little better than some people, but certainly nothing to show off about.

Dora said that for most of the 1950s, everything was pretty harsh with all the show trials, and all the denunciations and witch-hunts of communists against communists. Many were tried and executed, a lot of them Jews. Dora kept her head down and didn't overreach or offend anyone. Stalin died. Shortly thereafter so did Klement Gottwald. He was replaced by a succession of colourless leaders and things became gradually less harsh. The secret police and the goons were still around, but as time passed the chest-beating faded away. It was mainly a question of keeping your mouth shut, and not going around asking any questions. And Dora did that very ably until one day in August of 1968.

Dora told me she'd always thought the Prague Spring was going to be trouble. It had been obvious from the beginning that the big boys in Moscow didn't like it and weren't going to put up with it for very long. Above almost everything, communist bosses do not like anybody challenging them on anything, and the Czechs, with their flowers and talk of love and free speech and 'socialism with a human face', were doing just that. They knew if they let the Czechs get away with it, it would spread like mould to Poland and Hungary and East Germany, then, what, Bulgaria, Romania, Ukraine, Belarus? Russia itself? The republics? You began to understand that the people in charge were thugs and goons, and that thugs and goons all act the same way to anyone weaker challenging them. They come down hard. And they did.

She remembered looking out the window of her flat in the middle of the night and seeing an endless stream of two-engine aircraft roaring overhead, obviously flying into Ruzyne airport, which was normally shut down at that hour. The aircraft were Russian, filled with assault troops, along with jeeps and light tanks. At the same time, thousands of Russian, Polish, Hungarian and Bulgarian tanks along with hundreds of thousands of soldiers were pouring into Czechoslovakia, all believing they were there to liberate their Czech and Slovak brothers and sisters from the clutches of the capitalist revisionists.

Dora told me how she turned on the radio and what she heard on the air was her colleagues, broadcasting news of the Soviet invasion as it was happening to them. Her colleagues. Dora was shocked. Everybody she worked with at Radio Prague had spent their professional careers doing what she did: toeing the party line on everything, keeping their heads down and not doing anything that might get them into trouble, written up and sent down to the labour office for reassignment more suitable for malcontents. Now they were reporting from the barricades and manning microphones in all the different studios in different languages, telling the world what was happening in Czechoslovakia; how the people were protesting and how crowds of civilians were standing up to the tanks.

Dora knew what she had to do. She got dressed, kissed her husband and daughter goodbye and walked down the Zizkov, past all the people, the tanks and the Russian and Bulgarian soldiers, and up Wenceslas Square, over to Radio Prague's offices and studios. For three days Dora read the news in German, English and Russian. For some reason the Russians hadn't located their offices, even though they had tanks and troops on the street outside their door. Eventually they wised up, but by then Dora and some others drove out in a borrowed Skoda to a remote emergency broadcasting site, which the Russians also didn't know about, where they continued broadcasting for another day. When they knew the Russians were coming for them, they all fled. Dora and two others drove the Skoda to the German border, where they walked across. A couple of days later, refugee passport in hand, Dora Slaba found herself back in London.

But it was not the London she remembered. The Cold War had changed it in unimaginable ways. The best job she could get was teaching French in a girls' school. After two years, she'd had enough and went back to Prague. They'd promised her she could have her job back at Radio Prague if she returned. It lasted a week. The following Monday, Dora was told her position had been cancelled and she was sent down to the Labour Ministry for reassignment.

Dora was sent to a basement office at the Czech Academy of Sciences where she spent the next fifteen years as an English language tutor for members of the academy needing to publish, or deliver speeches, in English. It was, in Dora's opinion, the lowest of the low. There was a crying need for fluent English and German speakers and writers in state trading companies and other groups. But Dora was not considered 'politically reliable', so she remained a tutor of moss-backed academicians.

'And that's what you did until now?' I asked.

For a moment I thought she would just say 'yes', that that was her life since 1968. Then there was a pause. Dora looked at me like she had a question she wasn't sure she wanted to ask. Then she asked me if I'd ever heard of an American writer named Martha Dodd.

I told her I hadn't and asked who she was. Dora replied that she wasn't sure, only that she had been a writer and journalist who'd written some bestsellers, and that she had lived in Prague for a long time before her death just two years earlier. I frowned and told Dora that she didn't sound like anyone I'd heard of. Why? Dora answered that she'd been her secretary for a while just before the Revolution. That struck me as odd. I hadn't thought that outside of embassy staff and the like there were any Americans at all living there during the Cold War. Dora informed me that there had been a handful living in Prague. So you worked for her? Yes, for about a year and a half. What was that like? She lived in a villa in Prague 5. She was very old, rich, widowed, and had servants. Servants? Really? I didn't think that sort of thing was allowed under communism. Dora made a gesture somewhere between a grimace and a smile, and the subject changed to something else. As we walked back to the paper, I remember thinking to myself that I ought to look into this whole thing sometime, but by the time we got back to the office it was already forgotten about. I'm sure it never crossed my mind once during the next six years. It was a very busy time.

Eventually, I went back to Dallas and for the next few years I wrote for different magazines and started writing books. I was researching a slapstick comedy set in Nazi Germany during the final days of the Third Reich. Most of it took place during the three-week period immediately after Hitler blew his brains out. It was something I'd done much research on years earlier. The internet had since come into existence and by now there was enough up there that I could do a good amount of research online … and that's where I stumbled across Martha.

If memory serves me, the name of the website had been something like 'Hot Babes of the Third Reich'. Mostly it was girl-friends and wives of various Nazi bigwigs: Eva Braun, Magda Goebbels, Leni Riefenstahl, Hanna Reitsch, Hermann Goering's first and second wives and Heinrich Himmler's mistress, along with numerous actresses. And there she was, among them all: Martha Dodd, the American woman Dora had worked for right before the 1989 Revolution. It had her listed as mistress of Ernst Udet, the famous dive-bomber ace, playboy and one-time Hollywood stunt pilot. But then it also turned out she had been girlfriend of the head of the Gestapo. It didn't stop there. She was also known to have slept with more Nazi generals and more high Nazi functionaries than could be listed. It mentioned that Martha Dodd had even briefly dated Hitler. Her father had been the American Ambassador, appointed by FDR early in his presidency, before the threat Hitler posed was fully understood. It noted that after cutting a wide swath among the young Nazi blades in Berlin, Martha Dodd surprised everybody by falling madly in love with a Soviet diplomat she'd met, and in the course of it got recruited as a spy for Moscow. When she returned to America, she wrote two bestsellers about her time in Germany. She married a millionaire whom she subsequently recruited. Together, they were part of a Soviet spy ring operating in America during the Second World War. It went on to say that somehow the FBI got wind of their activities and put them under surveillance, which went on for years. Even so, she and her husband managed to slip away from the FBI, not once, but twice, and both times with all their money, which was how they ended up in Prague, where they lived for 30 more years until their deaths. So Martha Dodd, the American woman Dora had worked for, was a Soviet spy who had gone to ground!

It's funny, but during the six years I was reporting from Prague, I spent surprisingly little time dealing with the Cold War, even though my reporting often put me in front of spooks, StB, and old communists of every sort. Its legacies were always there, but that was different. We were focused on the here and now, and not on sorting out the past. Getting to the bottom of Cold War mysteries was a sure-fire means of going broke and starving to death.

I sold my book about post-Hitler Nazi Germany and made enough money from it to allow my wife and I to move back to Prague for a couple years. I managed to hunt down Dora Slaba and ask her what she remembered about her old boss. Dora told me she remembered everything. Oh? Did she know about Martha's time in Berlin? No. Did she know about Martha dating Hitler? No. Did she know about her dating the head of the Gestapo? No. Did she know about her being a Soviet spy? No. Each time she said it like none of it particularly surprised her.

Then I asked Dora if she had ever thought of asking her why she was living in Prague. At this, Dora's voice took on a sad, pitying tone. 'Brendan,' she said, 'that was a question you just didn't ask. You didn't even wonder. That was how Communism worked.'

'Tell me what you remember about her.'

There was a long pause and then Dora started telling me of her time with her. I'll never forget the way she began:

'She was a bitch.'

1. THE FLYING HAMBURGER

Back in Chicago, the *Tribune*'s foreign editor had told Martha that, with the Nazis now in power, she could forget about Berlin's legendary social scene. It was dead. As a result, when they packed for the move, Martha and her mother brought only a few of their gowns and dresses. They also didn't bring any furniture or household items with them, which diplomats normally did, so the small amount of baggage the Dodds brought aboard the SS *Washington* made them seem more like tourists than the family of a US ambassador travelling to a new duty station.

They did, however, bring along the family car, a not-new Chevrolet. Martha's father, William E. Dodd, simple, resolutely unadorned man that he was, cringed at the thought of being seen riding inside any of the grand limousines which the embassy kept for the ambassador's use. His idea was that, whenever there might be an official function to attend, he'd use the Chevvy with his son, Bill Jr, acting as chauffer. One of the points Dodd had stipulated to President Roosevelt when he'd offered him the ambassadorship was that he be allowed to live within his salary. FDR agreed right off, like it went without saying. But then, hadn't he been the one who had said his reason for sending a Jeffersonian Democrat like Dodd to Berlin was so that Hitler and the Nazis would see what America was about?

The Chevvy was at that moment in the ship's hold, and once they were docked and passenger disembarkation was underway, a dockside crane would lift it out and set it gently down on the pier.

They'd load it up and Bill Jr would drive it down to Berlin to their hotel. Then Dodd and some embassy bigwig named Gordon would go off together on some special train called 'The Flying Hamburger' for a briefing on 'the political situation', which needed to be discussed right away and in private. As for Martha and her mother, there'd be people from the embassy who'd come up with Gordon and would get them on the regular train, and they'd all travel down to Berlin together.

Her father's appointment had caught everyone in Chicago by surprise, since no one in the Cook County political machine had ever heard of him. All anyone knew was William E. Dodd, a Chicago Democrat, university professor, eminent historian and apparently one of President Roosevelt's personal friends, had been appointed ambassador to Berlin and FDR's personal envoy to Adolf Hitler! Since no one knew who the Dodds were, it didn't take much for the Chicago papers to grab the few available facts and concoct an engaging and acceptable narrative. The Dodds were an All-American family: *Mom, Dad, Buddy and Sis off to Berlin to show Mr Hitler just what America is all about.* It worked. Readers ate it up. But then, strangely, the story got picked up by the papers in other cities,[1] so by the time the Dodds reached New York, they discovered they were celebrities. When they boarded their ship, the SS *Washington*, the next morning, there was a crowd of people, mostly strangers, gathered at the dock to see them off, along with numerous press photographers. As the lines were cast off and the ship's screws began churning the water, some of the photographers, seeing the Dodds looking down from the rail, shouted at them to wave goodbye for the cameras. The Dodds obliged and the photographers snapped their picture. The shot that made the papers appeared to show the new ambassador and his family giving 'Heil Hitler' salutes. But as the ship headed out of New York Harbor and into the Atlantic, a calm finally came over everything and the Dodds' brush with celebrity was ended.

The voyage from New York lasted nine days. The whole time the sea was calm and for Dodd, it was a time of quiet reflection about what lay ahead. He hadn't used his German in years and now, in an effort to quickly regain his former fluency, he had his wife and children sit with him in his stateroom for an hour or two each morning while he read aloud to them in German. The rest of the time he spent going through the thick sheaf of reports and briefing documents which the State Department had prepared for him.

As for Martha, for the first two days at sea she 'wept copiously and sentimentally' for things and people she'd never come back to. There was the comfortable, if anonymous, middle-class existence which the Dodds had led up until then, and for Martha, there were the many friends and more than a few lovers, and even, it turned out, a husband she hadn't quite gotten around to telling her parents about. There was also her job as Assistant Books Editor at the *Chicago Tribune*, a plum position she'd only recently started but had already grown bored with.

As for what lay ahead, Martha had no idea, either. Her life's dream had always been to be a famous writer, and even though she was now, officially speaking, a newspaperwoman, she'd never had any interest in journalism. As for all that was going on in Germany, Martha had given it very little thought. Her interests lay in literature and poetry, not politics. It didn't matter that she'd grown up in an intellectually vibrant household, alive with endless spirited discussions about history, politics and economics, none of it particularly interesting to her. Hitler was, to Martha, little more than 'a clown who looked like Charlie Chaplin... who burned books and had set up a dictatorship'.[2]

Martha's basic indifference to world affairs and the situation in Nazi Germany was largely lost on the poet Carl Sandburg, one of her father's closest friends and, apparently, one of Martha's occasional lovers, who extolled her to 'find out what this man Hitler is made of, what makes his brain go round, what his bones and brains are made of!'[3] What Martha made of Sandburg's sage advice at the time is not known. For her, it was enough that she was going on an adventure abroad in a faraway, exotic place, and at the same time extracting herself from her secret marriage and other personal complications, which she hoped might then sort themselves out without any great participation on her own part.

It wasn't that she no longer loved the man she'd married. She did love him, but it had been done on a whim a year earlier. She loved him just as she loved other men too, and with all of them, she blew hot and then cold. Mostly Martha loved the art of pursuit and of being pursued. But much as Martha loved men, there were never any whose company she preferred over her father's and no place she'd rather be than with her family.

After two days, Martha's weeping ended and once again she was ready for fun. Franklin Delano Roosevelt Jr, the President's son, was also aboard, on his way to spend a summer in France. He fit the bill perfectly for a shipboard playmate. They danced, they drank. If it went beyond that, neither mentioned it afterwards. When the SS *Washington* docked at Le Havre, she got off with him and walked with him to the train station before returning to the ship.

⁂

While Martha claimed to have had 'not the faintest idea of anti-Semitism. in either its mild or vicious forms',[4] prior to entering university, the same could not be said of her father. William E. Dodd considered himself a liberal democrat, but only in the 'Jeffersonian' sense. His interest and sympathies were with the 'yeomanry': farmers who worked their own smallholdings with, at most, the help of a hired hand or two. These and the mechanics and tradesmen who supported them and made an agrarian economy possible was what he cared about. Dodd opposed slavery, not so much because of its inhumanity as its inherent inefficiency. Unlike many Southerners, Dodd professed no warm feelings for Black people, or for the teeming ethnic masses who lived in cities and toiled in factories. A perfect America was, in Dodd's mind, one peopled by men and women from the British Isles and northern Europe. This was particularly so for the Jews. Dodd's anti-Semitism was of the mild, socially acceptable form. He probably didn't have it in him to be mean to Jews, or vicious. While he read the reports in the newspapers of what the Nazis were doing to Jews in Germany, he mostly took a dim view of those reports, just as he had of the entreaties of different Jewish leaders he'd had meetings with in the days before his departure. If there was any truth to it, Dodd couldn't help but believe it was something they'd probably brought on themselves.

⁂

When the SS *Washington* reached Hamburg on the morning of 13 July 1933, a crowd of Germans and Americans were there on the United States Lines terminal pier after traveling up from Berlin to greet, or at least get a glimpse of, the new American Ambassador and his family. Many brought flowers, though probably no one there had ever met or seen the Dodds before this. They'd come because the arrival of a new American Ambassador was a very big deal. Sackett, the last ambassador, had been extremely popular, and in a city that viewed itself as 'almost-American', he was seen as a sort of spiritual godfather. With all that was going on with Hitler and the Brown-shirts, people couldn't help but wonder whether this new ambassador might have the same kind of magic as his predecessor. Everyone hoped so, but some had their doubts.

Among the crowd was a small delegation of embassy staff, headed by George Anderson Gordon, the notoriously tightly wound Counselor, and Ambassador Dodd's soon to be chief subordinate. In Gordon's mind, the success or failure of the new ambassador's mission rested in no small way on how well he listened to and did what Gordon told him. As political appointees went, Frederick Sackett had been close to perfect, even though he couldn't speak German and knew next to nothing about the country. Ultimately, none of that mattered, because Sackett knew how to listen, especially to his experts and advisors. Not that he always did as they suggested, but at least he operated on the information with which he'd been furnished. It wasn't surprising, since he'd previously been a Republican Senator from Kentucky and a business tycoon before that, so Sackett knew all about dealing with people of all kinds and giving them a good face. And that was something the Germans had needed, after the years of war and economic and political disruption.

But Sackett had been far more than just a good listener and a friendly face. President Hoover had sent him to do everything he could to bolster the democratic Weimar government and Heinrich Brüning, its Chancellor, and to make sure the German government didn't stop making interest payments on the massive loans it had taken out from all those American banks, which were themselves on the verge of going under. In this, he had been quite successful, right up until the end of January when the democratic government finally collapsed and that gutter politician Hitler became Chancellor.

By then, of course, Sackett was already on his way out, following Hoover's defeat to Franklin Roosevelt in the 1932 presidential elections that November. While Hoover was in the White House and Germany remained a democracy, Sackett did everything he could to keep it that way. He shelled out plenty from his own pocket, which was of course one of the requirements for the post. But Sackett had no intention of shelling out in support of Franklin Roosevelt, especially not if the recipients were going to be a bunch of Nazis. Sackett remained at his post another month following Roosevelt's inauguration, but once it became clear no one in Washington had any idea when a replacement might be coming, Sacket folded up his tent and went home.

Oh, but the man had style! Once, Sackett and his wife put on an afternoon tea in which they'd served lobster. Lobster! It made the evening papers, something Gordon personally took a dim view of. But it paid off because people were still talking about it.

After Sackett left, for the next four months, George Messersmith, the Consul General for Germany, sat in the ambassador's chair, and during that time seemed to do all he could to drive Hitler crazy. Messersmith had never made a secret of despising Hitler and this was something he was free to do, because unlike Sackett or Gordon or anyone else associated with the chancellery, he was consular and not so bound by protocol. Hitler knew he couldn't complain to the ambassador about Messersmith, because Messersmith was the ambassador. Hitler, being a bully, avoided confrontation unless he already knew he'd come out on top. He knew Messersmith was a vicious little terrier who'd relish the opportunity to show him what for.

George Gordon and George Messersmith. Depending on how you chose to look at it, they were either complete opposites or simply cut from different ends of the same cloth. George Gordon was a Harvard-educated Alabama aristocrat, tall, with a formidable mustache that matched his bearing, and a temperament that varied between 'difficult' and 'explosive'. Still, he was a keen observer and analyst, highly respected by those who read his reports. Messersmith was also considered difficult. In later years, there would be a saying that there were only two types of Foreign Service Officers: those who'd heard George Messersmith was an ogre to work for and those who knew it for a fact! Messersmith was a harsh, vindictive and petty taskmaster, something he'd apparently picked up teaching in rural, one-room Delaware schoolhouses.

Unlike Gordon, who had been born of wealth and attended the finest schools, Messersmith, a Pennsylvania Dutchman, grew up in poverty. Unable to afford university, he went instead for a teaching certificate and within a few years had gone from teaching in a one-room schoolhouse to being assistant superintendent for Delaware's public schools. Then, one day, he surprised everyone by joining the State Department's consular service. His first post was a mostly disused border crossing in Fort Erie, Ontario. Then the First World War erupted in Europe and Messersmith was reassigned to Curacao in the Caribbean. Being Dutch and therefore neutral, Curacao was a hotbed of spy activity and Messersmith soon found himself drawn into it. At one point he was approached by what he called 'a disreputable young German-American man', who was actually an American double agent requiring his help in busting a spy ring, since, as it turned out, Messersmith had a natural skill in breaking codes. After the war, Messersmith bounced between posts in northern Europe and South America before being appointed Consul General for Germany, the Consular Service's highest post.

While Gordon confined his interactions to Germany's uppermost political circles, Messersmith spoke with absolutely everyone else. Ogre as he might have been to work for, outside the office George Messersmith was an affable fellow whom people were naturally drawn to. Kings, generals, businessmen and clerks found him easy to confide in, which was fortunate, since Messersmith had also been born with his ear to the ground. For all their apparent differences, in the end, when it was time to write reports and draw conclusions, the ones Gordon and Messersmith reached were about the same: that Hitler and the Nazis were the real, immediate threat, not the communists and socialists as Washington insisted. Hitler was not simply a flash in the pan. Hitler meant everything he said about the Jews and what he would do to them. Hitler would kill them and anyone else who got in his way. And he would start another world war. Anyone who thought it was just political posturing was wrong.

Now, standing with all the others on the dock, watching the large ship approach, Gordon must have wondered, like everyone else, why Roosevelt had picked him for the job. Dodd was just a history professor with neither the stature nor the means to do it properly. Berlin was, after all, a 'millionaire's post'. When Hoover asked Sackett to take the post, Sackett knew in advance he'd be continually shelling out on banquets and receptions. So why Dodd? He obviously didn't have money. What had the new President been thinking?

And what was he doing coming with two adult children in tow? In Gordon's world, adult children didn't accompany their parents on foreign postings. They had lives of their own. Dodd's son and daughter were both in their late twenties and unmarried. Apparently the son was also an academic, with what looked like two one-year teaching appointments, neither of which had been renewed. Why? Then there was the daughter. Martha Eccles Dodd was twenty-five and had studied poetry and literature at the University of Chicago without graduating. She had been working at the *Chicago Tribune*, but quit to be with her parents. This couldn't have looked good in Gordon's eyes, being someone who undoubtedly took a dim view of unmarried women in their mid-twenties, or 'career women' of any age and, most of all, anyone in the press.

Gordon had already exchanged many cables with Dodd, but still wasn't sure how well he grasped the current situation. If Dodd did, he would listen to what Gordon told him. He needed to understand that in the world of diplomats, protocol was paramount; that you didn't just do things because they felt right at the moment. Everything had to be measured, and there had to be a strict delineation of whom one talked and did not talk with. An ambassador had to limit his contacts to the uppermost circles of power: to the Head of State and the Head of Government. That meant the President, the Chancellor, and, if applicable, the Vice-Chancellor, but that was it.

Gordon had made it clear to Sackett that talking to the opposition parties was not part of his job – 'opposition', of course, meaning Hitler. Of course Sackett went anyway, but at least he waited until Gordon was away. A secret meeting with Hitler[5] was set up. The idea apparently was for it to be a 'meeting of the minds', where Sackett and Hitler would spend a couple of hours together, getting to know each other and examining ideas. In the end, all Sackett got was Hitler ranting, like he was addressing a crowd of several thousand, not pausing, even once, for the translator to catch up or even asking a question. Sackett left, two hours later, certain of one thing: Adolf Hitler was a dangerous nut, who must never be allowed to ever take power.[6]

Of course, now that Hitler was Chancellor, Dodd would be required to meet him. Hopefully there'd be no need for a second meeting. Hopefully it wouldn't be long before Hitler got booted and replaced by someone else. Brüning would be ideal. Sackett had worked with him quite closely for years. No reason to think a Brüning–Dodd partnership wouldn't work. Again, it was mainly just a question of this Professor Dodd listening to what Gordon said. And of course, they would also have to find a way of getting Brüning or even one of the others back in power.

'The others' meant the other previous chancellors: General Kurt von Schleicher, and Franz von Papen, currently Hitler's Vice-Chancellor and Prussian Premier. To consider either of them as being on the side of the angels required far more naïveté than Gordon possessed. Both were arch intriguers and opportunists, whose endless cynical machinations had inadvertently gotten Hitler into power in the first place. After Brüning, they were the best Germany could hope for, and if working with either of them was how you got rid of Hitler, then it might well be necessary. Von Schleicher and von Papen were among the top items Gordon planned to discuss with Dodd during their first briefing. They would need at least an hour alone without any interruption and Gordon had a plan for achieving this: the Flying Hamburger

The 'Flying Hamburger', or 'Fliegender Hamburger', was a high-speed diesel-electric train which had just started running between Berlin and Hamburg that spring. It consisted of just two streamlined coaches, each with its own engine, and was capable of reaching speeds of up to 100 mph, making it the fastest train in the world. He'd suggested it to Dodd during their continual exchange of cables, even informing him, in case he didn't know, that the ship's purser could make the necessary arrangements. He presented the idea to Dodd in a telegram and Dodd readily agreed to it.[7] So that was all set. All he had to do was go to the ship's purser and buy himself a ticket. Yes, he and Dodd would ride the Flying Hamburger and Mrs Dodd and her children and the rest of the embassy delegation would ride together on the regular train.

Then there was the matter of a residence for the Dodds. As there was no official ambassador's residence at the time, the assumption was that Dodd would continue doing as Sackett had done and live at one of the city's top hotels – either the Adlon, the Bristol, or the Esplanade. But Dodd, it turned out, wanted no part of luxury hotels, insisting, as Messersmith put it, that 'he wished to have modest quarters in a modest hotel'.[8] Messersmith and Gordon knew this was not realistic. 'Mr. Dodd was a man of very exaggerated ideas about the way an Ambassador should live,' wrote Messersmith years later. 'He felt that he should live most inconspicuously and modestly. While I understood this and how he felt about it, I knew that the German officials and German people would not understand it.'[9]

Being friends with managers from several of the city's leading hotels, Messersmith suggested Gordon leave this matter to him. Messersmith then contacted the manager of the Esplanade who, eager for the added prestige, offered a deal so friendly that it was practically free.[10] Messersmith figured Dodd would be pleased.

⚜

Gordon hoped that riding together aboard the world's fastest train, Dodd would grasp what Gordon needed to tell him about how Hitler had turned a democratic republic into a full-fledged dictatorship; how less than a month after being named Chancellor, someone, probably one of Hitler's thugs, set fire to the Reichstag and burned it down, giving Hitler all the pretext he needed to declare an emergency, suspend key sections of the constitution, give police powers to his Brownshirts, and then arrest communist and other opposition members of parliament. In just a couple of deft moves, Hitler dismantled rule by law. Weimar democracy was dead. The Brownshirts, who were now auxiliary police, went about beating up Jews and anyone they considered insufficiently enthusiastic about the new Nazi regime. They'd set up secret impromptu jails, often in empty apartments or in abandoned factories. People would disappear from the streets and be taken to them. If they were lucky, they might reappear days or weeks later, dazed, beaten, naked or in rags. Other times they'd be found floating in the canals. But just as often, they'd never be seen again. And now with the summer holiday season in full swing, American tourists were occasionally catching the Brownshirts' wrath. When it happened, often as not the German police stood around, doing nothing.

Telling him this might jolt Dodd into understanding that he was no longer just a university professor but a diplomat, the President of the United States' personal envoy to a madman bent on dragging the world back into war.

Again, it was mainly a question of what Dodd wanted, and in a few minutes, Gordon supposed, he would start finding out what that was.

❧

The big ship sidled up to the dock, aided by the harbor tugs. Lines were thrown down, fore and aft, from the main deck, looped around the mooring posts on the dock and then drawn taut. The gangway was attached and the large hull door opened; the passengers began disembarking. As the Dodds descended the gangway, the press photographers' flashbulbs began popping. The crowd cheered and waved their flower bouquets at them. While Dodd and his wife seemed to take it all with a good-natured, if slightly bewildered, grain of salt, Martha reveled in it. Celebrity fit Martha Dodd perfectly. She felt the spotlight on her and knew it was where she belonged.

But then, just as they stepped off the gangway onto the pier, a man came forward to greet them, a tall, stiff, almost comical figure, with, as Martha would later describe him, 'gray-white hair and mustache which looked curled, elegant dress, gloves, stick and proper hat, complexion of flaming hue, clipped, polite and a definitely condescending accent … a gentleman of the most extreme protocol'.[11] It was Gordon, stiff and formal as an 18th-century courtier, with the rest of the embassy delegation behind him.

Dodd responded the way he did to anything reeking of pomp and classism: with his farmer's puncturing informality. Martha and Bill Jr may have giggled or burst into outright laughter, or just stood there fighting back silly grins as Gordon addressed them with his ridiculous formality.

History is not supposed to deal in 'what ifs'. It's still hard not to wonder how different things might have turned out had the Dodds managed to muster up some gravitas for the occasion. Perhaps then their relations with Gordon and the rest of the embassy staff might not have been permanently poisoned for the four-and-a-half years that Dodd spent as ambassador. But the Dodds could not, and left Gordon so offended that 'his rage almost – not quite – transcended the bounds allowed by his rigid code of behavior'.[12]

Everything about the Dodds seemed to exasperate Gordon: from their flippant informality to the miniscule amount of luggage they brought, the decidedly modest Chevrolet they'd insisted on bringing, and Dodd's painfully earnest intention of using it instead of the embassy limousines – and then having his son be his chauffer. Only after the car had been lowered down onto the dock and the customs official started examining it, did it emerge that Dodd hadn't bothered acquiring any of the licences or permits necessary for operating automobiles in Germany. He had simply assumed its Illinois registration and plates were enough. Keeping his explosive anger in check, Gordon managed to prevail upon some customs officials and got them to issue a temporary waiver allowing Bill Jr to drive the automobile down to Berlin.

But then, once Gordon had that problem solved, he learned Dodd hadn't bought tickets for the Flying Hamburger. Through an apparent miscommunication, both had assumed the other would take care of it. Dodd shrugged it off with amiable sheepishness, but Gordon was fuming. They tried buying a ticket at the station, but they were already sold out.

Gordon and Dodd ended up riding the ordinary stopping train to Berlin along with everyone else. They rode together in one compartment while Martha and her mother went in another, which had been filled with bouquets of flowers from their many well-wishers. Gordon gave Dodd a thorough briefing on the current political situation along with a serious talking to about his role as an ambassador and the importance of altering his behavior accordingly. But by all indications Gordon's admonitions had little effect.

When the train finally pulled into Berlin's Lehrter Bahnhof, George Messersmith was waiting on the platform. Accompanying him was Bella Fromm, one of Berlin's leading journalists and a close friend of Messersmith. He saw to it that she and Dodd had a friendly chat while the baggage was loaded aboard the embassy limousines which Messersmith had brought. She immediately liked Dodd's dry wit and precise observations. But then when the subject of Hitler's treatment of the Jews inevitably came up, he surprised her by insisting that he 'hadn't been charged to speak up for the Jews'. He added that his understanding was that the 'horror tales' he'd been reading about their mistreatment in the American press were exaggerations. Fromm, herself a Jew, calmly informed Dodd that if anything, the situation regarding the Jews was far worse than anything the newspapers dared print. 'He seemed upset when he heard that the "horror tales" are innocent fairy tales compared to the actual goings on,' she later wrote.[13]

While Dodd and his wife rode with Messersmith in one limousine, Martha shared the backseat of another with a 'nervous young man, one of the embassy secretaries, who, fearing the driver would report their conversation to the secret police', attempted to hush her anytime she asked a question or ventured an opinion. When she didn't stop, he sharply told her she needed to start learning 'to be seen and not heard'.[14] It was advice she would never follow.

2. SKIN IN THE GAME

Whatever topics may have been discussed during Gordon and Dodd's train ride, what almost certainly wasn't raised were the Soviet spy rings which, until only a few months earlier, had been operating with impunity. They were now, apparently, all shut down following Hitler's mass arrests of communists and other leftists. Even though Gordon probably knew quite a bit on the subject, the reason it was likely not brought up was that at the time the US had very little skin in that particular game. Officially, there were no American spies operating in Germany at the time. Unofficially, George Messersmith could have counted as one, though he certainly would have blanched at the suggestion. Something similar could have been said of the British at the time. The French, however, were a very different story.

For more than a dozen years, Soviet spies and spy networks had operated almost without interference throughout Germany. That they could do so was an unintended result of the secret alliance which had been going on between the two countries since shortly after the end of the First World War. While it would have been difficult for Hitler not to know about the secret alliance, what he knew about the networks themselves is less of an easy guess. He had to have known that Soviet spies were around and in large numbers, but as for the quotidian details about their structure and organisation, it is entirely possible he might not have been that interested.

When Hitler began ordering the arrests of large numbers of communists and other leftists, shortly after becoming Chancellor, he also, in one fell swoop, put the Soviet spy networks out of business, which in turn forced Moscow Center to devise a radical new 'American strategy' for staying in the German game. Though it had not been its intention, the effect of this new strategy would soon spread over to the United States, where its repercussions would continue to be felt long after the Third Reich was gone.

✦

The Russian–German entente had its beginnings inside, of all places, Berlin's Moabit prison following the German government's brutal suppression of the communist-led Spartacist Uprising of January 1919.[1] It was there, in the detention cells, among the hundreds of arrested communists and leftists, that a police official recognised Karl Radek, a top Comintern[2] official and close colleague of Vladimir Lenin. Radek had illegally entered Germany to help organise the insurrection, which the Bolsheviks had hoped would turn Germany into a fellow Soviet state. Germany did not have diplomatic relations with Russia at that point, which made Radek the closest thing there was to an emissary. They decided to find out if Radek had anything to say. It turned out he did. Radek started getting visits from German government officials, among them Foreign Minister Walter Rathenau, head of the army General Hans von Seeckt, Turkish envoy Enver Pasha,[3] and others, all interested in exploring areas of common interest with their fellow pariah state. It didn't take long to realise that they each had what the other needed.

After the war, Germany's industrial base was at a standstill for want of raw materials and hard currency to pay for them, and markets to sell to. Russia, on the other hand, was a massive, hungry market. It wanted to construct, from scratch, an entire industrial base and on a gigantic scale: factories, steel mills and power plants; everything. Its military needed modern weapons: aircraft, tanks, artillery and the know-how to use them effectively. Russia lacked foreign exchange, but was rich in raw materials. The Germans also needed weapons, but because of the peace terms dictated to them from the West, they also now needed hidden places to develop them, build them, and develop tactics using them, far from the Allied

Control Commission's eyes. Again, Russia had what they needed. The problem was Germany and Russia had always been mortal enemies. Was it possible they could find a modus vivendi? Radek and his visitors talked about it at length and decided they might.

Over the next several months, accommodations were reached. In the 1922 Treaty of Rapallo, Germany and the Soviet Union formally recognised each another, renounced previous territorial claims and cancelled their pre-war debts. Elaborate barter systems were devised to work around their lack of foreign exchange. As a result, Germany received raw materials and Russia acquired industrial machinery, know-how, and sometimes entire factories.

In the military sphere this new relationship proved particularly fruitful. *Zentrale Moskau*, a joint secret organisation, was established with offices in both capitals to facilitate military cooperation. After that, the Red Air Force established a flying school at Lipetsk, 250 miles outside Moscow, staffed by German civilian instructors. In remote Kazan, a tank school was set up for the Germans in which the future Wehrmacht's panzer force gestated.[4] A Trade Enterprise Development Company, deceptively named *Gesellschaft zur Forderung Gewerblicher*,[5] or GEFU, contracted with the Soviets to manufacture aircraft engines, artillery shells, small-caliber ammunition and other war materiel, the output of which the two countries shared. GEFU also sent hundreds of military and civilian specialists into Russia to help production.

Understandably, this arrangement did not ride well with OGPU's (OGPU was the Joint State Political Directorate, an early security and political police force in the USSR and forerunner of the KGB) counter-intelligence branch, being that GEFU was in their eyes an arm of the German military, and from communications they'd intercept, it was apparent some of its specialists were engaging in espionage. But for the moment, their concerns had to take a backseat to economic and foreign policy considerations.[6] Of course, the Germans weren't the only ones engaging in espionage. As cooperation grew throughout the 1920s, Soviet intelligence found new opportunities to insert agents into Germany. Soviet trade delegations often included spies who, once inside the country,[7] would promptly split off and disappear. Their papers would get taken over by other agents without the German police ever noticing their absence. They would then acquire local papers and new identities and begin recruiting German communists and left-wingers as agents.

Soviet intelligence relied heavily on assistance from German communists and other sympathisers. From the moment the German Communist Party was created in November 1918, there was a symbiotic relationship between them and the Soviet intelligence services. Members were appointed to work as liaisons with spies who'd been sent in. At their direction, they would help recruit other agents and participate in clandestine operations.[8] Communist student organisations became a source of young, eager recruits. So were German engineers responding to newspaper adverts for employment in Russia?

Probably the most productive method for acquiring large amounts of usable intelligence was through *Betriebs-Berichterstatter* (Worker-Correspondents), or 'RABKOR', in which local communist newspapers invited workers to share their knowledge of inventions and new technologies they were involved with. In early 1928, *Rote Fahne*, the German communist paper, boasted having 127 Rabkors.[9] By the end of that year it claimed several thousand. At one point the German Ministry of Foreign Affairs estimated that the Soviets were stealing $250 million worth of industrial secrets per year. Nevertheless, they chose to keep quiet about it rather than disturb their productive relationship with the USSR.[10] During this period the Soviet spy presence was so commonplace that German communists had nicknames for the two organisations operating there. Red Army Intelligence, the GRU, was *'Klara'*, while the Cheka's foreign branch, the INO, was *'Grete'*.[11]

❧

Hitler became Chancellor on 31 January 1933, and suddenly Grete and Klara's day was over. Once the arrests of KDP members started,[12] the people making up the Grete and Klara networks were either on the run or in prison. Hitler continued to be largely ignorant of the arrests' full effect on the networks. At one point the German police raided one of the German–Soviet joint ventures, not realising what it actually was.[13] The Soviet Ambassador protested and Hitler promptly apologised, explaining that they were only interested in

German communists and that the Nazis wanted to maintain good relations with the Soviets. The Soviet Ambassador accepted Hitler's apology, telling him that they did not want to interfere in German internal affairs.[14]

It wasn't that Moscow Center hadn't seen Hitler coming. Sometime in mid-1932 they instructed Comintern to start setting up escape routes and to prepare to evacuate as many key KDP members as they could,[15] providing them with false identities and moving them either to neighboring countries or to the Soviet Union. Still, they hadn't expected Hitler to move as quickly as he did, and Moscow Center very quickly found itself cut off from much of its best sources of clandestine information. Realising they needed to come up with a new strategy, Moscow Center sent two of its best men to Berlin to see what they could salvage from their old networks and start putting together a new organisation.[16] It was here that the 'American Strategy' was born.

The Soviet 'legals', spies operating under diplomatic cover, continued functioning as before, but in greater numbers. Replacing the massive old 'illegal' system was a much more compact organisation, based on small groups of spies operating under foreign cover, usually as businessmen, with a small number of local agents, many operating singly, serviced by a large network of couriers who were either foreigners or Russians with foreign passports. Finding couriers was, in some respects, a fairly easy task. Comintern would scout out suitable candidates back in their home countries and do the recruiting.[17] Young people were often the best candidates as it was easy for them to come to Germany as tourists and then get student visas upon arrival.[18] As long as they behaved themselves and said nothing subversive to their neighbors, who could be counted on to report to the police everything about their behavior, their comings and goings could be relatively unimpeded. For the purposes of being either a courier or operative, by far the best nationality to be was American.[19]

During the 1920s, Moscow Center's interest in the outside world fell into three categories. First were the western countries directly bordering Russia: Romania, Finland and Poland. Then came the three major European powers: Britain, France and Germany. And finally there was Japan, Russia's only real rival in Asia. The United

States wasn't even on the list. This didn't mean that Soviet intelligence wasn't interested. They were, but since they didn't yet view the US as a threat, OGPU's American presence was limited to only three or four 'illegals' working out of some small, secret location in New York City. Their activities focused mainly on industrial espionage. Stealing American technical secrets was not that difficult a task. Knowing how to make use of them was.

The American industrial behemoth filled Russia with desire. They saw America's automobiles, trucks, steam shovels, locomotives, and earth-moving equipment and wanted them for themselves. But much as they craved them, the Russians knew that what they needed more were full-up factories where they could build them for themselves. American industry was eager to sell Russia whatever it wanted, but since the US did not formally recognise the Soviet Union, it couldn't extend it credit or any of the other normal avenues of trade finance, limiting trade to cash-and-carry. Since Russia lacked hard currency, it would have preferred setting up with the US a system of reciprocal barter and counter-trade arrangements similar to what they had with Germany. But America's appetite for Russian fur, bristles, platinum, benzine, caviar and lumber wasn't remotely large enough to pay for the full-up car factories and tractor plants the Russians wanted to buy. Instead, the Russians were forced to find markets elsewhere to raise the capital necessary to pay for immense projects, like the Ford Motor Company's recreation of its River Rouge car plant in Nizhny Novgorod or the Lubertsy tractor factory which International Harvester built outside Moscow.

The 1920s and early 1930s saw not only massive direct transfers of American technology to Soviet Russia, but also thousands of American engineers, technicians and industrial workers going to help run the factories and provide know-how. At the same time, unbeknownst to everyone, the US State Department was secretly allowing thousands of Soviet engineers and industrial workers into the US to work in American factories in order to gain knowledge and hands-on experience that could be used back home. All of it went through AMTORG, a Soviet state trading corporation, with offices at 165 Broadway in New York. AMTORG conducted trade and at times even acted as a stand-in for an embassy. Normally, a state trading company like AMTORG would also have been a front for espionage, but at this point, AMTORG's legal activities were still of such vital importance that Moscow didn't want to jeopardise any of it by running spies.

From its earliest days, the American communist movement was a raucous, fractious, ethnically diverse group, and given neither to party discipline nor to a uniformity of beliefs. Grete and Klara generally left them to the Comintern to try to control. Moscow knew that too many things could go wrong and that the limited benefit wouldn't be worth the risk. Ever since the Palmer Raids of the early 1920s, the US government made a practice of deporting, without trial, anyone whom they suspected of being a 'red agitator', regardless of the citizenship status.

Even so, in the event of contingencies, there was something built into the structure of every nation's Communist Party that almost no one knew about, and which, at least for the American group, had barely ever been used. It was called the 'Secret Apparatus', and it existed entirely for the benefit of Moscow Center.

The collapse of the German networks created a need for American couriers and 'American' agents. This in turn required having operatives capable of creating agent identities and then acquiring passports for them. To accomplish this, the GRU began activating the American Secret Apparatus and manning it with Communist Party members recruited to perform secret work for them.[20]

Perhaps if Hitler had been the only opponent that Stalin faced, Soviet espionage in America might never have ballooned the way it did during the 1930s. Up until the day in June 1941 when he turned his armies on Russia, Hitler was, in Stalin's eyes, a fellow power-hungry dictator, not unlike himself, whom he could get along with. As a result, Moscow Center's approach to spying and infiltrating the Nazi German target was kept to a measured level. On the other hand, what did bring out the worst in Stalin's paranoia was a fellow Bolshevik named Leon Trotsky.

Ever since Stalin had removed him from power and forced him into foreign exile, Trotsky had become an even bigger pain in Stalin's side. A tiny faction of communists across the world had come to consider Trotsky's brand of Bolshevism truer to their movement's founding ideals and he gathered passionate supporters everywhere. This did not go unnoticed by Stalin, who saw them as a far greater threat to his rule than the anti-communist Whites whom Trotsky's Red Army had defeated and sent into exile ten years earlier. Trotskyism found particularly fertile ground in the US and with every American Communist Party member that switched over to his banner, Stalin saw yet another enemy with whom he would now have to contend. Once again he turned to the American Communist Party's Secret Apparatus to launch a secret war against the Trotskyites. Even as the first American couriers began reporting for training in Berlin and Paris, Stalin was sending his own operatives, disguised as Americans, into the United States to look for more recruits and to oversee operations against Trotskyites and anyone else regarded as a potential threat. For the first time, the US ranked as an actual target for Soviet espionage.

⟪✦⟫

For all its elegance and comfort, Dodd did not care for the Hotel Esplanade. As a proud son and grandson of North Carolina dirt farmers, its splendor irritated him, and being extremely frugal by nature, he worried about the bill. He relented a bit after Messersmith told him how little it was actually costing. But the nervousness soon came back and Dodd announced his intention towards eventually finding a more modest residence.[21]

Martha, on the other hand, adored the Esplanade and the Imperial Suite. It was sumptuous and the hotel staff treated her like royalty. Plus, all day long important people would come by, dropping off visiting cards along with invitations to cocktails, receptions, dinners, and tea dates.

For Martha, falling in love was almost never a slow-building thing. It either ignited in an instant and burned hot until it went cold or it never happened. So it was for her when it came to Berlin and Germany. She loved the towns, cities and countryside that she observed from the window of the train. And she loved the people, who all seemed so kind and welcoming. For her, it really started when she and her mother boarded the Berlin train and found their compartment. It had been filled with dozens of bouquets, put there by the people who'd come to see them at the pier. Martha was moved, knowing that each one was meant as a greeting by an individual German, none of them wanting anything other than to show their hospitality.

In her memoir, Martha recalls how, after dinner in the Esplanade's dining room, her father took them on their first evening stroll in the city. Heading towards the Tiergarten, they walked up Siegesallee, which ran northward, and then to Puppenallee, lined with the 'rather ugly and pretentious statues of previous rulers, flanked by busts of their advisors'. Even though Martha thought Puppenallee was ridiculous, it didn't matter because she loved it. The dull glow of the streetlights had the feel of a small American town late at night. Despite what she'd been told to expect, there were no soldiers on the street. 'Everything was peaceful, romantic, strange, nostalgic. I felt the press had badly maligned the country.'[22]

She woke up the next morning with a bad cold and stayed in bed for the next two days. Then there appeared at her door an American woman, short, buxom, and absolutely frenetic, with bright blonde hair that cascaded well past her shoulders. Her name was Sigrid Schultz and she demanded an immediate audience with Martha.

Martha knew very well that Sigrid Schultz was the *Chicago Tribune's* Berlin and Central Europe bureau chief, but what she probably didn't know was that Sigrid Schultz was also one of the most-respected, most senior, and also best-liked foreign correspondents in Germany. She'd come to give Martha a briefing about the situation in Germany, because she naturally assumed that the only reason a young colleague from the *Tribune* would accompany her parents to Berlin was to use the opportunity to report from there. Anything else was inconceivable! Martha invited her in and, over tea, spent the next two hours listening dumbfounded as Schultz told her about everything from the assaults on Jews, the kidnappings, the killings, the secret prisons, the way Jews were being systematically stripped of their rights, their professions and ability to participate in civic life. She told her about the growing tension between Hitler and Ernst Roehm, the thuggish, openly homosexual head of the SA. She told Martha about how Hitler had suddenly lost interest in the great revolution they'd been fighting for in the streets for more than a decade and was now currying favor with the capitalists and the industrialists, whom the stormtroopers had always considered as bad as the Jews, along with the conservatives and monarchists and everyone else they despised. Sooner or later, this was all going to come to a head, and it wouldn't just be Nazis killing Jews and leftists, but Nazis killing other Nazis!

None of it was what Martha had wanted to hear. In the short time she'd been there, Martha had already fallen head-over-heels in love with Nazi Germany. Everything she'd seen seemed perfect, until this strange little woman had barged in, intent on ruining it all for her! Looking back on it years later she admitted, 'I didn't especially like her at first.'[23] But she also knew how important Schultz was. She knew everybody worth knowing and she was not only giving Martha a top-level briefing, she was also welcoming her into one of the most exclusive and exciting fraternities in the world.

Two days later, a lanky, red-haired Texan named H. R. Knickerbocker took Martha out on a tea date at the nearby Eden Hotel, where, between dances, she was given another high-level briefing. Like Schultz, 'Red' Knickerbocker had been reporting from Berlin for years. His German was flawless. He knew the scene and had the sources. He'd also put in time reporting from Moscow. His analysis and coverage of the Soviet Five-Year Plan had earned him the Pulitzer Prize the year before. Like Schultz, he'd interviewed Hitler numerous times. In Russia he'd even managed to have an interview with Stalin's mother, who, speaking through an interpreter, told him that her famous son was as much a mystery to her as he was to the rest of the world. Now he was sharing his insights with Martha.

What he told Martha couldn't have been much different from what Sigrid Schultz had told her several days earlier: that Germany had now all but become a police state; how Hitler had used the Reichstag fire to introduce 'enabling acts' to bring on a state of emergency, suspend the constitution, and give the police powers to arrest anyone they wanted and even execute them on the vaguest grounds; how the Jews were losing their professions, their rights, their citizenship. He told Martha how on the night of the Reichstag fire, Goering was there, johnny-on-the-spot before the fire was even put out, shouting how it was all the communists' fault and that they needed to be crushed. It was all the pretext Hitler needed to get President Hindenburg to issue an emergency decree suspending civil liberties and allowing the mass arrests of communists and leftists, including parliamentary deputies, which overnight turned the Nazi Party's plurality into a majority, allowing them to start consolidating power. Knickerbocker could also have told her that there was plenty of evidence suggesting that it was actually the Nazis that started the fire and not the communists they had fingered.

Red Knickerbocker also might have told Martha how the SS were beginning to emerge as a force. Officially they were just a sub-set of the SA, providing security for Hitler and other senior Nazi officials at rallies and other public events, and in terms of sheer size, their mere thousands might seem insignificant compared to the SA's millions. But they were making all their moves independent of Roehm. Its head was Heinrich Himmler, a mousey little non-entity with all the charisma and presence of a lavatory attendant, but whose organisational skills were second to none, and his ability to quietly acquire power positions without Roehm, his titular boss, noticing, was uncanny. Clearly, something was going on.

Knickerbocker likely also told Martha that, despite everything, Hitler's hold on power was still far from absolute. It wasn't just Roehm and the SA that could dislodge him. The army could. Hindenburg could remove him from office. He could cancel the ena-bling acts, he could order the freeing of the jailed communist and left-wing deputies and return them to parliament. It was really just a question of someone taking the initiative. The problem was that the spheres which should have been standing up to him – the conserv-atives, the military, the monarchists, the industrialists, the church – were all letting themselves get played, because Hitler was making them all think he wanted them as partners and could be made to do things *their* way.

Martha listened to her briefing and at one point confessed that she really didn't know that much about politics, but her new friend didn't seem to hear it. He kept talking; she kept listening and trying to take it all in.

Returning to the Hotel Esplanade and the Imperial Suite, Martha was delighted to find a new batch of visiting cards and invitations for drinks, receptions and dinners. Back in Chicago the Dodds had never counted as 'society'. Society was something they'd lived alongside but had never been part of. Now, suddenly, people with 'von' attached to their names were all seeking to make the acquaintance of Martha Dodd, the young, pretty, vivacious and, as far as anyone knew, unmarried daughter of the American Ambassador. Just by showing up, Martha had attained high social standing. She began accepting some of the invitations and soon found herself surrounded by new friends and admirers. Night after night there were receptions, parties, and dashing young men eager to show off their excellent English. Martha Dodd had arrived.

3. THE ANNA RATH INCIDENT

Despite what the foreign editor had told Martha back in Chicago, Berlin's legendary social scene was neither dead nor moribund. It was heavily curtailed, with many of the best nightclubs shut down, but at the ones still running, things were as frantic as they'd ever been. During their long decade of struggle, the Nazi rank and file had largely been kept out of Berlin's fun side. Most had spent the years ill fed, with nothing much in their pockets and all their drinking done in crummy stormtrooper pubs. But now, finally, the glittering life was theirs and they were eager to catch up on all they'd missed.

One of her favorite nightspots was Ciro's, since it was the one remaining club featuring a jazz orchestra of 'Negro' musicians. Martha loved going there to dance. If she found someone she met at a party suitably engaging, she'd suggest they leave and go there or some other nightspot. After that, if she felt like it, they might go have sex someplace, or if she wasn't quite ready to go home just yet, she'd go hang out with the foreign correspondents.

The community of British and American reporters in Berlin numbered over two dozen, and when it came to gathering news and scooping each other they were highly competitive, but outside that, they mostly enjoyed each other's company and liked hanging out and drinking together once they'd filed their stories or finished the evening's round of receptions and cocktail parties. There was a popular Italian restaurant on Kurfurstenstrasse called 'Die Taverne', which had a large round table, a 'stammtisch',[1] reserved for them where they'd usually gather to shoot the breeze into the early hours.

Martha was welcomed into the club, presumably on Sigrid Schultz's say-so, and quickly fit in with the smart-talking, hard-drinking crowd. She even picked up a string writing human interest features for Hearst.

Snubbed by the embassy wives and everyone else, about the only American friend Martha had outside the journalists was Mildred Fish von Harnack, of Madison, Wisconsin. Mildred was an academic who spoke flawless German and taught American literature at Berlin University. Born and raised in Madison, she was tall, painfully thin, with long blonde hair and piercing blue eyes. They met at an afternoon tea the embassy held for the American Women's Club of Berlin, which Mildred ran, just as she ran the local chapter of Daughters of the American Revolution. She and Martha immediately hit it off. Mildred's love of books and literature meshed well with Martha's and they became fast friends.

Mildred was a tireless networker and organiser with a lot of personality, and though not at all without humor, she was, nevertheless, in everyone's estimation, a serious person. So was her husband, Arvid von Harnack, a respected but penniless economist and aristocrat.

By the time Martha met them, both were already signed up as Soviet intelligence agents. It had happened earlier that summer and now, at their handler's direction, they were being publicly supportive of Hitler in order to better speed their penetration into the Nazi structure. Neither Mildred nor Arvid had particularly communist leanings. Both were, in fact, deeply religious, liberal Christians. But they'd agreed Hitler had to be stopped and there was no other way to do it.

Martha didn't know anything about this, at least not for a while. All she knew was they were the nicest, most intelligent people she knew.

For the first few weeks Martha was in Germany, most of Berlin was on its summer holiday. During most of August, the stammtisch was half-empty, but still welcoming to Martha. One of the reporters she became friends with during this time was Quentin Reynolds,[2] an ambitious young American on his first overseas assignment, who'd arrived in Berlin at about the same time as Martha. Reynolds wrote for Colliers and Hearst's International News Service and though only a few years older than Martha, he was already a veteran newsman, with a nationwide reputation for his sports writing and human-interest features. He'd been chosen because his editors heard he spoke German, although in his memoir he claimed it was only 'saloon German' – only good enough for ordering drinks and telling the bartender '*der andere mann besalt*'.[3] Nevertheless, the Bronx-born, Brooklyn-raised Reynolds was quickly accepted into Berlin's foreign correspondents' ranks and was soon a stammtisch regular. He and Martha quickly became friends. In her memoir, Martha described him as: 'A big hulk of a man, with curly hair, humorous eyes and a broad beaming face ... sharp and tough and unsentimental ... an excellent newsman.'[4]

By now, attacks on civilians by groups of Nazis on the streets were increasingly commonplace, but whenever reports appeared in the foreign press, the foreign correspondents who wrote them would get blasted either by propaganda minister Josef Goebbels or the Harvard-educated, half-American foreign press chief Ernst 'Putzi' Hanfstaengl, who'd dismiss the reports either as complete fabrications or, when they could not be denied, claim that they were done by individuals angry, perhaps over-enthusiastic in their support for the regime, but in no way organised or operating under the direction of the Nazi leadership. They all knew it was a lie, but they needed proof, and finding it was no simple task. To begin with, they were already walking on thin ice, since the Nazi regime was notoriously thin-skinned and did not like criticism. They had ways of making foreign critics feel unwelcome and uncomfortable. Reynolds knew the reason he'd been sent was that his predecessor had gone too far and had been shown the door by the Nazis.[5]

Martha, at this point, was well into her first forays among Berlin's new social elite. She went out most nights, bouncing between receptions, dinners, cocktail parties and going out dancing. Often as not she'd top it off by dropping in on Die Taverne and partaking in the repartee of her journalist friends into the early hours before finally heading home. If she thought her escort was presentable or sufficiently entertaining, she might invite him along and see how he handled himself. With the newcomers, who'd joined the party out of opportunism, it was fine, but the more doctrinaire Nazis might get flustered or uncomfortable.

But much as she might have liked being part of their smart company, she didn't yet see eye to eye with most of them about Hitler and their assessments of the political situation. Martha remained wildly enthusiastic towards Hitler and the Nazis and nothing that her new friends said could dissuade her.

At one point in late August, with still not much going on in Berlin, Reynolds suggested an extended road trip to get a first-hand look at the country outside Berlin, and perhaps even a wander into Austria and dropping in at the Salzburg Music Festival. Bill Jr agreed to come, possibly at his sister's behest. Then the parents decided to accompany them as far as Leipzig, since Dodd wanted to show his wife the city where he'd studied 30 years earlier. On Sunday, 13 August, Reynolds and all four Dodds loaded themselves into the family Chevrolet and hit the road.

After dropping off Mr and Mrs Dodd in Leipzig, Reynolds, Martha and Bill Jr travelled the lesser roads, wandering and going wherever they fancied. For several days everything went wonderfully. It was the height of summer and the German countryside was in its full scenic glory. People were outside, working in the fields and in their gardens. In the towns they drove through, Nazi banners and flags were usually present. 'We saw a lot of marching men in brown uniforms singing and shouting and waving their flags,'[6] she wrote, adding: 'These were the now-famous Brownshirt Storm Troopers through whose loyalty and terroristic methods Hitler seized power.' Of course, at the time she was witnessing all this, Martha was still an enthusiastic supporter of Hitler and the new Germany and delighted at everything she was seeing.

Wherever they went, the locals noticed them and would start waving and greeting them with *Sieg-Heil*s as they drove past.[7] Martha, caught up in their jubilation, enthusiastically *Sieg-Heil*-ed back. For Martha, it was a heady experience. If she'd felt any uncertainty about Germany following her briefings by Schultz and Knickerbocker, this seemed to dispel it completely. In all the small towns and villages they drove through it was the same story; everyone seemed to be happy with the National Socialist revolution transforming Germany.

Late one evening, they pulled into Nuremburg. From previous experience Reynolds knew it was a town known more for going to bed early than for its nightlife. But even though it was late in the evening,[8] the streets were full of people in a festive mood. When they came to their hotel, which was on the Koenigstrasse, they asked the desk clerk if there was going to be a parade. Hearing their question, he laughed good naturedly, so much so that the long curls of his mustache shook.[9] Then he responded with a sly smile that, yes, 'it would be a kind of parade', adding, 'they are teaching somebody a lesson'.[10] After bringing their bags upstairs to their rooms, they became aware of the sound of a brass band in the distance outside. The three decided to go back out and see what all the gayety was about.

Outside, the street was lined with people waiting for the parade. Everyone was smiling and seemed happy. The music of the brass band got louder as it approached, punctuated by the sharp *crack-crack-crack* of hob-nailed jackboots against the pavement. Down the street, Martha could see the approaching columns. Stormtroopers: the vanguard holding swastika banners, followed by stormtroopers with torches, while behind them, the band continued playing festive music. Around her, all the smiling faces had hardened into ugly grimaces. *They are teaching someone a lesson.* People started pointing and she could see a figure being dragged along, between two tall stormtroopers.[11] Martha's first impression was that it was a clown. The person was in costume and their head had no hair and was covered in some kind of a white powder. Only it wasn't a costume and it wasn't a clown. It was woman, her hair shorn, her dress half torn off her, her face frozen in a mask of fear and humiliation. A sign hung around her neck that read: 'I have offered myself to a Jew.'

The crowd roared with excitement. A double-decker bus drove up, full of people eager to witness the spectacle. For several minutes Martha, Reynolds and Bill Jr watched as the woman was cursed and spat on. In disbelief, Martha looked at the crowd. These were the same nice German people who'd been smiling and waving at her earlier that day, who had made her feel welcome and like she was part of something wonderful. 'Here was something that darkened my picture of a happy, carefree Germany,'[12] Martha wrote.

Eventually, it wound down. The band played the *Horst Wessel Lied* and after that, everyone went home. It was late. The three repaired to the hotel bar and started drinking. At one point, Reynolds quietly asked the bartender what he knew about what had just happened. The bartender whispered back that the woman's name was Anna Rath and that she'd made the mistake of trying to marry her Jewish fiancé. He also told them the whole event had been staged by Julius Streicher, the local Nazi Party chief and publisher of the Jew-baiting, half-pornographic newspaper *Der Sturmer*.

After the bartender moved on to other customers, Reynolds explained to Martha and her brother that what they'd just witnessed was the proof he and all the other reporters had been looking for: that the attacks on Jews and their friends were indeed being orchestrated at the top. This was a major scoop!

Hearing him say this, Martha got very upset and begged him not to file an article about it.[13] What they'd witnessed was indeed a terrible thing, but Hitler's people weren't all like this, and painting them all with the same brush would be wrong. Martha got very emotional and laid it on so thick that in the end, Reynolds relented and promised not to write it.

But then, after phoning his editor and conferring with him, he wrote it, judiciously leaving Martha and Bill Jr out of the story. And rather than cabling it to New York, Reynolds mailed it.

The three continued their holiday, driving into Austria and enjoying themselves. When they returned to Berlin a week later, the story still hadn't run. Then, a day or two later, Reynolds got summoned to Hanfstaengl's office, where he got screamed at for writing a story with no basis in fact. The incident, he told Reynolds, had been 'investigated' and they hadn't been able to find even a single person in Nuremburg who could attest to witnessing it. Reynolds dryly told him he could name two people who had. When Putzi asked for their names, Reynolds told him Martha Dodd and Bill Dodd Jr. After that, Putzi's built-up anger seemed to deflate. Up until then, Reynolds and Hanfstaengl had been somewhat chummy. After that, relations between the two became more coldly correct.

Looking back on it in her memoir, six years later, Martha would say that what she witnessed that evening in Nuremburg was something she couldn't shake. 'The ugly, bored brutality, I thought would only make a superficial impression on me – but as time went on I thought more and more of the pitiful, broken creature, a victim of mass insanity,'[14] she wrote. The Anna Rath incident, she said, marked the beginning of the end of her flirtation with Nazism.

Even if this was the case, the end was still a long time coming.

∾⬥∾

Two weeks later, Ambassador Dodd finally had his meeting with President von Hindenburg, who had been convalescing from an illness at his country estate. Dodd, accompanied by Gordon, both in top hats, presented his credentials and then he and von Hindenburg talked for a while on various topics. Dodd was impressed by the breadth of the old man's knowledge and his great desire for peace and cooperation among the nations, which only a few years before had been locked in the worst war in human history. Dodd also thought he detected in von Hindenburg's words indications of strong disapproval of Hitler and the Nazis.

While Dodd's meeting with Hitler would not come until October, he was now officially in place as the American Ambassador to Germany. Initially, much of his working day was spent receiving his fellow ambassadors making their official visits, which he would then be obliged to reciprocate with a visit to their embassies. Most meetings were little more than exchanges of niceties and friendly intentions, but some turned out to have some meat on them. The most notable was with the French Ambassador Andre Francois-Poncet, probably the most experienced and best informed of all the diplomats in Berlin. He was also better acquainted with Hitler than anyone else, having already met with him many times, even spending weekends with Hitler as his informal guest. Poncet arranged for an hour-long meeting with Dodd, arrived early and left after fifteen minutes. But during that brief period, while endlessly smoking cigarettes, he probably told Dodd more than all the other ambassadors combined.

By now attacks on Americans were a near-daily occurrence. Whenever it happened, Dodd would send an angry protest to Hitler and the Foreign Minister, who would inevitably respond, either by denying any knowledge of the incident or blandly explaining it hadn't been authorised, or by apologising and explaining that something would be done about it, and that it would never happen again.

Dodd felt his warm feelings for Germany increasingly turning bitter and his sympathies for the Jews, people he'd never much cared for, growing daily.

While there wasn't much Dodd could do besides protest, the task of finding out the details of an incident and getting it resolved fell onto the shoulders of George Messersmith and his consular staff. It was their job to find out what happened, what the charges were, where the victim was being held, the extent of injuries, who had instigated the incident. They made the calls to the police to find out what had happened, then went to visit the victim, either at the hospital or in their home, to get a statement from them and one from the doctor so they could make a report of it. Often the victim would be in jail on trumped-up charges, in which case they'd try to find out who was in charge, whose jurisdiction it fell under, and then do what they could to get the charges either reduced or dropped altogether. Messersmith often already knew the local police president personally and could get through to them, get them to see to reason and find a way to get the matter settled.

Messersmith knew from the first that Hitler was no good and that he meant everything he said about the Jews and about bringing war back to Europe. The way Messersmith saw it was simple. Hitler needed to be taken out; gotten rid of. In letters to Washington, he all but explicitly stated it. It would be a really good idea, and not that difficult to accomplish if done right away. The whole time he'd had his eye on the Nazis, he'd never once seen anything positive about them to report back. But just recently Messersmith found himself wondering if he might, just now, be detecting a positive trend within the Nazi Party's mid-levels.

Being a member of the Rotary Club and an active participant in the Berlin chapter put Messersmith on a 'luncheon-buddy' familiarity with a great many up-and-coming German businessmen. So many of them had told him they had joined the Nazi Party. All of them were good men, not bigoted or stupid, or drawn to gutter politicians. He knew they didn't hate Jews. No, they were Rotarians; men of decent character, integrity, ability and moderation. Could their inclusion impel the Nazi Party to be better?

This spark of moderation was something Messersmith thought he also detected in Rudolf Diels, the young, highly intelligent and ambitious head of the secret police whom he and his staff were now dealing with on a daily basis. Anytime an American national was arrested or grabbed by an SA jump-out squad and no one knew what happened or where they were, Messersmith knew if they could get Diels on the phone, he would look into it and find out, and even get the whole matter dropped. In Messersmith's experience, top Nazis would always promise to be helpful, but it was just the empty talk they all seemed to excel in. Diels got on the phone and even if the issue was outside his jurisdiction, he'd do his damnedest to deliver.

Before the Nazis came in, Dr Diels was a nobody lawyer running an obscure office[15] inside the Prussian Interior Ministry under Severing, the Social Democrat. But then Hermann Goering took over the ministry and all Severing's people were sacked, except Diels, who suddenly emerged as head of the entire Prussian state secret police apparatus. Now, he and Goering were consolidating all of Germany's many different state secret police organisations into a single, unified entity which people were calling the 'Gestapo'. To Messersmith, the Gestapo was a positive development, particularly when compared with Roehm's SA, which wasn't answerable to anyone, including Hitler. They grabbed whoever they wanted and did to them whatever they felt like. The SA didn't keep records or issue warrants of receipts. The Gestapo operated on the rule of law, or at least tried to, which by this point was saying a lot.[16] Not that the Gestapo were saints – far from it, their brutal side was all too apparent. But at least their brutality was accompanied by a certain degree of nuance and circumspection, something Roehm and his stormtroopers clearly lacked. 'Moderate' was of course all relative, being defined by the extremes it was set against. Berliners already had a joke going around about preferring a beating by a gentleman because he'd at least let you first fold your coat – supposedly a reference to Diels.

The Gestapo kept records and followed procedure. Messersmith knew the Gestapo weren't averse to torture, but being a man of the world from Delaware, Messersmith also knew beatings and torture were something police interrogators did everywhere in the world. He also knew that Diels' previous boss, a Social Democrat, hadn't been any different.

It also helped that Diels was educated, with refined manners, an engaging personality, topped off with a striking appearance: tall, thin, his once-handsome face crisscrossed with dueling scars from his student days. He liked dropping by in the afternoons to chat with Messersmith or anyone else if Messersmith happened to be tied up. Messersmith encouraged this. Good relations with Diels helped ensure the safety of Americans. Diels seemed to be genuinely interested in America and always had a question or two about American history, government and society and what they thought about America's democratic institutions. Messersmith found that talking with him was a lot like talking to German Rotarians, leading him to suspect Diels was not the only moderate among the Nazi elite. There had to be others, and now they were starting to come to the fore and, in the process, become a positive force. At least he hoped it was the case. Messersmith genuinely liked Germans and hated the idea of having to go to war with them again.

⚬❈⚬

Ambassador Dodds' quest for more modest quarters turned out to be a ridiculously easy one. With so many of Berlin's Jews fearing their safety or outright trying to flee, it was a buyer's market, and the Dodds could afford to live anywhere they wanted. Tiergartenstrasse 27A was a modern, spacious, elevator-equipped, four-storey villa belonging to one of Berlin's most prominent Jewish families. Alfred Panofsky owned a private bank which, despite the Nazi's efforts to remove Jews from the public and commercial spheres, continued operating, as the Nazis were heavily dependent on its services. Like a great many people, the Panofskys were confident the Nazis' tenure would be short, so they decided to wait it out in Berlin. What they needed was protection, and in their minds the best possible protection was having the American Ambassador and his family living in the bottom three floors of their house.

The ground floor had a large living room and a library with a fireplace. Back in Chicago, the Dodds did not so much entertain as have their home open to a small circle of literary and intellectual friends who were free to drop by anytime. Almost as soon as they had settled into Tiergartenstrasse 27A, their new home was opened to a new batch of acquaintances, drawn by seeming magnetic attraction to the lively family of the new American Ambassador. The way Martha described it, their new circle included writers, artists, dissidents, Jews, diplomats and Nazis. Since Dodd and his wife were homebodies and hated going out in general and to diplomatic functions in particular, most of the new crowd were people Martha had met at the many receptions and parties she attended. Often she'd bring them home and the party would continue into the early hours. Sometimes the parents were still awake, though most nights they'd usually turn in early.

About the only people who never seemed to drop in was anyone from the American Embassy. Dodd's relations with the staff never recovered from his initial encounter with Gordon that first day in Hamburg. His ill feeling toward Gordon and other senior staff deepened after he learned most employed a full retinue of servants in their households. Unlike Dodd, who lived on his salary, most of them were wealthy and had their own private incomes. To Dodd, their display of wealth was a betrayal of American egalitarianism, an idea which, in Dodd's mind, they were supposed to represent. They didn't care for that. After that, he limited his interactions with them. Writing about it years later, Messersmith thought it was a shame the way it turned out, since for all his marked eccentricities and imperiousness, George Gordon was an able and thoroughly professional officer whose reporting was very highly regarded. Dodd should have availed himself of Gordon's insights.[17]

Dodd made numerous efforts to institute changes in the way his staff did things. He slashed the budgets for food and drink and embassy receptions and parties, and required the counselors and secretaries adhere to the established office hours, even directing that they not keep their golf clubs in their offices, since he rejected the idea that important discussions got carried out on the golf links. It didn't take long for Dodd and his family to become objects of ridicule among the embassy staff.

By now, stories were also starting to seep in about Martha's social activities. She'd gotten into the papers in the company of various apparent beaux, nearly all members of the new Nazi elite. Someone at the embassy came up with a nickname for her: 'The Nazi Penetration of America.'[18]

Messersmith had also heard the rumors. There wasn't much he didn't hear. A lot of names came up, but thankfully, most were easy to dismiss, since they were only mentioned once. But the beaux that kept getting mentioned he found particularly troubling. There was fighter pilot Ernst Udet, top of the list of most popular Germans outside Germany. Udet had been a fighter pilot during the war and afterwards, had done barnstorming and stunt flying in Hollywood films. Udet was a playboy, though he was married, something Messersmith found offensive. While most considered him an affable fellow and a bon vivant, as far as Messersmith was concerned, Ernst Udet was nothing but an opportunist; someone who viewed Hitler and the Nazis as the gravy train he needed to get aboard. Now, word was going around that Martha Dodd, the ambassador's daughter, was Udet's mistress. Messersmith asked around and found it was true.[19] This wasn't good. It made her father look bad and also gave the impression that the United States might already be in Hitler's pocket. Messersmith wondered if he should broach the subject with the ambassador himself. Unlike everyone else, Messersmith got along well with Dodd and could speak with him candidly about a lot of things. But speaking to him about his daughter? That was an entirely different matter.

Since most of the reporters were friends of his, Messersmith knew about Martha being in the journalists' gang now and a regular at Die Taverne stammtisch. She seemed to be fitting in well with that group. He'd heard she was witty and had apparently not had any difficulty getting accepted by them.

Now they were telling him that she was not only linked to Udet, but Martha had lately been dropping by with a new boyfriend in tow, a handsome young lawyer, a *herr Doktor*, with a devilish wit and a face marked with dueling scars. He'd been a Social Democrat with the Prussian Interior Ministry, but now he was heading the *Geheime Staatspolizei*, the Gestapo!

Messersmith already knew his name. It was Rudolf Diels.[20]

4. THE DEVIL YOU KNOW

Martha once asked Diels how he'd managed to get in with Goering at a time when all the other Social Democrats in the Prussian Interior Ministry were getting tossed out. Diels simply told her that after impressing Goering with his skill at playing the stock market he'd been asked to stay. It wasn't exactly that Diels' answer was a lie, it was just a remarkable version of the truth.

Hermann Goering was an extravagant man with extravagant tastes and vision, but no money of his own. This made him dependent on others for financial support. For years he'd enjoyed the largesse of steel magnate Fritz Thyssen, but once Goering took power, he felt the need to begin turning his dreams into reality. One was an early medieval-style castle, hunting lodge and great hall combined with a mausoleum for his late wife in whose honor it would be named 'Carinhall'. Needless to say, it didn't take him long to realise its cost was far beyond his benefactor's resources. The way future Abwehr intelligence officer and anti-Hitler conspirator Hans Bernd Gisevius tells it, Goering ordered Diels to come up with an idea for generating money. Diels' solution was brilliant in its utter crudeness:

Diels went to the Berlin Stock Exchange and asked to see whoever was in charge. Diels introduced himself impudently and made it clear to the directors that he expected his orders to be obeyed. Then he brashly named the stock he wanted to fall one day and to rise the next. They did as they were told

and over several trading sessions, Goering made himself a
tidy sum and soon construction on Carinhall got underway.
In the truest sense, Diels bought his way into indispensability
under Goering, though the purchase price was not with his
own money.[1]

⤞✦⤟

History, the fickle bitch, has not been generous to Rudolf Diels.
He's someone you're not likely to see mention of, unless you're
drawn towards obscurity or if the focus of your interest in Third
Reich history happens to be Hitler's first two years in power. Diels'
glory days lasted just fourteen months, between February 1933 and
April 1934. After that he got kicked upstairs, given a post in the
Cologne police presidium and the impressive-sounding rank of SS
standartenfuhrer to go with it, except that the rank was as empty as
the job that came with it.

Rudolf Diels was born in 1900 and fought in the Great War.
When it ended, he entered Marburg University and spent the next
ten years first studying medicine, then law, but mostly drinking, dueling and engaging in affairs with women. Gisevius, who knew him
well, says even then, 'he was creating an image for himself as a clever,
insolent renegade whose stunts included biting off the tops of beer
steins'.[2] But for all his displays of daring and cleverness, Gisevius
doubted Diels had what it took to push things to the limit.

After completing his law degree in 1930, Diels joined the Social
Democratic Party and then went to work for Carl Severing, Interior
Minister for the Prussian Free State. Severing had played a key role
in reforming the Prussian state police force, making it operate in
line with the norms of a democratic state. Doing so, nevertheless,
required keeping a firm control on both communists and right-wing
groups such as the SA, Stahlhelm[3] and countless other militias. This
involved keeping extensive intelligence files on right- and left-wing
extremists. That was the function of a small, under-funded,
under-staffed detective bureau known as Abteilung 1A,[4] to which
the young, newly hired Dr Rudolf Diels was occasionally assigned.
In April 1932, state parliamentary elections were held in Germany
and for the first time since 1918, the center-left coalition lost its

majority. With the communists and Nazis holding over half the seats between them, but not cooperating, the situation quickly turned in a crisis. Open clashes between the SA and the communists took place in the streets. On 17 July a three-sided gun battle took place on the streets of Altona between the communists, the SA and SS, and the Prussian police, in which eighteen people were killed, nearly all of them communists and all by police gunfire. Three days later, German Chancellor Franz von Papen staged a coup, using seditious notes taken from a secret government meeting, given to him by Diels, as pretext for replacing Prussia's democracy with a right-wing dictatorship. Von Papen declared martial law and had Severing arrested. Diels became the new master of Abteilung 1A. A quick peek at the files and Diels quickly realised he was sitting on gold. Abteilung 1A didn't just have files on communists, it had files on everyone.

Eleven days later, there were parliamentary elections. The parties supporting the government did poorly, and while the communist and Nazi parties fared better, neither had any advantage over the other. A stalemate ensued. In November 1932, Franz Bracht, Severing's replacement as Interior Minister, issued a secret decree containing names and addresses of the leadership of all the different radical organisations. Diels got invited to speak at a War Ministry conference on what they'd do in the event of a civil war. He spoke about handling mass arrests. A month and a half later, in an effort to break the deadlock, Hindenburg accepted von Schleicher's resignation as Chancellor, the position he'd manoeuvred von Papen out of after von Papen had seized the Prussian premiership. The man Hindenburg replaced him with was Schleicher's rival, Adolf Hitler.

Hitler, in an apparent show of modesty, immediately formed a coalition government with another right-wing party, and let them have all the important cabinet posts, taking only the Interior Ministry, a then-powerless post, since police powers were jealously held by the individual states.[5] It went to Wilhelm Frick, a prominent Nazi and former police official in the Reichstag, while a ministry-without-portfolio post went to Hermann Goering, who was also appointed to the lesser post of aviation commissar in the new government. Goering was also offered the Prussian premiership, the post which von Papen currently occupied. Goering turned it down, taking instead the lesser post of Prussian Interior Minister. By then, Goering knew where the actual power rested and knew he didn't need to be the Prussian premier to own Prussia.

Later that day, Hermann Goering strode into the Prussian interior ministry building, accompanied by his faithful bodyguard, driver and aide Paul 'Pilli' Hoerner, and announced that, except one Dr Rudolf Diels, all the liberal and Social Democratic section heads who hadn't already left were herewith fired. He and Diels then had a meeting during which Diels allowed Goering a peek at the Abteilung 1A files. Goering had no difficulty seeing how Diels might help him against his enemies, particularly Josef Goebbels. Almost immediately after that, Rudolf Diels became part of Goering's very tight inner circle.

Drawing on information from the 1A dossiers, Goering began purging the Prussian police, ridding it of socialists, liberals and anyone of the left. At the same time, he put together a large 50,000-man paramilitary police force, mostly of SA men, and with them took over Prussia, leaving von Papen in place as a puppet prime minister.

Shortly after that, someone set fire to the Reichstag. Although a suspect was immediately arrested, it has since been shown that the fire had probably been set by someone else. Some, not all, point toward Diels, working at Goering's direction. Whether or not he did it, what is probably more important is that when the suspects were conveniently caught, it was Diels who led the investigation and conducted the interrogations.

The day after the fire, Hitler submitted a decree to President von Hindenburg, which Hindenburg promptly signed, declaring a State of Emergency and suspending the seven key sections of the constitution guaranteeing individual and civil liberties, thereby making it possible for communists, socialists and anyone else deemed subversive to be placed into 'protective custody'. It also allowed the Reich to take complete power in the federal states when it was deemed necessary and even to impose the death penalty for offences as minor as disturbing the peace. With the communist and leftist deputies gone, the Nazis went from a plurality to a majority, and for Hitler, a rubberstamp.

In her memoir, Martha couldn't pinpoint exactly where and when she and Diels first met. It was either in the late summer or early autumn, and probably at one of the dinners and receptions she'd gone to during her first weeks in Berlin. What she mainly remembered was how tall and thin he was, with black hair and a face 'sensitive and beautiful, but broken', with a 'sinister scar that marred his cheek and disfigured his mouth'. He was, she said, a 'human monster' who 'fascinated and intrigued' her.[6] Martha responded the way she did and promptly went head over heels.

The two started going out, and for a couple of months everything was great. Diels spoke perfect English and he was charming and handsome, with a wonderful, devilish wit and excellent manners. He would take her dancing and on long night-time drives outside Berlin. Afterwards they'd usually come back to 27A, her parents having gone to bed hours earlier, and settled in inside the library, where Fritz the butler usually left a fire going.

Diels was great fun at parties, but he also had a touch of the Mephistophelian which he relished switching on just to put people on edge. He'd never make a conventional entrance if he could help it. 'Parties would be going full-swing, people talking, drinking, dancing, eating,' Martha wrote. 'Then suddenly, late in the evening (he always came late), you could almost feel a chill in the room and Diels would appear at your elbow in all his dark and horrible glamour.'[7]

Martha asked her new friends if they felt it too. 'Though some of them say that when you got to know him, he was quite gay and informal and charming, they all acknowledged the sinister quality of every meeting with him.' Martha felt their unease, but instead of being frightened or repelled by Diels, she felt excited.

Diels quickly made himself a fixture at the Dodd home. With so many people always there, Fritz the butler began letting him in without bothering to announce him. Diels got along well with Martha's parents. They liked his manners, his geniality and wit. That he was married and head of the Gestapo didn't seem to bother them.

Diels loved talking to Martha. 'He described to me many times the intrigues and inter-party struggles and hatreds,'[8] she wrote. One evening he even took her to Gestapo Headquarters where 'on the desk in an unpretentious, large and somewhat bare room', she saw a bank of American-made Dictaphones which they used to listen to secretly recorded conversations, not only between 'subversives', but also other Nazis, innocent civilians, and sometimes even foreign diplomats. 'He gave me the impression that spying was done, not only by the Secret Police Department, but by every department.'[9]

One of the things Martha learned from Diels was that Germany was not merely a police state, but one in which its many different police organisations were in fierce, even deadly, competition for political power. With so much at stake, everyone was suspect. No one was out of bounds, especially not diplomats. 'I began to realise … that all diplomats were analyzed in files that kept growing – their activities and points of view watched and reported.' The Dodds weren't exempt either. 'He convinced me through indirection or otherwise, that our embassy office and residence were wired for Dictaphones, either in the walls or in the telephone. I soon learned not to say a thing over the telephone.'[10]

❧

By now, Berliners had begun adopting the practice of giving a quick look over their shoulders before talking about anything remotely sensitive. From her journalist friends, Martha learned all about the realities of the Gestapo's activities. Competitive as they were with each other, it had become an article of faith among them to share certain information and insights about Hitler and the Nazi's campaign against the Jews. By now most of the communists who hadn't already been arrested had vanished into Czechoslovakia and other neighboring countries.

'Murderous stories began to circulate to which I lent more and more of an ear as I became wise to the ways and methods of dictatorship; of cars, driven up in the middle of the night, SS men had jumped out and in a moment had come down … with a man or woman who was never seen again.'[11] Even so, it didn't dampen Martha's fascination with Diels.

❧

Of course, Diels wasn't the only man Martha went out with that autumn of 1933. There were other young men, including army officers, whom she described as 'extremely pleasant, handsome, courteous and uninteresting',[12] men from the SS, the SA, and polished Nazi diplomats-in-training from the Foreign Office, including one whom she later heard had actually been with the secret police. She described him as 'particularly assiduous in his attentions and subtle arguments ... handsome, blond, innocent and enthusiastic with a slightly more devious and trained mind'.[13] Then there was 'a young SA boy from the Spreewald, who'd been in the Hitler movement for several years', whom she thought might be Slavonic, with 'a beautiful, broad, childlike face', and, she added, 'a no more than an average brain'.[14] There were others as well, but Martha doesn't bother naming them. However when it came to rubbing shoulders with the Nazi *nomenklatura*, Martha was more forthcoming.

Initially, only one member of Hitler's early inner circle spoke English.[15] Ernst 'Putzi' Hanfstaengl was Hitler's self-appointed foreign press chief, whom everybody knew, many grew to dislike, and by the end, all dismissed as a blowhard and clown. Early on, Martha's journalist friends told her Hanfstaengl was someone she needed to know. She asked Quentin Reynolds to introduce her, but he said he couldn't since they were no longer friends. He suggested she attend a party one of their British colleagues was throwing. Since this colleague and Putzi were friends, Putzi would likely be there. She could go and introduce herself, which was what Martha did.

'Call me Putzi!' Hanfstaengl told her and she did, and that was that.

Everyone knew Putzi. He was a towering, garrulous giant of a man. Everything about him was oversize: his height – he stood nearly seven feet tall – his presence, his personality, his appetites, his ability to entertain and draw attention to himself, his boundless eccentricity and fondness for skirt. Putzi was the son of a prominent German art publisher and an even more prominent American mother.[16] He was born in Munich, educated at Harvard, and married to a woman from New Jersey. A talented pianist and a born entertainer, Hanfstaengl supposedly once destroyed a White House piano by playing it too energetically during an impromptu party put on by his classmate Theodore Roosevelt Jr, the President's son.

Unlike nearly everyone of his generation, Ernst Hanfstaengl hadn't fought in the Great War. He was living in America when it broke out in 1914, and though he could easily have returned to Germany at any time during the first couple years of the conflict, he stayed where he was, not returning home until almost a year after the Armistice. But no sooner had he returned to Munich than he suddenly experienced a flowering of patriotic conservatism and loathing of Weimar democracy, seeing it as weak and incapable of standing up to communism.

What led Hanfstaengl to Hitler was that, back in 1920, at the behest of his close American friend Truman Smith, a US Army intelligence officer stationed in Munich, Putzi attended a Nazi Party rally to report back what he'd found out about Hitler. Instead, at the rally, Hanfstaengl found himself mesmerised by the strange man's amazing oratory. In an epiphany, Hanfstaengl knew that he, Adolf Hitler, was Germany's future.

Hanfstaengl became an early Nazi supporter and one of Hitler's close friends. Hitler saw him as someone who could open doors for him, bring him beyond the gutter and beerhalls and introduce him to the industrialists with money. Hitler loved Putzi's piano playing. It calmed his soul in ways nothing else could. As is often the case with closeted male homosexuals, Hitler was more or less chastely in love with Helene, Putzi Hanfstaengl's wife. For much of the 1920s, Hitler was a constant presence in their house, playing with their son Egon so much he'd address him as 'Uncle Adolf'.

But of course that was ten years ago, and now, with Hitler in power, Putzi Hanfstaengl was quickly being marginalised. His title as 'Foreign Press Chief' was essentially something he'd come up with himself and it came without any power other than ready access to the Fuhrer. Hanfstaengl reinvented himself as a gatekeeper, the shaper of opinion, the go-between, the one who could make or break a foreign correspondent's tenure in Germany. He could arrange an interview with Hitler or some other top Nazi for a journalist of sufficient stature, but it always came with an implicit understanding that the journalist in turn had to 'play ball' and mute any criticism or they'd get cut off.

So, for a while, Martha let Putzi squire her around at parties. Not that it was an ordeal. Putzi was fun and his presence was much sought after since he had a way of making every party a success just by being there. He loved making dramatic entrances and dominating whatever space he occupied. If there was a piano in the room, and there usually was, he'd take it over and start pounding out music, inevitably drawing a crowd in the process. For Martha, Hanfstaengl was her admission ticket to meeting Germany's new elite, and the price of the ticket wasn't anything she wasn't already accustomed to. Of course, this isn't something she discusses in her book, but then *Through Embassy Eyes* was never meant to be a kiss-and-tell. That wasn't actually something Martha believed in. She told stories and dropped names, and what the reader might surmise from it was their business, not hers.

It didn't take long for George Messersmith to get word of Martha's running around with Putzi Hanfstaengl. His initial reaction was to dismiss it as essentially harmless, especially since on many of the occasions he'd heard about, she'd had her brother Bill Jr accompanying her. Martha was, apparently, pursuing a career in journalism; dealing with Hanfstaengl went with the territory. But as time went on, he found it increasingly troubling. In a letter to J. Pierrepoint Moffat, a colleague in Washington, Messersmith wrote:

When Mr. Dodd first came to Berlin and brought Martha and William with him, the two young people formed intimate contact with a number of the Nazis, among whom was Hanfstaengl. While I saw no harm in their having these contacts and saw some advantage in it, I did not feel that the close, constant, contact with Hanfstaengl was in our best interest. It aroused a certain amount of comment and did create a certain amount of reserve among certain people who could otherwise have been more frank with the Ambassador. While having every confidence in him, these people did not have the same confidence in Martha and William and feared indiscretions on their part.[17]

By this point, Messersmith already knew about Martha's escapades with Udet, Diels and others. His writings never reflect direct knowledge of an affair with Hanfstaengl, though it's a safe bet he'd made that conclusion privately. While Martha kept her fling with Putzi out of her memoir and apparently never discussed it with anyone, the same couldn't be said about Putzi, who bragged about it enough that his son recalled being told about it.[18] But this was years later. Initially, it appears he was quite circumspect in what he said publicly or even privately about Martha. Like Diels, Hanfstaengl was playing a long game when it came to Martha Dodd. He knew that, despite the top Nazis' near-universal indifference to what the outside world might think about them, acceptance of Hitler by the outside world was absolutely critical if Nazi Germany was to survive. To this end Hanfstaengl started developing a plan, one that would ultimately end up involving Martha.

Then there was Armand Berard. Officially, Berard was Third Secretary at the French Embassy. He was handsome and young, but despite being not much older than Martha, Berard was somebody senior people in the diplomatic community listened to. Martha met him at a formal dinner she attended with her parents in Counselor George Gordon's home.[19] Immediately they hit it off. After first asking her parents' permission, Berard began calling on Martha and inviting her out, and, after a fashion, they became occasional, but long-term lovers. Sometimes he'd take her to the movies or on long drives in the country outside Berlin. His manners and gallantry fairly swept her off her feet. Martha wasn't used to being treated with so much courtesy. She, of course, never mentioned to him or anyone that she was actually married. 'I suppose I practiced a great deception on the diplomatic corps by not indicating that I was a married woman at that time. But I must admit, I rather enjoyed being treated like a maiden of eighteen knowing all the while my dark secret,' she wrote.[20]

Berard had secrets of his own, though the biggest was more or less an open one in Berlin. Berard was deputy to Ambassador Andre Francois-Poncet, probably the best-informed foreign diplomat in Berlin.[21] While most ambassadors usually had no more than a single official conversation with Hitler during their time in Berlin, Poncet probably had dozens, including long, informal ones during occasional weekend get-togethers at the Eagle's Nest. Berard acted as Poncet's personal communications conduit with the British and

Americans. But more importantly, Berard was widely presumed to be the French Secret Service's top Berlin man. Martha started becoming aware of this whenever she'd introduce him to any of her acquaintances. 'The Germans began telling me he was a spy ... and that he was head of the French Secret Service in Berlin.' But Martha, being awash in what she called 'irresistible foreigners', was having too much fun for any of it to be, for her, anything but a delicious game.

Then one day, Putzi Hanfstaengl came to Martha with a brilliant idea. Hitler needed to get married, and the best thing would be if he married an American woman. That woman should be Martha.

5. MARTHA, THE FUHRER
NEEDS A WIFE

It wasn't that Hitler didn't like women. He did, though only up to a point. He liked being around them and talking to them and they certainly liked talking to him. But that was about as far as it went. The women, of course, were crazy about him. Everyone said it was his eyes. In this regard, he was like a Valentino.

People with any sophistication generally took it for granted that Hitler was homosexual. Anyone who knew what to look for saw it. It wasn't that Putzi lacked sophistication, it was just that he was old-fashioned in asserting that all Hitler needed was to find the right woman and settle down. The problem was that Hitler still wasn't really comfortable around women. Until just a few years earlier, Hitler's adult life had been spent entirely among men. Whether it was in Viennese flophouses and workingmen's dormitories, or army barracks and frontline trenches, his was a world almost completely away from women. Things being what they were, it was that way with a lot of men. It didn't necessarily have anything to do with sexual orientation. But now, with the ladies screaming for him by the thousands, it turned out Adolf Hitler had no idea what to do with them once he'd got them on the couch. Hitler insisted that there was magic behind his ability to take a woman's breath away and that the magic depended on his celibacy.

Putzi of course knew all that was horseshit and that it was just a question of finding the right girl, one who'd make a man of Adolf

Hitler. And sweet experience told Putzi Hanfstaengl that the right girl in this case was Martha Dodd.

He and Martha had, of course, done the deed, and as far as he was concerned, Martha was absolutely fantastic; if anybody could make Hitler see the light, it would be Martha. He also knew how these things worked. Hitler would fall in love with her, they'd get married and everything would be happily ever after.

<hr />

Hitler's close relationship with Putzi and Helene went on throughout the 1920s during his rise to power, but as soon as he became Chancellor, he began distancing himself from them. At Goebbels' urging, Putzi got taken off the inner staff list. Putzi reinvented himself as 'Foreign Press Chief', which he was uniquely qualified for, especially since Goebbels didn't have anyone whose foreign contact list came near Putzi's. But Putzi was just starting.

Putzi knew Hitler's grand, romantic image involved presenting himself as an unmarried man, untroubled by carnal desires, whose energies were wholly focused on Germany and the fulfillment of the Aryan race's cosmic destiny. Putzi thought that if Hitler had an American wife, he would be so much more acceptable to the outside world as well as to modern, outward-looking Germany. Hitler with a good-looking, witty and sophisticated American wife was the best thing to ensure that the Thousand Year Reich got off to a good start.

It galled Putzi that a thrice-married cow like Magda Goebbels could have herself called 'The First Lady of the Third Reich'. Well, if Putzi had any say in it, the title would belong to Martha Dodd.

<hr />

'Hanfstaengl had been calling me up and wanting to arrange for me to meet Hitler,' Martha wrote. 'Hanfstaengl spluttered and ranted grandiosely: "Hitler needs a woman. Hitler should have an American woman – a lovely woman could change the whole destiny of Europe. Martha, you are that woman."'

Intrigued, Martha agreed to Putzi's offer, and a few days later the arrangements were completed and she and Hitler were scheduled to meet for tea at the Kaiserhof, a luxury hotel on the Willehmstrasse. On the assigned day Putzi drove Martha to the hotel. He parked and they walked to the hotel terrace. There, she was taken to Hitler's table. Hanfstaengl waited in the lobby. Less than an hour later, it was over. Of Martha's time with Hitler, not too much can be said. They had tea and he talked with her a little. In her very bad German, she more or less understood what he was saying. Up close, she didn't find him that impressive. He didn't look amazing or anything, and he had bad breath. 'He seemed modest, middle class, rather dull and self-conscious,' Martha wrote, 'yet with this strange tenderness and appealing helplessness.'

Hitler's eyes, on the other hand, were something else. 'Certainly the eyes were his only distinctive feature. They could contain fury and fanaticism and cruelty. They could be mystic and tearful and challenging.' Perhaps, but not this time. This particular afternoon, she wrote, he was excessively gentle and modest in his manners.

Not that she ever said anything about it, but it probably took Martha Dodd all of about two seconds to know, with complete certainty, that fucking Hitler would be a really bad idea and not any fun, either. He had all the signs. She knew from experience that the best you can ever hope for in things like this might be 'pathetic', but only if he tried, and she'd rather not.

After a while Adolf Hitler and Martha Dodd stood up from the table. He bid Martha goodbye. Martha left and headed for the lobby. Putzi spotted her, got up and walked out with her.

When I left the Kaiserhof with the ecstatic and towering jitterbug Putzi, I could only lend half an ear to his extravagant, senseless talk. I was thinking of the meeting with Hitler. It was hard to believe that this man was one of the most powerful men in Europe – even at this time other nations were afraid of him and his growing 'New Germany'.

Martha and Hitler never met again. But she never forgot his eyes. In her book, Martha wrote: 'Only in the mad burning eyes could I see the terrible future of Germany.'

Autumn in Berlin was, for the Dodds, a time of both beauty and foreboding. Throughout October, the trees in the Tiergarten were vivid in their autumn colours. The air had a delicious bite to it mixed with the pungent smell of coal smoke. As happy as things appeared, the realization that their home was undoubtedly the target of wire-tapping and surveillance put the Dodds into a state of perpetual unease. Even though life largely went on as before, conversations lost their usual gay spontaneity and became muted and strained. They started keeping a lidded box near the telephone so they could put the telephone into it before engaging in sensitive conversations in case someone was listening in. Once, Diels observed Martha covering a telephone with a pillow. When he gave her a bewildered look, she put her finger to her lips. Diels smiled back approvingly. She was learning.

For the first time they began to suspect what everyone else had assumed from the beginning: that Fritz the butler might be a police plant. He seemed to always be around, but hidden, possibly listening in on their conversations. They also noticed that he seemed to let in Diels without introduction whenever he appeared at their door. Wisely, they decided it was best to do nothing about it. Better the devil you know.

6. IRON BOOTS

Moscow Center had gotten many of its people out well before Hitler launched his crackdown of German communists. Yet even months after the takeover, there were chunks of the illegal networks still in place, languishing, awaiting instructions. Moscow knew it would be only a matter of time before the Gestapo found the networks, and then after breaking them, turned them around and fed them back, unnoticed, into the Soviet apparatus. If and when that happened, Russia's German spy game would be ruined for years to come. Sometime during the late summer or early autumn, Moscow Center sent in the first of two experts to salvage what it could of the Grete networks. His name was 'Bruno' Grunfeld and beyond that nothing is known about him, other than that the purpose of his mission was to find the surviving segments, amputate the 'infected' parts and then 'cauterize' the adjoining 'good' network segments and move them away to prevent the Nazis from ever finding and infiltrating them.

It wasn't that Grunfeld was unsuccessful in his efforts, but something he was doing, either his reporting or all the expenses he was running, displeased Moscow Center, so they decided to send in someone higher up the food chain to take over his operation. His name was Gregor Rabinovich, and since he would later figure prominently in a number of major intelligence operations in America, quite a lot is known about him.[1] Louis Budenz, a leading American communist who worked with Rabinovich before defecting, recalls him as a 'sad-faced cosmopolitan that wore elegantly tailored suits'.[2] A medical doctor by training, Rabinovich also had a background in technical intelligence, which was particularly useful in this case, since the bulk of the old network's activities was industrial espionage. It was also important because many of the 'left-behinds' were involved in technical support activities, such as printing and document forging, and getting them relocated and up and running again required a lot in the way of logistics and reorganisation, something spies often aren't geared toward.

Rabinovich's mission was to streamline what Grunfeld had saved into new networks a fraction of the size of the earlier ones. Where previously there had been hundreds of 'worker-correspondents', now there were only about 25 agents on the ground. The networks' 'back end' operations: forging and printing got moved to Denmark, Holland, France and Czechoslovakia. Also, rather than pass messages to the embassy in Berlin, message traffic now went to Moscow via Paris. This increased the need for more couriers capable of crossing borders without arousing suspicion from the Gestapo. In other words, what they needed were more people with American passports and American identities.

In November 1933, diplomatic relations were formalised between the US and USSR. A Soviet Embassy opened in Washington, DC, along with consulates in New York and other major cities. And with that, AMTORG ceased being a diplomatic and consular stand-in and became nothing more than a Soviet-owned trading company and front for clandestine activities. More of its staff could now devote more of their time to espionage without having to worry quite so much about upsetting diplomatic apple carts.

Among AMTORG's crew of industry experts, technical intelligence gatherers and second-story men was an ardent individualist named Jacob Golos. His working hours were devoted to creating identities of non-existent people for whom he would then obtain genuine US passports, which would go to Soviet intelligence officers awaiting deployment, first to Germany and then later in the US. Because his product was so much better than the forged passports that were usually provided to its spies, Golos' genuine passports had a nickname within the community: *Zelezniye Sapogi* ('Iron Boots') – solid, unbreakable and guaranteed to work.

Golos identified as an American; even his Soviet employers considered him one. But, much like the identities he invented for a living, it was a creation he'd pinned on himself. Born Yakov

Naumovich Reizen in the Ukraine in 1889, he had been an early Bolshevik. Caught running an illegal printing press in 1906, he was sentenced to eight years' hard labour, which then got turned into permanent exile in a Czarist prison colony in Yakutia, northern Siberia. Reizen escaped, made his way across China, then boarded a Japanese freighter and smuggled himself into the US. Somewhere along the way he acquired the name Jacob Golos and an American identity. He worked in printshops in San Francisco and New York. He picked fruit and organised agricultural workers in California. He belonged to different socialist and left-wing political parties before becoming a founding member of the Communist Party of the United States of America (CPUSA).

Golos spent much of the 1920s in Russia, but then returned to America in 1930 to act as a CPUSA liaison with Soviet intelligence in America. As such, he was one of only a small number of CPUSA members with any real knowledge of Soviet intelligence activities in America. Since Moscow liked keeping things tightly compartmentalised, it might be assumed that what Golos knew was probably limited to his own sphere of activities. However, working at AMTORG put him more or less at one of the centers of Soviet intelligence operations in North America; it's a safe bet he was aware of quite a lot more.

Golos was also manager of World Tourists Inc., an AMTORG offshoot which arranged tours to the Soviet Union and other destinations. With Golos at the helm, it also got into the business of acquiring and then smuggling American passports and other critical identity documents into the hands of Moscow Center.

Golos had befriended a clerk at the passport office in Brooklyn named 'Johnny' who, it turned out, had a problem with gambling.[3] He was continually owing money to bookies, and Golos, kind, pragmatic soul that he was, would help Johnny out by lending him money. They soon came to an arrangement where Johnny, together with a colleague in Washington, would process and deliver bona fide, fully registered passports on demand for whatever identities Golos created with a turnaround time of only three days. To make it even better for the normally tight-fisted Soviets, the cost per passport was, by any standards, remarkably reasonable.

Another palm Golos greased was James Sullivan, a clerk for the Supreme Court for Kings County (Brooklyn) New York, whose job was to take oaths from the passport applicants. It isn't known precisely how or why Sullivan agreed to accept the oaths from the non-existent applicants which Golos brought to him. The operation went on through most of the 1930s before finally being shut down. By the time the FBI arrived to investigate it, Sullivan had already been dead for several years.[4]

✧

Back in Germany, trouble was brewing within the Nazi movement. Though things seemed peaceful on the surface, there was growing tension between Hitler and the SA. For years Hitler had preached Revolution. But when the time came, he conquered Germany with almost amazing ease. Now, for all intents and purposes, Germany was theirs. But as far as the SA was concerned, the revolution hadn't gone far enough. There were still millions of unemployed and the industrialists and the landowners and the rich still held the power, which the SA wanted redistributed. They wanted a second revolution to bring it about. But Hitler didn't want it. As far as he was concerned, the SA had already fulfilled its purpose. What he had to do was allay the fears of the industrialists and business owners, to let them know the socialist part of 'National Socialist' was mainly window dressing. Early in July, Hitler gave a speech to Nazi state governors in which he insisted that the 'revolution is not a permanent state of affairs, and it must not be allowed to develop into such a state'. 'The stream of Revolution,' he said, 'must be guided into the safe channel of evolution.'

This did not please Roehm. On 6 August, taking advantage of Hitler's absence, he staged a massive SA rally at Templehof Field, just outside of Berlin, in which he not only refuted Hitler's earlier statement, but tossed down the gauntlet before 80,000 Brownshirts. 'There are still men in official positions today who have not the least idea of the spirit of the revolution. We shall ruthlessly get rid of them if they dare to put their reactionary ideas into practice ... Anyone who thinks that the tasks of the SA have been accomplished will have to get used to the idea that we are here and intend to stay here, come what may!'

Roehm had plenty of reason to be brazen. He now led an army of 2 million men more loyal to him and the idea of a left-wing Nazi revolution than to Hitler, and he was certain they shared his opinion that if Hitler wasn't willing to bring them to it, then Roehm was the one who would. Many were beginning also to share Roehm's opinion that Hitler was, as he put it, a 'limp rag'.

⁂

Ambassador Dodd's relationship with the embassy staff never improved. He'd come to Berlin with strong ideas about how everyone at the embassy should represent American values while working there, but about all he'd succeed in doing was alienating them. They didn't like Dodd and Dodd didn't like them. His feelings toward George Gordon were permanently poisoned the moment he realised the aristocratic Gordon was a millionaire with a dozen servants at his house, even though it was only Gordon and his wife living there. Gordon was everything Dodd despised, even besides being difficult and explosive. But Gordon was also an expert and very, very good at his job. He'd been around for years and personally knew everyone who truly mattered, or at least used to matter, and his judgement on Germany and Europe was sound. Sackett hadn't particularly liked Gordon either, but he at least recognised his value and listened to what he had to say. Gordon in turn maintained a fairly favorable opinion of Sackett. Dodd didn't listen to Gordon except to dismiss whatever he'd say. Dodd's relationship with George Messersmith was different. Certainly, he never felt the deep class-antagonism toward him he did toward Gordon. Dodd and Messersmith had grown up in poverty and had gotten where they were purely by hard work. But while Dodd respected Messersmith and would listen to him, he was too set in his ways to learn from him.

Rather than working well with his staff, Dodd turned instead, as he always did, back to his family. By then, Bill Jr had moved out and found lodging elsewhere, to better concentrate on his studies. But Martha was there. As always, he could depend on her for wit and counsel. Being her father's confidant was something Martha was proud of. 'We love each other and I am told state secrets,'[5] she bragged in a letter to Thornton Wilder.

Martha would occasionally show up at the stammtisch with the reports and freshly decoded messages which her father shared with her. Often she'd read them aloud and compose replies in the other journalists' presence. It was all good fun and, in a way, it must have seemed at least a little equitable to them, since by now most of them had met Dodd and were readily sharing their information and insights with him. Having cut himself off from Gordon and most of the embassy's more formal information streams, Dodd found that in many respects, the information the reporters were providing her was as good, or better, than what the embassy had been getting.

❧

When Diels first met Martha in the autumn of 1933, everything seemed to be going in his favor. In the space of just a few months, he'd parlayed his collection of dossiers into the creation of the Gestapo, already considered the world's most-feared secret police organisation, with tentacles reaching into every town in Prussia and already spreading into the rest of Germany. But as powerful as it made him, Diels remained a pawn in someone else's struggle for power. And Goering, whose pawn he was, was at that moment being out-played by Heinrich Himmler and he didn't even know it.

Heinrich Himmler wasn't visibly anywhere near the top rungs of power at the time Hitler took over. Those rungs were occupied by Roehm, Goering, Goebbels, Hess, Streicher and a handful of others. In everyone's eyes, Himmler was merely a Roehm underling – in charge of bodyguards and security during rallies and that was it. Goering, being hierarchically minded and fond of titles, probably regarded Himmler as being simply too far down the Nazi Party food chain to bother thinking about. But whether or not Goering recognised it, Himmler and his numerically inferior SS were already well on their way to becoming the most powerful single group in the Nazi universe.

Looking at him, there was nothing about Heinrich Himmler to inspire fear or respect. Scrawny, pallid and near-sighted, he viewed the world through thick pince-nez eyeglasses, giving him the appearance more of a rheumy owl than an Aryan superman. Himmler had an oddball fascination with everything occult: karma, astrology, Nordic runes, Tibet. But for all his fascination with the ethereal, he was deeply obtuse and incapable of grasping nuance. He could show considerable initiative in carrying out orders, but couldn't think for himself.

The SA had always been a street-fighting brotherhood, mostly combat-hardened war veterans. For all the street brawls Himmler had participated in, he'd never seen front-line combat. This normally would have marginalised him, but Himmler had something the other stormtroopers didn't: an extreme knack for organisation and strategic thinking. After a stint as a full-time Party secretary and propaganda assistant under Gregor Strasser, Himmler joined the SS in 1925, when it was still primarily the SA's meeting hall guard detachment. A year later, its first head, Julius Schreck, handed the leadership of the SS over to co-founder Joseph Berchtold, preferring instead to simply be Hitler's chauffer. Hitler, who by this point already distrusted the SA, privately directed Berchtold to start making the SS more dynamic and distinctive. But Berchtold's efforts were stymied by the SA leadership, which wanted to keep them as nothing more than a somewhat specialised SA unit. After a year, Berchtold resigned and was replaced by his deputy, Erhard Heiden, a known 'former police stool pigeon of unsavory reputation'.[6] Under Heiden, everything started falling apart. Its numbers fell from roughly a thousand in 1926 to just 290. Hitler then made Himmler Heiden's new deputy. Himmler quickly turned the organisation around and soon its numbers were climbing back past a thousand. Then Heiden resigned, leaving Heinrich Himmler as the new Reichsfuhrer SS. At that time the SS membership stood at 2,000 members. In 1931, when Reinhard Heydrich became his deputy, it was over 10,000. By the time Hitler became Chancellor in January 1933, the numbers had again doubled. Man for man, the SS was tiny compared with the 2 million SA men Ernst Roehm commanded, but Himmler was infinitely more selective and strategic in terms of who he recruited into his ranks.

Himmler, like Hitler, was expert at making incremental moves nobody noticed. It is unlikely Roehm paid attention when Himmler opened a department called '1-c' inside the SS and appointed a recently cashiered naval officer named Reinhard Heydrich to run it. 1-c's purpose was counter-intelligence: it was the Nazis' first intelligence organisation. A year later, it was renamed *Sicherheitsdienst*, or SD, one of the most-feared internal security organisations in history.

Roehm likely also didn't pay any mind when Himmler convinced Hitler to let him run the SS as a separate organisation, since it technically remained subordinate to the SA, and to give him the rank of Obergruppenfuhrer, which, technically, also made Himmler equal to Roehm, which was laughable, since the SA was still easily twenty times larger than Himmler's SS. Nor did Roehm pay any mind when Himmler and Frick, the new Interior Minister, began creating a unified German police force. Why would Roehm care, since the police were already subordinate to the SA? If Roehm noticed when Bavaria made Himmler head of its police and that when he did, Himmler named Heydrich head of Bavaria's secret police, then he also noticed when, right after that, all the other states followed suit. But maybe he didn't. At the time, Roehm was enjoying the pleasures of his office. But now, Himmler and Heydrich controlled the police and secret police organisations for every single German state except Prussia, which belonged to Goering and his secret police chief, Dr Rudolf Diels.

If Roehm didn't notice, it was because his mind was focused on merging the SA with the army, without letting the flames of their Nazi Socialist revolution burn out, since it seemed all Hitler was doing was getting into bed with the capitalists. The army wanted the merger as much as Roehm did. Under the terms of the Armistice, the army was kept to only 100,000 men, a humiliation for a country that large. The SA numbered nearly 3 million rough and tumble streetfighters, decidedly lacking in the army's spit and polish, but they were experienced war veterans and all ready and willing to return to being professional soldiers. It was a question of who'd be leading this dance. Roehm couldn't see why the Reichswehr should lead, since they were obviously the junior partner. Besides, the SA was a revolutionary army, nationalist and socialist; an army of real men, and yes, an army of lovers – the fiercest, purest warriors of all! It wasn't something Roehm and his men were willing to give up, just for the Reichswehr's respectability.

As one might expect, the Reichswehr generals' view of the situation was almost exactly the opposite. While they acknowledged the Brownshirts were tough, seasoned fighters, they also viewed them as professional armies always view irregulars: as undisciplined scum. They also didn't like that Roehm and his leadership were openly and militantly homosexual. No, for this particular dance the army was going to have to lead!

Perhaps if Goering hadn't put so much on his plate, he might have noticed what Himmler was doing. But Goering had Prussia, he had aviation, and he was a minister without portfolio. Building political power required him to stay close to Hitler and remain in his favor. Prussia was running itself. The aviation office still didn't require much hands-on attention, but the Gestapo did. So would establishing primacy over the SA.

Roehm, restive over Hitler's foot-dragging over the Second Revolution, had been dropping hints all summer about not actually needing Hitler's say-so to start it. Hitler, being aware of this, had in turn started dropping broad hints to Goering that it might soon be time to put Roehm in his place, or that perhaps the best way might be to let him put together his little planned merger with the army and then, once he was done, yank him out and replace him with someone more suitable; someone like Goering. Goering liked the idea of being in charge of the whole Reichswehr: army, navy and soon-to-be-created Luftwaffe.

But while Goering and Roehm grandstanded and paraded about, Himmler was standing on the side, like a waiter, seemingly oblivious to the slights and snubs of his betters, but remembering them all, storing them all away, until the time came to settle accounts. The SS might have held the secret police powers in every single German state except Prussia. Goering might have insisted Prussia and the Gestapo were his and that he was not interested in giving them up to Himmler. But Himmler had other ideas.

⚜

One evening in October, the SS made its move against Diels. Knowing he was still at work and that his wife was at home by herself, a group of SS men broke into his apartment. His wife ran into the bedroom and locked herself in. Rather than come in after her, they found Diels' personal papers at his desk in the living room and began going through them, searching for anything they could use against him.

From their bedside telephone,[7] Frau Diels phoned her husband and told him what was happening. By the time he got there they had left, having taken with them all the papers they could find. Diels made a few calls and found out the raid had been led by an SS Hauptsturmfuhrer named Herbert Packebusch, someone Diels already knew plenty about. He knew Packebusch had previously been in the SA but that his artistic and literary leanings had led him to ditch them for the more elite and style-conscious SS.[8] Diels quickly assembled an armed counter-force of police and drove over to SS Headquarters at Potsdammerplatz. Entering the building with guns in their hands, they were let in without any fuss, walking right past the SS men guarding the entrance.

They found Packebusch at his desk in his shirtsleeves, scribbling down notes as he went through Diels' personal papers. He looked up to see Diels pointing his pistol down at him. Diels ordered him to put up his hands and stand up. With a nod from Diels, one of the policemen began searching Packebusch. He found nothing. Retrieving his papers, Diels informed Packebusch that he'd be coming with them. Packebusch asked if he could take his jacket. Diels ordered one of the cops to grab his jacket and give it to him. He did so, not bothering to first check it. The group walked out of the building without attracting any attention from the guards.

Under interrogation back at Gestapo Headquarters, Packebusch made it clear he wasn't intimidated by Diels' threats. Soon the two were shouting at each other, which went on for a while, until finally Packebusch snarled at Diels that he was a traitor. He whipped out a pistol hidden in his jacket and probably would have shot Diels had there not been a large dog sitting quietly in the corner next to Diels. It lunged at Packebusch, overpowering him, giving Diels enough time to yank the pistol from Packebusch's hands. The interrogation continued, though Packebusch was no more forthcoming now than he'd been before. Finally, he was let go.

❧

Diels might have won the opening round, but he knew he was in the loser's corner, a victim of his own success. He'd set up a secret police apparatus designed to put fear in people and it had worked. Everyone feared Diels, even Goering. The problem was that nobody liked him. Having no friends meant Diels had no protection. Given the choice, it was in everyone's interest to have Diels out of the way.

For the rest of October, Diels was a neurotic, paranoid, drunken mess. Even though he was a constant presence at the Dodd home, he wouldn't let Martha or Bill Jr in on any of the real details about what he was frightened of. 'Many times in these weeks, Diels seemed to cling to me, my brother, and the Embassy in a sort of desperation when his mind and imagination were harassed with fears and fantasies of having been poisoned by his enemies,' wrote Martha.

One day, Martha and her brother went to meet with Diels at a restaurant in Wannsee. When they got there, his distraught appearance shocked them. 'He told us dramatically that he anticipated being shot at any moment,' she wrote. 'We didn't take too seriously what he said, thinking that he was a melodramatic sort of fellow. And that his job was one in which anything might cause him to become hysterical or paranoiac. But it seemed a little strange to us that he didn't want to be seen in the city or among crowds.'[9]

At one point, he got up, excused himself and left the table. Once he was gone, a man came over whom Martha recognised as one of Roehm's adjutants. He told them Diels was in trouble and Martha 'should not antagonise the Nazis by being seen with him'.[10]

It wasn't the first warning Martha had received about Diels. At a recent cocktail party, one of her friends, a 'very nice Jewish boy', told her that what she was doing was 'very silly' and that she was 'playing with fire'.[11]

'You are being used by Diels, perhaps because he actually needs some protection,' he said. 'In any case, it is very dangerous to take sides in such a manner or to identify yourself with any particular man in the Nazi group. There is some sort of trouble ahead and you may get yourself unwittingly involved.'

Martha knew he was right. From what Diels and the journalists had been telling her, the Nazi leadership was endlessly plotting against each other and there were more factions than anyone even knew about. But the intrigue had seduced Martha. She loved being part of it and the price of admission had only been her body.

7. GESTAPO TO THE RESCUE

Sometime in the autumn of 1933, as her affairs with Berard, Udet and Diels were all heating up nicely, yet another swain entered Martha's life. Unlike the others, who ultimately all came and went, this one would change her life. His name was Boris Vinogradov and he was a Russian.

Boris was tall, thin and blond-haired with deep, blue, soulful eyes. Unlike most Soviet diplomats, he was polished, gregarious and with a devilish wit which endeared him to the newsmen, especially since Boris was also press spokesman at the Soviet Embassy. In her memoir, Martha never actually names him, but he's alluded to several times and, one gets the sense he is endlessly present at dinners, bierabends, in nightclubs and driving her around in the Ford roadster which for some mysterious reason the embassy allowed him to have.

Looking back on it years later, Martha couldn't be sure where they'd first met. Boris thought it might have been at a pub, in which case it could very likely have been the stammtisch at Die Taverne, since Boris was someone the reporters all knew and liked. It would have been nothing for one of them to have invited him along one evening. Boris spoke German, but no English. Martha still barely spoke any German, certainly not any Russian. Nevertheless the chemistry was there and they immediately decided to go dancing at Ciro's. Within a very short time, Martha and Boris had become 'an item'. She continued dating Diels and Berard and whoever else caught her fancy. Diels knew about this and presumably so did Berard. If either of them objected to it, they wisely kept it to themselves. Boris, on the other hand, was not so circumspect. He did not like sharing Martha and told her so, even though he himself was married and known to have other lovers. They fought. They made up. They fought more, followed by the inevitable making up. Such was the texture of their relationship during the four years that they knew each other.

It should have been obvious to anyone familiar with Vinogradov that he was a spy. Why else would the Soviet government allow him such liberties? Everyone else at the embassy seemed to have the personality of an automaton, permanently fearful of saying or doing anything which might get construed as disloyal. None of them ever went out alone. They were always in groups with minders present. Boris Vinogradov was free as a bird. He wore nicely tailored suits and always donned leather motoring gloves when he was behind the wheel of his car. Like Diels, whenever he was in the Dodd home, he seemed to have his own bantering relationship with Fritz, the family butler and presumed secret police informer. The newsmen either didn't suspect him of being a spy or they simply didn't care. Soviet spies weren't their problem just yet.

As for Diels, most of the time he seemed withdrawn and downcast. When he'd drop by the consulate for a chat, they could see his nervousness. With the summer tourist season over, and fewer SA assaults on Americans, Messersmith and the others weren't requiring his assistance as much. Then, in early November, Diels suddenly emerged from his depression and went on the offensive, staging a series of police raids on some of the impromptu prisons the SA and SS had set up, which Hitler insisted he had no control over. At an SA barracks they raided on 10 Hedemannstrasse in Berlin, the fourth floor had been turned into a torture chamber.[1] They found prisoners half-dead from starvation, who had been kept standing for days inside narrow cupboards.[2] In the cellar were more prisoners, whom the torturers had finished with, lying on the floor, beaten, bones broken, bleeding, their faces unrecognisable. They'd been left there to die. Diels ordered them to be released and then went looking for more. No one had any idea how many makeshift prisons there were.

On 4 November, he sent out Gunther Joel, one of his lieutenants, and a group of Gestapo and Prussian state police to an SS-run concentration camp called Borgermoor, in the barren wetlands near Papenburg in Lower Saxony. Its thousand-odd prisoners were mostly

Social Democrats and communists, many of them Jews, engaged in what was termed 'land reclamation'. Joel brought his force to the camp gate, showed his warrant and demanded entry. The commandant refused and a gun battle ensued, which went on for ten minutes before he asked for a ceasefire.[3] Soon after, the SS men marched out and the Gestapo and Prussian police took it over.

Himmler's revenge took an odd form. A couple of days after the incident, he met with Goering and Diels and presented them with a sheaf of what he claimed were communications between different communist conspirators, proof, he claimed, of a 'Trotskyist plot' to assassinate Goering. If Diels was such an expert on communists, why wasn't he aware of it? Diels knew what he was insinuating, that Diels had turned a blind eye to it because he was still a left-wing socialist. After that, Himmler and Heydrich presented President Hindenburg with a dossier highlighting Diels' many moral failings: his drinking, his womanising and his erratic behavior as a student. It was enough for Hindenburg to demand Diels' resignation as director of Gestapo, but in the end it was only a 'paper' demotion. Someone else had the title, Diels still had the job. Himmler had yet to make his real move.

One morning a few days later, while driving to work, Diels spotted two of his aides standing on the curb, frantically waving at him to pull over. When he did, they ran up and told him a force of men from the SS and SD had taken over Gestapo Headquarters. They had a warrant for Diels' arrest and were at that moment searching his offices for incriminating evidence. Diels thanked them, turned his car around and drove away.

That night, Diels drove across the Czechoslovakian border in the company of a 'Frau von Clemm', the vivacious, adventurous and soon-to-be-divorced American wife of a prominent German-American businessman.[4] Frau von Clemm constituted half of Diels' cover. The other half was an American passport apparently given to him that very day by Messersmith, who had discretionary access to blank, unissued American passports.[5][6]

The two decamped to Karlovy Vary, the west Bohemia spa town. Reading *Bohemia*, the local German newspaper, Diels learned he'd been replaced by Paul Hinkler, the one-time Nazi police president of Altona, well known as a hopeless, mentally unbalanced alcoholic. A surreptitious phone call to Pilli Koerner, one of Goering's most trusted lieutenants, had Koerner telling Diels that it had all been a terrible mistake and begging him to come back. Hinkler was a disaster and it had all been Himmler and Heydrich's fault.[7] They'd tried to prove to Hitler that both Goering and Roehm were communists and the evidence they'd presented against them had turned out to have been nonsense. The crisis was over.

Diels knew if he returned to Germany, he'd be right back in the hornet's nest. Himmler still wanted the Gestapo, and losing a round wouldn't deter him. They'd be after him, he'd be alone. Last time, Goering hadn't lifted a finger to protect him.[8] If it happened again, why would Diels think he would do anything differently?

Still, he knew he couldn't stay where he was. Karlovy Vary was already filling up with Jews and other political refugees with whom he didn't particularly wish to associate. Once they figured out who he was, things would get very unpleasant. Besides, if Himmler was that determined to rub him out, he could just as easily do it there as in Berlin.

Another call to Koerner had him put through directly to Goering who implored Diels to come back so he could get rid of Hinkler right away. Diels wanted to know why Goering hadn't just handed the Gestapo over to Himmler and was told Himmler had changed his mind and 'wouldn't think of it'. So Diels and Frau von Clemm packed their bags and returned to Berlin.

When Diels returned to work the next day, Hinkler was already gone. A day or two later, Goering took Diels to see Hitler. The Fuhrer's confidence in Diels seemed to be as strong as ever.

⁂

In early December, Bella Fromm spotted Diels with other top Nazis at a large social event in Berlin. 'It was rather amusing to watch the Nazi leaders spying on each other,' she observed. 'Himmler from Munich was there, and Gestapo chief Diels. There are more. None of them can trust the others. There's a constant race on to be the first to inform on the other fellow and get his job.'[9]

By then, of course, Martha and Diels were back at it. Both were adept enough at juggling lovers that finding time for each other was not difficult. But during their times together, Martha couldn't help but notice how nervous Diels still seemed. Gone was much of his fun-loving wickedness, though he did continue to drop by at Tiergartenstrasse 27A, very often unannounced, and to have cordial relations with Martha's parents as well as with herself. He continued to make himself available to officials at the embassy and consulate, always ready to solve any of the many problems which seemed to increasingly befall American tourists and residents.

But Diels was getting desperate. The American card was about all that was left in his hand. Evidently he had concluded that staying close to the Americans might be the only good way to ensure his own safety. Early in December, Martha learned that Diels had approached Messersmith and her father, requesting letters of recommendation attesting to all the help he'd been to the American Embassy as well as to the American community in Berlin. While both affirmed to Diels that he had indeed been of great help to them, they nevertheless felt writing such a letter 'would not be appropriate'. While Diels left empty-handed, he continued to be a presence.

By now Boris commanded most of Martha's attention, but Diels was never far from her mind. In the middle of December she wrote a letter to Thornton Wilder describing the situation. 'The snow is soft and deep lying here – a copper smoke mist over Berlin by day and the brilliance of the falling moon by night. The gravel squeaks under my window at night – the sinister face, lovely lipped and gaunt Diels … must be watching me.'[10]

***

Somewhere in the course of their time together Martha started slipping Boris reports and cables she'd taken from her father's desk. It probably first happened during one of the evenings where Martha was entertaining the gang at the stammtisch. Perhaps Boris had witnessed it himself. Perhaps he'd heard about it from someone else and asked to be invited along to see for himself. Either way it had to be the answer to his prayers. When she'd finished her performance, he probably asked if he could look at it and then neglected to give it back. Or perhaps he pinched it – swiping documents is something spies are known to do. She may not have noticed it was missing, or if she did, she likely didn't care. She was probably inebriated, and even if she wasn't, it's unlikely she held the embassy in any great regard. Besides, she and Boris were in love.

8. THE MAN WHO KNEW TOO MUCH

November turned to December, and from then through February, things were mostly quiet. Christmas came, and for the Dodds the serenity of the season was almost enough to put all the ugliness out of their minds. In his diary, Ambassador Dodd noted 'Christmas trees at public squares and in every house' and cynically mused that 'one might think the Germans believed in Jesus or practiced his teachings'.[1] By now, they had been in Berlin a little over five months and it had been an eye-opener for them. Dodd had brought his family to Germany sure that Hitler and the Nazis had been getting an unfair rap in the press and that whatever woe was being visited upon the Jews was something they'd brought upon themselves. But it hadn't taken very long for him to recognise that the country he'd loved so much was descending into pagan barbarism and the people he'd never much cared for, the Jews, were its hapless victims. Now, without even wanting to, Dodd was standing at the front lines fighting for them.

For Dodd's wife Mattie and son, it was different. Mattie mostly stayed home and her opinions rarely went beyond the family circle. Being wife of an ambassador did require her attendance at events, but her participation in them was mostly perfunctory. As for Bill Jr, it hadn't taken him long to hate his new surroundings. Rather than try to live amid Tiergartenstrasse 27A's unending social swirl, he found lodging elsewhere, focused on his studies and his own circle of friends.

Martha's eyes had also been opened by what she'd seen. But she'd let herself fall in love with Germany, the same way she did with the men she fancied. It had worked for a while; in fact it still did work. As aware as she was of much of the evil growing around her, Nazi Germany never stopped exciting her. Martha loved being at the center of all the glamour and attention and endless intrigue. Besides, she was getting from it an education she knew she'd never get anywhere else.

An amnesty was declared in the weeks before Christmas, and as a result nearly all of the remaining political prisoners in the illegal camps were released. Diels made a point of travelling to a number of the camps, giving speeches to the inmates and hailing their return to freedom. All in all, the impression it made on the world press was positive. Hitler was pleased and, through Goering, let Diels know he had big plans for him.

Even though Martha and Boris Vinogradov were officially 'an item', it didn't stop her from going out with Diels, and anyone else she fancied. It was all Diels needed to continue being a frequent presence at the Dodd home as well as at the US Embassy and Consulate General. The events of the autumn caused Diels to realise he'd put himself in a bad situation and in a way, the American Embassy crowd were about the only friends he had left, so he stayed close to them. His long skirmish with Himmler had left him permanently paranoid and bitter. Winning one battle against Himmler didn't mean much since Himmler's people were everywhere and once the gloves did finally come off, he'd be dead. Diels figured that the best way to protect himself was to hug the diplomatic limelight, which meant staying close to the Americans.

Of these days, Martha wrote: 'Many times in these weeks, when Diels seemed to cling to me, my brother, and the Embassy in a sort of desperation. When his mind and imagination were harassed with fears and fantasies of having been poisoned by his enemies. And now, in these weeks he was like a frightened rabbit.'2

Even with Martha's ever-deepening involvement with Boris Vinogradov and the fact that she was already occasionally giving him embassy documents, she remained sympathetic to the Nazis. She'd often discuss her feelings about them with her father whenever the two of them were together. Dodd would listen to her making excuses for all the Nazi excesses. 'My father would look at me a bit stonily, if tolerantly and gently label me a young Nazi,' she wrote. 'That put me on the defensive for some time and I became temporarily an ardent defender of everything going on.'

❧

With the new year, speculation started appearing in the foreign press about possible friction between Hitler and Goebbels on one side and Goering on the other.[3] There were rumors Goering hadn't received New Year's greetings from Hitler, an indication he was falling from favor. As the weeks passed, speculation only increased. Word on the street was that the army would stage a putsch and replace Hitler with Goering. At the same time there seemed to be a consensus among 'the informed' that President von Hindenburg might call for a Hohenzollern to return to the throne, while keeping Hitler around as Chancellor along with a national assembly of some sort.

❧

While Hitler pit Goebbels against Goering, and Himmler against both of them, Roehm remained his bigger concern. His discussions with the generals about merging the SA with the Reichswehr remained at an impasse over which of them would lead the dance. Hitler let everyone know he supported the merger, he just wanted someone besides Roehm in charge once it was accomplished. He even suggested to Goering he might be the man for the job. Possibly for this reason Goering castigated Diels for his close ties to Roehm. Then he ordered Diels to carry out an investigation into Roehm and the other SA leaders on their corruption of members of the Hitler Youth: 'The SA is the pace maker in all this filth.[4] You should look into it more thoroughly.'[5] Later that month, Diels and Goering travelled to visit Hitler at Obersalzberg, where he presented his report detailing how Roehm had been conspiring not only with Hitler's old-friend-turned-rival Gregor Strasser, but also Kurt von Schleicher, who'd directly preceded him as German Chancellor. The report also suggested that the French government had paid Roehm 12 million marks to overthrow Hitler.[6]

Hitler was furious and fumed that 'Strasser and Schleicher, these arch-traitors have survived to this day'. After leaving the meeting, Goering told Diels: 'You understand what the Fuhrer wants? These three must disappear and very soon.'[7]

⁕

Then in March, after months of lying low, Diels launched new raids against the SA and SS prisons. Following one at a shut-down tire factory in Stettin,[8] Diels and Hanfstaengl held an informal get-together with members of the Foreign Press Association, where he described to the reporters the ragged, beaten, starving prisoners they'd found in the camp; how in the previous year, 30,000 Germans had been imprisoned by the SA and SS. By now, he said, all but 5,000 had been freed and most of the rest would soon be let go. He said the Gestapo believed in humanitarian treatment, not force.'[9]

⁕

Being favored with an important assignment from Hitler should have given Diels a sense of invulnerability. But if it did, it didn't last long. Himmler resumed his quiet offensive against him and Diels quickly crumbled. One morning in April he invited Martha to come see him at his home. Not having any idea what to expect and wary of a confrontation with his wife, she brought her brother along. Diels' wife met them at the front door and let them in. She was, Martha wrote later, 'a rather pathetic, passive-looking creature' and Martha guessed she 'must have gone through hell living with Diels'.[10]

Frau Diels brought Martha and Bill Jr into the living room where they found Diels lying on a couch with two loaded pistols within reach on a nearby table. Diels dismissed his wife and then invited them to sit. Once she was gone, he gravely told them 'the hit was on'. He'd had it on very good authority that Heydrich would be sending his goons to arrest and kill him. 'Today, maybe tomorrow, but probably today,' he told them. If Diels showed his face outside, they'd shoot him down on the streets. If he stayed there, inside his home, it might take a little longer, but eventually they'd storm in and kill him there. The only real question was whether they would shoot his wife in the process. They might or they might not. Either way, Diels was a dead man.

Diels showed them a map of Germany he had with him on the couch. Marked all over it were what Martha called 'the nuclei of the secret police agents and organization'. To her, it was a terrifying spectacle because by now she knew that: 'All the lines and designs spelled brutality, torture, sacrifice of innumerable human lives – it was a vast spiderweb of intrigue, carefully and effectively spun, woven with the blood, sinew, brain and nerves of thousands of Germans.'[11] But her lover did not see it this way.

'Most of this is my work,' Diels told them, with bitter pride. 'I have really organised the most effective system of espionage Germany has ever seen.' Martha looked up from the map at Diels and wondered how he could ever have been a Social Democrat, someone who had once been chief of police under Severing, the respected Prussian minister who 'had given his mind and work to a supposedly humanitarian and democratic system'.[12] Now Diels was 'teary-eyed and fearful' and on the verge of breaking out into a fit of weeping because the totalitarian police state he'd devised was about to be taken away from him. Martha asked Diels how he could be so fearful when he had so much power in his hands. 'Because I know too much,' was his mournful reply.

Martha and her brother didn't stay long and once they were back outside, she thought over Diels' predicament and she suddenly knew what she had to do. Saying goodbye to her brother, Martha went to see the one person she'd heard might be able to help her.

❧❦☙

George Messersmith was neither delighted nor surprised to learn Martha Dodd was outside his office at the Consulate General, wishing to see him. He'd been aware of Martha's involvement with Diels and other ranking Nazis for some time and was fairly disgusted at her behavior. Being both a very blunt man and one schooled in discretion and keeping secrets, he wrote of the incident years later, just before he died, but refrained from actually naming her, referring to her instead as 'the daughter of a prominent American official in Europe':

> She started to weep and she told me that Diels, the head of the German Secret Police, that is the Gestapo, was about to be arrested during the course of the day and that it was almost certain that he would be executed. When she was able to compose herself she asked me to see Goering immediately and tell him that Himmler was going to have Diels knocked off during the course of the day, as he wished him out of the way in order to have himself made head of the Gestapo and in this way take away some of Goering's power. She said that I was the person and the only person who could tell this to Goering without being in danger of his own life, and that as it was so important to Goering she wished me to see him immediately.[13]

When Messersmith told her there was nothing he could do for her, Martha became hysterical, pleading with him, begging for him to save her lover's life. Writing about it, he admits he 'felt no real sympathy for her because I felt that she had behaved so badly in so many ways, especially in view of the position held by her father' and that it was 'only with a great deal of difficulty that he was able to get her out of his office'.[14]

But once Martha was gone and Messersmith had time to think about it, he realised she had been correct. Diels was, after all, one of the best in the regime, as was Goering, and if anything happened to Diels and Himmler came in, Goering's position would be weakened and with it what Messersmith considered 'the more reasonable element in the party'.[15] Messersmith also realised that with Himmler as head of the Gestapo, US government representatives would have a great deal more difficulty dealing with cases of attacks on American citizens, 'for Himmler was known to be even more cold-blooded and ruthless than Dr. Diels'. Messersmith knew he had to do something.

It was almost noon, and Messersmith had a luncheon engagement at the *Herrenclub*, Berlin's most exclusive 'English style' gentleman's club. He had been invited the week before by General von Fritsch and General von Seeckt, the heads of the army. Messersmith had not been told the reason for the luncheon, but knew it had to be something very important. But much as he needed to attend, he knew it was imperative he speak with Goering. He made a phone call to Goering's closest lieutenant, Erhardt Milch, whom he already knew fairly well, and asked if he could get an immediate meeting. Milch answered that Goering had just left for the *Herrenclub*, where a luncheon was being put on in his honor. Realising that this had to be the same luncheon he'd been invited to, Messersmith rang off, grabbed his hat and coat and headed out.

⚜

It was just a little after twelve when Messersmith arrived at the *Herrenclub*. The luncheon had not yet begun. He found Goering standing in conversation with the two generals who were hosting it. Goering saw him approach and immediately broke off his conversation with the generals, walked up to Messersmith and put his arms around his shoulders like they were old pals. 'Gentlemen,' Goering declared, 'this is a man who doesn't like me at all, a man who doesn't think very much of me, but he is a good friend of our country.'[16] Goering and Messersmith joined with their hosts and chatted for a few minutes, but then as soon as the opportunity arose, Messersmith asked Goering if they could have a moment aside as he had something to say to him which was of 'some importance'. 'I told him in very few words that a person in whom I had absolute confidence had called on me that morning and told me that Himmler was bent on getting rid of Diels during the course of the day and that Diels was actually to be bumped off. I did it in the plain language that Goering was accustomed to use himself and which I knew would leave no doubt as to the character of the information which I had.'

Goering thanked Messersmith for the information and promptly walked over to the two generals and told them 'that something had come up which required his immediate attention and that to his great regret he would have to forego the pleasure of having lunch with (them)'. Goering departed and the luncheon, which, it turned out, was to have been in his honor, 'went on just as though nothing had happened'.

At around five o'clock, the late edition of the *Berliner Zeitung* came to Messersmith's desk with headlines that proclaimed that Rudolf Diels, head of the Gestapo, was being transferred to Cologne as *Reichs Reigerungs Prasident*. He had resigned his post which would now be filled by Reichsfuhrer SS Heinrich Himmler.[17] Goering had apparently suffered no visible fall in prestige.

A few days later, on 20 April 1934, there was a ceremony in Berlin in which Rudolf Diels, wearing the splendid black uniform of an SS *oberfuhrer*, formally handed over control of the Gestapo to Heinrich Himmler, who now controlled all the police in Germany.

A few days later, Messersmith was promoted to ambassador and sent to Vienna to replace the American Ambassador to Austria who had suddenly died. Though he was gone from Germany, his presence continued to be felt. It was not to be his last unpleasant encounter with Martha either.

Writing about it in a letter to Undersecretary of State William Phillips in Washington, George Messersmith wrote: 'The real story of this is that Diels is really a decent man, who, as long as five months back insisted that order could not be brought about unless SA men were punished the same way as others. The long and short of it is, of course, that Diels was too decent for the political police and that an SA man like Himmler, who could be depended upon to do anything, must take his place.'[18]

Martha and Diels did continue to be occasional lovers, even though he'd been knocked down a number of rungs to a post which was mostly without any power. Diels' facial scars continued to exert their magic on Martha. While Boris Vinogradov and other lovers would largely replace him in Martha's affections, Diels was the one she would write the most about in both her bestselling memoir and the screenplay which, for a while, came very close to being turned into a major motion picture. As for Boris Vinogradov, the uncontested love of her life, there was no mention at all.

9. RECRUITS AND 'IRON BOOTS'

'Tell Boris Vinogradov that we want to use him to carry out a project that interests us,' read the message from Moscow Center to someone at the Berlin Embassy codenamed 'Arkhip'. The 'project' was his American lover, Martha Dodd. 'According to our information, the sentiments of his acquaintance have fully ripened for her to be recruited once and for all to work for us.' Arkhip was to direct Boris to write Martha 'a warm, comradely letter', inviting her to travel to Paris, where an operative whom Boris knew personally would meet with her and 'will take the necessary actions to recruit Martha for our work'.[1]

Although Boris presumably did as instructed, there isn't any evidence Martha actually went. What happened? Could she have taken the trip without mentioning it to anybody? It's entirely possible. Martha had, by this point, learned the rudiments of tradecraft and the importance of keeping her mouth shut. Could Martha have suddenly gotten cold feet? Or did she simply refuse to go because she had no interest in spending her own money traveling to a city she didn't care for to meet someone she didn't know?[2] Since this took place at around the same time that Rudolf Diels, Martha's main boyfriend then, was going through all kinds of hell with the SS, she may have felt her first duties were with him and not with some supposed friend of Boris'. It's all possible, but there is no way of knowing.

Or it also might have been that, willful woman and inveterate 'player' that she was, Martha wasn't one who liked being told what to do, or being expected to accept the first offer she was presented with. One of the first things a Communist Party member is supposed to learn upon joining is giving unquestioning obedience to orders from above. Martha hadn't yet joined the Party, but either way, it was one of those virtues she never quite picked up during the more than 50 years she considered herself a good Stalinist. Blindly following orders would never be her forte. Martha Dodd might have been an 'easy' woman, but she was never a pushover.

Or perhaps Martha simply wished for something better. Again, there is no real information to go by, but a couple of things do stand out. The fact that they wished Martha to meet with someone in Paris would suggest she was being considered for the 'illegal' networks in Berlin, possibly as a courier, since Paris was where all the illegal operations against Germany were based. Boris Vinogradov, being with the embassy, belonged to the fleshier, 'legal' operation. In the Soviet spy world, the legal and illegal operators never, ever mixed. They kept clear of each other, particularly since the illegals were usually, by appearance, from somewhere other than Russia. Had Martha gone to Paris and joined the illegal apparatus it would likely have necessitated an end to her relationship with Boris. Perhaps having consulted with him on this point, she thought it might be better to pass on the invitation and instead take her candidacy directly to the top, so they, and not some mid-level agent runner, might immediately recognise her true potential and aim her to a higher slot. Again, there is no way of actually knowing.

Signed-up agent or not, Martha continued slipping Boris reports and cables from her father's desk. Over the next several months Boris reported back only twice about Martha. The first was on 25 May with news that 'tense relations have taken root at the American Embassy'. The second was on 11 July when he reported that Martha 'plans to leave soon for the USSR as a tourist'.[3]

There is also no way of knowing who the person in Paris waiting to recruit Martha might have been. Was he actually an acquaintance of Boris or was that simply what he was told to tell her? Paris had been a hotspot of Soviet espionage activity for years at this point, but aimed at the French target, whom Moscow had initially considered a more serious threat than Germany. But now, with all that was happening in Germany, some of its best people who'd been there working against the French were now being redirected against Germany.

Of course, what little is known about these activities are only stray fragments; orphan pieces to a lost puzzle. But among them all exists one good-sized chunk crying out to be fitted into the larger picture, and since the man residing within that chunk eventually figures significantly in Martha's later career, the urge to connect it to her is naturally very strong.

⁂

On 15 February 1934, SS *Washington*, the same United States Lines steamship which, seven months earlier, had carried the Dodds to Germany, once again departed the New York docks on its regular Hamburg run.[4] Among the several hundred passengers aboard were Edward Joseph Herbert, his wife Sarah, and their infant son, Peter, whose photograph was included in the mother's passport. Herbert, whose birthdate was listed as 26 April 1898, was 36 years old. He was described as having blond hair, blue eyes, and a height of five feet, seven inches. His profession was listed as 'salesman'. Sarah Herbert, née Graff, born on 18 May 1906, was 28, with black hair, dark brown eyes, standing five feet, three inches tall. Her stated profession was 'housewife'. Both were born in New York City and lived at 217-21 133rd Rd in Springfield Gardens, Long Island. Their plan was to visit Europe for a couple of months and then return home.[5]

At least that was the understanding at the New York Passport Office when the passports were issued to the Herberts just three days earlier. Truth be told, the Herberts weren't actually aboard the SS *Washington* when it departed New York. Nor were they in New York or even, for that matter, anywhere in North America. The truth is, Edward and Sarah Herbert didn't actually exist, at least not for a couple more months. At the time the ship set sail, the people whose faces were on the Herberts' passports were living in Paris, but slated for Berlin. Neither was born in New York City, nor did they live in Springfield Gardens, Long Island. An Edward Joseph Herbert and a Sarah Graff had been born on the dates indicated in the photostatic copies of the birth certificates which had been submitted with their applications. That both had died in infancy was, on the other hand, not reflected anywhere in the paperwork. As far as the applicants were concerned, it was an unimportant detail and not pertinent to the business at hand. What mattered was that the two passports issued to them were genuine and now could be used without any difficulty for the remainder of the 1930s and well into the 1940s. For the couple purporting to be Edward J. and Sarah Herbert, these passports were their 'iron boots', the proud work of Jakob Golos.[6]

At that moment, the Herberts were Jaroslav and Elizabeta Kocek, a Slovak couple in the advertising business who had emigrated from Copenhagen, Denmark, a few years earlier. The Koceks were, in fact, intelligence officers with OGPU, *Obyedinyonnoye Gusodarstvennoy Politicheskoye Upravleniye*, or Joint State Political Directorate. The organisation's name had been around since 1922. In another couple of months, it would change to 'People's Commissariat for Internal Affairs' – *Narodny Komissariat Vnutrennikh del*, or NKVD. In another twenty years, it would be renamed *Komitet Gosudarstvennoy Bezopasnosti* – 'State Security Committee', or KGB – which it would keep using until the collapse of the Soviet state in 1991. But to everyone who worked for it, its real name was the one it had started out with during the earliest days of the communist state: *Cheka*.

Cheka stood for *The All-Russian Extraordinary Commission for Combating Counter-revolution, Profiteering and Corruption*. While its name would change many times over the years, the organisation largely stayed the same. It was the secret police agency working for the Central Committee of the Communist Party of the Soviet Union, and for as long as it existed, its members called themselves '*Chekists*'.

Both Vasily Mikhailovich Zarubin and Elizabeta Zarubina, the real names of the couple purporting to be Edward J. and Sarah Herbert, were Chekists, both in the Service since the Russian Civil War. Vasily had previously been deployed in Finland, the Far East and China.[7] Elizabeta had fought in Romania, worked in New York and Turkey, and attended the Sorbonne in Paris. She spoke many languages perfectly, including English.[8] He spoke almost as many languages, though not as perfectly. His English was still rough and heavily accented and would need work before he could hope to pass himself off as American. But Vasily Zarubin thought very well on his feet and was nothing if not intrepid. He could be curt and inconsiderate and frequently rubbed people up the wrong way. Liza, as she was called, was just the opposite: kind, nurturing and very empathetic; she was someone people naturally turned to, to settle conflicts. But she was also known to be icily ruthless when necessary.

They had married shortly before being sent to Copenhagen. It was her second marriage, his third. No one expected Cheka marriages to last, although of course sometimes they did. Over the years, Vasily and Liza had worked singly and with others. Between deployments they mainly socialised with other Chekists. In 1934, it was still more a fraternity than an organisation. Later would come times of fear and purges and betrayal, but this was the golden time. For now, Chekists were all family.

The baby boy whose picture appeared on Sarah Herbert's genuine American passport was their sixteen-month-old son, Pyotr Vasilyevich. Like his parents, little Peter Herbert had supposedly been born in New York City. He had actually been born in Paris as 'Petr Kocek',[9] since his parents were, at that time, disguised as Czechoslovak emigres and part-owners of an advertising agency that took them all over France and even sometimes Germany on business. They'd emigrated from Denmark in 1929 where they'd been involved in the same work for a number of years.

During their time in Paris, they had recruited a number of agents and grabbed a good quantity of secret French government documents. A tennis fanatic, Zarubin, as Jaroslav Kocek, had joined a leading Parisian tennis club and sometimes even made it into tournaments that took him to other cities. The club provided an opportunity to get acquainted with, and ultimately recruit, rising young French politicians. Meanwhile, Liza did the same with an underpaid and overworked secretary at the German Embassy and soon had access to key communications coming in and out of the German Foreign Ministry.[10]

The whole time there, the Zarubins worked their covers perfectly, maintaining a low-key, but not invisible, presence. They made friends, entertained sometimes, did business locally. Zarubin patronised a local pub and socialised a normal amount. It was the best way of not attracting attention. People, if asked, had things to say about them – good things, normal things.

Ever since the Armistice, Moscow viewed France as its most likely enemy and therefore its number-one intelligence target. Germany didn't rate quite so high, as its army was both small and already engaged with them in the secret entente. The British, being off by themselves on a large island somewhere between Ireland and Belgium, didn't quite rate either. No, it was the sneering, ever-belligerent French who, for an entire decade, had posed the direct, existential threat to Russia. But now Hitler had put an end to all that.

Though the Russian–German entente continued apace, and despite Hitler's assurances that crackdowns against communists were meant only for *German* ones, and that anything that might have been visited upon Russian communists in Germany was a mistake deeply regretted, Germany was suddenly now the greater threat. Moscow Center began redeploying its resources aimed at the French and directing them against the Germans. And with a wave of Moscow Center's magic wand, the Zarubins would cease being the Koceks and become Edward, Sarah and Peter Herbert of Long Island, New York.

While the task of successfully situating couriers in Berlin was not an overly difficult one, doing the same thing for full-up intelligence officers like the Zarubins was going to require more than an American passport. They needed to create for themselves a presence big enough to 'hide' behind. They'd need a reason for being there: a business, or better, a large, well-known company back home that they could say they were representing. And because Edward Herbert was a businessman and not a student, he'd need a full, respectable residence: an apartment and not just a room somewhere. He'd also need a business address: an office with phones, and a local bank. To have all those, they'd have to have either a real employer or something which at least passed for one. They'd also need to have a background, a legend. These were not the easiest things in the world to acquire.

With all this in mind, Moscow Center sent word to AMTORG and the newly opened consulates to keep their eyes open for people who might be able to help provide backgrounds for their agents. Sometime during the spring of 1934 word came back to Moscow from someone on the staff in the New York consulate, codenamed 'Osip', that they might have just found someone who could help them.

A man had recently visited the consulate, a Russian-born American business executive, requesting help sending food parcels and other items to family members back home. From the way he carried himself, Osip knew right away he had to be someone important and not just another nobody, such were most of the people coming through their doors seeking help. Osip invited the man to lunch.

The man said his name was Boris Morros and that he was a top executive at Paramount, the giant film and entertainment company. Over lunch, Osip listened enraptured as the man regaled him with endless stories of movie stars and show business. Each tale seemed to spur another, and another one after that, all of them full of glittering detail, colour and confidential information. The point of all of them seemed always to be how important he was and how everyone in the business – that is, everyone that mattered – knew him personally: producers, directors, movie stars, opera singers, theater owners, mayors, senators, impresarios; all of them! They all knew Boris Morros and trusted his judgement, because he knew business – show business in particular – from the ground up, something few of these smart boys could claim. And just a few years earlier, Boris Morros wasn't ashamed to admit, he'd been one of the nobodies himself. But because he had the drive and the ambition, plus the talent and a sixth sense about what the public wanted, he'd shot up to the top.

At one point Osip asked Boris Morros if he could tell him anything about Paramount's overseas operations. Boris Morros happily obliged, since naturally, he was involved there as well. Paramount was big! Paramount was global; their films were in cinemas all over Europe, Asia, Africa and South America. Sadly, Russia wasn't a customer, but he was sure that would change. Perhaps they could explore that topic further sometime? Osip agreed that it did sound like a good idea. He'd make sure to bring it up with his boss.

When Osip asked about Germany, Boris Morros admitted the situation there was problematic. The Germans had always been a great market for Paramount. It still was, in fact. Paramount films always did well with German audiences and all their experiences doing business with them were good. But once this Hitler came in with all his anti-Jew this, anti-Jew that rules, it got ridiculous and they'd decided to shut down their Berlin office. But that was last year, and now everything seemed to be settling down and the people in the government were starting to act reasonably and they'd probably be sending their people back in. Oh? said Osip. Then he asked if he thought it might be possible to get someone he knew hired to work in Berlin. Boris Morros shrugged like the question was nothing and said that he didn't see why not. Osip casually asked about other countries. Could he get jobs for people there? Where? Now it was Osip's turn to shrug like he hadn't had any place in mind specifically when he'd asked. Oh, for instance, how about Japan or Manchuria? Hearing Osip ask, the man didn't flinch or act like it was anything. Another shrug. He didn't see why not, like it wasn't that big a deal. Although Osip could barely contain his excitement, he managed to give a disinterested nod and move on to other, less imperative topics. As for those parcels Boris Morros wanted to send, if he could just write down the names of his family members and where they lived, so he could see about getting the parcels expedited to them, this being the sort of thing friends do for each other, right? After that the lunch wrapped up and the two men exchanged telephone numbers and agreed to keep in touch.

Back at the consulate, Osip excitedly told his boss, Peter Gutzeit, about his lunch with Morros and how he had all but offered to provide cover for the man they wanted to send to Berlin and then made it sound like getting people in place elsewhere would also be a breeze. Gutzeit congratulated Osip on his coup and in due course took over. After meeting with the man several times, he wrote up a report on him for Moscow Center. Gutzeit's enthusiasm was equal to Osip's:

> I instructed Osip to meet with M and ask him, in passing, if he could get a relative – and friend – of his a job at one of Paramount's offices. As you can see from the report, M is prepared to do so. I think M-s could be brilliantly put to use providing our workers with a cover. Of course they would have to have at least a rudimentary knowledge of the film industry's commercial aspects.[11]

Moscow Center seemed to share their excitement. New York was instructed to develop the source, to keep in touch with him and see about getting a firm commitment from him about getting jobs for their people. He was given the codename 'FROST' because the Russian word for frost was 'Mroz', which sounded like 'Morros'.

10. RUMORS OF A COUP

George Messersmith was gone. That spring, his promotion to ambassador had come through, a rare occurrence for someone from the Consular Service. Initially, the idea had been to give him Prague, but someone with more pull took it, so then he was reassigned to Paraguay. But when the American Ambassador to Vienna suddenly died, he was sent there instead. Fond as Dodd was of Messersmith, Messersmith's far superior knowledge of the German scene together with his strong opinions must have been intimidating to him, and his departure must have come as an enormous relief. Of course, Martha was probably even more relieved, having gotten an earful of what he thought of her scandalous behavior when she'd come to him seeking his help in preventing Diel's murder.

But Messersmith's presence would continue to be felt in Berlin. He stayed in constant touch with his many friends and sources who kept him abreast of what was going on in Germany. Though the consular staff were probably uniformly delighted at finally being freed from the ogre's iron hand, one of them, his successor, Raymond Geist, communicated with him on a frequent basis. Although Geist gets described these days as a *closeted* gay man, it might be more accurate to say he was a highly discrete, private person in a world where complete privacy was granted to people of certain classes. But perhaps more to the point, Geist was something of a chameleon: adept at presenting himself to whomever he was meeting as whatever they needed him to be in order to get what he needed.

In many ways, Geist was cut from the same cloth as Messersmith: extremely capable, hard-working, and not at all lacking in force of personality. Geist came from a family that was moderately well off, but not rich, and he grew up loving art and theater. In university, first Oberlin and then Harvard, Geist studied many things including acting, performing there and later professionally for a while. Theater, as anyone knows, has always been a place populated by forceful, often flamboyant personalities and one can assume that whatever Geist was, he was nobody's shadow. Then the US entered the First World War, and like millions of young American men, he flocked to the Colors. He joined the army, entering as a private and leaving pretty much the same way. Geist never saw combat during his time in the army, but was part of the American delegation to the Versailles Peace Conference. After that he was seconded to Herbert Hoover's privately run famine relief program. There Geist, still a private, essentially single-handedly ran famine relief for Vienna. In the process, he became someone everyone there was familiar with. Just before going home, the city of Vienna threw Private Geist a parade. Sometime after that, Geist joined the Consular Service and eventually found himself working under the notorious Messersmith. Somehow, possibly because of his own extreme competence and appetite for working long hours, Geist wasn't fazed by the legendary ogre.

Unlike the embassy, the consular wasn't governed by protocol or position. Mostly it was low-key, done on the ground and on the spot and required the ability to charm and yet be firm, especially with the Nazis in control. By now Geist had, like Messersmith, long lists of people he knew on a friendly, personal basis. Many were people he was revolted by, though they never knew it. But he knew he could talk to them and that if he did it the right way, they might do what he asked: a prisoner's release, a copy of a report, a list of the people who'd been arrested, brought into the hospital, *the name of the man whom the police had initially arrested, but let go, or that they didn't let go, but then the SA grabbed them, or was it the SS? Did he give his name? Did he say he was American?*

But unlike Messersmith, Geist succeeded in making contacts within the SS, including with Heydrich and even Himmler himself. With the SS in ascendency over the SA and others, this was an important gain for Messersmith's shop. After Messersmith went to Vienna, Geist became Acting Consul General for Germany. The two continued corresponding and discussing things just as they'd always done, only now Geist was one set of Messersmith's eyes in Berlin.

On 14 June 1934, Geist wrote that 'the air is loaded with something that is supposed to happen in July'. He went on to explain how, recently, an agreement had been reached between the Reichswehr and the SA in which, as a prelude to their merger, the army would start taking in individual SA men for recruit training in its upcoming draft. The idea was that the SA would enter the army's ranks as individuals rather than by whole units. But as it turned out, the latest draft of recruits didn't include any Brownshirts at all! What was going on? Why weren't they there? Was the army suddenly digging in its heels against Roehm? Geist found the news troubling.

Geist's contact informed him that Roehm and Hitler had been having one-on-one talks, with some very frank exchanges between them, but now, apparently, everything seemed patched up. Hitler had gotten Roehm to agree that the entire SA would go on vacation at the beginning of July. During this time they would take off their uniforms and go everywhere as civilians. Roehm had agreed to this in order to cement the reconciliation. 'Roehm has taken a sick leave and the whole of the SA is supposed to go on vacation during July. All this gives rise to uneasiness,' Geist wrote.

Then word started flying around that the putsch was still on, and that when it did take place, the Reichswehr would lead it and Goering would be its primary beneficiary. Did this mean the Reichswehr was bent on replacing Roehm or Hitler? The rumor, of course, wouldn't say. It was easy to see Goering as head of the SA. It was a post he'd already held. With him there, the army would have the confidence and reassurance they'd need for the merger. Could Goering end up replacing Hitler in the chain of command? Suddenly people began recalling the reports from the beginning of the year that Hitler and Goering were on the out and that Hitler had pointedly not sent New Year's greetings to him. Suddenly that very old bone was dug up and endlessly chewed over until people gave up trying to parse it for still-unnoticed clues.

At around the same time, Dodd decided the first week of July might be a good time to stage a 'stag dinner' as a way of returning the favor to all the many 'bier abend' invitations he'd both accepted and declined over the last eleven months. He sent invitations out to numerous top Germans including Goering, Himmler, Goebbels and Roehm, and sat back and waited for the responses to come in.

11. ABOUT BORIS MORROS

It is said the Dutch boast that, while God created the world, they, not He, made Holland. One has to wonder if in their heyday, Russian Jews, themselves a people also not particularly known for modesty, made similar assertions about themselves and Hollywood. Certainly, they would have been entitled to. After all, when they'd first arrived in the early twentieth century, there hadn't been much there aside from some semi-desert scrub. They were real pioneers, those early Jews.

Boris Morros was one of them, even though he didn't show up until a full generation later; in fact, not until the talkies were almost done kicking silent films aside. But a pioneer Boris Morros certainly was. He forced the important step that made film music something more than incidental wallpaper. He made it part of telling the story. So, if anyone deserves grandfathering into the ranks, it should be Boris. Like them, he had the drive, ambition, vision and sheer greed and readiness to tell whatever lies he needed to tell, and always at the drop of a hat, to get the people with the power and money to believe whatever he was dishing out and then come back for seconds. And time and again they did. That Martha Dodd was one of the very few people never swayed or charmed by him speaks volumes of her.

Boris Morros was, like Odysseus, a man never at a loss. History might indeed be chock full of slimeballs, scoundrels and psychopathic, predatory creeps, but history hasn't produced many with the audacity to blow as much smoke way up so many asses on both

89

sides of the Cold War as he did. And for all this, in a perfect, fair, and just world, Boris Morros ought to be celebrated.

But, of course, that's also the problem with Boris Morros and his story. It's hard to deny his tale makes for a wild, comical and frequently absurd ride. It would be just a lot more fun if, in the end, so many innocent and somewhat-innocent people had not gotten their lives so callously ruined as a result.

Somewhere in the FBI's vaults in Washington sit dozens of cardboard boxes containing hundreds of thousands of pages of case files all bearing the name 'MOCASE' – 1950s FBI shorthand for 'Morros-Case', its investigations into Soviet spies and spy rings spurred by the confessions Boris Morros made to them prior to his recruitment in 1947.

While bits of the massive MOCASE files have been released, including some currently available at the FBI's online 'vault', the vast majority remain closed off to researchers, even though everyone associated with them is long dead. Perhaps someday researchers will be allowed to look at them, but it's not likely to be anytime soon. It would be one thing if all those pages did was make the Bureau look like jackasses and fools, but the Boris Morros files will make them look far worse than that. FBI Director J. Edgar Hoover was no fool and knew a liar when he saw one, especially when it was someone of Boris Morros' obviousness. When he put him before a Federal grand jury to testify about Martha Dodd and the other members of his spy ring, Hoover knew Morros would lie through his teeth, but Hoover needed a pretext to begin an investigation he could turn into a witch hunt, one that would ensnare not just former communists and leftists, but even liberals and progressives; anyone, as the saying went, to the left of Atilla the Hun. What was ultimately inflicted on the American nation was something it never truly recovered from. Because, in Hoover's mind, Boris Morros' lies served a much higher, nobler purpose than the truth, J. Edgar Hoover happily went along with the liar and his lies.

In his heyday during the late 1920s and 1930s, Boris Morros' name was continuously in the newspaper gossip columns as well as in 'the Trades'. He knew how to give reporters something to write about so that he stayed visible to people in the business. A natural raconteur, Boris Morros wasn't one for letting truth get in the way of a good story. Of his life prior to coming to America, he had plenty of colorful stories he'd tell,[1] none even remotely verifiable. Not that it mattered. In America, someone's foreign past wasn't something they were judged by. Unlike today, self-invention was not considered a sin. What you were judged on was whether you could deliver the goods, and that was something Boris Morros could do.

Boris Morros claimed he was born in St Petersburg,[2] though his biographer insists he was born in a grimy town in Belarus called Bobruisk.[3] His father was a lock-maker, an entirely respectable trade, but Morros preferred to say he was a teacher, descended from six generations of scholars, musicians and academics.[4]

Morros also claimed that when he was twelve he was recognised as a musical genius and enrolled into the St Petersburg Conservatory,[5] where he studied music alongside Jascha Heifetz and Sergei Prokofiev.[6] For all anyone knows, it may be true, it being the only major Russian music conservatory known to take Jews at the time. After that, Morros claimed he served as assistant musical director for the Imperial Opera Orchestra, and that its famous conductor, Eduard Napravnik, was so impressed by him, he recommended his appointment to a similar position organising musical activities at the Tsar's Imperial Court where, according to Morros, he got to know Grigory Rasputin[7] so well he gifted him with an amber rosary,[8] something Morros said he prized and kept for the rest of his life. It all may be true, there just isn't any record of it.

But Morros' story was just beginning. During the First World War, he claims he conducted a military orchestra[9] which played both for the Tsar and the Duma. Then came the 1917 Revolution and the Bolsheviks, for whom, he says, he ran a large military band. Then the Russian Civil War erupted and after even more adventures, Morros fled south to Baku, a petroleum-rich, independent enclave which had become home to hundreds of thousands of refugees, all, like Morros, seeking sanctuary from the chaos. There he met an actress and singer named Yekaterina Yefimova Modina, married, but on the verge of widowhood, with a son and daughter, both of them in their early teens. Her once considerable wealth now consisted of a small velvet bag of jewels kept around her neck.[10] Boris Morros started calling her 'Catherine', and the two of them fell in love or something sufficiently close to it. The husband apparently died, or something close enough that they got married, or at least claimed they did. They departed Baku, travelled on to Constantinople, then down to Ataturk, bought their way aboard a steamship and shared a third-class cabin with three other families. On 8 December 1922, their ship arrived in New York and it is only here that the documented, verifiable part of Boris Morros' history actually begins.

Stepping ashore onto Ellis Island with his bride and her two children, Morros and the other disembarked passengers were shepherded inside a large hall where immigration officers waited to process their entry. They would ask their names, find out where they were from, inspect them for disease, deformity, imbecility, and assess their likelihood of becoming public charges. There, to the immigration officer at the other side of the window, Morros spun his grand story about once conducting the Tsar's royal court orchestra, about how he was a maestro, a certified, conservatory-trained genius who'd composed and conducted countless symphonic and orchestral pieces, and not a nobody like everyone else trying to get in. He was Boris Morros, a somebody!

It isn't known if the immigration officer was impressed or merely taking the path of least resistance, but he began dutifully filling out the landed-immigrant admission form for the four Morroses. Asked his age, Morros initially told the man he was 32, but then asked to change it to 31.[11] Although short, fat and bald, Morros put his height at an amazingly optimistic five-foot-four, the hair which had long deserted his head was described as brown while his eyes were put down as 'blue'. As for his wife, well, suddenly she was his cousin.[12] The two children? Hers. Her husband had a mattress factory in Philadelphia and had promised Morros a job. Asked for the name of his nearest relative back home, Morros gave one 'General Pelle, High Commissioner of France'.[13]

Somewhere between the docks, Pennsylvania Station and Philadelphia, Catherine's son Constantin left them, striking out on his own, never to be seen or heard from again. The cousin in Philadelphia had nothing for them, but suggested an acquaintance in Boston who might. On his recommendation, Morros, his wife and daughter went on to Boston and for a while settled there.

⚜

In the ten-odd years since he'd left, Morros had had very little contact with his family in Russia. Sometimes letters got through, but mostly they bounced back. When a letter did come, he couldn't help noticing the wording was more guarded than informative, and the feeling he got was things were bad for them. A little earlier, his friend and fellow impresario Sol Hurok, on one of his many trips to Russia, had brought food and money for members of Morros' family. But when he met with them, they adamantly refused to accept any of it. Hurok recounted to him how his brothers, Serge and Savely, 'both engineers, but both of them were shabbily dressed ... They are either shy or very proud men. I told them you had asked me to give them anything. They seemed pleased. But when I opened my trunks and laid out ties, warm clothing and pipes on the bed, they shook their heads ... When I asked them about your parents and the rest of the family, I could learn nothing. Perhaps, like everyone else in that terror-filled world, they are too frightened to say anything – or even think.'[14]

Hurok recommended Morros try sending food packages through Union Tours, knowing it was a subsidiary of AMTORG, the Soviet government trading company which, until now, had been a stand-in for an embassy. Union Tours mainly handled tourist trips to Russia; the package thing was more a sideline than anything else. Hurok had recommended he speak to the man who ran Union Tours, a Mr M. B. Horton. In reality he was Yakov Golos, a Ukrainian-born American national, fervent communist and currently Moscow Center's on-site wizard for creating bona fide US passports and identities to go with them. And at this very moment, Golos' attention was wholly focused on acquiring a business identity for one of their most important Chekist officers. Golos only knew him as 'Edward Herbert', the American identity which Golos had created for him. His real name was Vasily Mikhailovich Zarubin.

12. NIGHT OF THE LONG KNIVES

Among the many odd beliefs about life the ancient Romans held was one called the 'Day of Virtue'. It posits that every man, regardless of how cowardly and wretched he might be, is accorded at least one day where he will do the right thing and perform it with full, 'manly' virtue. For Vice-Chancellor Franz von Papen, as singularly miserable and spineless a man as ever lived, his occurred on 17 June 1934, when he gave a speech at Marburg University sharply criticising his government's oppressive policies and calling for the restoration of freedom of the press, rule by law, and other basic civil rights. Even though the speech's text was kept from the press and not mentioned on the radio, it still got out and its effect on the German populace was riveting. That the one giving the speech was the gutless, two-faced von Papen must have made it more extraordinary.

The speech was written by two of Papen's secretaries: Edgar Jung and Herbert von Bose, with help from Erich Klausner, head of *Catholic Action*, one of Germany's most influential centrist Christian organisations. Their goal was to express the discontent felt by the majority of Germany's Christians and conservatives, who, until now, had been silent and obedient. This, they knew, was their last opportunity to force a change and return Germany to the rule of law and sanity. The text of the speech had been sent to Hindenburg ahead of its delivery and he had wired them his approval. Jung, von Bose and Klausner prayed it might induce him to remove Hitler from power, using the army.

Instead, Hindenburg merely summoned Hitler to his estate for discussions. Just before he went, von Papen went to see Hitler to tell him he'd spoken not as Vice-Chancellor, but as 'a trustee for the President'.

The next day, 21 June, Hitler flew to Hindenburg's east Prussian estate. He found, to his surprise, Blomberg was there to talk with him before he'd have his audience with the President. Normally one of Hitler's more fawning lackies, Blomberg became, for the occasion, a very stiff, stern Prussian officer, warning Hitler that unless he got things quickly under control, Hindenburg would declare martial law and place the government in the army's hands. Then Hitler was taken in for a few minutes alone with Hindenburg, who repeated everything Blomberg had just said. It was all Hitler needed to know. Back in Berlin, he met with Himmler and Goering, who had lists with names of people needing to be 'taken care of' and a plan of action already worked out. They then convinced Hitler of the enormity of Roehm's plot against him. Not present was Goebbels, apparently still fence-sitting.

On Saturday, 23 June, Dodd held a luncheon. The guests included Phipps, Schmitt, one of the non-Nazi cabinet ministers and the widow of a one-time Weimar chancellor, along with journalists Louis Lochner and Sigrid Schultz. Writing about it later in his diary, Dodd noted that there was no useful discussion, but that the rumors flew.

On Monday, 25 June, Army Commander-in-Chief General von Fritz called a state of alert, cancelling all leaves and confining the troops to barracks. Goering called up Diels and pointedly suggested he leave town and go on vacation somewhere out of the way. Diels took the hint and booked himself into an out-of-the-way guesthouse in the Eiffel to wait things out.

On Friday, 29 June, an article appeared in *Volkischer Beobachter* written by Blomberg proclaiming: 'The army stands behind Adolf Hitler ... who remains one of ours!' Later that day Hitler flew to Godesburg, outside Bonn. Meanwhile, back in Berlin, Goering met with Himmler and together they activated a number of special police units. While some were SS, most belonged to Goering's personal police force, the '*Landespolizeigruppe General Goering*'. Once they agreed everything was in readiness, Himmler departed, travelling first to Westphalia to visit some Labour Service camps, then to Godesburg where he joined up with Hitler while Goering remained in Berlin.

Josef Goebbels arrived in Godesburg, having chosen his side. To help cement his position, he brought with him some 'threatening intelligence'. Karl Ernst had gotten wind of their plans and had alerted stormtrooper units outside Berlin to be ready to defend themselves in the upcoming putsch. It was shocking news to Hitler. Ernst had always been one of Hitler's favorites, but now, conveniently, Ernst had become one of the enemy. It was all a lie, of course, like nearly everything else being fed to Hitler at that moment about the SA's intentions. But it was the lie Hitler wanted and needed because it provided the necessary justification to strike hard and fast against his enemies, including the loyal servant who, in the faithful execution of his duties, had come to know way too much.

Muscular, brutally handsome and probably not all that overly bright, Ernst, at the time, held an SA rank equivalent to a three-star general. Not many years earlier, Ernst had been a bell-boy and bouncer at the El Dorado, a fabled gay nightclub and hotel. Apparently it was there he became acquainted with Roehm and joined the SA, becoming part of Roehm's personal army of lovers. Martha never said where she met Ernst, but like Diels, he was riding the Berlin party circuit at its height and meeting and partying with Martha was inevitable. She mentions him in a chapter in her memoir titled 'Young Blood of Berlin Social Life', where she mostly talks about the dashing young SS men with perfect manners who seemed to be all over the Foreign Office. But while Ernst might have passed for one of them, they were actually at the bottom of the food chain; he was at the top, something Martha was no doubt quite aware of. If Putzi Hanfstaengl had told her what he had told others, then Martha knew something about what Ernst was privy to. As commander of all Berlin's stormtroopers, Ernst also did whatever he wanted. If he wanted to grab anyone off the street and lock them up, he did. And when he felt like beating them to death or just shooting them in their cells, he'd do that too. His loyalty to Hitler was absolute, but now he'd become inconvenient.

At that moment, truth be told, defending against a putsch was about the last thing on Ernst's mind. Karl Ernst had gotten married just two weeks earlier. Hitler himself had attended and may have even acted as best man. Now Ernst, Ernst's bride, and Ernst's best friend were driving north to Bremerhaven, where one of the Kriegsmarine's newest warships was waiting to take them to Tenerife for their honeymoon. Like Roehm and everyone else in the SA, he was looking forward to a month of vacation.

On that same day, 29 June, Dodd gave another small luncheon which Martha attended. This time guests included von Papen, Goebbels, Luthor, the German Ambassador just back from Washington, and Mme. Cerutti, the brilliant, vivacious Italian wife of the Hungarian Ambassador, who sat on Dodd's right. Everyone, it seemed, was on edge. Cerutti told Dodd how, a week earlier, she'd travelled with Hitler's party to Venice and had witnessed, first-hand, a testy meeting between Hitler and Mussolini. She told how Mussolini had upbraided Hitler for all the unrest and the bad state of the German economy, which Hitler hadn't taken well. Surveying the other guests for a moment, she then leaned in and told Dodd 'it was obvious they were all on a volcano'. Where was all this heading? 'The Germans are again in the position of July, 1914,' she told Dodd. 'We may be plunged into war again. These people are simply crazy.'

Not quite two weeks had passed since von Papen had delivered his Marburg speech, but he was still man of the hour in everyone's eyes. Looking at him, Dodd observed that giving the Marburg speech had definitely been courageous. He had probably also just pinned a huge target on himself. Something was obviously about to happen and when it did, he would probably catch the brunt of it. Shortly before leaving the luncheon with Luthor, Dodd heard von Papen snapping to another guest, 'Anyway, I shall not be torpedoed.'

That evening, Hitler phoned Roehm, telling him he would be arriving Saturday morning at eleven and that he should have all his leadership assembled there for an important conference. Roehm agreed and told Hitler he'd see some vegetarian dishes were prepared for him for the banquet following the conference. Hitler hung up. Roehm, interpreting it as an indication relations were still good, sent out telegrams summoning the other main SA leaders to come right away. Roehm then had his doctor give him a shot and went to bed.

At 2am on Saturday, 30 June, Hitler, Himmler and Goebbels flew from Bonn to Munich, landing an hour before dawn at the Oberwiesenfeld Airdrome, where a force of SS and regular police was waiting for them. They drove to the Hanselbauer Hotel in Bad Wiesse where Roehm and his followers were staying. Hitler led them into the building. He had one of them knock on the door to Roehm's room. When Roehm opened it, Hitler pointed a revolver and told him he was under arrest. Others were awakened, arrested, forced into a caravan of commandeered trucks and driven back to Munich. Throughout the morning SA leaders arrived at Munich's main train station, where they were promptly arrested by waiting SS men and taken to Stadelheim prison, where Roehm and the others were being held. With the first part of the operation completed, Goebbels phoned Goering in Berlin and, using the prearranged codeword *Kolibri* (Hummingbird), let him know it was time to begin the next phase. Goering sent a joint force of SS troops and his police into the SA's Berlin Headquarters, seizing it without any resistance. Once secured, Goering arrived and strode down the building's hallways, pointing out the SA men he wanted arrested. They were taken to the cadet school at Lichterfelde Barracks, outside Berlin, which had been turned into a jail for the occasion.

Throughout Munich and Berlin, teams of SS men and police appeared outside people's homes, demanding entry or simply kicking the doors in and arresting, or shooting, on the spot, whoever was on their list. One of the first to be killed in Munich was the former Bavarian state commissioner who had crushed the Beer Hall Putsch ten years earlier. Another team seized a priest, Father Bernhard Stemfle, and dragged him into a forest where his body was later found, neck broken and shot three times. Stemfle's crime? Knowing about the affair Hitler had with his niece, Geli Raubal.

In Berlin, an SS unit stormed the vice-chancellery where they found and shot Herbert von Bose, von Papen's assistant and primary architect of the Marburg speech in his office. His associate, Edgar Jung, was taken from his ransacked apartment and never seen or heard from again. His housekeeper found the word *Gestapo* penciled on his bathroom wall. Another group of SS men found Dr Erich Klausner at his desk in the Labour Ministry and informed him that he was under arrest, then shot him. Klausner fell to the floor, wounded. They tried placing the gun in Klausner's hand to make it look like a suicide. During the hour it took Klausner to bleed to death, no one was allowed to enter the room. Franz von Papen was arrested at his home, but instead of shooting him, he was placed under house arrest. Guards were stationed around his villa and his phone lines were cut.

At 1.30pm, five plainclothes Gestapo men arrived at Gregor Strasser's door and arrested him while he was having dinner with his family. They told his distraught wife that he was being taken to his office so they could search it. Halfway there, he was handed over to a squad of SS men who then drove him to the Gestapo jail on Prinz Albrechtrasse, where he was shot several times and left to bleed to death. A month later, his family was delivered a regulation Gestapo urn bearing his ashes with no explanation about how or why he died.

Around this time, Karl Ernst, his bride and best friend arrived at the Bremen docks. They walked up a gangway onto the warship that was to take them to Tenerife. But once aboard, they were met with a group of SS and Gestapo who arrested them, put them in handcuffs and took them off the ship. Initially, Ernst believed it was nothing more than a mix-up of some kind and assured his captors everything would be straightened out once they got to Berlin. Taken to Lichterfelde, Ernst found himself in the execution queue. The fact that Hitler had been his best man only a couple of weeks before did not save him.

That afternoon, Schleicher's friend and confederate General Ferdinand von Bredow was sitting at the Adlon Hotel's bar. Seeing him, one of the waiters, a Gestapo informant, used the telephone behind the bar to make a short call. Arriving home, von Bredow was killed by gunmen outside his door.

Sometime that afternoon the executions began. Some came following a sham legal proceeding involving a Nazi judge or magistrate, others didn't even bother with that. Either way, it was done quickly without anything allowed in the way of defence. Some were shot in their cells, others were used as target practice. Many died shouting out 'Heil Hitler'.

That afternoon, Goering gave a press conference where he announced that a mutiny by Roehm and the SA had been successfully stopped. He noted that von Schleicher had unfortunately been shot and killed while resisting arrest. Goering didn't mention the killings were still going on. In fact, they'd barely started. Accounts were getting settled with anyone Hitler considered an enemy – editors who'd been critical of him, along with journalists and lawyers and several police chiefs and others who knew things about Hitler or Goering or the Reichstag fire. The only foreign reporter present was Louis Lochner. Once Goering finished, he went to his office, phoned London and began dictating the story, getting in the last sentence before being cut off.

As for Martha, that Saturday, 30 June was as beautiful and warm a day as they'd had that year. Martha and Boris Vinogradov agreed it was the perfect day to go find a place to have sex in the great outdoors. He picked her up that morning in his Ford roadster. They took down the top and drove out to Gross Glienicke and spent the day frolicking in a private spot and later having a picnic. At six o'clock, Martha and Vinogradov decided they'd had enough sun and began driving back to Berlin. It didn't take long before they started to notice something was going on. Everything suddenly seemed different. There were fewer people on the streets and those they did see were often in 'curious, static groups'. Then they started noticing all the cops. 'There was an unusual number of police standing around. As we drove nearer and nearer in the heart of the city, we saw many army trucks, machine guns, many soldiers, SS men and especially large numbers of the green-uniformed Goering Police.'

What they didn't see were any SA men. Where were they? Why were the roads blocked? What was happening? They were now only a few blocks from home, on Standartenstrasse, a street slated to be renamed in honor of Ernst Roehm. But it was blocked by barbed-wire barricades and 'Goering Police'. Somehow Martha found a payphone and called home. Bill Jr answered it, telling her that von Schleicher had been shot. 'We don't know what is happening. There is martial law in Berlin,' he said. Eventually, they found a way through. After dropping Martha off at the front door, Boris Vinogradov beat a hasty path back to the Russian Embassy. Her father, mother and brother were all together, doing whatever they could to stay informed. They'd all been listening to the wireless, then endlessly getting on the phone, calling up people to find out what they were hearing. One of Bill Jr's friends who lived in the suburbs, near the prison at Lichterfelde, reported how it 'had been transformed into shooting gallery with human bodies as targets'. 'He told us that a court-martial had been set up in which a few Nazis, including Goering, were the judges. The charges were made and the sentence passed – without the defendant having a chance to say a word – and the victim led to the firing squad.'

Afterwards, Martha noted being told by many people how 'the shots from Lichterfelde could be heard most of the night'. Sometime that evening, her father received an RSVP from Roehm, regretting that he would not be able to attend Dodd's upcoming stag night.

By Sunday, most of Roehm's leadership was dead, but the executions continued. Hitler returned to Berlin and threw an impromptu garden party in the chancellery gardens. Though Hitler was intent on only making small talk with his guests, Rudolph Hess was never far away, as a reminder to Hitler that a decision still needed to be made about Roehm, who was languishing in a cell in Stadelheim prison. Hitler knew why Hess was there, but continued dithering about Roehm. As Hitler continued chatting with the ladies at the garden party, Hess' presence became increasingly like an impatient waiter's. Finally Hitler waved him over and muttered to him something like 'Get it done'.

A few minutes later, two SS officers entered Roehm's cell. They tried handing him a revolver loaded with a single bullet, hoping he'd do them all the favor. Roehm took one look at it and sneered back, 'If Adolf wants to kill me, let him do his own dirty work.' The SS men left and returned a few minutes later, pistols in hand. After ordering him to his feet and ripping the torn brown shirt from his body, they fired their pistols. Roehm fell to the floor. Dying, his last words were *'Mein Fuhrer, mein Fuhrer!'* At around the same time, Martha's father drove out to von Papen's villa. Although the guards would not let him through, they did allow him to drop off his visiting card.

On 3 July, von Papen looked out his window and realised the police were all gone. He left his house, got in his automobile and went for a drive over to the Dodds. Though he didn't say much in front of Martha, he did have a long conversation alone with her father. Later, when she asked him what he'd been told, Dodd just shook his head gravely and told her he'd sworn never to talk about it. All he would say was that what had happened to von Papen was truly horrible.

The next day was the Fourth of July. The Dodds threw an impromptu garden party and everyone who showed up was greeted with 'Oh, so you're still alive!' A fews day later, Diels and the few others who had hidden began emerging, and to their surprise, found they were no longer being looked for. They went back to what they were doing and nothing more was said.

Martha thought it was strange how quickly everything reverted back to an approximation of what it had been like before. For the whole week, nobody would say anything. But then, the following Saturday, exactly one week after the massacre, Martha Dodd surprised everybody by stepping aboard a Junkers trimotor airplane and flying alone to Moscow.

13. JAZZ RECORDS FOR MOLOTOV

Martha had booked a vacation package which Intourist, the state-run tour operator, called 'Tour #9', a month-long, all-inclusive tour featuring two days in Leningrad, four days in Moscow, a four-day steamer trip on the Volga, and then on and on through the Caucasus, Crimea and ending in Kiev.

She'd told the handful of close friends who knew beforehand that she wanted to see for herself if there was any truth in all those ridiculous stories in the Nazi-controlled press about famines and Russians eating babies. Martha's parents, for once, were not encouraging. Her father dismissed the idea of calling it a 'fact-finding trip'. What it really was was a 'wild goose chase', while her mother couldn't bear even thinking of Russia, which she regarded as a horrible, wild, dirty place rife with infection and disease no one in their right mind would ever visit. The German authorities were also not happy. Until then, everyone had assumed she was in the Nazi camp. Now, suddenly, they had reason to wonder whether Martha's loyalties might lie elsewhere.

Except for Boris and the von Harnacks, no one had any idea her real reason for going was to introduce herself to some of the biggies at Moscow Center. Martha would need to sell herself to them and make them understand all that she could do for them, both now and afterwards, when she'd return to America. At Boris' suggestion, she'd even packed some jazz records to give to Molotov, the Soviet foreign minister whom Boris said had been his mentor and friend in earlier days. Then, when all that was completed, she and Boris would go to Caucasus for their summer holiday.

Intourist had been providing tourist packages like Tour #9 since the 1920s. Loath as the paranoid Soviet leadership might have been about having any foreigners, even sympathetic, left-leaning ones, nosing around, they allowed it because package tours generated a modest, but welcome hard currency stream at relatively little cost. Tours also made political sense because they helped build favorable international public opinion. Most of the people taking them were already favorably inclined toward communism and the Soviet Union. They came needing to believe what Stalin was doing there was for the good of the whole world. It was mainly just a question of controlling what they saw and didn't see, which, by and large, wasn't that difficult. The guides were professionals with a sense of mission. They knew what to tell the visitors. There was also another, less obvious reason to bring in package tour groups. Foreign tourists came with foreign passports, which, when needed, could be stolen then doctored and used by Moscow Center operatives not important, or fortunate enough, to rate genuine American 'shoes'.[1]

Normally tour groups consisted of between one and two dozen people, all closely shepherded by their Intourist minders. But the sparse way Martha described hers, only making mention of three or four other people travelling with her, suggests it might have been a 'special tour', such as Intourist reserved for guests important enough that their favor was being courted, or, as in Martha's case, being considered by the NKVD for recruitment and training, but only after their behavior was first observed.

Martha devotes a full chapter of her memoir to her Russian trip. She mentions visiting museums, palaces, churches, collective farms, a tractor factory and even a 'prophylacatorium' – a home for retired prostitutes.[2] She records how workers were well fed, well dressed, not overworked and how concerts, plays and other cultural activities seemed to be available to them at little or no cost. But aside from the mostly glowing, but ultimately canned things she says about what she saw in Russia, Martha doesn't actually say much. Normally a fervent name-dropper, the one name she drops is American Ambassador William Bullitt, who invited her to lunch. She mentions their young female guide, and a couple also making the trip, but that's about it. Interestingly, she mentions going out to dinner with 'two or three friends' during her last night in Moscow, but Martha's words somehow make it sound like they weren't her tour-mates. If that is so, who were they? If her book doesn't tell, it seems files found in the KGB archives apparently do.

Martha never mentions Boris anywhere in her memoir, let alone during her Russian visit, but according to the KGB files, when her tour group reached Moscow, Boris and two friends were waiting there for her, probably as arranged. They went somewhere and talked. Martha declared her willingness to work with them. They must have discussed what the work would involve. Somewhere in the process they took her shopping and possibly gave her some quick training in miniature photography and other bits of spycraft.

From the letters they exchanged afterwards,[3] we learn Boris appeared in Moscow with two 'friends', quite possibly the same two or three whom she mentioned having dinner with. They were also apparently the Moscow Center recruiters who'd invited her to meet with them in Paris. From a report found in the KGB archives by Western researchers in the early 1990s, Boris' friends were very impressed by her.[4] There may have been more meetings, with higher-ups, as she'd hoped. Her letters don't say.

What Martha's Moscow Center file says was that they had extensive discussions about cooperation with them and that 'during "Liza's" visit here, we gave her 200 American dollars, 10 rubles and bought her 500 rubles' worth of gifts. Liza herself requested permission to come to Moscow for a few days in order to arrange her future work in America.'[5]

But after that, things took an unexpected turn for Martha. Having, she thought, successfully sold herself to the Moscow Center leadership, she was ready for some vacation fun with Boris. But it turned out that Boris had other vacation plans. He sheepishly informed Martha that while he was indeed heading for a resort in the Caucasus, she wouldn't be the one accompanying him. He'd be going with someone else, either with his wife and daughter, or maybe with another girlfriend. He wouldn't say.

It is likely Martha was under observation during the rest of her trip. Martha described the lazy, four-day steamer ride down the Volga. They got on in Kazan and visited Samara, Saratov and finally Stalingrad. From the way Martha describes it, there weren't many on the boat besides herself and the young woman who was their guide. She mentions several other people, but the only one she actually describes is an elderly German-American communist who, though nice, was extremely long-winded. She mentions helping herself to whatever food they provided on board. She tried sunbathing but ended up with a sunburn.

Russia was, in Martha's eyes, 'a democratic country in spirit'.[6] 'There was no race hatred, no class antagonism, no grinding down of individuality under brutal economic laws that kept the poor always poor and the rich always richer,' she wrote.[7]

All told, what Martha writes about her month in Russia is mostly boiled-down and canned and positive without getting carried away. While she never says anything negative, Martha cites one tiny incident to signal readers that the Russia she visited was not perfect. The boat had just tied up at Kazan when Martha noticed a peasant woman in apparent distress, though no one around her bothered to notice. Martha asked about it and was told she had been aboard the ferry crossing the river and had somehow, in the course of it, lost the few kopeks she'd brought with her. Apparently they were all she had and now they were gone. Reflecting on it, Martha wrote that it was only then that she began to understand both the staggering level of poverty plaguing Russia and the correspondingly massive indifference people felt toward strangers.

Still, Martha makes it seem that package Tour #9 had been enjoyable and interesting, even if it's more likely that she didn't enjoy herself very much. Martha liked the bright lights and the glitter and swank of exciting people. Here she was, travelling with uninteresting people in a gigantic country that was mostly massively boring and not exactly sparkly-clean.

Martha probably spent most of the tour stewing about Boris and how he had ditched her in Moscow. This, of course, led to discontent about other things. While floating down the Volga, she apparently knocked off several angry letters letting him know she didn't appreciate what he had done and having to spend three-and-a-half more weeks with these nobodies while he was having at it with someone else. And Russia being not exactly the way he'd endlessly described it. She'd never have thought it would be the dreary, boring, utterly messed-up dump it was. She'd had it with him; she threatened to go back to Armand. That always got Boris. Her relationship with him had always been combative. They fought, made up and fought more. It was the way they liked it. As far as Martha was concerned, there was never any thought of fidelity. When they were together, she was his and it was heaven like she had never known. But they couldn't be together that much. His job basically took up all his time. And of course, there were other women. They also argued about everything possible. Politics particularly.

Excursions like Package Tour #9 were supposed to be tightly controlled and curated, so that the visitors saw the Russian Economic Miracle the government wanted them to see, and not the rickety reality. Apparently Martha's letters to Boris indicated this. With all this understood, one cannot but wonder if what she saw made her have second thoughts about her recruitment as a Moscow Center operative. She'd done it at Boris' urging, yes, but her close friends Mildred and Arvid von Harnack back in Berlin must have also had something to do with her decision. If it wasn't for them, she would probably have never developed her commitment to fighting fascism. The von Harnacks must have made Martha realise there were only two sides. There were the fascists and the capitalists on one, and everybody else on the other. And right now the only people in the world facing up to the fascist threat were Soviet Russia and the World Communist Revolution. That was it. Martha knew from what her father told her time and again that the only thing anyone in Washington cared about was whether Germany would make good on its loans. The capitalists were all on the side of Hitler, it was a fact!

14. ZARUBIN IN MANHATTAN

On 17 July 1934, at the same time Martha Dodd was having her Russian vacation, the Norddeutscher Lloyd liner SS *Bremen*, out of Cherbourg, docked in New York City. Among those disembarking were three American nationals: a man, woman and child. According to the passports presented to the immigration and customs officials, their names were Edward Herbert, his wife Sarah and their infant son Peter. They'd been travelling about in Europe since February and now their plans were to go back to what they were doing before they'd left. He was in sales, she was a housewife and mother. They could be reached c/o Schichtancz, 217-20-133rd St, Springfield Gardens, Long Island. But it doesn't appear they ever made it to Springfield Gardens. An investigation years later indicated that no one at that address had ever heard of them.

Edward and Sarah Herbert were, of course, Soviet spies Vassily Zarubin, his wife Elizabeta Zarubina, and Petr, their infant son. They were there so Boris Morros could give Zarubin a crash course in the business of being a Paramount Pictures film executive in Germany. The idea was to do it over the summer and then deploy in Berlin come autumn. They quickly found lodging, probably furnished rooms in Manhattan where the weekly rent was paid in cash. No doubt they went and saw the sights. Everything they could do to build up their American cultural identities would pay off once they were operational in Germany. Elizabeta probably saw to it that her husband intensively worked on his spoken English, as it was far behind his French and German, which were flawless.

Things were probably fairly relaxed for the Zarubins during their time in New York. They knew their covers weren't anything they'd overly need to sweat. They were transient people in a world of transients. Being anonymous was nothing new in New York. Edward Herbert was just another guy with a heavy accent. While they were there, it's likely Vassily and Elizabeta got together with some of their Chekist comrades doing their jobs in America. At that time it was still a tightly knit brethren. It's also quite likely that an understanding existed that following completion of the Berlin assignment, their next would be in America, as was the case with Ovakiman and a couple of others there. It's not known if Zarubin had previously spent time in America, but Elizabeta definitely had. During the late 1920s she worked as a clerk at AMTORG and probably still had friends there.

It is known that it was Petr Gutzeit who was tasked with developing a productive relationship with Boris Morros and also handing Vassily Zarubin over to him for training up into the movie business. Gutzeit had been having discussions with Morros about getting jobs for Moscow Center operatives in Paramount offices overseas for several months, and every time they met, Morros would sound extremely positive about the chances of making it happen. The point he kept making was that for Berlin, the person would have to not be Jewish, speak at least some German and know something about the film industry. Morros told him that the head of Paramount's foreign department was a good friend of his and he could talk to him about it once he got back. There'd be another meeting. Morros would always say everything was going great. Everything was about to be settled. 'As soon as the Foreign department head arrives, we will meet again and the matter will be settled once and for all,' Gutzeit wrote to Moscow Center. In another week, or ten days, or two weeks. Good, wrote back Moscow Center, who in that case would also ask them about openings in other parts of Europe, Scandinavia. To that, Gutzeit replied that 'until the business with getting Katya [Zarubin] a job has been settled, we should not discuss this with Frost [Morros]'.

By now, more than a month had gone by and they hadn't even met with him once. Morros was always too busy. Gutzeit was getting impatient. Finally he decided he'd had enough. Using his connections, Gutzeit found out where Morros was going to be and brought Zarubin along with him. It worked. Gutzeit made the introductions and that was that. 'At the moment, negotiations to get Katya a job have taken such a definite tone that we already took Katya to see Frost to learn the nature of the upcoming job,' he reported.

Boris Morros remembered the story differently in his memoir, *My Ten Years as a Counterspy*. He claims the meeting took place in 1936 and not 1934, and in Hollywood, not New York. Visiting Morros at his studio, the man calling himself Edward Herbert raises the matter of the Nazis.

'You are against the Nazis, aren't you?' he asked.

I told him of course I was and that everything Hitler stood for was an abomination in my opinion. Then he said he lived in Germany and was organizing the underground anti-Nazi work there for the Soviet government.

'Isn't that dangerous?' I asked thinking of his Russian accent.

'Very,' he said. 'But you could make it less so.'

'I can?' I said, in astonishment. 'How?'

'To fight the Nazis effectively,' he said, 'I should have some sort of occupation that makes it legitimate for me to move around freely.'

I could see his point but couldn't imagine what he wanted of me. 'I should have some sort of trade or profession,' he kept saying, and then, 'Don't you want to help a man who is devoting his whole life to fighting the Nazis?'

'Of course I do, but what are you getting at?'

'Haven't you talent scouts looking for musical talent all over the world?'

I nodded.

'Make me your talent scout in Germany.'

Herbert reminds Morros how his brothers back in Russia were in trouble with the government: 'But they will not be prosecuted if you help me now.' And he went on: 'What possible wrong can you be doing to your company, your country, or anything else by helping me?' Having the proposition framed that way, Morros saw the light. 'In my own handwriting that day and on the stationery of Paramount Studios of Hollywood California. I wrote the letter he wanted, certifying that he, Edward Herbert, was authorised to act in Germany as talent scout for my department. I signed it, "Boris Morros, General Music Director."'

Boris Morros' memoir never mentions anything about teaching Edward Herbert about the movie industry, but material in Soviet archives indicates they met a number of times during the late summer. Probably Boris Morros took him out to lunch two or three times and went on long walks through Manhattan, and maybe they got together in other ways. Zarubin had lots of questions and got lots of answers. Morros would answer Zarubin's questions and he'd tell him about Hollywood and dealmaking. Zarubin was amazed at the kinds of things Boris Morros knew about. He was a natural operator. Even with his big, big mouth going all the time, he had control of things. Vassily Zarubin, a man who many times owed his own survival to his ability to see things straight and to recognise bullshit when it was there, was profoundly impressed. The two got along really well.

'There is neither vacillation nor fear on [Morros'] part, though he knows and understands that this is not a usual service [performed] for a Soviet official,' Zarubin told Gutzeit. They continued to meet through September. Morros kept going forth about the movie business and telling lots and lots of stories, all of which, he insisted, had a point. Zarubin continued to be impressed with Morros. Finally, he gave Morros a fat wad of $50 bills and told him it was to be used to pay him $50 a month. Also to send him business letters in Germany, every week or so, to maintain his business cover.

Boris Morros nodded, put the money in an inside coat pocket, smiled and wished Edward Herbert a nice trip. Not long after, on 6 October 1934, Edward Herbert, Sarah Herbert and their infant son, Peter, boarded the SS *Europa* and sailed back to Cherbourg.

❧

Martha's river trip ended at Stalingrad, where they toured a tractor factory, which, unbeknownst to everyone, would, eight years hence, acquire a kind of immortality as the site of some of the bloodiest fighting of the Second World War. From Stalingrad, they took a train to Rostov-on-Don. Visiting Ordzhonikidze,[1] Tiflis, Batumi, Yalta, Sevastopol, Odessa and finally Kiev.

Martha's Russian vacation ended when the train she'd ridden from Kiev finally came to a halt at 7.22pm on Tuesday, 7 August 1934 at the Berlin train station. Stepping off the train, she saw her parents waiting for her on the platform. They didn't recognise her at first, Martha says, because of the 'brilliant Asiatic cap' she was wearing.[2] They'd assumed she was someone else.

15. SUSPICIONS

Among the mail waiting for Martha when she returned from Russia were several letters from Boris Vinogradov written in response to the irate ones she'd written him after Moscow. In addition to being angry that he was vacationing with someone besides herself, Martha had apparently been aghast at what she'd seen during the tour. His responses were, in turn, apologetic and chiding. 'I am very sad that you do not like everything in Russia,' he said in one. 'You ought to review it with completely different eyes than America. Please, dear Miss, look "inside" a bit deeper.'[1]

As for the matter of spending his holiday with someone else, he pointed that she, not he, had been 'the one who said we do not have to meet each other in Russia'.[2] To her suggestion that she would be going to Armand Berard, Boris responded, 'After your angry letter I am more than sad. Why did you do that, Martha? What happened? Can you not be two months without me.'

Boris' pleading had to have riled Martha, which, if anything, only propelled her into her French lover's arms as she'd threatened. Still, whatever Martha's conflicting feelings were over Boris and Armand, they couldn't have had much effect on the happiness and deep contentment she felt being back with her parents and brother. Never happier than when they were all together, the Dodds decided to make the most of it and take a road trip together. Saturday morning, three days later, they loaded up the family Chevrolet and hit the road, driving first to Koln, then up the Rhine to Mainz. All the way the roads were good and the weather perfect. They lunched at

Eisenach and then Martha and her father ditched Mattie and Bill Jr and explored the old Luther Museum. After that they drove to a resort town near Kassel and spent the night in a modern hotel that only charged them five marks each. The next day they headed to Frankfurt, looked in on the local consulate and then visited Goethe's home. From there, Heidelberg, Stuttgart and Württemberg.

For Martha and Bill Jr it was almost like the long drives the family took each summer to and from their farm in Virginia. They were always happy times with singing, story-telling and endless jokes. It was also a time for talking at length about history and politics. It is likely during this time there was plenty for the Dodds to talk about candidly, knowing that no one would be listening in on their conversations. Undoubtedly Martha regaled them with tales from her Russian trip, though it's unlikely she said much about Boris being there or about the NKVD recruiters.

No doubt the Dodds discussed the massacre during their trip. Six weeks had passed and for Dodd, it had fundamentally changed his relationship with Germany. It stripped away the last illusions he had for the country he passionately loved. Much as he despised German militarism, he'd always believed the German people were themselves fundamentally good and decent, with a wonderful culture and a strong sense of rationality and order. But now he'd seen with his own eyes how meaningless all that was. They'd made an idol of a deeply evil man who was putting not just Germany, but the whole world on a path of destruction. Messersmith had been so right on that; but even Messersmith had gotten things wrong. He had pinned his hopes on the idea that moderate Nazis would come to the fore and take over from the fanatics and make them something worthy of a place among the Family of Nations. Moderate Nazis either didn't exist or if they did, they simply didn't matter. It wasn't how things worked. Either way, as long as Hitler or any of his brutal gang were in charge, there'd be nothing but killing and terror. The massacre had made that obvious.

One of the things that irked him right after the massacre was how quickly everything returned to normal. That very Sunday, when the executions still hadn't finished, people were showing up for garden parties. That the dead were public figures, people they probably knew, didn't stop them continuing their lives as usual. The endless procession of American business leaders coming to see Dodd in his office all seemed uninterested; they continued to be dazzled by Hitler. It didn't seem to bother any of them that they were all brutal murderers. He probably told Martha about sending reports on the killings to Washington, and their responses were always the same. They only wanted to know whether it would affect Germany's debt repayment obligations.

Martha's mother, Mattie Johns, was also disgusted with Germany and its people. How nice they'd all seemed. Nice, decent, hospitable and Christian, and then they turn right around with their *Heil Hitlers* and their Hakenkreuz and their self-satisfied, thin-lipped smiles at seeing Jews being beaten. Wanting nothing more to do with them, Mattie did what she always did. She retreated into her family and home. Bill Jr was also overcome with disgust. Like his sister, he'd initially been enthusiastic about the new Germany. At first he went out a good deal with Martha into the social swirl. Messersmith and other chroniclers mention his presence beside her at social events. But it very quickly soured. Unlike Martha, Bill Jr wasn't any good at pretending to enjoy the company of people he utterly despised. To avoid the unceasing social swirl and festivities at 27A Tiergartenstrasse, he found lodging elsewhere and only rarely accompanied Martha to parties, preferring to spend his time either studying or with a small circle of friends. All Bill Jr wanted at this point was to complete his doctorate as quickly as possible, leave Germany and never come back.

Dodd travelled with his wife and children for three days. On Monday evening, they reached Stuttgart. The Dodds booked themselves into a modern hotel, had dinner and then dawdled for a while longer until their father bid them farewell and walked by himself to the train station, where he booked himself onto the sleeper back to Berlin. The next day, Martha, her brother and their mother got back in their Chevrolet and went on for another week, visiting southern Germany, Austria and Hungary.

Boris still hadn't returned when Martha got back from the road trip, but another of his letters had trickled in. In it, he let Martha know his time in Moscow hadn't exactly been a bed of roses, that his overlords were not overly pleased with his work, and that, in fact, he never got to the Caucasus. 'I could not spend my vacation together with you,' said Boris in one letter. 'It was not possible for various reasons. The most important reason: I had to stay in Moscow. My stay in Moscow was not very happy,' he confessed, adding 'my destiny is unresolved'.[3]

Was this true? Was Moscow Center unhappy with Boris' work? If so, why? Boris Vinogradov was a 'legal' spy. He was a Third Secretary at the Berlin Embassy and its press spokesman. Diplomatic cover allowed Boris to operate openly as a 'social agent'; a 'Romeo Spy'. Unlike nearly everyone else at the embassy, who knew that being seen talking to the wrong people would likely get them shot, Boris went to receptions, dinners, parties and, when he wanted to, frequented cafes and tony nightspots. His job was to win friends and influence people, especially journalists and the socially important. Boris' brief included seducing and sleeping with prominent women whom he could turn into sources and agents.

Nailing the socially prominent daughter of the American Ambassador had to have been a major coup, especially since she was also supplying him with high-level documents and other information. How could they have been unhappy with him after producing someone like that?

The answer might be that much as Moscow Center liked big scores, they preferred it not to come with any great disruption. Cheka had its methods for recruiting agents. They didn't like flashiness or anyone standing out too much. Events like Martha's surprise appearance might have unforeseen consequences, incurring suspicion and with them ending up in front of a firing squad.

Perhaps they were aghast at Martha making a big show, coming on like a movie star? And with a bunch of jazz records that she was expecting to give Comrade Molotov personally? Who gave Martha that idea? What had Boris told her that would make her do such a thing? Or perhaps it was something else.

Over the years, Moscow Center probably had its share of 'Champagne Spies', but strictly speaking, Boris Vinogradov wasn't one of them, since everyone already knew he was with the Soviet Embassy. Boris dressed well, drove a sporty car, had enough money and didn't seem to worry who he mingled with outside the embassy, something which could not be said of any of his co-workers. For most members of the press corps, Boris was the only person at the embassy any of them actually knew. He was fun and good company and most of the newsmen thought well enough of him, though he was known to say strange things when he was really drunk.

Boris' job was to get around, be friendly with people and use his charm and good looks to his advantage, especially when it came to women. That meant that while quality was nice, and clearly Martha Dodd was 'quality', quantity was also nice. Perhaps Boris Vinogradov was low on his count. And not to make too fine a point of it, nice as quality is, much, much nicer is quality brought in faster and with less fuss. This could have been achieved much sooner if he'd made her take the train to Paris four months earlier and gotten her through the recruitment process discreetly. Not like right now. There were pictures of Martha in afternoon papers, waving from the doorway of a Junkers trimotor on her way to Moscow.

Perhaps Boris explained that while a spy's survival does require sneakiness, not all sneakiness is low-key. Martha was indeed sneaky, just not in a quiet way. Martha was high-profile, but apparently she got results. Even so, she should have gone through Paris.

When Boris Vinogradov was finally back in Berlin, Martha, as promised, was with Armand Berard. But it didn't last long. Once she saw Boris again the thing with Armand fell apart and Armand went back to the 'occasionals'. Martha and Boris' relationship resumed, pretty much as before. They fought constantly, they made up and made love. Neither was remotely faithful. They were happy.

Not long after Martha's return from Russia, Pierre Huss, one of the American correspondents and a stammtisch regular, met up with Karl Boemer, head of the Propaganda Ministry's Foreign Press Department. Boemer was upset. Huss asked him what was wrong. Boemer told him it was about Martha.

Now, as far as the Nazi elite went, Boemer wasn't that bad. He could almost have been a moderate, except, of course, he wasn't. He spoke excellent English, was educated, had very polished manners and preferred to understate things. He could also be quite candid when no one was listening in. He'd get dragged to the stammtisch from time to time and he was usually a good addition. For an hour or so he'd be one of the boys and that was fine. They'd drink and smoke and shoot it back and forth and it was usually all quite witty. And sometimes, later on, if the planets were lined up right, when it was just him and you and maybe one or two others, Boemer might open up for ten minutes or so and let slip some serious insight into what Josef Goebbels was thinking and what he had on his plate. And when that happened, it would be utterly enlightening. You just had to be careful what you gave back to him in return.

It was no secret he and Martha had a thing going. But then, so did damn near everybody at one point or another. However, Boemer's thing with Martha was more or less ongoing. The problem was, it had gotten noticed recently and was suddenly a big deal. Because of that Russia trip of hers, she was now being investigated by the Gestapo.

Boemer told Huss how he'd been brought in for questioning and put through an interrogation he was still shaking from. Apparently Martha had been asking a lot of very pointed questions about Nazi intentions in foreign affairs. The Gestapo men wanted to know about what had gone on between him and Martha. *You two were lovers? What had she been asking you about and what did you tell her? What did he tell her? Well, lots of things. Little things, silly things, things that really had no value. Things like what? What did she say about her trip to Moscow? Tell us!*

And needless to say, Boemer pled hopeless innocence and told them anything and everything he could remember, which wasn't very much, but he stretched it out and padded it as best he could. 'That was yesterday,' Boemer told Huss. Huss nodded sympathetically. 'I don't dare see her again,' Boemer said. Under those circumstances, he supposed he wouldn't, either.

Martha did have a way of surprising people. Huss remembered his very first impression of her, thinking she seemed nice enough and even that she might be a virgin. Then he and everyone else found out that was definitely not the case. Huss also saw how she'd light up at the sight of guys in Nazi uniform. Brownshirts had her damn near rapturous.[4] Of course it wasn't the first time he'd witnessed this. Nazis just did it for some women, and Martha, apparently, was one of those women, only perhaps more so. Simple, really.

Only, it turned out, not so simple. Here's Martha all hot for Nazis. *What was the nasty little nickname those embassy people had for her? 'The Nazi Penetration of America.'* And Daddy-the-Ambassador either not knowing or caring. But then, suddenly, off she flies to Russia for a month's holiday under the questionable pretense of investigating rumors of people eating babies? That explanation didn't fool anyone, at least no one at the stammtisch. Fact was, Martha Dodd might have had a couple of strings, but she was much more of a hanger-on than a real journalist. Real newshounds might not get up with the birds, but they certainly didn't get out of bed at eleven as she was known to do. Obviously Vinogradov had put her up to it. He was the only Russian anyone had ever seen her with. He was the only Russian any of them had much to do with. Everyone else at the Russian Embassy was far too frightened to ever talk with any of them. He was a charmer, old Boris.

And now the Gestapo was asking about her.

⋯

The Germany Martha had returned to was very different from the one she'd left a month earlier. Hindenburg was dead and now Hitler had total control. While Hindenburg had still been alive there'd been a possibility, however faint, of some restraint on Hitler. Even after the 30 June massacre, some still nursed an ember of hope that the Old Man would direct the army to crush him. But now, with Hindenburg out the way, Hitler's rule was absolute. People suddenly had to be much more careful about what they said and did – and who they did it with. Nowhere was this more true than with the prospective young Nazi blades Martha had been partying with. If they wanted their careers to continue ascending, they would start putting distance between themselves and the wild, willful daughter of the American Ambassador.

The Gestapo was no longer the genteel bunch of thugs who'd hold your coat for you while beating you half to death. They no longer raided SA prisons and freed political prisoners. Those prisons were now theirs, and while they weren't as random in who they chose to arrest, those they did weren't in for any fun. Now they were part of the SS and their eyes were out for people who were neither Jewish nor communist, but whose loyalty was questionable and who might in fact be traitors; people like Arvid and Mildred Fish von Harnack, Martha's best friends.

The Harnacks were, at this point, already in the process of turning their study circles into active resistance groups. As it was, they lived just down the street from Columbia House, still a police torture center. From their window they could see the Gestapo cars coming in and out. There were a lot more of them than before and they seemed to be running all the time. It was enough to make the Harnacks want to find another flat.

⚜

Sometime in the autumn of 1934, Vassily Zarubin, his wife Elizabeta and son Petr arrived in Berlin. Presenting themselves as the fictitious American nationals Edward and Sarah Herbert and their son Peter, they quickly found a place to live along with office space from which to work. Zarubin then reported to the local police presidium to register and get the necessary permits. He next went to the Propaganda Ministry and presented his credentials as a fieldman for Paramount Pictures, and ended up having a chat with one of Goebbels' assistants who complimented him on his excellent German. Zarubin also, apparently, dropped by the US Consul General offices and introduced himself there as well. There, according to Cheka folklore, Zarubin was warned by the consular staff to exercise caution in hiring staff, since the Nazi secret police would make every effort to put in informants.

With all that out of the way, the Zarubins went to work running the Berlin illegal rezidentura.

According to Edvin Stavinsky, Zarubin's Russian biographer, Zarubin was prohibited from recruiting new agents in Germany and was to only work with the agents and sources transferred to him. All communications would go to Stanislav Glinsky, the legal rezident in Paris.[5]

Little is known about the Zarubins' activities during this period, but a few things are known about the rezidentura prior to their arrival. For years it had been a large and bustling operation with probably dozens of agents and other operatives working for them. There were espionage efforts taking place all the time along with counterfeiting and forgery operations. But now all that had been either shut down or dispersed to outstations. What remained was essentially a skeleton operation. Nevertheless, it was still one of Moscow Center's most important stations.

The legal side of the operation might communicate directly with Moscow, by cable or radio. The illegals sent everything by courier through Paris. Zarubin's predecessor, Fyodor Klaren, had brought in two American women to handle this.

Much of the Berlin operation ran out of a tobacco shop managed by a German named Karl Gursky. The tobacco shop also operated as a mail drop. They likely ran a number of agents, but the only ones anything is known about are a former German police official, later codenamed 'Rauppe', and an unidentified Gestapo employee they called 'Papasha'. Among the tasks on Zarubin's list was to hunt down remnants of the deep-cover networks from the old days.

If Zarubin's tradecraft in Paris is any indication, he made the requisite effort to establish his cover in Berlin as somebody in the film industry. He doubtless introduced himself to his neighbors, along with his wife. They socialised at least a little. Zarubin found a neighborhood pub and frequented there enough so that locals wouldn't become suspicious of him.

As he had in Paris, Zarubin found a socially desirable tennis club, joined it, and no doubt was soon playing against a number of young men who were up-and-coming in the new Hitler regime. It's likely that after sessions he wouldn't say no to beer or coffee, entertaining the men with stories of Hollywood and show business in general. He also joined a bicycle racing club and was soon attending meets and races, sometimes travelling to events in different cities in Germany. Quite likely he'd use these trips to meet agents and to search for those gone to ground.

Since he was officially in the movie business, Zarubin did what he thought he should do to bolster his professional profile. It is therefore likely that he also put in time at the local watering holes favored by members of Berlin's film community. One such spot was the café on Kurfurstenstrasse called *Die Taverne*, where the Brit and American foreign correspondents had their stammtisch. Part of the fun of going there was listening to what these correspondents had to say. Since English was Edward Herbert's first language, he probably entertained whoever he was with by telling them what the Amerikaners were talking about. It is not altogether unlikely that Zarubin made the acquaintance of a certain stammtisch regular named Martha Dodd.

16. 'TO MARTHA, MY WIFE!'

It didn't take long for word of the Gestapo's interest in Martha to spread. Many of her young, up-and-coming swains began to think twice about the effect further association with her might have on their careers. Of course, it wasn't just Martha. The same thing was happening to lot of Germans who until then hadn't worried about mixing openly with foreigners. Now they had to start limiting and sometimes outright avoiding interactions with those they might get asked about later. Word was also out that the American Embassy was somewhere to stay away from. More and more, invitations sent out for various embassy events now came back unopened with 'Moved Away' written on the envelope.

But while the Gestapo rumors about Martha might have frightened off the young-bloods, it only stoked the ardor of her lovers higher up the Nazi food-chain. For them, being seen with a woman of Martha's dubious caliber only bolstered their stature as true men of the world. Adding a hint of international intrigue made her that much more attractive. Goering still invited her falconing, Udet was happy to fly her up in his new airplane. Von Reichenau squired her at parties and athletic events, plus all the others. Martha's dance card was anything but empty during the autumn of 1934.

But Martha was also spending more time with Mildred and Arvid von Harnack. They had become her refuge; her other family. Everything else in Martha's life might have been crazy, but when she was with them, everything was real and serious and had balance and meaning. Like her own family, they cared about intellect and ideas.

Theirs was a place where good writing mattered and truth was The Truth.

For all their obvious differences, Martha and Mildred immediately bonded when they met. Each felt the other was the only person in Berlin who cared as much about writing, poetry and literature as themselves. For a while, the two jointly ran the *Berlin Topics* newsletter and organised events where visiting British and American writers came and gave readings and led discussions about books. They did all they could to make German writers and other intellectuals feel safe to venture out and attend these occasions.

While Mildred's literary criticism had frequently appeared in German newspapers, she was primarily an academic writer. Her writing was disciplined; her structures all thought out and logically presented. Martha, on the other hand, had no discipline at all. She wrote when it pleased her, but it seemed she was born already understanding the magic of words. Martha was the artist, Mildred the artisan. Mildred's work was engaging and brilliantly constructed, but it was clear to her, at least, that she didn't have the creative spark which, it seemed, Martha could effortlessly summon.

Boris didn't approve of Martha's friendship with the Harnacks. It made him nervous. He told Martha that with all that was going on, being seen with them could put Mildred and Arvid under suspicion. They were actively in the process of passing themselves off as loyal Nazis.

However, Martha knew the real reason he didn't want her hanging around with them. During one of their recent get-togethers, he and Arvid had gotten into a nasty argument about communism. After much thought and deliberation, Arvid had declared himself a communist. Having studied it as both an economist and humanist, he saw how communism could create a workable, equitable, just society and he was willing to give his life to the cause. But much as he might agree with, or be willing to support all its tenets, he wasn't going to join a cult-of-personality for Comrade Josef Stalin. Stalin might be the leader, the man in charge, but that was it. He was only the leader and you were loyal to the leader and not the man. Boris Vinogradov needed to accept that Arvid was a communist, but not a Stalinist.

But Boris Vinogradov was not all right with it. Not at all. You can't do that, said Boris. You can't think that. Everything Stalin does and thinks is good. Everything. You never question what Comrade Stalin says because there's never a need to. So never, ever question anything he orders. No deviations. At which point Arvid probably said something about needing to 'agree to disagree', to which Boris answered, No we don't agree to disagree. You must agree. But Arvid kept shaking his head, no. Martha listened to them arguing and since her German still wasn't very good, she might have gotten the gist of what they were arguing about, but why it was such a brutal topic she wasn't quite sure. Boris suddenly didn't want Arvid, or Mildred either for that matter, talking to Martha and influencing her about things she shouldn't concern herself with, like Comrade Stalin.

Of course Boris had a point. Martha knew she was being followed, but then, everybody got followed; it was just one of those things. But she also guessed it might be more than that. The question was, how much more? She didn't know the answer, but she wasn't going to let Boris order her around. Besides, Martha had diplomatic immunity.

She and Boris continued dating that autumn. As he had earlier, Boris continued taking Martha out to top nightspots. They were a crazy, passionate couple. No one had ever physically excited Martha near as much as Boris did. They enjoyed themselves – not that it stopped their endless arguing. A good deal of what they argued about stemmed from his jealousy over Martha's other lovers, but more than a little of it was about what she saw in Russia. Eventually she came to accept Boris' argument that everything had been incredibly worse under the Tsars.

As far as the recruitment process went, Martha was somewhere not quite in the middle. Everything was still very preliminary. There had been initial discussions in Moscow where she told them what she knew and what she could do for them. She might have been given some quick lessons in spycraft and using miniature cameras. There might even have been talk about dead drops and couriers when she got back to Berlin. She had probably been told she'd be working for an intelligence branch of Comintern. It was a lie. But beyond that, Martha probably didn't get told much, certainly not anything about 'konspiritsia', which for Chekists was a sort of guiding principle; an approach. Martha was not yet an operative; she was mainly a source. Boris would continue being her handler. Konspiritsia would come later.

Much as Martha might have believed her usefulness as a spy rested in her ability to wheedle secrets out of important men, mostly it was the secret US government reports and cable traffic coming across her father's desk. Martha had been asked to keep her eyes peeled particularly for reports about Japan, Poland and of course Germany – political, economic, military, and a lot of financial stuff too.

A lot of material she gave directly to Boris whenever they'd get together, which was fairly often. This material was great as far as Moscow Center was concerned, but at the same time, except for some of the cables, it generally wasn't time-sensitive. Boris would have written brief reports on their meetings, but what shows up in the files is sparse. Boris writes that at one point Martha had told him the atmosphere at the American Embassy was 'quite tense'.

In another note, Boris informs Moscow Center of Martha's planned trip to Russia just one day before her departure. Had he only learned of it then or had he been simply holding back on telling them? Following that, his meetings with her only generated a couple of one- or two-sentence reports. Towards the end of the year he informed them that she'd told him 'about her father's trip to Switzerland to meet with the American Secretary of Agriculture'.[1] In reality, Dodd and Bill Jr had secretly driven to Konstanz on the Swiss border in order to discuss the situation in Germany with one of President Roosevelt's close advisors, Rexford G. Tugwell, also, less importantly, the Assistant Secretary of Agriculture.[2] If what Vinogradov sent back was all they got of it, then they were completely missing out on quite a few fairly juicy tidbits. Quite likely, Martha sent on the full report to them by other means.

꧁꧂

At the end of the year, Boris Vinogradov was transferred to Bucharest. Martha could not have been pleased, but what could she do? There were goodbye parties, including a lunch at the Soviet

Embassy, apparently a great affair with some drinking. The stammtisch gang was there. Among them was Agnes Knickerbocker, H. A. Knickerbocker's wife who, years later, recalled seeing an inebriated Vinogradov loudly raising his glass and offering a toast 'to Martha, my wife'. Agnes noted how Martha 'neither blushed nor felt angry in the least'.[3]

It was by no means the end of things between Boris and Martha. They continued to correspond and he came to visit several times. Occasionally he'd even call Martha long-distance and they'd talk and tell each other things, knowing full well there were people listening in on them. Still, he was gone.

With Boris out of the way, Martha played the field, with Berard, Diels, Udet and others. The man Martha was most often seen with was Louis Ferdinand, Prince of Prussia, engineer, playboy (after a fashion) and unenthusiastic pretender to the abolished German Crown. 'He was one of the most interesting men I was to know in Germany and one of my dearest friends over the long four-and-a-half year period,' Martha wrote of him. She also 'felt his personality was out of touch with Nazi Germany'.

Called by some 'the American Hohenzollern', Prince Louis Ferdinand was, at the time Martha first met him, fresh out of Detroit where he'd been a senior executive at the Ford Motor Company. Louis Ferdinand hated Nazis and he loved America; he loved Ford, the automotive industry and production lines as a concept. He'd have stayed in Detroit given the choice, but he had been called home following his older brother's renunciation of his right of succession of the cancelled Hohenzollern crown in order to marry a member of the minor aristocracy. His grandfather, the Kaiser, had renounced the crown and gone into exile in order to end the First World War. His father had had to renounce it as well. Now, with his brother also stepping away, Louis Ferdinand was the next in line should it get reinstated.

Not that Louis Ferdinand wanted to be king. He'd looked on at all the monarchist intrigue with a good-natured sort of bemused detachment, knowing it was all taking place because the damn game had to be played and the monarchist card, for better or worse, was what they'd been dealt. They let Hitler take their money and then use them to help further his aims. If they wanted to believe the Fuhrer might soon find reason to reinstate the crown, well, that was entirely their business. Louis Ferdinand didn't believe any of it and even if he did, he wasn't capable of pretending that he didn't despise Hitler or his gang. But he also knew that on the off-chance something did happen to remove Hitler from office, he might need to be there to fill the kingly role, should it ultimately be called for. It would be wrong to be outside Germany at this hour.

Regardless of any possible outcome, Martha was there as his good, with-benefits, pal. By all indications their friendship was real. He liked interesting, intelligent people. Martha was of that sort. The Prince was a dashing man of the world who liked people talking about ideas and engineering. It seemed everybody liked him and were delighted anytime he might show up, just before dinner. Both Dodd and Messersmith mention setting him a plate and then talking with him into the evening. Messersmith, who had known him ten years earlier in Buenos Aires, considered him a son. If Messersmith and his wife knew anything about the Prince and Martha, he never mentions it. But then, Louis Ferdinand was seen with a lot of different women. As Prince of Prussia and more or less – but mostly less – heir apparent, he knew he'd eventually have to marry so that the imperial line would continue, but it didn't have to be now and it didn't have to be Martha or anyone else. He was free to have fun and he did. They'd been introduced shortly after her arrival in Berlin and the two immediately hit it off. The pictures of him from that period show an exuberant young man-about-town in a monocle. He could have come out of a P. G. Wodehouse novel: jaunty and exuberant; aristocratic without being stiff; a young man who had made his own way in the world and was comfortable being with people of all stripes.

Louis Ferdinand, Prince of Prussia, spent his days studying the German aviation industry trying to figure out ways to apply what he knew about automotive assembly lines to building aircraft. In the evenings he might frequent nightclubs and parties, but he continued just dropping in on people around suppertime and maybe making an evening of it. For the former, he'd take Martha or some other woman. For the latter, he usually went alone.

17. A WOLFE AND A BULLITT

Author Thomas Wolfe loved Germany and everything about it: the land, the culture, the poetry, the rationality and the romanticism. He loved the philosophy. He loved the music and loved what Goethe said about literature and about writing the novella. But Thomas Wolfe especially loved the German people. He loved Germany and didn't like Jews and was favorably disposed toward what was happening in the country. It wasn't exactly that he favored Hitler and the Nazis; it was more like he was just very enthusiastic about how Germany was changing and getting back to itself – to 'Blood and Soil'. Germany was achieving greatness once again and that was a very good thing. So if this was all because of Adolf Hitler and the Nazis, then it was hard to say Hitler was a bad thing. Still, there was something conditional about his approval of Hitler. Seeing this, Mildred and Martha decided he was ripe for conversion.

Wolfe had visited Germany several times over the years, usually for two-week periods, and now was coming over for two months. He needed to. His first novel, *Look Homeward, Angel*, had been a great critical and commercial success and now he had a second one coming out, *Of Time and the River*, looking certain to be another hit. Wolfe's muscular romanticism was approved by the Nazis as well. The German edition of *Look Homeward, Angel* had generated massive sales on publication, but because of currency restrictions, he couldn't export his German royalties. He had to spend it in the country, which was the main reason for the trip. Rowohlt, his German publisher, had put together a large publicity campaign to celebrate his visit, which the reading public was excited about.

Martha and Mildred were rapt with curiosity and enthusiasm for his upcoming arrival. They decided to stage an event for him, a literary tea, at the embassy. Martha sent him a letter on embassy stationery, through Scribner's, his publisher, asking if he could come.

To their great surprise, Wolfe agreed. Martha's letter had apparently intrigued him, especially when she told him that both her father and brother were historians and that she was herself a writer. Martha and Mildred began setting up the event. They invited the press. The rest of the invited guests were writers and critics who hadn't yet sold themselves. It was what was left of what had been a community and was the last time most of them would be together.

The many notches on Martha's bedpost included several famous authors: Carl Sandburg, Stephen Vincent Benet and others.[1] She was primed to throw herself at Wolfe. But Mildred also had her eyes on him, though her aims weren't carnal. When Wolfe arrived in Berlin, Mildred was at the hotel, wishing to interview him. The two immediately clicked. They talked through the evening about literature and American writers: Hemingway, Sherwood Anderson. Wolfe talked about being a writer and spoke some length about Maxwell Perkins, his by now legendary editor at Scribner's. It went on for hours. Wolfe was impressed with the questions Mildred asked and the ideas she presented to him. He loved talking with her. In a way, he was captivated and hoped their conversation could continue.

The tea party was a success, even though only two members of the German press were there: Bella Fromm and another. But the stammtisch crowd was in attendance and a good number of others – writers and intellectuals who were now mostly avoiding each other. Wolfe realised that Martha and Mildred were friends, probably best friends. He evidently also surmised that Mildred was happily married and Martha was not.

Martha was no Mildred. In one of his mentions of her to Perkins, he dismisses her as 'a little Middle Western flirt with a little "sure that would be swell" sort of voice'.[2] Martha had other qualities which he soon found endearing. She knew where to go, and for the next two months took him out, usually with Mildred, her brother, and Ledig-Rowohlt accompanying them. It was, he said later, a 'wild fantastic whirl of parties, teas, dinners and drinking bouts, newspaper interviews, radio proposals, photographers, etc'.[3] He and Martha also engaged in a tempestuous affair. By the end of it, he was writing to Perkins and telling him: 'Martha is like a butterfly, hovering around my penis.'[4]

It didn't take long for Martha to get on his nerves, especially when she'd chide him for his drinking and what she considered to be the wasting of his talent. She let him know she expected him to confide in her his fears and loneliness. It was as though Martha felt that having sex with him, housing him, feeding him and driving him around gave her some proprietorship over his behaviour. Wolfe let her know he was neither particularly afraid nor lonely and that if he was, he was hardly going to share it with some young thing he'd just met, which miffed Martha a bit – though of course not enough to send him on his way. Wolfe also didn't think much of Martha's opinions, particularly her political ones, since he felt she was leaning too much leftward.

However, his conversation with Mildred continued and grew deeper. Often the two would go on long walks in the Tiergarten, discussing literature and the whole business of writing and how he did it. She ended up writing a number of articles for different publications based on her extensive interviews with Wolfe. In the course of it, Mildred began working in the politics, making Wolfe understand why Hitler was such a bad thing. Bit by bit, his support for Hitler and the Nazis was worn down. Still, his love for Germany and for German ideas and culture never faltered.

⋯✦⋯

Shortly after Wolfe left, Mildred and Arvid were approached by someone newly transferred to the Soviet Embassy named Boris Gordon, who asked if they'd be interested in working with him. They said they would be. The Harnacks must have impressed Gordon with their ability to assemble many small, intersecting circles of like-minded Germans. Gordon might have been able to link her with some of the people which the KDP had hidden within its own independent secret apparatus. As with Martha, the Harnacks were probably told they would be working for the 'Comintern'.

❧

While Wolfe had been around, Martha sent Boris Vinogradov letters letting him know who she was having fun with. But the fact that she was rubbing it in Boris' face didn't mean she wasn't still aching to be back in his arms. Martha never stopped wanting Boris. Once or twice he took the train up from Bucharest and they'd have a couple of days together. But it was never enough. She wanted to be with Boris permanently. She made sure he knew. Boris presumably wrote the required reports on their meetings, though none were found in the KGB files when they were opened up half a century later. Presumably Martha fed whatever dead drops were set out for her during this period, not that the files make any mention of it, either.

The files also make no mention of what it might have been that caused Moscow Center to send a message to Boris Vinogradov in June 1935 asking him to 'clarify the nature of his "working" relationship with Martha Dodd'.[5] From Bucharest Boris wrote back that: 'The situation with the American woman (Martha Dodd) at present is as follows: She is currently in Berlin, and I have received a letter from her in which she writes that she still loves me and dreams of marrying me. It is possible to work with her only with the aid of a "good relationship".'[6]

Around this time, Bill Jr received his degree from Berlin University. Fancy European doctorate finally in hand, he immediately went back to Virginia, to the farm. But within a few weeks he boarded another ocean liner and returned to Europe, bolting through France, Germany and Poland, arriving in Russia and embarking on a package tour like the one his sister had been on the year before. A few days after returning stateside, he began a one-year teaching contract at William and Mary College. It was the result of his father prevailing upon one of his friends to give a job to his son.

❧

Boris Vinogradov visited Berlin for a few days in early October 1935. As usual, they fought. When Martha saw him off at the Berlin train station on 8 October both were angry.

On the evening of 7 November 1935, the Soviet Ambassador threw a high-profile bash at the Radziwill Palace, which Martha attended, arriving alone in a chauffeured limo. The first to greet her was the TASS (the Soviet news agency) man Sergei M. Kudryavtsev,[7] who escorted her to the main reception hall, where he presented her first to Ambassador Nicolai Skwarzekev, then to Vladimir Pavlov, just in from Moscow. He was Josef Stalin's preferred English-language translator and, some believed, his illegitimate son. Martha spent the evening talking to high-ranking Russians, always with Kudryavtsev beside her, translating and making witty quips. What was discussed isn't known, but one can guess how it went. Likely, Martha hit them with both barrels about what she knew, what she heard, who she knew and what she could do for them. Pavlov listened to her, then asked her some questions. How long would she be in Berlin? When would her father go back? Was it true she knew President Roosevelt and his family? What did she plan to do after her father left? What about remaining in Berlin?

The special treatment accorded to Martha at the Russian Embassy bash did not go unnoticed. Among those who observed her was Sir George Ogilvie-Forbes, one of the big dogs at the British Foreign Office who happened to be in attendance and was probably hoping for a word with Pavlov himself. He'd heard about Martha. Odd girl.

One has to wonder if Pavlov had been there in an extra-official capacity as Stalin's personal envoy, his *Fritz Wiedemann*. What did he think of Martha? How did he assess her wanting to be a comrade and serve the World Communist Revolution? What would she be willing to do for them? Was she an adventuress, like in the movies? Pavlov was extremely curious. What did she want? What could she do? What kind of a person was she? *What would Comrade Stalin have me tell her?*

It was probably also during this reception that Martha was introduced to her new case officer.[8] Officially, Dmitry Bukhartsev was a correspondent for *Izvestia*, but in reality he was an NKVD officer. According to Rudolph, 'They got acquainted at a reception in our mission. Martha (in future "Liza") willingly agreed to the suggestion by Bukhartsev (in future "Emir") to get together outside the mission. "Liza" continues to inform "Emir" along the same lines that she did when she was meeting with "Alexander".[9]

Shortly after that, Bukhartsev reported in with news about a visit by the American Ambassador to Moscow, William Bullitt: 'I have seen Liza several times over the past 2–3 weeks. At the first meeting she described to me Bullitt's "swinish behavior" during his visit to Berlin. According to her, Bullitt scathingly excoriated the USSR at the American Embassy, arguing that in the next few months the Japanese will take over Vladivostok, and the Russians, he said, won't do anything about it. Then, according to Martha, Bullitt had a discussion with François-Poncet, where he tried to convince the latter of the necessity of cooperating with the Germans against the USSR. All this greatly angered the American Ambassador Dodd, who sent an appropriate letter to Washington.'[10]

❦

Shortly after the Soviet Embassy party, George Ogilvie-Forbes was having drinks with Pierre Huss. He told him what he saw. Huss nodded. Everybody had 'Martha stories'. He let Ogilvie-Forbes know he lately hadn't had much to do with her outside the stammtisch. But mysterious Russians? High-level Nazis? Who knew? With Martha, anything was possible. She'd brought some amazing people by at one time or another.

'She is a strange girl, it seems to me,' said Ogilvie-Forbes, musing aloud. Huss agreed.

18. REPLACING THE NEW
CASE OFFICER

Bill Jr's teaching job at William and Mary College did not work out. For two semesters he taught a handful of classes in American history with only a couple of students taking them. He quickly became popular with students when they learned about his experiences in Berlin. The faculty did not share their enthusiasm, viewing him as a leftist radical. Bill Jr's one-year appointment was not renewed and he returned to Round Hill to lick his wounds and figure out what to do next.

By coincidence, his father happened to be in Washington for consultations and came down to see him. Dodd intended to give his son a talking to, to upbraid him for his lack of decorum and professional behavior, and then, once he was sure Bill Jr understood his mistakes, finding him another teaching position. But to Dodd's surprise, his son told him he was no longer interested in teaching. What really mattered to him was politics and political activism. He'd been offered, and accepted, a position with the Paris-based *La Rassemblement Universel Pour la Paix* (The Universal Peace Campaign, or RUP). More than a little taken aback, Dodd wished his son well in his new pursuit. Learning how little it paid, he also agreed to help subsidise him.

That June, Bill Jr sailed back to Europe. By the end of July, he and his group were in Shanghai, from where he wrote Martha that they were 'having more success than I could have expected'. He also mentioned meeting their friend Franz von Papen Jr, son of the former

Vice-Chancellor, who, inexplicably, happened to be living there at the time. The group then returned, travelling through Russia, stopping in Moscow, then Berlin, just long enough to see his family at the station, before continuing on to Geneva. If they'd had more than a few minutes together, Bill Jr might have mentioned something that had happened to him in Round Hill shortly after his father's visit.

Someone claiming to be a reporter in New York called wanting to interview him about joining the international peace campaign, which he somehow knew about. Bill Jr invited the reporter down to the farm, if he wished to interview him on the subject. The reporter showed up and they talked at length. He revealed that he was a Moscow Center operative and wished to recruit him. Bill Jr declined the invitation, saying that at the moment he wanted to just focus on the peace campaign, though it was quite possible he might later. Before the reporter left, he told him he knew that his sister, Martha, was already working for them.

❧

Martha met with Bukhartsev through the spring and summer. He reported her willingness to provide them with information and even how she was 'now intensively studying the theory of communism, poring over Stalin's "The Issues of Leninism", with the aid of Arvid Harnack, "her teacher"'. But he also reported on her sexual escapades and her justification: 'Although Martha insisted she was now a fervid Communist, she reported that this doesn't prevent her from maintaining a rather intimate relationship with the crown prince's son, Louis Ferdinand. According to Liza, this is a wonderful cover, because those who were previously suspicious of her because of her overt relationship with Vinogradov now consider her past infatuation to have been from the "heart" rather than "political".

'Martha asserts that she is a committed supporter of the Communist Party and the USSR. With the State Department's knowledge Martha helps her father in his diplomatic work and is up to date regarding everything he is doing. The entire Dodd family hates the National Socialists. Martha has interesting contacts that she uses to obtain information for her father.'[1]

That summer, Nazi Germany hosted the 1936 Summer Olympics. For the entire month of August, the Nazis held off on their usual in-public oppression of the Jews. Thomas Wolfe returned to Berlin and though he did resume his meetings with Mildred, he did not continue his affair with Martha.

Also that summer, Boris Vinogradov was transferred from Bucharest to Warsaw, which put him much closer to Martha.

⚹

For Soviet intelligence officers working undercover, taking over agents from other handlers was a basic part of the job. Naturally, there'd need to be some adjustment. The new handler needed to be respectful but firm in establishing procedures, making them understand what was now expected, along with whatever new procedures would be used. Martha's training under Boris had probably been hit or miss. Martha had to have been a challenge for Bukhartsev, who probably preferred agents who did their best to be invisible. But Martha was that rare spy who preferred having the spotlight on her. Also, of course, was the fact that her previous handler had been a 'Romeo' and that their passionate affair was woven into the very fabric of their professional relationship. Doubtless, there must have been some concerns in this regard on Bukhartsev's part. Possibly for this reason, as part of her recruitment, Bukhartsev directed Martha to explain things about herself, which Martha did, including her many lovers. In an undated report, Bukhartsev writes:[2]

> She has intimate relationships with several acquaintances. Her contacts are:
>
> 1. A. Berard[3] – a secretary at the French Embassy in Berlin. He is in charge of intelligence.
> 2. Diels.
> 3. Berger.
> 4. Jung.

Despite what the file entries might suggest, things were not fine between Martha and Bukhartsev. There was a problem and Martha made a point of mentioning it to whoever it was she knew at the Soviet Embassy, who, after listening, agreed Bukhartsev didn't cut it. 'Emir didn't meet the station's expectations regarding the work with Liza,' reported Rudolf in a message to Moscow Center sometime in September 1936. Bukhartsev got replaced by the embassy's new press secretary, Yevgeny Gnedin, codenamed 'Pioneer'.[4] He and Martha apparently worked out fine, and there were no problems after that.

As for Bukhartsev, he was sent home, whereupon he was immediately arrested, tried and shot.

So what had been the problem? Knowing Martha, it's hard not to wonder if sex had something to do with it. Had they 'done the deed'? Had something gone wrong, or could it simply have been that Martha didn't want to sleep with him and he thought she should. It could easily have been that. Or, nothing at all might have happened in that department. It's also possible that the problem wasn't even between the two of them. Whatever it was, we'll likely never know.

On 29 October, one '*Rudolf*' wrote to Moscow Center that the professional relationship between Martha and her new handler seemed to be working out: '"Liza" was very pleased with our little gift – we gave her the book "Chapayev" from her friends in Moscow. "Liza" said she is ready to follow all of our instructions. She agreed that if her father moves away she will stay here, if we find it necessary, to work for us.'[5]

But while everything was harmonious between Martha and her new handler, relations between Martha and Boris were still tumultuous, even from a distance. At some point when Moscow Center realised the extent of the relationship, they directed the lovers to conduct all their correspondence through them. After learning, presumably through one of her contacts at the Soviet Embassy, that Boris had been transferred from Bucharest to Warsaw, she sent him one letter so breathless that it alarmed them:

Boris, this week marked a year since I last saw you. I kissed you goodbye at the train station on the 8th, and we haven't seen each other since. But never for a minute have I forgotten you or everything you gave me in life.

Every evening this week I thought about you – every evening – and that evening, when we had such a foolish and unseemly quarrel – did you forgive me? I was scared and in a weird frame of mind that evening, because I knew that I wouldn't see you for such a long time. I wanted terribly for you to stay with me that evening and forever, and I knew that I would never be able to have you. What have you been doing all this time, did you think about me, and did you wonder what course my own life took? I know from various sources that you will soon go home.

Will you pass through Berlin? Write me and let me know your plans. I would like to see you again. On 8 December I will be home the whole night. Won't you call me, won't you talk with me from Bucharest for a few minutes – I want to hear your voice again so much – and the 8th will be the anniversary of our foolishness, we must curse our cowardice for this separation. Please call me that night. You may have heard about me by indirect means. I have lived through and thought over many different things since I last saw you. You must know about this. Armand is still here – but you should know that he can't mean anything to me now – as long as you're alive – nobody can mean anything to me while you're alive.

I still love you, and I always will, and I will go with you if you have the courage to take me with you. Now everything is different, but you should know this. Martha.'

At the bottom of the letter one of its readers left the following comment: 'Decision: We need to put an end to this immoral behavior.'[6]

Evidently, Martha's drama alarmed the wise men of Moscow Center. Martha had the makings of a great asset. Important men all seem to share the same weakness for pretty, young, attentive women, all characteristics Martha possessed and which made her so effective. But she also required special handling. Martha's charms needed to be reserved for the target, not the handler. Martha and Vinogradov needed to be separated. They were both told that, whatever they were doing, to knock it off and stay away from each other, at least for the time being. For a while it worked.

Several months went by without Martha hearing anything from Boris. Christmas passed without a word, as did New Year's. 1936 became 1937. Then, in late January, Bill Jr showed up in Berlin, looking shabby in a worn-out suit, but brimming with enthusiasm from his time with the peace campaign. The last six months had been exciting. He had witnessed, first-hand, a German ship supplying weapons and ammunition to Franco's forces in Spain and had testified about it at the House of Lords in London. Listening to him, Martha found herself wishing she could join him. Her own experience as an erstwhile spy paled in comparison to what he'd been doing and she started thinking about giving it up and joining him. Martha's envy was not shared by her parents. Glad as they were that Bill Jr was doing something meaningful, they didn't like him showing up looking dishevelled like this when they were bankrolling him.

With her brother there with her, Martha decided it might be a proper occasion to give Boris a call so all three of them could chat. Late that evening, Martha put through a long-distance call to the number she'd been given, but when the phone was answered, Boris was not available, so she left a message for him. Boris wrote back a day or two later, unsure if the call had actually come from Martha. In a letter to Boris dated 29 January 1937,[7] Martha wrote:

Darling, I was so glad to hear from you and find out that you are finally in Warsaw. Yes, I called you then late in the evening ... my brother was in Berlin and we thought that it would be nice to chat with you. He left this morning for Brussels and Paris. In a few days he will move the offices of the International Peace Conference to Geneva. Then later, I think, he will travel to America for them ...

You cannot imagine, darling, how often you have been with me, how I constantly thought about you, worried about you, and sought to see you, how I adjusted to the inevitable when I heard the initial news, and how happy I was when I learned the truth. I want to see you so much, darling. Could I come before the end of the month? I would like to come on the 6th of February, a Saturday I think, and stay for about a week. It's extremely important for me to see you, and I promise to do it as soon as possible. I'd like to stay somewhere in a small hotel not far from you, and I don't want anyone to know I'm there, because I don't want any diversions. I only want to see you, and as incognito as possible. Maybe we could leave Warsaw for a day or two and drive into the countryside. I would come by myself, of course, and my parents completely agree that I do as I wish – after all, I'm 28 years old, and I'm very independent!

In early March, Martha took a train to Warsaw to spend some time with Boris. Apparently this time they had a wonderful time together without any fighting. At some social event they'd attended Martha flirted with a 'Prince Sapieha',[8] who subsequently invited her to visit his estate that April. Martha then took another train, this one to Moscow. According to KGB files, Martha arrived on 14 March. Unlike her previous visit, this one was pure business.

In his report to Moscow Center, Boris writes: '"Liza" left today for Moscow, since her father will retire sooner or later, she wants to work in her own country (in the US). She established contact with Browder,[9] who invited her to work for him. She has also established contact (through her brother) with the World Peace Committee in Geneva, and has become close to Comintern officials Otto Katz and Dolivet. In order to persuade her to stay in Europe and work only for us, we need to arrange for an authoritative comrade to have a talk with her.'[10]

Beyond the fact that she stayed at the Savoy Hotel, the KGB records don't tell much about Martha's time in Moscow, only that her meetings inside Moscow Center were with some high-level people, and even though very little of true substance was discussed, it's safe to assume her presence there did generate discussions at the very highest levels of power. Being in a world where nobody liked surprises or anything coming from out of left field, Martha's presence likely generated more unwelcome disruption than anyone cared for, at a time when purges were thinning the ranks and everyone's neck was on the chopping block.

Soon after arriving in Moscow, Martha submitted what she said was their joint request for permission to marry:

To the Soviet Government
Statement.
I, Martha Dodd, a citizen of the USA, have known Boris
Vinogradov for three years in Berlin and other places, and
have agreed with him to officially request permission to get
married.
Martha Dodd, Moscow, 14/3-37[11]

Unlike other personal requests from agents, Martha's, owing to her
perceived importance, entered at very nearly the top levels of Moscow
Center's bureaucracy. The high-ranking NKVD officials examining it
probably weren't sure exactly what to make of it. They weren't accustomed to having operatives making such requests and especially not
directed to no less a comrade than Stalin himself! Under other circumstances, it might have been buried or lost. But coming in at such a
high level, things didn't get conveniently lost or forgotten about. But
then what should they do with it? Likely they didn't know. Had they
checked the file and seen what Boris Vinogradov, her intended groom,
had to say, they'd have been aware of his distinct lack of enthusiasm
for what Martha was requesting, not the least since he was already
married with a daughter. Somehow it was decided Comrade Martha
should have the opportunity to state her case to Yezhov, head of the
NKVD, who would listen and decide whether to pass it on to Stalin.
    In a subsequent report to Comrade Nikolai Ivanovich Yezhov,
the People's Commissar of Internal Affairs of the USSR General
Commissar of State Security, Martha is introduced and allowed to
argue her case for how she should be deployed in the future:

> Some time ago, we recruited Martha Dodd, the daughter of
> the Amer. ambassador in Germany. We made use of her brief
> trip to the USSR for detailed talks with her and determined
> that she has highly valuable capabilities and can be actively
> used by us on a broad scale. At our request, she has set forth
> herself her position in society, her father's position and the
> prospects for her future work for us

Martha began by repeating her original offer of service made months
earlier and then brought them up to date about her access: 'At present

I have access mainly to the personal confidential correspondence of my father and the State Department, as well as the President of the US. The source of information on military and naval matters, as well as aviation, is solely personal contact with the personnel of our embassy.' Martha then admitted that, while she still remained in close contact with other journalists, she had lost almost all contact with ordinary Germans, except perhaps for chance encounters and meetings in society which, she admitted, 'yields almost nothing'. Martha went on to say that most Germans, foreign diplomats and even the personnel at the embassy 'are suspicious, hostile and (with regard to the Germans) insulting toward us' ... 'Is the information that I get from my father, who is hated in Germany and isolated among foreign diplomats ... really important enough for me to stay in Germany?'

It was all Martha's way of hinting that it was time to let her leave Germany, 'unleashing' her on the American target. Failing that, there were also the international organisations, like the ones her brother was in. Perhaps she could serve in one of those? The best, she suggested, would be one with 'bourgeois cover'? 'In America I'm not suspected of anything,' she told them.

Then Martha gave her predictions about the future:

Roosevelt must grant positions to many diplomats and capitalists who financed him. Among them are Davies (who is seeking a post in London), Hugh Wilson (Switzerland), Messersmith in Austria, Cudahy in Poland, Thomas Watson (International Machines Corporation, a big friend of Germany), not to mention govt. officials like Roper (secretary of commerce, a fascist) and members of business circles in NY and other places. Since he has little experience with regard to European politics, Roosevelt will probably name one of these people, or from these groups, who will be, in the final analysis, dangerous now as well as during wartime ... Nevertheless, my father has great influence on Hull and Roosevelt, who ... [12]

My father has certain guidelines regarding people and will exert pressure in order to make them follow his instructions, but if there is information regarding our candidates, it would be important to find out whose candidacy for the post in

Germany the USSR would like to push, if this person has at least the slightest chance, I will try to persuade my father to push his candidacy.

It would be interesting to know what Yezhov made of it. By then the Great Purge was well underway and as head of the NKVD, he was busily carrying out mass arrests, torture and executions. The wishes of a highly entitled American comrade must have struck him as an exceedingly odd distraction, especially in view of everything else going on at that moment. He might well have wondered how anyone could have thought themselves so important. But at the same time, it might also have occurred to Yezhov that, since he couldn't be sure what kind of regard Comrade Stalin might hold for her – after all, her reports were going directly to his desk – dismissing or mishandling her request might have adverse unforeseen consequences.

With this in mind, Comrade Yezhov wrote to the man at the very top, Josef Stalin.

29.III.37
Top secret. Eyes only.
To Comrade Stalin:
Secretary of the Central Committee of the VKP(b) Department 7 of the GUGB of the NKVD has recruited the daughter of the American ambassador in Berlin, Martha Dodd, who arrived in Moscow in March 1937 for business talks. She has outlined her position in society, her father's position and the prospects for her to work for us in the future in her own report. In forwarding a copy of the latter, I request instructions regarding the use of Martha Dodd.
Yezhov.

Stalin's response is not known, but Martha left Moscow and returned to Berlin convinced permission to marry Boris was all but in her hands. Despite Boris begging them to disabuse Martha of this, Moscow Center decided it was best to keep her on the hook. They hadn't exactly said yes, but it was good enough for Martha.

Apparently though, shortly before she left, Martha did have meetings with one or several senior NKVD officials about what she should do once back in America. After convincing them of her family's high standing within Democratic political circles and close friendship with FDR, it was determined Martha should focus on infiltrating the inner circle of First Lady Eleanor Roosevelt. Her assignment in hand, Martha Dodd took a train back to Berlin to wait out the months until her return to America.

The Berlin Martha returned to wasn't the wide-open city she'd come to four years earlier. Fear and suspicion were everywhere. Just as she'd explained in Moscow, she'd become cut off from nearly everybody in Berlin, except for the journalists and a few others. She didn't even have any connections at her own embassy. Their icy, polite condescension had only grown worse and she hated the way they looked down their noses at her. In letters to friends, she'd make references to the snobbery she had to endure. She had few real friends there besides Mildred and Arvid, and she had to keep away from them, though occasionally she and Mildred did meet up in different, out-of-the-way places. One of the ways they kept in touch with her was whenever they'd take one of their trips outside Berlin, Mildred would fill up a postcard with her musings and send it to Martha unsigned. Martha and Boris also kept apart, though they'd send each other letters through the required channels so Moscow knew what was going on between them.

❧

The passenger-cargo ship *City of Baltimore* wasn't a glamorous ocean liner like the ship which had first carried the Dodd family to Germany four years earlier. It was a much smaller steamship working the cargo and mail route from Hamburg to Southampton to Havre, across to Baltimore and ending at Norfolk. It was a ship you took if you didn't want to call attention to yourself. It was the ship Dodd took when he sailed back alone to America on 24 July 1937.

Officially Dodd was going for consultations, but actually he just needed a long rest. His time in Berlin had ruined him, physically as well as mentally. By now he suffered from endless headaches and stomach pain. His mind had grown feeble. More than anything, he wished to return to Round Hill and concentrate on writing his history of the Old South. Pressure to quit was coming from both sides: from inside the State Department and from the German government. But Dodd was determined to continue. To resign was to admit failure and he was too proud to do that.

After arriving at Norfolk on 4 August,[13] Dodd went directly to Round Hill where he spent a week engaging in physical labour around his farm, getting his strength back. By 11 August, when he drove up to Washington to meet with President Roosevelt, he was already feeling much better. Roosevelt was deeply troubled by all the 'war talk' going round. Dodd spoke frankly with the President and there was nothing he could tell him that would instill any optimism for the future. The President told Dodd he wished him to remain at his post another two or three months, after which he'd bring in a replacement. After that, Dodd met with Secretary of State Cordell Hull, who told him about the complaints delivered against him by Hans-Heinrich Dieckhoff, the new German Ambassador. Dodd drove back to his farm for another week of rest. Roosevelt had invited Dodd to his home in Hyde Park on the 19th and even suggested he bring along his son – apparently Roosevelt was aware of Bill Jr's involvement in the International Peace Campaign and wanted to meet him. A week later, Dodd and Bill Jr drove up to Hyde Park and spent the afternoon and evening with the President and his family. That night, as they prepared to depart, Roosevelt told Dodd to write him personally. 'I can read your handwriting,' he said.[14]

When Dodd sailed back to Germany in late October he expected to remain in his post until at least March. But almost as soon as he was back in Berlin he received instructions to wrap things up and leave Germany before the end of the year. Martha sent word on to Moscow Center that her father's tenure as ambassador was ending soon. She also let Boris know, along with her expectations that he would soon join her in America, fighting fascism and capitalism as a married couple. He was quick to let Moscow Center know his displeasure: 'In her letter to me "Liza" writes about marriage again. When she left for Moscow [earlier that year] I wrote you that such promises shouldn't be made. Yet such a promise was made to her and now she expects the promise to be carried out. Her dream is to be my wife, at least a de facto one, and for me to work in America, and she would help me.'[15]

A week later, Boris Vinogradov took the train from Warsaw to Berlin for a last visit with Martha. Apparently he did so on Moscow Center's instruction, since he brought with him information she'd need for making contact with her new handler in New York City. Upon his return to Warsaw, he sent this message to his superiors in Moscow:

> The meeting with 'Liza' was successful. She was in a good mood. She is leaving on 15 December for NY, where a meeting has been arranged with her ...
>
> 'Liza' continues to be occupied with marriage plans and is waiting for me to carry out our promise, despite the fact that her parents have warned that nothing will come of it. The journalist Louis Fischer, who is not unknown to you, has proposed to 'Liza'. She is not giving her consent, since she hopes to marry me. But if we tell her that under no circumstances will I ever marry her, then she will not be averse to accepting Fischer's proposal. I don't think she can be left in the dark regarding the real state of affairs, because if we mislead her, she could become embittered and lose faith in us.
>
> At present she consents to work for us, even if it becomes clear[29] that I won't marry her. I offered 'Liza' money, but she refused it.[16]

⁕

The last time Martha saw Mildred was shortly before departing for America. They met at a busy restaurant in a park.

> We found an inconspicuous table and talked quietly for an hour, about books, ourselves, fascism and the future ... Quietly she related that she and Arvid had succeeded in influencing and bringing into the underground many intellectuals, writers and professionals, the only groups with whom they could have close contacts (through their own relatives they reached into diplomacy and the army).[17]

Although Mildred travelled to the United States early in 1938, it does not appear the two met anytime during her visit. Mildred had arranged to meet with numerous other friends who had relocated there from Germany, but inexplicably, she failed to show up for several of them. Mildred had also hoped to get together with Thomas Wolfe as well, but he died shortly after she arrived. It would be Mildred's last visit to America.

On 15 December 1937, Martha Dodd left Germany.

19. THE WIFE OF A WEALTHY MAN

Boris Vinogradov had hoped that when Martha returned to America, she would do as she always did and find someone else. He hoped that nature would take its course: she would settle down and put him out of her mind once and for all. Martha, to her credit, did give it a whirl. She found someone, fell in love, and very quickly married him. Even so, Martha never managed to forget about Boris.

Alfred Kaufmann Stern was a millionaire and a Jew, nine years older than Martha, divorced, and heavily involved in progressive politics. His business was investments and he dabbled in them quite successfully from an all-but-empty office at 30 Rockefeller Plaza. Alfred gave money, signed petitions, and sat on boards and committees. Many considered him pedantic, a bore and know-it-all. He had made himself an expert on public housing and had already served as housing commissioner for Chicago. Alfred Stern lived alone in a five-room apartment at 155 Central Park West for which he paid $3,800 per year – not a trifling sum.

No one can say at exactly which leftist, progressive fundraiser it was that he and Martha met. Whichever one it was, the two immediately clicked, because a very short time later they were driving down to Ellicott City, Maryland, to get married by a local justice of the peace. Martha was now Mrs Alfred Stern, the wife of a wealthy man.

Which is, of course, not to say that Martha didn't already have things going on with other men when she met Stern. Whatever money she'd possessed had largely dried up by then. She had begun writing a memoir of her time in Germany, and in order to stay in New York, she had shacked up with a leftist writer named Sydney Kaufman. A professional writer and serial womaniser, ever on the hustle, Kaufman had somehow also gotten himself on the hook to the FBI and, along with everything else he was doing, wrote reports informing on anyone and everyone he knew. Though his reports on Martha have never been found, from what he later told people, he put in whatever she told him, adding that she was, in his estimation, 'a sex maniac'.

As was her custom, Martha usually got up late, rarely before 11am. She spent her days writing and her nights partying. Alfred Stern came close enough for entrée into New York's liberal, left-wing social elite and soon she made her place among them.

∘⊰❖⊱∘

As for Martha's mission to infiltrate the First Lady's inner circle, it never got out of the gate. She disembarked in New York three days before Christmas, eager to set the capitalist world on fire, and for the next two weeks she waited, expecting, at any moment, word from her Moscow Center contact. But Christmas passed, as did New Year's, and still not a peep. Her parents arrived on 8 January, but wasted little time there before heading back to Round Hill. One morning shortly after that, someone knocked on the door of the house on Irving Place where Martha was staying and asked to speak with her. When she appeared, he said to her, 'I want to give you regards from Bob Norman.' Martha froze. It was the 'contact protocol' she'd been told to wait for months earlier, back in Moscow.

∘⊰❖⊱∘

His codename in correspondence with Moscow Center was 'Jung'. He may have introduced himself as 'Michael Green', 'Michael Adamec', 'William Grienke', or any of several other cover identities which he went by, but probably not by his real name, which was Iskhak Abdulovich Ahkmerov. Ahkmerov was the station chief;

the 'rezident' of the NKVD's illegal operation in New York City. Although Ahkmerov had already been briefed about Martha, it does not appear he knew the nature of her assignment; he didn't need to. What he'd been told was that she'd been recruited by Boris Vinogradov, that it had been a 'romantic' recruitment and that she now fully expected she would be allowed to marry him. Moscow Center did this in order to continue managing Martha's expectations.

Over coffee they told each other about themselves, but mostly he let Martha talk about her time in Germany, her work there, about Boris and how she hoped that once they got married, they'd be able to work together wherever he got assigned, though Martha no doubt suggested the best place to start would be there in the United States. At some point Martha brought up her mission to get into Eleanor Roosevelt's inner circle. He likely feigned interest in the different ideas she had about achieving it. Ahkmerov went over a few basic rules she needed to observe to maintain her cover. He likely repeated Moscow Center's admonition to refrain from officially joining the Communist Party or establishing too-direct ties with anyone in it. Rubbing elbows with them at receptions and parties and political events was all right, but only up to a point. The FBI had its eyes out, as did the NYPD's 'red squad'. Her job was to be a liberal, not a radical; leftist, not communist.

Martha listened to it all politely, wondering why it all seemed so vague and roundabout. It was almost as if he was stalling, dragging out this inconsequential stuff that rightfully seemed to belong toward the end of the conversation. Martha knew from experience how preliminary conversations of this sort had a peculiar logic of their own. Still, her instincts told her he was stalling by letting her run the clock. Martha decided to force the issue and asked Ahkmerov if he was going to be her case officer.

It took him a moment to marshal his response. No, he told her. As a matter of fact, there wasn't one available just yet. The case officer who'd been slated to take her on had been called home for consultations on short notice and she'd have to wait until he got back before officially starting on her mission. But he reassured Martha it shouldn't be long; a couple weeks, at the most.

Martha came away from the meeting a little unsettled. What did he mean when he said it'd just be a couple weeks before her handler got back? Was it the truth, or was he just saying this? The weeks passed, and no word came of the case officer's return.

⁂

Martha's new circle of acquaintances included Earl Browder, head of the Communist Party USA. Shortly before leaving Berlin, she had contacted him and he'd written back telling her to get in touch once she was stateside. CPUSA loudly proclaimed itself an independent, American organization, and while it might have been true on some level, like communist parties everywhere, CPUSA had its 'secret apparatus' which ultimately took its orders from Moscow. Browder was himself an operative for Moscow Center,[1] as were many members of his family, including two sisters, a brother and a niece.[2] Knowing he was 'in the game', Martha asked Browder to see if he could find out anything on Boris' whereabouts. Browder duly passed it on to one of his contacts within the Soviet consulate in New York, who duly passed word of it back to Moscow. Once Moscow Center got word of Martha's inquiries, there was an immediate flurry of discussions. Unbeknownst to Martha, Boris Vinogradov was at that moment under arrest and facing trial as an 'Enemy of the State'.

Western researchers found a message inside a file within the KGB archives in Moscow from someone in New York codenamed 'Gennady' writing that 'Luiza' had gone 'to the Communists' with a request to learn the fate of Boris Vinogradov, 'her close, familiar friend'. Gennady adds: 'she is supposedly writing a book about her life and intends to mention him in it. She asks how Vinogradov had worked with her.' Below the message is a handwritten note suggesting 'a letter from B. Vinogradov should be taken to her',[3] followed by three additional notes. The first states: 'read 'Luiza' [Liza – Martha Dodd]'. The second states: 'Entrust contact with Luiza to a worker whose failure would not be very damaging to us; if Liza is not giving valuable materials – leave her alone.' The third: 'Also: Before contacting her, it is extremely important to determine a key fact about her previous work, namely: *was she a deliberate accomplice in work with Vinogradov, and if not, did Vinogradov use her without letting her in on the nature of the work.*'

Obviously, Moscow Center was starting to entertain doubts about Martha and what to do with her. Bukhartsev had ended up before a firing squad and now it looked like Boris might be facing one himself. Officially, Bukhartsev was guilty of transporting messages between Leon Trotsky and Karl Radek, but word on the street was he'd been flipped by the Gestapo. Martha's involvement with Diels, the former Gestapo chief, was no secret. Were they worried that she might have had something to do with both men's downfall? There was no way of knowing, but they still needed to come up with something.

The NKVD's interrogators were busily sweating Boris Vinogradov about his perceived criminal activities. He had probably, by this point, surmised that he was doomed and that nothing was going to save him from the same fate that befell Bukhartsev and so many others. Whatever he might have actually felt towards Martha, he was at least determined not to drag her down with him. Whatever he was guilty of, he told them, Martha Dodd had nothing to do with it. With that in hand, Moscow Center passed the word on to New York. New York duly wrote back, 'Upon receiving your message that Vinogradov denies "Liza's" participation in his criminal activities, we decided to make contact with her. Contact with her will be maintained by "Igor".' [4]

On 29 May 1938, Martha's mother, Mattie Johns Dodd, died suddenly and unexpectedly, less than six months after returning from Germany. Her health had never been good, and the four-and-a-half very stressful years she'd spent in Germany had hastened her decline. Even so, Mattie might have lived a little longer had it not been for the unending aggravation brought on by Bill Jr's continued involvement with the International Peace Campaign. She'd hoped when he returned to the US that he'd put his political activism aside and either find another teaching job or something else fitting for someone with his level of education. But instead he continued on with another anti-fascist group. They all had different names, but they always seemed to concern the same people. Mattie Johns had absolutely no love for the Nazis, even the nice, polite, affable ones that flocked toward Martha. But she wasn't too crazy about the communists either, especially not the people Bill Jr insisted were his friends. They were the ones imploring him to get his father to give speeches to different groups, when they knew full well her husband was too worn down from all he'd been through. He'd already done enough! But they wouldn't have it and Bill Jr always went along with them.

Shortly after her husband had received his orders to return home, Mattie wrote her son an angry letter, upbraiding him for his injudiciousness: 'I am sorry that you got him into "your affairs",' she wrote. 'You should not have taken advantage of the situation and of his naïveté. All this ... placed him in an almost impossible situation here and injured greatly his prestige as a diplomat. [The anti-fascist movement has] used your father's position to advance their ends, and he even has to help you, because they will not pay you enough to live on decently.'[5]

The final straw came when Bill Jr announced he was running for Congress. Virginia's 8th Congressional District, which was nearby, had a hardline old Democrat named Howard K. Smith representing it. Smith had been there forever and, as a rule, was against nearly everything Roosevelt's New Deal stood for. Somehow Bill Jr's left-wing friends had convinced him he could get all the 8th District's FDR supporters to vote for him instead of Smith. Mattie knew right away it was a harebrained scheme. She knew the reason Smith had retained his seat, election after election, was because 8th District voters were just like him: bigoted and arch-conservative. The fact that he'd been there so long was because he was connected to all the local power structures. He knew everyone and got things done for everyone who mattered. Why did anyone think Bill Jr stood a chance? But apparently someone did think he stood a chance. Suddenly he had $3,000 in campaign contributions! But from who? When Mattie pressed him, he admitted that one thousand came from Martha's new boyfriend. Another thousand came from Rabbi Stephen Wise – obviously it was his way of thanking Mattie's husband for all his help getting Jews out of Germany and standing up to Hitler. Mattie felt sick and disgusted that they had prevailed upon the rabbi to give them the money, obviously using her husband's good name. What about the remaining thousand dollars. Bill Jr smiled a little sheepishly and said that it was a secret. A secret? Some secret person or persons gave a thousand dollars for an election he couldn't possibly win. Who could be that foolish? She asked again, but Bill wouldn't say. It didn't make any sense and that made Mattie Johns worry even more. She died soon after that.

Martha came down for the funeral, remaining home for a while to look after her dad. Mattie had been the glue which held the family together all those years. It wasn't that she lacked for intellect. Mattie could hold her own with her children and husband, she just had no desire to share it with the world by writing or teaching. But now with her gone, it started coming apart. She might have quietly prevailed on Martha to rethink her new beau's suitability, just as she'd gotten Bill Jr to quit giving in to his friends' asking to get his father to give anti-fascist speeches. But now, with Mattie gone, his friends were once again free to prey on the old man to show support for 'The Cause'.

At one point while she was in Round Hill watching over her father, Martha took a day trip to Washington and paid a visit to the Soviet Embassy. She had a meeting with a counselor, where she asked if he knew anything about Boris' whereabouts and if, in his opinion, she should continue waiting for permission to come to marry him. The counselor admitted he had no idea what had happened to Boris, but said he doubted that they would get permission to marry.

When Martha returned to New York, she heard that someone from the illegal residency had been trying to contact her. Using the protocols she'd been taught back in Moscow, she set up another meeting. The man who met with her was someone she hadn't encountered before. The first thing she asked him was about Boris. Had he been arrested? The man acted like he was surprised by her question. He assured Martha that Boris Vinogradov hadn't been arrested; that he was fine and working in Moscow. Martha repeated what she'd told the embassy counselor in Washington: that she hadn't heard from Boris in over a year, that he'd promised to marry her once he'd obtained permission and that she'd been waiting all this time to find out what the answer was. She told him about Alfred Stern, how he wanted to marry her. Was there some way she could send a telegram to Boris and ask him, because if he told her to wait, she would. What should she do? Then she asked him about her case officer. When was she going to get one? What about her mission to infiltrate Eleanor Roosevelt's inner circle? She told him about Stern and how he was rich and had already done things for the Communist Party and that she didn't think marrying him would get in the way of performing her mission. It might even help. What did he think?[6]

The man shrugged and said he didn't know what to tell her about whether she should wait for Boris or marry Stern. As for her case officer, everything was on hold right now. It might be a while before another was available. But she should go ahead with whatever she was doing. They'd be in touch.

Martha walked away from the meeting wondering what was going on back in Moscow. The next day, Martha and Alfred eloped to Ellicott City, Maryland, where, late that night, a justice of the peace married them. Bill Jr came with them and acted as best man.

Not long after that, Martha received a letter from Boris.

Until now I have lived with the memory of our last get-together in Berlin. What a pity that is was only 2 nights long. I want to stretch this time to the rest of our lives. You were so nice and kind to me darling. I will never forget that ... How was the trip across the ocean? One time we will cross this ocean together and together we will watch the eternal waves and feel our eternal love. I love you I feel you and dream of you and us. Don't forget me. Yours, Boris.[7]

Soon after, Martha wrote back:

Boris, darling! Finally I got your letter. You work in the press office, don't you? Are you happy? Did you find a girl you can love instead of me? Did you hear that my mother died in late May totally unexpectedly? You can imagine how tragic it was for me. Surely, you know better than anybody else how we loved each other and how close we were in everything. The three of us spent time together perfectly, and I remember how sweet she was to both of us when you were in Berlin. Mother knew very well how deep our love was and understood all the meaning that you had and will have in my life. She knew that I loved nobody before and thought that I would never love again but hoped that I would be happy anyway. You haven't had time yet to know that I really got married. On June 16, I married an American whom I love very much. I wanted to tell you a lot, but I will wait until our meeting. We are supposed to be in the USSR in late August or early September this year. I hope you'll be there or will let me know where I can meet you. You know, honey, that for me, you meant more in my life than anybody else. You also know that, if I am needed, I will be ready to come when called. Let me know your plan if you get another post. I look into the future and see you in Russia again.

Your Martha.[8]

Boris never got to read Martha's letter. He was already dead. His letter to Martha had probably been written with a gun to the back of his head, and once he'd finished writing it he was executed as an Enemy of the People.

20. FROM 'BOY' TO 'PRESIDENT'

If there was ever such a thing as a 'typical' wealthy, left-leaning New York Jew, it wouldn't have been Alfred Stern. He was a Westerner, born and raised in Fargo, North Dakota, though by way of Harvard, Phillips-Exeter and wartime service in France. His family had owned a bank back in Fargo, but his own wealth came from marrying Marion Rosenwald, heiress to the Sears-Roebuck fortune. During the dozen-odd years they were married, they had two children and he managed investments for the family's charitable foundation. What led her to end the marriage and his job is not known, but she apparently paid quite generously to be rid of him. The divorce settlement became his investment 'grubstake' and Stern apparently did quite well with it.

As 'limousine liberals' went, Alfred Stern again defied the stereotype. He didn't just write checks, attend benefits and lend his name to funding appeals, Stern got involved. A few years earlier, he'd been heavily involved with the founding of the American Labor Party, a pro-FDR party of 'right-wing socialists' who supported progressive Republican Fiorello LaGuardia in his run for New York mayor against the more conservative Tammany Hall. At the suggestion of his close friend and ALP founder Vito Marcantonio, LaGuardia appointed Stern housing commissioner.

Alfred Stern was even a man of action sometimes. He travelled to Nazi Germany once, risking arrest and imprisonment, in order to secretly hand over funds to an anti-Nazi resistance group. On another occasion, he drove down into Mexico and then back

157

across the border with one Otto Katz, a member of the International Peace Movement who'd been denied an entry visa into the US. Even though Alfred Stern was not yet a member of the Communist Party, he was a comrade. Okay, so he was also there for the sex, but then wasn't everybody?

The problem with Alfred Stern was that he tended to think he was 'the smartest guy in the room', which wasn't quite true. As a result, he was seen by many as overbearing and arrogant, leading some to roll their eyes and refer to him as 'the genius'. Also, later it turned out that the International Peace Campaign was a communist front group and Otto Katz, the official he smuggled in, was actually a Comintern biggie and a Moscow Center operative to boot. Of course, Stern knew none of it when he did it, but it proved he was a comrade and friend of the World Communist Revolution, something which ultimately meant a lot more than his lack of a pleasing personality. It was also enough to convince Martha she could reveal her mission to Stern without worrying about him getting cold feet and blabbing it to the authorities. Not only was Alfred Stern not a fink, but once Martha told him she was a Soviet spy, he told her he wanted in as well.

This gave Martha the pretext she needed to get back in contact with the New York rezidentura. In her last meeting with them, when they informed her that getting a handler wasn't anywhere on the horizon yet, as a parting gesture of consolation she was told she could nevertheless continue providing them with valuable service as a talent spotter.

Martha had evidently concluded there was no point sitting around waiting for a case officer to be provided to her, because at the rate everything was going, it might just take forever. By now Martha might even have seen the writing on the wall and logically concluded that her mission to infiltrate Eleanor Roosevelt's inner circle had simply gotten lost in the shuffle and forgotten, what with all that was going on back in Moscow. Martha decided instead to take the initiative and create a situation they'd want to take advantage of. What would that be? What would be the best thing Martha could imagine? Simple. Being a diplomat again.

Martha longed to return to the diplomat's life. Her dream had been to marry Boris and become the glamorous American wife of a Russian diplomat, charming the world together, engaging in high-level affairs and teasing secrets from her lovers, the kind which made the world operate. Well, if she couldn't have that life with Boris, perhaps she could have it with Alfred. And maybe if she could get them a posting in Moscow, their power duo could become a trio; a diplomatic menage a trois! It was just a matter of getting Alfred appointed as Ambassador to the Union of Soviet Socialist Republics. How hard could that be? Only a few months earlier, FDR had given London – Ambassador to the Court of St James – to Joe Kennedy, that Boston Irish rum runner. Of course, Joe Kennedy was a major campaign contributor. His wealth was far beyond Alfred's and it was no secret he'd given the Democratic Party a lot of money. Well, her Alfred might not be Joseph P. Kennedy, but he wasn't a nobody either. He had lots of political friends in New York and back in Chicago. And besides, she was an ambassador's daughter, and that also accounted for something. So Martha told Alfred her idea. It appealed to him and they agreed to look into it.

❧

Martha had been put on the shelf. It wasn't surprising. With word out that Martha was not just difficult to work with but also likely to get you put in front of a firing squad, it made sense, especially once you understood just how risk-averse most Chekists were as a result of the purge. But even that didn't quite explain why instead they had put their money on Martha's brother, Bill Jr. It turned out that mysterious thousand-dollar campaign contribution he'd received came from Moscow Center. They had high hopes for him, so much so that they'd also changed his codename from 'Boy' to 'President'.

As anyone will tell you, electoral politics in America is a two-pronged exercise in marketing: marketing to voters and marketing to donors. What appeals to one is rarely what appeals to the other. Except for the handful of New Dealers living there, Bill Jr's candidacy had next to zero appeal with Democratic voters in the 8th Congressional District. Which is not to say Bill Jr didn't have appeal elsewhere. He was running against someone the New Dealers regarded as an active roadblock to their legislative agenda. Bill Dodd was offering himself as the weapon to dislodge him and they took it.

FDR had been aware of Bill Jr's political activities since returning to America. It was one of the reasons he'd asked Dodd to bring him along on his visit up to Hyde Park the previous autumn. Apparently he'd made some impression on the President, who now asked Harold Ickes, his interior Secretary and one of his closest advisors, to have a look at the campaign and perhaps give him some advice. Ickes did meet with Bill Jr and gave him encouragement and advice, though it doesn't appear he contributed any money to the campaign, having possibly concluded that Dodd's campaign was, like the Confederacy, a lost cause.

It was different with the Soviets. To begin with, of course, their grasp of American politics was poor. The fact that Bill Dodd was running on a 100 per cent New Deal platform against one of FDR's foes must have made him look like a shoo-in. Loathe as Moscow Center was to spend a thousand dollars in hard currency on anything, spending it on Bill would be worth it to them if it could enlarge their footprint on Capitol Hill. It would be money well spent, because in the long run it would save them a fortune.

Moscow Center already had a man on Capitol Hill, but they really didn't like him. His name was Samuel Dickstein, a Democratic congressman from New York. For the past year or so, Dickstein had been handing the Soviets mostly useless information and demanded they pay him a $1,200 a month 'retainer'. Having no real recourse, Moscow Center agreed, paid him, and gave him the codename 'Crook'. They hoped that with Bill on the Hill, they might gain some real access and influence without the endless squeeze. But none of it worked out. Bill Jr's campaign never made it past the 2 August primary. In the end, he was outvoted three to one by Smith's supporters. The Soviets were disappointed, but continued to believe he had possibilities and retained great faith in him.

Martha spent her days writing. The book was going well and she already knew there wouldn't be any trouble selling it. A lot of her writing she did in the apartment; other times she'd hole up with Sidney Kaufman or someone else. Evenings, she and Alfred often went out. They constantly rubbed shoulders with interesting and important people. When they did, there was some great repartee and Martha was never shy about talking up her book or telling them how great her husband was.

From some different people she talked to during all this, senior people with the Democratic Party, she was told ambassadorships were doable. How much would it matter where you were made ambassador to? To Moscow? Well, now, you know they just sent Laurence Steinhardt there to replace Davies, who just replaced Bullitt two years ago. Three, four months ago it might have been a different story. Just have to wait and see how the current one works out. Is there some other place you might consider? Bangkok? Asunción?

On 1 December 1938, someone at the New York illegal rezidentura sent a letter to Moscow Center about the changes in Martha Dodd's life since marrying Alfred Stern:

> Since becoming the wife of a millionaire, Liza has experienced significant changes in her lifestyle: she lives in a luxurious apartment on 57th Street in New York, has two servants, a chauffeur, and a personal secretary. She is very excited about her plan to travel to Moscow as the wife of the American ambassador. According to her, her husband is ready to give 50 thousand dollars to the Democratic Party fund if that post is promised to him. He hasn't heard anything concrete yet. He is currently seeking a means of getting to President Roosevelt through Wall Street. We already wrote to you that so far, his chances are very low.[1]

Moscow Center was at a loss when it came to Martha. They weren't sure what to do. The idea of having their people among the very top ranks of American capitalist society was so appealing to them. To infiltrate Eleanor Roosevelt's inner circle was the very stuff of dreams. She was confident she could do it and it sounded like she had done amazing things in Berlin. But at the same time, Martha was trouble, difficult to control. She also had a sense of entitlement and an unnerving habit of writing or going to the embassy or nearest consular office if she happened to feel she wasn't being treated right. Agents weren't supposed to do things like that. But no, Martha was the daughter of an ambassador and not someone to be trifled with.

Of her three previous case officers, two were already shot. Just because the last one wasn't, didn't mean there was a lucky streak going on yet. Whenever Igor met with her, he had to keep telling her he wasn't a case officer, that he was just a comrade assigned to carry messages and he couldn't tell her when her case officer would be coming. At one point he did let her know that Moscow Center had asked that she remove any mention of Boris Vinogradov from her book. Martha agreed, then asked if Igor knew anything about Boris' whereabouts. Igor didn't think he did. So far, so good.

Now suddenly Liza thinks she can get her husband an ambassadorship. It might take a while. Martha has another idea. How about visas so she and Alfred could visit Russia? She could do some reporting there. There are plenty of magazines she could sell stories to. It would be swell. Also one for her brother, Bill Jr. What do you say?

What should they say? What should they do? They had no idea, except now circumstances demanded they start seriously assessing Martha with all the information they had and make a full, measured judgement on whether or not to proceed with her.

In an undated memorandum to Moscow Center, Akhmerov reports and pleads:

> 'Liza' has sent embassy counselor Umansky a private letter in which she has requested assistance in obtaining a visa for the USSR to meet with Vinogradov. Umansky stated that she shouldn't go since Vinogradov is under arrest. We are trying to convince 'Liza' that her trip to the USSR is inadvisable from the standpoint of the interests of our work. She continues to stand her ground and to demand reasons that are persuasive to her. She and her husband should be denied permission to enter the USSR.[2]

Another Moscow Center memorandum about 'Liza' states that while 'she considers herself a Communist and ... recognises the party's program and statutes, in reality ... "Liza" is a typical representative of American Bohemia, a woman who has become sexually depraved, ready to sleep with any handsome man.'³

Again, they chose not to go ahead.

❧

It didn't particularly trouble Moscow Center that Bill Jr lost the election. To them, what mattered was he was willing to take on an ogre like the racist, fascist, capitalist Southern *judge* Howard K. Smith. It showed Bill had guts, grit and sneered in the face of the odds when they were that much against him. So he lost. But then he got up, ready for another go. That's what Chekists are all about! Try again, Comrade *President*! Get in any way you can and work your way up! Bill Dodd, they were convinced, was going to take them places.

Bill told them he wanted to run again when the seat opened up once more in 1940. Meanwhile, he needed to build up his own career in the New Deal. Moscow Center urged him to do that. Who could he talk to? His father had plenty of influential friends in the government. Could he go to one of them? Bill Jr guessed he could. How about President Roosevelt's close advisor, Ickes?

Bill Jr asked for a meeting with Ickes. One was arranged. He told Moscow Center, and in a memo someone remarked, 'The conversation with him will be a test to see how Roosevelt's people treat "President". If it doesn't work out, we will give him a directive to try to join the leadership of the Democratic Party.'⁴

It's doubtful Harold Ickes' opinion of William E. Dodd Jr mirrored that of Moscow Center. Having met with him, largely at President Roosevelt's behest, Ickes probably came away underwhelmed. No doubt the son of the former ambassador was a deeply committed and passionate young man, decent and well-meaning. He just wasn't a do-er. Ickes knew all about hard partying, but he also knew you had to do the roadwork. You had to get out there, bang on doors and talk to people. Bill Jr hadn't done that. Sure, he was just then getting over the death of his mother, but if he'd been a real politician, he would have done it anyway.

Winning political campaigns requires savviness and drive. Bill Jr had neither, and while there were some races which money could win, the Virginia 8th Congressional District race wasn't one of them.

Smith was too strong and Dodd was too ... ineffectual. Ickes would have liked to see someone giving Smith a run for his money. But Bill Dodd wasn't that man.

Now Bill was asking for a job in government. Ickes made a call and got him a job as an assistant in the personnel department of the Works Progress Administration. It was not the sort of job that would ever cause anyone to accuse him of nepotism.[5] Bill Jr took it, figuring it was as good a way into government as anything else.

~~~

Not long after starting at the WPA, Bill Jr made a fortuitous discovery. The *Blue Ridge Herald*, a local family-owned weekly newspaper in the 8th District, was being put up for sale. It occurred to him that perhaps the best way of serving the Revolution might be by molding public opinion. Being an assistant clerk in the WPA's Personnel Office did not really agree with Bill Jr. The work itself was tedious, and the pay not much better than the peace committee. The job would not take him anywhere, except very slowly. The beauty of community papers was that, for people living in the area, they'd be a key source for the news and opinion that mattered most to them. And as for political direction, well, that was something its owner got to determine. The *Herald* could be had for a mere $5,000. The more Bill thought about it, the more he saw the opportunity it represented. Early in March 1939, he pitched the idea to his case officer and they seemed warm to the idea. They in turn passed it on to Moscow Center with their recommendation: '"President" plans to start a small weekly newspaper in his state. It is possible that this newspaper will be published on behalf of the League of Democratic Youth, of which "President" is being nominated chairman in the State of Virginia. "President" does not have money of his own. The money will have to be raised. We think it is essential to give him 3–4 thousand dollars for the aforementioned purpose.'[6]

Moscow Center initially seemed to like the idea and earmarked $3,500 towards it. The rest Dodd would have to come up with himself. Could he? An inquiry was sent about Bill Jr's current situation. The rezidentura answered back. 'At present, he lives in his father's house in Virginia' and 'has no means of his own'. When they asked about how he planned to make it work, New York's answer was that, 'He is counting on enlisting the free services of prominent Washington journalists and of his sister.'[7] 'The direction of the newspaper will depend entirely on us. We will work out every detail of the newspaper's agenda with "President".'[8] Moscow Center started mulling it over. They ruminated on it throughout the summer and then came back with, 'It should not be too left-wing, and it should not be pro-Soviet – nor, it goes without saying, should it be anti-Soviet. A moderately liberal local newspaper with a direct connection to liberal Washington journalists and their participation in this little newspaper.'

Halfway into December, they decided against it. It was too much money. It was not the time. Also, a lot had changed in the months since. In March 1939, the world was merely teetering on the edge of war. Now they were in it. Just days before Hitler launched his invasion of Poland, Stalin astounded the world when he had Molotov, his foreign minister, sign a non-aggression pact with Ribbentrop, his Nazi counterpart. In the blink of an eye, the Soviet Union went from being Nazi Germany's only true opponent, to its one almost-ally.

And then the war started. Germany attacked Poland. Britain and France came in with Poland. Poland fought for a while. The Soviets came in with Germany and helped themselves to a nice chunk of Poland. And that seemed to settle that. A border was drawn. Both sides shook hands, pledged cooperation, discussion and even staging joint manoeuvres at one point. By December, the war was pretty much ground to a near-halt. They'd bomb, shoot at each other, mostly with light bombers, attacking this and that. At this point nobody could say what would happen next.

Within the anti-fascist world itself, Stalin's pact with Hitler succeeded in cutting a very deep line which, after this, would divide them.

People felt incredibly betrayed. They had become communist because communists were the only ones fighting fascism and capitalism and other ideologies that made the world so unnecessarily terrible. They didn't like Stalin one bit, he was the opposite of what they stood for, but still they pledged to him because he was the one leading the fight. And now Stalin has joined with Hitler. Did this mean the people were no longer anti-fascist? Comrade Stalin is our Great Leader! We do what he says and we like it. Don't think, obey.

⁂

The line cut deep among the American Left. In America, it came down to 'Which Side Are You On, Boys?' If you're a real communist, you suddenly cannot be against Hitler. No, you cannot, not if you're for Stalin. And a lot of Americans were. If you're a communist, you've already pledged to obey. So they did. But a lot of Americans wouldn't, and starting then, a lot of connections to Moscow began unravelling. The ones who did disconnect and those that didn't never saw each other quite the same way again.

For Martha, Alfred and Bill Jr, there was never a question of which side they were on. They were with Stalin. They'd picked their side. They weren't going to change. That wasn't who they were. Martha wondered what Boris thought about the world right now. With any luck they'd be together again soon.

⁂

That year, Alfred Stern made his own unsuccessful foray into congressional politics. The 'right-wing socialist' American Labor Party had him run for a New York congressional seat. ALP had been set up a few years earlier to elect progressive Republican Fiorello LaGuardia as mayor against Tammany Hall while continuing to support FDR and the New Deal. It was headed by Stern's close friend Vito Marcantonio. Stern took his defeat on the chin and moved on

⁂

Somewhere in the course of all this, the FBI opened files on Bill Jr and Alfred Stern. It was all strictly routine. They'd both run for political office and had demonstrated some kind of left-wing proclivity. That was enough. Now, anytime their names appeared in a newspaper or on a bulletin or in a mass appeal, it got clipped and noted and put into the file. And each time the file was put away until the next time. The files just sat there, usually for years, growing or not growing, with no one ever looking inside them.

⊶❈⊷

In 1939, Martha's book came out. *Behind Embassy Eyes* was an immediate bestseller. It seemed everyone in America wanted to hear what Martha had to say about Hitler and his inner circle of goons. Martha, of course, had plenty to tell about them, and from up close. Martha told of the parties and the receptions and outings rubbing shoulders with the top Nazis and of her one fleeting rendezvous with Hitler. War was coming. Then it came, but that only whetted the public's appetite for Martha's dishing. Once again, Martha was being written about and taken seriously. There were more interviews and her opinions were frequently given voice in the papers. Moreover, she was being taken seriously as a writer. Within a year of publishing *Behind Embassy Eyes, Ambassador Dodd's Diary 1933–1938* came out.

Diary is a purposely edited, not-altogether-completely-accurate collection of Dodd's writing from that period, placed into 'official diary' form. It was also a bestseller. While *Diary* is made up of his writing, Dodd himself had no real role in the book's edition. By then he was too weak and worn out to do any of it. Everything was done by Martha and her brother. As much as anything, Dodd's *Diary* cemented the importance of his place in the history of that period. There was interest from Hollywood for a film adaptation.

Martha and Alfred had become a popular couple within left-wing high society. Their friends were New York politicos, along with the known artists, writers and journalists of the day. Martha turned their Upper West Side apartment into a literary salon and it drew them all, the interesting and the important.

Not that it didn't come without a certain amount of ill-wishes. Martha was well aware how universally disliked she'd been by everyone at the embassy in Berlin. All of them, it seemed, had turned their noses up at her and her family. The scorn she'd had to pretend she didn't see. She learned to adopt a certain imperiousness in her manner that said to them, *I'm an ambassador's daughter and don't give a fuck what you or anyone thinks!* Still, Martha couldn't forget its sting.

167

Alongside her fame and elevation, Martha noticed some of the old Berlin snobbery and hurtfulness coming her way in the form of snide comments from people who acted like they had her number.

When once she bragged to famous author and publisher Bennett Cerf about the size of her book sales, he crisply responded that apparently all those men she'd slept with were buying her book. On another occasion she phoned Thomas Wolfe and invited him to come to a benefit she was holding. He hung up on her and then told the person with him, 'A benefit for sharecroppers? I hardly think so!'

Even so, Martha had it all. She wasn't just a hostess and political activist. Martha had standing. What Martha didn't have was a case officer. She should have one. She was halfway to Eleanor Roosevelt's inner circle. If not now, when?

21. DITHERING THROUGH
THE WAR YEARS

The SS *President Coolidge* was a luxury ocean liner operating in the Pacific since the early 1930s, normally sailing from San Francisco to Honolulu, to Kobe, then Shanghai, Manila and back to San Francisco via Honolulu. Though owned by the US President Lines, it had been under the control of the US Maritime Commission since that June. With relations worsening with Japan and the war now spreading across China, the runs to Kobe and Shanghai ended and the *President Coolidge* mainly ferried in troops and equipment to the Philippines and took out civilians and military dependents who'd been ordered to evacuate. During the autumn of 1941, it made three runs in and out of the Philippines. Its final voyage left Manila at the end of November. Among the passengers boarding it that day was Vassily Zarubin, his wife Elizabeta, and their young son Petr. Though once again on their way to America, this time they were not Edward, Sarah and Peter Herbert. They weren't even 'illegals', but official, accredited Soviet diplomats. Even so, the wise men of Moscow Center couldn't send them off without changing their names, albeit only marginally. They were not the Zarubins, but the *Zubilins*: Vassily, Elizabeta and Petr, Vassily Zubilin being the newly appointed Third Secretary at the embassy of the Union of Soviet Socialist Republics in Washington, DC.

They arrived in San Francisco on Christmas Day after spending nearly a month zig-zagging across the Pacific, following the ship's departure from Manila late in November. In that time much had happened in the world. A week after leaving Manila, the Japanese attacked Pearl Harbor, followed almost immediately by attacks on the Philippines, Hong Kong, Singapore, Malaya and the Dutch East Indies. Twelve Days later the ship put in at Honolulu, Hawaii. Entering Honolulu harbor, they got a good look at the devastation the Japanese aircraft had wrought on the American fleet, which had been anchored nearby. They could see the sunken battleships: some half-submerged, some overturned, superstructures smashed. They were there just long enough to take aboard 125 critically wounded sailors along with a group of nurses and Navy doctors. A week later they reached San Francisco, on Christmas Day 1941.[1]

Years later, when it was dawning on them what the Russians had managed to steal, and suddenly the FBI needed to find out who this long-gone Vasily Zubilin had been, they found people who'd been aboard the *President Coolidge* back at the time of Pearl Harbor to see if anyone could remember them, and it turned out quite a few did. They all remembered the Zubilins as a friendly, open, fun-loving couple. Both spoke excellent English and he even had an American accent, though he insisted he'd never previously been to America. Wallace Carroll, a veteran journalist also taking the long way home after covering the Russian Front for the Associated Press, recalled Zubilin telling him about being interviewed by Stalin who, he said, had treated him as if he were 'a small boy'.[2] They were knowledgeable and curious. They were expansive and asked everybody to tell them about America. They themselves talked about lots of things, but never politics. In the month they'd been aboard together, many grew to know the Zubilins quite well, even now considering them close, personal friends. Many expected their friendship to continue afterward, and admitted being puzzled when they never heard from them again.

※

Following the Japanese attack on Pearl Harbor, America was again caught up in a global war, and as a result, the lives of millions of Americans changed in ways few could have imagined. Millions of American men and women from all walks of life entered military service. Many went overseas, others to bases and installations far from their homes. Those who didn't go to war went to work in factories, shipyards and assembly plants, building tanks, jeeps, warships and combat aircraft, and always in massive numbers. They found themselves surrounded by strangers also in a similar situation. Teachers became soldiers. Housewives became welders, dishwashers became machine operators or secretaries or nurses. Everyone's lives changed. But not Martha's.

Martha probably could have had a 'brilliant war' if she'd wanted. Many she knew did. With her social-sexual connections and background, she could have situated herself into something interesting. Martha could have talked her way into the Office of Strategic Services without anything in her background bothering Bill Donovan or anyone in its leadership. Any of her many journalistic contacts would have vouched for her to receive press credentials to cover the war with any of dozens of newspapers. Martha could have found her way onto the staff of plenty of important men. But for some reason she didn't. For a while before Pearl Harbor she tried acquiring a visa to work as a journalist in Russia, covering the war. But when that wasn't forthcoming, Martha more or less dropped the whole thing.

She and Alfred spent the war doing exactly the same as what they'd been doing since 1938. They lived in their luxury Central Park West apartment. They had servants. They entertained, went to parties, dinners and other functions. He went to his office. She woke up late. She wrote sporadically and had her flings. They spent their weekends and summers at their big country house just on the Connecticut border. And they waited for the activation call to come from Moscow Center. But the months passed and the call never came. Not that Martha didn't have things to do. She'd put out two bestsellers in very short order. Now she was going to have to come up with something new. She thought about all the men she'd known in Berlin and wondered who she should use as the basis of a fictional story. Diels? Blomberg? There was no way you could make a tragic hero out of either of them. Hanfstaengl? Better not. She wanted her novel to be serious, not farcical. Besides, Putzi was in Washington, now, working for FDR. Louis Ferdinand? Please! Who, then?

Udet. She'd use Udet. Udet was perfect: heroic, dashing, loved life and everything that came along with it. He was probably the best aerobatic pilot in the world, certainly in the movies! How to write about him? Simple, just add tragedy, because that was what was bound to happen now with him. Udet could have stayed away. He had a good thing going in Hollywood, but he had to get on the gravy train. It was just too good, because they needed Udet more than Udet needed them, so they made it worthwhile. He'll have everything and then it'll all turn ... Martha began writing her novel about Udet. She would call it *Sowing the Wind*. Mostly, though, she waited for Moscow Center to activate her.

Martha's brother Bill wasn't around much at this point. He was living in Washington, DC, married and starting a family. Bill's personal life had been rocky since his return. His job in the WPA's personnel office led him to one at the War Production Board and he stayed there just long enough to be hired as an editorial assistant, researching and writing news at the Federal Communications Commission's Foreign Broadcast Information Service. Approaching a year in that job, he was now also broadcasting and his bosses informed him that he'd probably be sent to London by the end of the year. Moscow Center was happy 'President's' journey into the heart of the capitalist imperialist beast was now underway.

Martha made a point of keeping in touch with the rezidentura. Occasionally 'Chap' would meet with her. He was someone she didn't much care for. It wasn't that Chap wasn't intelligent, he was just lowly and having him assigned to her made her feel like she'd been 'downgraded'. After all, he wasn't actually an intelligence officer – she complained about it to the Russian Ambassador on at least one occasion, which then got passed back to Zarubin via Moscow Center cable. However, she did all she could to make a good impression on him. As they'd requested, she'd bring a list of people she'd recently encountered whom she thought might be good candidates for recruitment. Sometimes she'd ask why she hadn't been activated and the best he could do was shrug. Sometimes she'd give him messages to bring back.

During the first weeks following Pearl Harbor, Martha endeavored to make herself indispensable to them by suggesting useful people for Moscow Center to contact:

Louis Aragon in France is of course too well known for me to add anything further. I do know that Lion Feuchtwanger (living on North Amalphi Drive, Los Angeles) is a very reliable and able worker and writer. Having lived in France for many years after his exile from Germany, he must have at his fingertips many, many French names useful for us. I am sure he would not hesitate to cooperate fully if he knew the source asking for it. In England I unhesitatingly recommend Jurgen Kuczynski, who can be reached through the London School of Economics. He is a brilliant scholar, a Jew, and economist of deep Marxist conviction, who was exiled (or left I am not sure) from Germany around 1936. I know him to be perfectly reliable from the Harnacks and from my own observation and experience with him. He worked for the Freedom station at one time and as far as I know has never deviated an inch on any matter whatsoever. At the outbreak of the war the English sent him to an internment camp. Through my pressure and others, Lord Lothian exerted himself to free Kuczynski and succeeded. He has not since been in any trouble with the British authorities and is working quietly in London on a seven volume history of labor. He knows not only Germany but the continent and England and would be more valuable and trustworthy for us than anyone I know besides the Harnacks in Berlin. He is tall, slender, dark, ugly, very brilliant and very stable politically. (35 years approximately).[3]

Coming ashore at San Francisco on Christmas Day, the Zubilins spent two days there before taking a train to Los Angeles to attend a gala event honoring the Soviet Union. Then they travelled back to San Francisco and from there took the train east, disembarking in Washington, DC, probably just after New Year's. Two days later, they took a train to New York City. While they were in San Francisco, it's likely they met with Gregory Kheifits, who ran his podrezidentura out of the Soviet consulate, which was also where the local GRU man had his office. The Zarubins already knew Kheifits, having worked with him in France. Kheifits had an excellent operation, with a network of operatives with their ears to the ground, watching the ports and waterfront all the way up and down the coast. There were also numerous maritime courier networks anchored in San Francisco which reached all over the Pacific. What Kheifits ran had largely been created by Comintern, back in the days when it had been more or less an independent entity serving the World Communist Revolution, and not simply Stalin. Either way, it was an impressive set-up. Its likely Zarubin told him about having his people keep their eyes out for anything about any exotic weapons being developed using uranium.

In Los Angeles, they met with his podrezident Vsevolod Vladimirovich Pastiyev, who, like Kheifits, was the Vice Consul and ran his operation from the consulate. The gala they attended was a big do at someone's place in Beverly Hills. It was probably the last party before New Year's Eve. America was at war and everyone was there, eager to proclaim their support for America's new, gallant ally, the Union of Soviet Socialist Republics. Outside was a procession of fancy cars and shiny limousines with rich, important people stepping out of them, attended to by valets. Inside was an onslaught. They were surrounded by swarms of elegantly dressed men and stunning women, precisely dressed waiters with trays hovering. Zarubin was introduced to the Russian contingent, mostly representatives of the embassy in Washington; two Soviet film industry executives, Antonov and Kalatsov; and a famous sound expert named Irsky; along with other dignitaries.[4]

And then he saw him, talking to some men, explaining something, using his hands like a puppeteer, their attention rapt. Boris Morros. And that brought it all right back to Zarubin. A golden afternoon walking through Central Park and the whole walk, Boris Morros in that same voice, explaining it all to him: 'Bubbie, how easy it is to completely blow smoke up people's asses, all the time, that those people in Berlin are not nearly as smart as they think they are. Listen, you and I both know you have the balls, right? Okay, then ... Again, bubbie, it's simple: Find out what they want to see and what they want to hear and then give it to them. That's not where you have to be sophisticated. That's a story for later unless you want to hear it now...'

Boris Morros and the man he was with laughed about something and Zubilin stepped forward, smiling. Boris Morros smiled back, but it was obvious he didn't recognise him. 'I want to thank you for saving my life,' said Zarubin, still smiling. Boris Morros looked at him again for a very long moment; his brain worked very hard and then he realised he knew who it was standing before him. Edward Herbert, that Russian secret police guy he'd written that letter for back in New York. Saved his life? Boris Morros remembered talking to him, but couldn't remember ever saving his life. Never mind Edward Herbert, he was now Zubilin, Third Secretary at the Soviet Embassy in Washington, and then he suggested they find somewhere to talk.

Zarubin was glad to see Morros there in his element. In Zubin's mind, Morros' glorified pep-talk had saved his life. Those hours they'd spent together talking were golden for Zarubin. Until then, he'd worried Berlin wouldn't be like all the other places he'd been sent; that his luck wouldn't hold against the Nazis. But Morros knew that they were still two of a kind, despite their different professions. He told him, and this had given him the confidence to face them. If Morros told him Berlin would be a snap, that Nazis were nothing special, then he was right. That's what would happen. And that's how it did happen. Berlin had been a snap, more or less. And he owed it all to Boris Morros.

But Morros hadn't gone the distance. He did what he did for Edward Herbert and when it was over he just walked away. He hadn't done what he had agreed to do. If things had gone bad at some point, not having a demonstrable stream of payments from Paramount Pictures might have gotten him a beating and a bullet in the back of the head. So he started out by chiding Boris Morros and letting him know just how badly he'd failed to perform his task. Luckily, of course, none of that happened. But Morros should have gone the distance. He should have written the letters. He should have sent money. It hadn't been too much to ask. If he'd fulfilled the little bit more that he'd pledged, then he'd be a fellow-countryman. Zarubin was now here to give Morros the opportunity to redeem himself. Was comrade Morros ready? Boris Morros nodded and said he was. Good. Zarubin would soon have some tasks for him to perform. When they come to him, he must see to it that they're done. Does Boris Morros understand? Boris Morros did understand. Good. Afterwards, he might have some business opportunities which he might be interested in.

Another thing, Boris. Starting now, you need to stay far away from anything Soviet. All these local Russians and Hollywood communists, you need to not have anything to do with them. It's not a suggestion, Boris. I'll see you again in a couple months.

❧

It would be a fair guess that Zarubin hit the ground running when he took over the rezidentura. A lot had to be done, and quickly. Pavel Klarin, who'd been running it, handed over the keys and then slipstreamed behind Zarubin as his deputy. The rezidentura was the biggest one he'd ever been in, with eighteen intelligence officers – most were in New York. But there were also podrezidentury in San Francisco, Los Angeles, Washington, DC, Mexico City and Ottawa. Zarubin's sub-deputies included operations officer 'Leonid' (Aleksei Prokorov), officially a diplomatic courier, and 'Twin' (Senyon Semyonov), an engineer with AMTORG, attending MIT and in charge of the 'XY' unit, which focused on acquiring science and technology secrets. Also running the XY line was Alexander Feklisov, 'Kallistratus', an operations and communications officer alongside another officer, Anatoly Yokovlev. Helping them was 'Sergei' Vladimir Pravdin, another operations man, officially a TASS correspondent. Within the New York City rezidentura there was another, separate XY line run by Leonid Kvasnikov, a civilian engineer with some background in atomic energy.

Coming in were several people he'd asked for. Ahkmerov returned, bringing back his girlfriend, Helen Lowry, now his wife and an officer herself. They were tasked with, among other things, finding the Ukrainian-born Soviet intelligence officer and US passport wizard Yakov Golos, patching everything up with him, figuring out what exactly he had in terms of networks, and then getting him to hand over some of them. Ahkmerov and his wife would set up their own station in Baltimore, furrier business as cover, and within easy distance of Washington for picking up material from all the rings operating out of there and getting it up to New York. For Ottawa, he picked Vitaly Pavlov, the young man who'd been his supervisor during his recent 'punishment' stint back in Moscow. Apparently he'd impressed Zarubin enough to give him a job.

Another person Zarubin asked for and got was 'Kitty Harris', one of Comintern's veteran couriers. Born in London to Russian-Jewish parents in 1899, she grew up in Canada, and by the time she moved to Chicago in 1923, she was already an established organiser and operative for both the Garment Workers Union and the Communist Party. In 1925, she married Earl Browder, an American and a senior Comintern official. But their work took all their attention and after a while they decided to divorce. She went into the Comintern, travelled to Shanghai and for much of the late 1920s crisscrossed Asia and the Pacific as a courier for the Pan-Pacific Trade Union's secretariat, a communist front group. In 1929, she was in New York working with AMTORG. There, she was recruited by Abram Einhorn, the 'illegal' rezident for Berlin. She arrived in Berlin in 1932 and worked for Einhorn until he was replaced by Fyodor Karin, who, after less than a year, was replaced by Boris Bazarov. She was in Berlin when Zarubin took over from Bazarov after he was sent to New York. In the time Zarubin ran Berlin, she impressed him enough that he asked for her to be assigned to him again for New York. She'd be focusing on Mexico. Then there were the probationers. Most were fresh from training. Most couldn't speak English very well; some not at all. The ones Zarubin could use, he used. The ones he couldn't were sent back to Moscow after a couple of months and replaced with fresh ones. Zarubin was travelling constantly, visiting different stations, meeting with people, talking to them, listening to what they had to say, chiding them, praising them, browbeating them to do what they were told.

Alexander Feklisov remembered Zarubin during that time as 'reckless', and that 'he liked men of similar character'. He 'loved bold behavior on the part of a young operations man, facing unforeseen circumstances'. His men, Feklisov noticed, seemed to be mostly French and Austrian. 'Under his supervision our rezidentura became one of the most productive of the entire NKVD.'

Meanwhile, Elizabeta, codenamed 'Vardo', worked her own side of the street, looking for recruits in science while keeping an eye out for Trotskyites. She travelled as work demanded. Unlike Berlin or Paris, they really didn't need to have much as cover. They were diplomats. Legal. *Yes, I'm officially assigned to Washington, DC, but I have been temporarily assigned to the New York Consulate. So much work!*

⁂

Then there was Jack Soble, whom Zarubin discovered more or less hiding in plain view in a town outside Montreal, Quebec. Fifteen years or so earlier, Abromas Sobelevicus had been among Moscow Center's more energetic fieldmen. Along with his brother Robert, he spent several years infiltrating the Trotskyite underground, worming his way into Leon Trotsky's inner circle in Istanbul. For a while it worked, but then it went bad and he returned to Moscow. He puttered around as a journalist for a few years, but even though he wasn't yet 40, he was already mostly used up. It was 1940 and he knew everything was going to get worse. He wanted a way out. His family back in Vilkaviskis, Lithuania, had been in the pig bristle business and Abromas knew the trade and that he could do it anywhere. Wherever there were pigs, there were bristles, and the trade in them was global. Sobelevicus was able to get exit visas not just for himself, his wife and child, but also his father, brother and a large chunk of his extended family. They were all allowed to leave because Moscow Center knew that no one in the bristle business was ever far from their reach. He and his group travelled across Russia to Kobe, Japan, where they stayed for several months before sailing on to San Francisco. From there, they took trains to Canada. Somewhere in the process, Abromas Sobelevicus became Jack Soble and he and his extended family started life over in a hidden corner of Quebec, hoping he might stay forgotten.

By early 1942, Jack Soble had a meager but satisfactory existence in Granby, Quebec. Looking back on it later, he wondered if he hadn't dipped his toe back into the trade and bought and sold a particular lot of Canadian pig bristles which had happened to come his way, perhaps he wouldn't have been discovered. But he did and they found him. It was only a little while after making the deal that a letter came to him from someone at AMTORG named Fomin proposing the sale of bristles. Soble wrote back and a meeting was set up with someone who turned out to be Zarubin, though during the nearly two years they would be together, the only name he ever knew him by was 'Vasily Mikhailovich'.

Vasily Mikhailovich started by asking him about the other members of his family who had emigrated with him. It was a subject Soble preferred to avoid, because during the time since landing in Granby, the clan were largely split on how they felt about the Soviets. Half were still favorable, out of gratitude for being let out. The other half resolutely hated Stalin and every Bolshevik who'd ever been born, excepting of course Abromas and Robert. Then Vasily Mikhailovich talked to Soble about the war, how neatly he and his family had managed to entirely escape it. He wanted to know whose side Jack Soble was on, the Axis or the Allies? Soble tried to say something, but Zarubin cut him short. You are at my mercy, he told Soble. Jack could come willingly or he would come unwillingly, but either way he was his. Soble, his wife and son were to relocate to New York City and take over a business – a small 'greasy spoon' in Manhattan they were using as a cover. Soble said he had no means to pay for such a move. Vasily Mikhailovich smiled and told him he did. There was an account with $14,000 at the Imperial Bank of Canada that had Soble's name on it. Soble answered that, yes, it was something his father had set up for him, but having his name on it didn't mean he could get his hands on it. At this, Zarubin evidently suggested to Soble not to worry. He'd take care of it.

So Soble, Myra and their son moved to New York City, along with his brother Robert. After moving into an apartment at 630 W 170th in Manhattan, they were taken to the S&W cafeteria, a run-down eatery on 38th and 5th Ave. Arrangements were made, after which Zarubin and Misha, his assistant Mikhail Chalaipin, drove a car up to Montreal, and, by means never revealed, successfully withdrew $4,000 from Soble's inaccessible account at the Imperial Bank of Canada, which they then took back with them to New York City. There they handed over the money to Soble, which he then used to buy the S&W Cafeteria from its previous owners.

Under its new ownership, the S&W was a decent cover operation because customers came and went. Things got dropped off and picked up. Nobody noticed anything, which was really all Moscow

Center cared about. Jack and Myra had to work long hours for not very much money, though they did get a monthly $150 salary on top of it from Moscow Center. But even that wasn't much. And it was also a lot of hours, especially since Zarubin started having Jack accompany him on some of his outings.

Over the course of nearly two years, Jack Soble met and had dealings with many, many different people whom Zarubin said were part of what they did, though whatever they did do was often not explained. There was Ilya Wolston, a Russian translator in the US Army, and Ester Rand, a very nice young lady who worked for different Jewish organisations. There was Prokhorov, who, along with Mikhail Chaliapin, was also a Zarubin assistant. Then there was Mark Zborowsky, some sort of scientist whose job was infiltrating different Trotskyite and Menshevik groups. Then there were all these others: Sylvia Callen Doxsee, a nervous, depressive young woman who brought in useful material; Zalmon David Franklin, who'd fought in Spain; and Stepan Choudenko, whom they called 'the Professor' because of the long coat he always wore. All in all, there were two or three dozen people and exactly what they did usually wasn't clear, since Zarubin never told him much.

As for Martha, Alfred and Bill Jr, apparently they were somewhere at the bottom of Zarubin's list; on the books, but that was about as far as it went. He'd see them mentioned in messages, and though he'd always intended to do something with them, he was so busy, he never got around to it. They remained on Zarubin's 'to-do' list all through 1942 and well into 1943. The messages kept coming in from Moscow, along with all the other suggestions, always nudging the rezidentura to find something to do with them:

For the past two years we have made unsuccessful attempts to use 'President' [Bill]. In various areas of work. Currently the paramount task for further use of these probationers is the need to break them up and use each one separately, which poses significant difficulties and requires a good deal of education work on your part. Even though 'President' has communicated with us for a long time, he remains a rough-edged probationer and requires a good deal of work both to teach him agent skills and to instill brutal discipline and the rules of covert work in him. The aim is to turn him into a journalist-commentator. To direct his appearances in the press and on the radio so as to earn him a more solid position and reputation. In order to detach him from 'Liza,' arrange a trip somewhere abroad (except for Home). Mideast, Turkey, China …

'Liza.' An able, intelligent and educated woman …, requires constant supervision of her behavior. It is essential to give her firm guidance, get her interested in our work and direct her energy toward benefiting our cause. Her use should proceed primarily on the line of getting leads … Let 'Liza' revolve in circles that interest us rather than circles that are close to the Trust, make new acquaintances, look for people of interest to us, etc. She must not only refrain from recruiting her husband for our work and letting him know about it, but must also not recruit him into the party, which, judging by your last letter, Liza she is stubbornly trying to do … Instructions should be given to 'Liza' about her husband – let her direct him toward obtaining a position of interest to us, an appointment to some diplomatic job, getting into a government. institution, etc.[5]

Zarubin stared at the messages: *requires constant supervision of her behavior … essential to give her firm guidance*; just thinking about what that was necessarily going to entail seemed to sap him of his energy. It all seemed like so much work, and as it was, he and his people were going full steam, day in, day out … *get her interested in our work and direct her energy toward benefiting our cause* … Why were these people so damn important that Zarubin was supposed to shepherd her into spy work?

Then there were her letters to Moscow Center informing them that Alfred was now attending a Marxist study group. *Marxist study group?* He stared at the words for a few seconds and wondered why anybody thought he needed to know this.

'I approached my husband Wednesday night about our work … He repeated several times that he must feel that he was doing something constructive and useful and that he was not yet sure he could function in illegal condition …'[6]

Then there were the letters about her from the embassy in Washington:

> She must also be oriented toward getting close and getting introduced to the president's wife, Eleanor, on the line of various public organizations, committees, societies, etc. Here we should make use of the special interest that the Roosevelts show in China and everything related to it. 'Liza' can play on this factor. Let her think over for herself the question of approaching Eleanor on the line of a committee to aid China or another similar committee and let her suggest herself a plan of action to achieve the objective that has been set ...
>
> President. and Liza should for now only be connected to the legal station
>
> ... 'Liza' was unhappy over the fact that the person who was connected to her ('Chap') was, first of all, not a Soviet operative, and second, not adequately developed politically and unqualified in her tasks and topics. 'Liza' was offended by the fact that we downgraded her work with us to such a level.

Zarubin stared at the messages and memos and wondered who this woman was that she was so important. What made her so entitled? And what was it about her that made Moscow Center so adamant a use be found for her? Zarubin promised himself he'd get to it, then let his attention focus on more pressing business. He didn't think about it again for several weeks, and then just fleetingly.

Martha Dodd relaxing at the beach, taken around 1930. (Library of Congress)

Above left: William Dodd, US Ambassador to Germany, 10 June 1933. (International News)

Above right: Young Martha Dodd. (Unknown)

Above left: The Dodds boarding the ship to Berlin. (Left to right) Martha Eccles Dodd, William Edward Dodd Jr. (Bill), William Edward Dodd Sr., and Martha 'Mattie' Ida Johns Dodd. (Unknown)

Above right: George E. Messersmith, US Ambassador to Austria, 19 September 1938. (United States Holocaust Memorial Museum, courtesy of National Archives and Records Administration, College Park)

(Left to right) Mattie Dodd, William Dodd and Martha Dodd, date unknown. (Sueddeutsche Zeitung Photo / Alamy Stock Photo)

Rudolf Diels, 1933.
(Bundesarchiv, Bild 183-K0108-0501-003 / CC-BY-SA 3.0)

Ernst 'Putzi' Hanfstaengl, foreign press chief, 1934.
(Bundesarchiv, Bild 183-R41953 / CC-BY-SA 3.0)

Above: Martha Dodd and Gestapo chief Rudolf Diels drinking wine at outdoor café, taken between 1933 and 1934. (Library of Congress)

Left: Ernst Udet, 1940. (Bundesarchiv, Bild 146-1984-112-13 / Conrad / CC-BY-SA 3.0)

Above: William Dodd Jnr. (Bill), 1941.
(International News)

Right: Mildred von Harnack, date
unknown. (Unknown)

Above left: Martha Dodd and Arthur K. Stern, late 1930s. (Library of Congress)

Above right: Boris Morros, 1937. (International Motion Picture Almanac 1937–38)

Vasily and Elizabeta Zarubin, date unknown. (Private album / Alamy Stock Photo)

Above left: Jack Soble, 1957. (Associated Press)

Above right: Myra Soble, with her son Lawrence, 1950. (Associated Press)

Lavrentiy Beria, head of the People's Commissariat for Internal Affairs (NKVD) of the Soviet Union from 1938 to 1946. Date unknown. (Unknown)

TOP SECRET PUBLIC SERVICE FEATURE!

THE SPY QUEEN WAS A NYMPHO!

1958 article in *Top Secret Magazine* by John Lewis Carver: 'The Spy Queen was a Nympho'.

Revealed for the first time—the biggest secret in the torrid life of Martha Dodd, the Reds' Mata Hari in the U.S.

By JOHN LEWIS CARVER

IN THE FALL of 1950, a short, clean-shaven, ebullient man had dinner behind closed doors in a Moscow office and while he was munching the excellent meal suddenly realized that this could very well become his last supper. In the midst of pleasantries he abruptly felt the cold gust of death breathing down his spine.

TOP SECRET magazine, in this special exclusive report, can reveal the details of that Moscow party and expose behind it the most extraordinary spy

drama ever staged. In the center of the story stands a fantastic femme fatale whose role in America closely resembles that of Benedict Arnold.

It is a story as spine-chilling for all of us as was the sudden change of a friendly dinner's climate for that man in Moscow.

He was Boris Mihailovich Morros, pudgy Hollywood composer of hits like "The March of the Wooden Soldiers" and the producer of smash movies like "The Tales of Manhattan" and "Carnegie Hall."

His host was a faceless Soviet general named Petro Vasilievich Fedotov, one

of the top ranking officials of the espionage department of the Soviet secret police.

Fedotov dined and wined Morros on receiving the composer into the inner sanctum of the Soviet secret service, because Morros was, behind his Hollywood mask, a secret agent of the Soviet Union. He joined the fold in 1945 and was the boss of a Soviet spy ring operating in the U.S. under a Russian spymaster named "Edward Herbert." This "Herbert" was none other than Vassili M. Zubilin, a lieutenant colonel in the Soviet secret service, masquerading in Washington as a secretary of the Soviet

Mr and Mrs Stern with their son Bobby at a press conference in Prague, refuting allegations made against them in America, 9 September 1957. (Keystone Press / Alamy Stock Photo)

22. ENTER JANE FOSTER

While Moscow Center never quite got around to deciding if they wanted Martha infiltrating Eleanor Roosevelt's inner circle, they did invite her to act as their talent spotter. It was something she was well suited for. Martha got around and knew lots of interesting and important people. She saw it as being about her only means of proving herself and staying in their sight. Often, when she'd meet with 'Chap' or someone else from the rezidentura, she'd present a list of people along with an explanation as to why she thought they would be good candidates as agents for the NKVD. They'd take the list, thank her, give it a look and that would be that. But truth be told, they mostly never did anything with the lists, and of all those she recommended, it appears only one was ever acted upon and brought into service.

Martha met Jane Foster during the summer of 1941 outside Carnegie Hall, in line to hear Sister Rosetta Tharpe. Jane's date, the writer Dexter Masters, spotted Martha getting in line and invited her to join them. Martha and Jane were introduced and the two quickly became close friends.[1] They had much in common. Like Martha, Jane had that flair for being a communist and a socialite without cheapening either. Her family were old-line San Franciscan and wealthy. She'd attended Mills College, a private woman's school in Oakland, and had then gone on to study painting in Italy. In the course of it she'd married a Dutch diplomat and settled with him in what was then the Netherlands East Indies. Disgusted at the brutality of Dutch colonial rule, she became a communist, which led to her divorce. Forced to remain there while the divorce processed, she spent her remaining time travelling extensively in the region, learning languages and the local culture. With the outbreak of the war, she returned to the United States. In New York, Jane held a succession of low-paying clerical jobs, plainly going nowhere in the process. Finding herself also at the bottom of the local Communist Party hierarchy, Jane often got 'picket line duty' and had to sell copies of *The Daily Worker* on the street, which she'd often do wearing a fur coat.

Jane Foster started coming to the parties which Martha and Alfred frequently hosted. At one party Martha introduced her to Earl Browder, who recognised her potential for secret work, and quickly urged her to 'muzzle' her 'public communism'. At around that time Martha pitched Jane to 'Chap', who passed her name up the line until it reached Zarubin, who instructed one of his people to meet with her and gauge her willingness to be recruited. A meeting was called; Jane was interested. They liked what they saw and the process began moving forward. But then, in the summer of 1942, Jane Foster moved to Washington, DC to take a research job at the Indonesian Section of the new Bureau of Economic Warfare. Soon Martha and Bill received a message, through 'Chap', to keep in touch with Jane when she was in Washington. Bill got her a room at the apartment of a married couple he knew – an old girlfriend and her husband, both of whom happened also to be of their fellow-countrymen network. Not long after moving to Washington, Jane was recruited by the new intelligence service, the Office of Strategic Services (the OSS), based on her expertise in Indonesian affairs. When she went into OSS training and then overseas, she effectively fell out of communication with her NKVD recruiters until after the war. But several months earlier, while she weighed up whether or not to join the OSS, a cable was being sent to Moscow Center from New York, informing them that the prospective candidate, Jane Foster, codenamed 'Slang', was now on their books.

What no one knew was that Soviet diplomatic cable traffic was being intercepted by the US Army's Signal Intelligence Service. Since it was encrypted, they had no idea what the message meant. It was one of many they kept and set their codebreakers to work to find out what the messages were saying. It would be years before they had even a partial decrypt, but when they did, things would begin to close in on Jane Foster and everyone associated with her, including Martha.

⸙

The likely reason Vasily Zarubin/Zubilin happened to run into Boris Morros in Los Angeles one evening in April 1942 was that he'd been making his circuit of the US and Canadian podrezidentury, dropping in on them, seeing how everything was going, praising and upbraiding them where warranted and making sure everything was getting ramped up for when the war really got going. Zubilin happened to be in Los Angeles that day. There just happened to be another gala evening do somewhere in Beverly Hills, also celebrating US–Soviet friendship, and likely being the ranking Soviet diplomat in California, he was automatically invited, so he went. Once again, Hollywood's sun-kissed communist contingent was present, along with a smattering of Los Angeles' more work-a-daddy Party members. The Vice-Consul was there, of course, along with his crew and whatever other Soviets happened to be around, some in Red Army uniform, all being lauded as the heroes of the hour. Also there, once again, happily hobnobbing with everyone, was Boris Morros.

With not quite as big a smile on his face as before, Zubilin approached and greeted him. Didn't he ask him to keep away from the communists? *Why is it so difficult to do as you're told?* Boris Morros, never at a loss, probably shrugged and said something clever. Then he promised Zubilin no more commies, from now on. And suddenly, almost before Zubilin knew it, the matter was settled and that was that! Zubilin repeated what he'd said before. He had important plans for Boris. Boris really did not need to be associated with Russians and communists. Boris agreed. But then, just before they parted ways, Boris confessed that he had heard from his family back in Omsk and was worried about them. If there was just some way ... Zubilin said he'd look into it.[2]

A month later, Boris Morros travelled to Washington, DC to visit with his son who was attending boarding school outside Annapolis. Knowing Zubilin was with the Soviet Embassy, he decided to drop by and see if he might be up for drinks or dinner.

But when he got to the embassy, they initially acted like they'd never heard of him, but then after he talked to them a bit, they relented and gave him a number to call. Boris Morros left, found a payphone and called the number. Zubilin answered, surprised to be hearing Morros on the other end. He asked how he'd gotten the number. When Morros told him, he could sense Zubilin's agitation. He gave Morros an address. Morros hailed a taxi. He was driven to a row house in the 'poor part of town'. Zubilin was there with a woman and child whom he introduced as his family. Looking around and seeing how mostly empty the place was, he surmised it was a safe house.

Zubilin's agitation had apparently subsided by the time Morros arrived. They all went out for dinner at a place Zubilin recommended. He started to relax. The conversation was genial and both Zubilin and his wife were enjoying themselves. At one point he asked Morros if he'd like to have his father brought in from Russia again. Morros asked if Zubilin could indeed do this and Zubilin told him that he could. But, he warned, it would require reciprocation from Morros. Was he interested? Morros said he was. Zubilin wouldn't say what the 'reciprocation' might entail, but began going over a protocol Morros was to follow next time he came east for business or a visit. Morros should first send a 'love letter' to a 'Leah Melament', one of Zubilin's people in New York who would be his 'girlfriend'. He should tell when he'd be coming to town and when and where they should meet. Also, when closing, he should sign the letter with a double clef. Morros would wonder what he'd just gotten himself into.

❧

On 24 June 1942, Moscow Center wrote Zarubin concerning his running of the rezidentura. 'The main deficiency in your work with probationers continues to be a lack of purposefulness,' they wrote. 'Apparently you are not pointing them toward coverage of the issues that are of primary interest to us, and you are not giving them specific assignments. Left to their own devices, the probationers often provide either outdated or completely worthless materials.'[3] After that, they listed the questions which they thought Zarubin's American agents should start finding answers to, like whether the US government had begun implementing its latest agreement it made with the Soviets.

> What groupings have formed within the government in response to this agreement? Is there opposition and who represents it ... Who is conducting practical preparations, and how, for opening a second front in Europe, when and in what location is it expected? ... How is the implementation of the law authorizing the shipment of munitions on loan or for lease proceeding? Which of the individuals who are directly handling the implementation of this law are trying to impede its implementation? ... What issues did Churchill discuss with Roosevelt? What are the disagreements between the British and the Americans regarding the main issues of the conduct of the war? ... What is the view of your country's leading circles regarding the postwar structure of Europe and, in particular, regarding our country's borders? What judgments are being expressed with regard to restoring the independence of the small countries currently occupied by the Germans, especially the countries that have borders with us? ... How are the subversive activities of the fifth column in your country (isolationists and others) manifesting themselves?[4]

Then the subject turned to Martha Dodd. They also weren't happy with the material she was sending them.

> 'Liza's' reports in the form that you sent them to us are of no practical value. We cannot make use of her connections in Europe – or rather, her acquaintance with the individuals with whom she was in contact while in Germany – because she hasn't known for 5–6 years already where these individuals are and what positions they hold. Judging by her own information, these acquaintances were superficial, and it is indicative that she devotes more attention to describing their appearance ('a blond man,' 'pretty eyes' and so forth) than to information about how these people could be useful to us in our work.

One has to wonder if, reading it, Vasily Zarubin rolled his eyes heavenward and told himself that this is what happens when you ask a book writer to write some simple reports: a shortage of facts and a wealth of description ... 'pretty eyes!' For the moment, at least, Zarubin was done with her.

⚜

A month or so after he returned to Los Angeles, Boris Morros started getting phone calls from Zubilin, which he ignored. But when he took a trip to New York in September, he followed the 'love letter' protocol and wrote to Leah Melament telling her when he'd be in town and the hotel he'd be staying in. When he and Zubilin met up, Zubilin requested a couple of favors. They needed someone to provide cover for two Soviet illegals, 'West' and 'Evgeny', currently in Switzerland. One of them had film industry experience, the other was a diamond trader. Could Boris do that? Boris guessed he could. Zubilin also needed him to provide cover for another illegal, codenamed 'Nora', who was already in Los Angeles. Boris said he could do that as well.[5] This gave Morros an idea. His latest film, a Laurel and Hardy comedy called *The Flying Deuces*, had been banned in Switzerland at the request of the Vichy French government, who objected to the way it satirised the French Foreign Legion. Could 'West', the Swiss film industry expert, since he was now, ostensibly my business partner, do something about getting the ban lifted before he came to America? Zarubin told Morros he'd request it.

When they had finished working out the details and Morros was preparing to leave, Zubilin had a surprise for him. His father was already en route from Vladivostok and would be arriving in America soon. Boris Morros was overjoyed. Zubilin smiled. One last thing, he said, as Morros prepared to leave. Zubilin wanted Morros to come up with a plan that would allow Soviet intelligence to bring their people into the US. It could be from anywhere, but almost certainly South America. Think about it and the next time we see each other, you can tell me what you've come up with.

Sometime after Boris Morros returned to Los Angeles, a telegram came from the State Department informing him that his father would be arriving in Seattle shortly.[6] Morros called an old business associate living in Seattle to find his father and put him on the next train to Los Angeles. He arrived a day or so later, old, gray, thin and very worn out, having been travelling for two months. Morros brought his father home to his place in Beverly Hills and made a point to not think about the debt he had incurred.

That December, he received a 'love letter' from Leah Melament chiding him for not writing. Boris Morros ignored it. Another letter came in January, which he ignored as well. One day in February 1943, Zubilin showed up at Boris Morros' door with vodka and caviar and asked to meet Boris Morros' father. They had a little party where Zubilin made no effort to discuss business. He just told Morros to meet him for lunch the next day at Perino's, a restaurant popular with the film industry crowd. Over lunch, Zubilin asked Morros if he had any thoughts for the idea he'd mentioned the last time. Morros suggested organising a contest of Latin American composers and then signing them to record deals and bringing them up to Los Angeles to record them. But before Zubilin could say anything, Morros nixed the idea, saying it would be more profitable and expeditious to purchase catalogues of works from individual companies and people. He was, in fact, just then in negotiations with the famous conductor Leopold Stokowski for the purchase of his catalogue, Morros claimed.

At one point Zubilin changed the subject and told Morros that he could obtain paintings from 'Great Masters' which Morros could then sell to raise operational funds. But Morros shook his head, dismissing the idea. It wouldn't work, he told Zubilin. With the meal finished, the two prepared to go their separate ways. Keep thinking about the idea. Look for something in the entertainment industry, preferably something with branch offices in South America. Don't worry about the financing, he told Morros. He might have someone in mind.

❧

Oakland, California, April 1943

Steve Nelson was a real communist and an organiser. He'd been in the Party since the 1920s, in both CPUSA and Comintern. Currently he was Secretary of the Alameda County Communist Party organisation. He made his rounds all over the Bay Area and always kept his ear to the ground, and the other day he'd heard something that made him wonder if it had anything to do with what Kheifits had talked about a year earlier. A comrade had mentioned hearing that funny things were happening at the Radiation Laboratory in Berkley. *Funny? Find who told you this and send him to me. Usual routine. Tell him to tell me his name is 'Joe'.*

A night or two later, a man showed up at Nelson's house in Oakland and said his name was Joe. Nelson invited him in. Joe explained that what was being explored at the Radiation Laboratory involved making a gigantic explosive. There were military guys who wanted the laboratory to prove something, which apparently they did. And now millions and millions of dollars of funding were coming into the lab. It involved uranium. Joe had also heard that the hardest part of the process was going to be the separation of materials, though Joe had no idea what that meant. That was all he knew. Nelson thanked him, let him leave and passed it on to Kheifits.

On 10 April 1943, another man showed up at Nelson's house. It was Zubilin. He said his name was 'Cooper'. Nelson invited him in. Zubilin let Nelson know he was with the rezidentura and wanted to ask him about something. Nelson pointed out that this actually wasn't how the protocol was supposed to work. As a Communist Party official, he was supposed to present a letter from Earl Browder, authorising him to ask his for help. Why didn't he have the letter? Zubilin smiled and told him he knew Earl Browder well, that he'd worked with his sister abroad, and assured Steve Nelson that Browder wouldn't mind at all.

Before he would talk about the Radiation Lab, Steve Nelson had something to say about how things were being run. There were big problems with the trans-Pacific courier networks. It wasn't just the war. It was deeper than that and needed to be attended to. Also Kheifits had two deputies whom Steve Nelson thought were more a hindrance than anything else. Zubilin patiently listened until Nelson finished his litany of observations and complaints and began telling him what he'd heard from the Radiation Laboratory. They were working on something, the aim of which was to create a big explosive using uranium, and that, while it was theoretically possible, they said the big problem was going to be separating materials. Zubilin told him to pass the word on to all the comrades to start getting jobs inside the Radiation Laboratory. If millions of dollars were suddenly being thrown at them, they would be hiring a lot of new people and probably not asking too many questions of the applicants. Tell them to get any kind of jobs they can, anything: clerical, technical, janitorial.

Exactly what Zubilin did after this is not known. Most likely he went and composed a special coded message which bypassed everyone and went directly to Comrade Stalin, informing him that his suspicions had indeed been correct. He might have sent it by wireless, since Kheifits had a radio transmitter operating inside the consulate. But Zubilin might also have thought it wiser to put it in a diplomatic pouch and have a courier take it to Great Falls, Montana, the first station of an enormous 'air bridge' recently set up for ferrying lend-lease aircraft and other war materiel directly to Russia. Each day several Soviet transports carried high-priority personnel along with about thirty large suitcases dubbed diplomatic pouches. The courier might have dropped it off there, but owing to the importance of the message, it is also quite likely he boarded the transport aircraft himself and flew to Moscow, giving the message directly to Stalin.

What is known is that once Zubilin completed his business in San Francisco, he went to Los Angeles. He contacted Boris Morros and arranged another lunch at Perino's. Things had changed, he told Morros over lunch. Everything had to be moved up and the operation they'd talked about previously needed to be up and running by July, or August at the very latest. There were six people whom Zubilin needed to get into the US. Also, he had not yet found someone to finance the operation, so Morros would need to take care of that as well. Boris Morros heard Zubilin's words, but was dumbfounded.

Suddenly he leaned over the table, a glass of vodka in his hand, and said, 'What about taking my men into your music company?'
I just stared at him.

'Don't look at me as though you didn't know what I'm talking about,' he said. 'You have a sheet-music company. It's at Sunset Boulevard and Vine Street. The office is on the Ground floor of one of the buildings down there, and the sign on the door say "Boris Morros Music Company". I have spent some time checking up on the people who go in and out of that door.'

'It is not mine,' I told him. 'I started it for my son, who's in the Army. I wanted to build it up so he'd have a nice little business started when he got out of the Service.'

'Sounds like the perfect cover. We could have men around the United States and a few in South America – all on your payroll.'[7]

Morros did his best to disabuse Zubilin of what he thought Morros could do. He had a business partner, managing the company on a 'salary and a percentage' basis. His songwriters worked on a 'salary and a royalty' basis. What was Morros supposed to tell them when these new people showed up?

It went on like this for a while, but in the end, Boris Morros left Perino's with nothing assigned to him more pressing than to keep his eye out for an entertainment-oriented company they could buy, preferably with a branch office in Buenos Aires. Zubilin promised to keep looking for someone with money to bankroll their enterprise.

<hr>

None of them knew this was all being observed. The FBI had had Steve Nelson's house bugged and under surveillance for months. It would be fair to say the FBI had it in for him because they knew he was a major local communist figure. They took it for granted he was up to something, and it turned out he was. They were there, watching, listening, and taking notes when Joe, from the Radiation Lab, came to his house in Oakland and told him about the strange goings-on and a uranium bomb. They were also there watching and listening as 'Cooper' was told the same thing by Steve Nelson. They had also been apprised that local members of the Communist Party were being urged to find jobs at the Radiation Laboratory at Berkley, which was at that moment undergoing a massive expansion, but they didn't know anything else about anything going on there.

Observing 'Cooper' coming and going from the Soviet consulate, they quickly learned he was really Second Secretary Vasily Zubilin from the Russian Embassy, and even though they were now allies, it really got the FBI's ears up. They followed him down to Los Angeles and observed him having lunch at Perino's with one Boris Morros, the Hollywood mogul. After that, some funny things happened.

The FBI started asking questions about the Radiation Laboratory. They soon confronted the US Army Security – plain-clothes at first, then in uniform – who crisply informed them everything was classified top secret – go away and don't come back; it's nothing Hoover and the FBI need to know about. Only it didn't turn out that way. FDR didn't care much for J. Edgar Hoover, but he dared not go against him. He let Hoover do what Hoover wanted to keep him out of reach. It meant, among other things, he got to hunt down communists and communist spies. Yes, the President is being informed about the different incidents of Soviet espionage. The Russians are going to steal everything they can. That's just the way they are. Meaning, Mr Director, the President wants you to go easy on the Soviets. But now, this was the exception. Hoover had the tool he needed for his battle against communists and those who hated America and would destroy it. And so it began.

For the FBI, Zubilin's meeting with Steve Nelson marked the beginning of the largest, most secret investigative operation in its history. However, his meeting a day later with Boris Morros was not, even by association, anything of interest. The FBI started a file on Boris Morros, and for a while their report on the lunch at Perino's was the only thing inside it.

In April, *Variety* reported that 20th Century Fox had announced it was going to make a film of *Behind Embassy Eyes*. It was getting a million-dollar budget and Otto Preminger would be the director, and the movie was going to be as big as *Mission to Moscow* from the year before. As part of the deal, the book's author, Martha Dodd, would assist in the writing – ten weeks at $400 a week. It wasn't bad.

Martha and Alfred Stern came to Los Angeles in early April. For two weeks they stayed at the Beverly Wilshire Hotel, then a furnished bungalow in Benedict Canyon. Martha was teamed with scriptwriter Fay Kanin. They apparently got along well. Each morning Martha would come to the 20th Century Fox studio's offices and she and Fay would work on the script through the morning. Fay would bring her around to meet people. At some point in the afternoon, everyone knocked off and there'd be drinks after work.

Fay knew everyone and introduced Martha to the community of Hollywood screenwriters. Soon she and Alfred became fast friends with many of them. A lot of them were communists, of course, but plenty weren't. If there were any Republicans or America Firsters, they kept real quiet. They went to a lot of brilliant parties and get-togethers, and Martha felt she was finally back in her element.

Once, on a Friday afternoon, Fay decided to knock off a little early and the two of them dropped in on someone she knew. He was a producer and music director named Boris Morros. He was the archetypal Hollywood producer, only a hundred times more personality-driven. And funny? Boris Morros was a scream. He kept them in stitches with his wisecracks. He listened very attentively as Fay and Martha told him about the project they were working on and Martha's book and her time in Nazi Germany. Martha was so impressed with Boris that twenty minutes after she and Fay left, she popped back into his office again with her husband in tow and introduced them, before leaving again.

It is unclear how much of the script Martha actually wrote. It appears Fay Kanin wrote the actual script on her own, because when the initial draft was completed, Martha wrote several pages of notes with corrections and suggestions. Martha pointed out that the family butler would not be addressed by his last name, as is the case in British households, but by his first name. Lots of little things.

Martha's ten-week contract ended in June. The studio agreed to another contract, this one for eight weeks. They expected it would be signed before the end of the month, but it got put off. Then it was July and everything that could started shutting down for the summer. Martha and Alfred hung on throughout June and took the train back in early July. At around that time, Otto Preminger stepped down from the project and handed the directorship to Archie Mayo, a second-stringer. Sometime after that, the wise men of 20th Century Fox decided to shelve *Behind Embassy Eyes*. The project's official cancellation didn't come until 21 March 1944, when Martha received a check from the studio for $1,600.

23. MEETING THE NEW BUSINESS PARTNERS

Sometime in August 1943, Boris Morros got a call from Zubilin ordering him to come right away to New York. Morros told him he couldn't, at least not right away; business commitments. Then when could he come? Morros couldn't say. Zubilin demanded he explain why he hadn't delivered the business plans he'd promised. Morros made excuses and spun it out as long as he could, then assured Zubilin he'd come just as soon as he could. After that, whenever Zubilin called, Morros reeled off more excuses, explaining that he wanted to, but just couldn't, putting Zubilin off another week, another month. At some point Zubilin must have realised what Morros was pulling on him and, in essence, read him the riot act. No more fucking around, Boris! Boris apparently took the hint. In November, Boris Morros sent the 'love letter' to Leah Melament, to say when he'd be in New York and that he'd be at the Sherry Netherlands.

As Morros expected, shortly after checking into his hotel, Zubilin showed up outside his door. He wasn't smiling. Without saying anything, he started looking around the room for hidden microphones. Finding none, he instructed Boris to come to Leah Melament's apartment at six o'clock that evening. Then he left.

Morros took a taxi to Leah Melament's place on the Upper West Side. He entered the building, found her apartment and knocked on the door. No answer, but the door was unlocked. He went in. Finding no one inside, he plopped into a chair and waited. After a couple of minutes, the door opened and a woman leaned in. Without saying anything, she motioned for him to come with her. Something about the woman told Morros it wasn't Leah Melament. So who was she? They walked several blocks to a movie theater, bought tickets and went inside. The lights were off and a movie was playing. The woman led him to a row where a man sat, halfway up the row, away from anyone else. She motioned for Morros to go in and waited until he'd taken his seat next to the man. It was Zubilin. Having delivered Morros, the woman left. He and Morros sat together for a few minutes, neither saying anything. Then Zubilin whispered to follow him outside.

They took a walk. Zubilin informed Morros he might have found someone to finance their operation. Then he asked Morros if he'd found a company with a branch affiliate in Buenos Aires. Morros told him he had. A music publishing and recording company with affiliates in Buenos Aires and other major South American cities! Zubilin looked relieved. He asked how much they wanted for it. Without missing a beat, Morros told Zubilin the owner would let them have it, lock, stock and barrel, for only $130,000. Zubilin nodded. It was a number Morros had pulled out of the air. He didn't mention the owner was himself and the company was something he'd set up several years earlier, but had never done anything with. In his book Morros claimed it had been worth $6,000, but even this might have been an exaggeration. As for the Buenos Aires office, he knew people everywhere; he'd figure that out when the time came. To Morros' surprise, Zubilin accepted the information with a nod, happy that he could now report that one key part of the problem was solved. Morros returned to Los Angeles.

A month later, Zubilin phoned again, telling Morros to come meet his new business partner. Morros dutifully made his arrangements and then sent a 'love letter' to Leah Melament telling her he'd be staying at the Sherry Netherlands hotel the last week of December and could be contacted there. A day or two after Christmas 1943, Boris Morros took the train to New York. Once again, shortly after checking into the Sherry Netherlands, he got a call from Zubilin who gave him instructions for their meeting. Following them, the next morning at eight o'clock, Boris Morros stepped out of the hotel lobby and walked up 60th and Broadway and then north to 70th Street.

After going almost ten blocks, he suddenly spotted Zubilin walking toward him. Catching Morros' eye as he passed, Zubilin signalled Morros to follow him. Morros turned and followed him at a short distance. Zubilin led him to where an automobile was parked. They got in. Depending on the version, the vehicle was either empty or Genady, one of the rezidentura's gorillas, was waiting behind the wheel. Zubilin, or Genady, if he was there, started up the engine and they drove off, heading out of town. Morros noticed that as Zubilin drove, he kept checking the rearview mirror. Also Morros found himself wondering about his new partner. 'I must admit, I was bedazzled by the idea that Zubilin's couple were willing to invest $100,000 or more in my $6,000 company,' he wrote. 'Where had he found people like that?'[1] He also wondered what they were expecting. Had Zubilin truly accepted the massively inflated $130,000 asking price without any question? And had they simply accepted it in turn? What had Zubilin told them? What promises had he given them? What should Morros expect?

By this point Boris had probably figured out that, worldly as communist spies like Zubilin might have appeared, they didn't understand the first thing about business or money. It wasn't something they ever thought or worried about. If there was nothing in their pockets one day, there'd be something the next. They were Chekists and such things were not their concern. And yet, Zubilin had somehow found his way into a nest of communist millionaires, surely among the strangest and most miraculous of God's creations.

In his book, Morros recounts the route they took: 'up the Henry Hudson Parkway, continuing north into Westchester County, turning off the Cross Country Parkway and then up the Merritt Parkway',[2] eventually reaching a small town on the Connecticut border named Ridgefield. Zubilin parked his car outside the Western Union office and told Morros to stay put. Zubilin got out and used the payphone to make a call. A minute or two later, he returned. Back inside the car, he told Morros that the man about to arrive was someone he'd met before, and that the man's wife was 'a highly intelligent woman whose father had been a prominent diplomat for the Roosevelt Administration'. Fifteen minutes later a station wagon pulled up and parked next to them. The driver's door opened and out stepped a lanky man in snow boots and a leather windbreaker. He had a pencil-thin moustache and his face was slightly pockmarked. Zubilin opened his door and the man climbed into the back seat.[3] Once he was seated he introduced himself to them. 'Alfred K. Stern.' Zubilin shook Stern's hand. 'Vasily Zubilin, Second Secretary, Soviet Embassy,' he said, grandly. Then, with a nod of his head in his direction, he introduced Boris as 'My good friend, Boris Morros!'[4] Stern and Morros shook hands. Up until now, Morros had assumed Zubilin already knew the couple they were meeting, but it appeared they'd never met each other before this. Also Boris Morros had been told by Zubilin that Stern and his wife were people he'd already been acquainted with. As far as Boris Morros could tell, he didn't know Alfred Stern from Adam.

Leaving Stern's station wagon where it was, they drove out of town and up a couple of different snowy country roads for several miles until they came to a large country house set back a hundred yards from the dirt road. He showed them where to park and then they all got out of the car. Walking together toward the house, Morros observed Stern and Zubilin silently regarding each other, like each was sizing up the other. If they'd never met before this, it meant somebody else had done all the legwork on the deal. Someone not present. Then the front door opened and out stepped a woman in her thirties, blonde, not quite petite, but with plenty of 'oomph' and dressed very smartly and 'to the manor born'. He guessed she was Mrs Stern. He also guessed the husband had to have been ten years older at least.

Then something happened which surprised everyone. Mrs Stern and Zubilin recognised each other from somewhere. They broke into broad smiles and fell into each other's arms. She kissed Zubilin and the two laughed like it was the most amazing thing possible. Morros observed this and saw how frozen Stern's face was. He obviously didn't like it, but knew better than to let it show, as if, perhaps, this wasn't the first time this kind of thing had happened. Then everyone paused and allowed the awkwardness of the moment to pass. Finally, before they all stepped inside, introductions were made: 'Vasily Zubilin, Soviet Embassy, Boris Morros, Hollywood producer. How do you do? How do you do? How do you do?' The woman shook Morros' hand hard, looking him in the eye as she did, like she'd been expecting something from him as well. And

Morros was supposed to already know her? He didn't see how. He drew a blank.

The Sterns presumably already had some refreshments laid out for their guests: coffee, tea and a platter of sandwiches to eat before they got down to the business at hand. For fifteen minutes or so, the four ate and drank and chatted about the weather and the drive up from the city. Inevitably, the visitors complimented the Sterns on their lovely house and listened to them tell how much they liked living there in rural Connecticut. It's likely they also talked a little about the war and FDR and where the war was heading; whether they thought he would open up the Second Front like he'd promised Comrade Stalin. But nothing was said that had anything to do with the beliefs they supposedly all shared. It probably amused Morros that everyone avoided the matter of how Zubilin and Mrs Stern previously knew each other. What was the proper response? How does it go? *We are all men of the world and such things do not concern us.* So if the wife had known Zubilin earlier, under different names, somewhere else, somewhere else like Berlin, did that mean she was herself some kind of spy? And what about this guy Stern, her husband? Was he also a spy, or just married to one? Morros guessed the latter. As for Edward Herbert, Vasily Zubilin, and whoever else he was, was he also the NKVD's big muckety-muck at the Russian Embassy; their *man-with-the-fuzzy-nuts*? So in their eyes, was being selected by him for secret work a great honour for the Sterns? It certainly demanded they bring out their nice dishes.

Morros let them do most of the talking, confining himself to pleasantries. As they were getting up to leave the living room and go to the library, Mrs Stern turned to Morros and said she had expected him to remember her. Morros was bewildered. Remember her from where? Had they met before? Yes, she said. They'd met that spring at the 20th Century Fox Studios in Hollywood. They had? Yes, she and Fay Kanin had dropped by his office one afternoon. Morros knew Fay and suddenly he remembered her. She was the woman who'd written that bestseller about being with the Nazis in Berlin. Hadn't her father been the American Ambassador to Hitler? So that's what Zubilin had been talking about! What was her name? What was her name? Then he remembered. It was Martha Dodd. Morros damned himself for not remembering her. He wondered if Martha Dodd was now going to hold it against him.

They went into the library, shut the doors and got down to business. Zubilin began with a convocation reiterating what he'd told Boris earlier: Stern and Morros were to set up a business as cover for secretly bringing in Moscow Center's people without the American authorities knowing or thinking anything. Nothing they currently had set up could do this, not with the level of secrecy required. They needed to bring in a lot of people over the next few years, but to start, they'd like six brought in between now and, say, June. Any ideas? Morros told them that if the idea was to bring in people, one, maybe two at a time, without attracting any attention, then a music publishing company would probably work. People from Argentina could come up as with master recordings, accompanying them to oversee their use. It was done all the time, but with more than one or two, you might start attracting attention. If you wanted to smuggle in larger numbers, then, in Morros' opinion, the best way would be through a combined music publishing and recording company. He explained how in the recording business, singers and musicians were coming in and leaving all of the time. The government authorities paid almost no attention to any of it. It was even more so with recording engineers. With so many of them in the army right now, there was a serious shortage. You could say they were sound engineers being brought in on short-term contracts. Nobody would question that. Combining publishing with recording and pressing, they could bring in dozens of people in a very short time and no one would ever know a thing. Isn't that what you want?

Morros' plan was to form a music publishing and recording company he would call ARA, for 'American Recording Artists'. Morros explained how he happened to be very close, personal friends with a large number of major recording artists, film and radio stars – Bing Crosby, Bob Crosby, Hoagy Carmichael, Peggy Lee, to name just a few. They'd sign to him in a heartbeat, because they appreciated the fact that Boris Morros knew music and was strictly prestige and always made money for everybody. At first, Zubilin seemed convinced, but then Alfred started asking questions about all the costs associated with operating a recording studio and record-pressing plant, and it didn't take long before it became obvious that going down that route was full of potential problems and costs. It didn't matter that Stern knew nothing about the music business; he knew about money and costs and cash reserves and how little things that went wrong often had very big implications. He and Morros argued about it at length.

In the end, Zubilin put his foot down and said no to ARA. The idea was never to start a new business, but to use an existing one, which was why their business would be called BMMC, for the Boris Morros Music Company. It already HAD its plaque up on an office building on Wilshire Boulevard. That's what was wanted. Zubilin noted that since Alfred was going to be vice president for the time being, he should also have a plaque up outside his office. Stern said he'd get one made right away. Zubilin told them that for the moment, their focus should be entirely on music publishing, period. They'll bring up the people that way. After all, Rome was not built in a day. Morros would do that and teach Alfred everything he needed to know about the music business. Then they'd start thinking about the other stuff.

The discussion then turned to how the company should be structured financially, with planning and budgets and reserves and incidentals. Stern started talking about wanting to be repaid using promissory notes in the sum of $50,000 bearing interest at 4 per cent per annum. Morros balked at that. They argued about it and none of it made the slightest sense to Zubilin. Stern tried to explain. He was a tedious explainer. Morros figured Zubilin had brought it on himself and excused himself. He went into the living room and dropped into a chair. Martha joined him. They talked. 'She was well-educated and imaginative, had a gift for telling phrases and did not lack humor by any means,' Morros wrote. 'And I kept marveling to myself, "what in God's name was this lovely young woman doing, married to a millionaire backer of a Russian spy ring?"'[5].

The discussions continued. Stern wanted to know lots of little details about how the money was going to be spent and the kinds of properties they were looking for. They broke for dinner. An hour or so later, they'd reached a basic agreement about everything and had written it up, but then both men decided they each wanted their lawyers to have a look at it before they signed anything. This was a business arrangement and it was why they had lawyers. They decided to go into town and take care of it in the morning. By

Morros' account, Alfred Stern drove while he, Martha and Zubilin shared the back seat. Zubilin had his hands on her the whole trip back. Morros was dropped off at the Sherry Netherlands. Where the party went after that Morros did not claim to know. It was, apparently, New Year's Eve.

What is known is that on or around 3 January 1944, Vasily Zubilin and Alfred and Martha Stern reconvened in Boris Morros' hotel room and in the end came to some agreement. The two signed a contract, with Zubilin as the unofficial witness. Alfred Stern and Boris Morros shook hands and Alfred handed Boris a check for $50,000 and Boris handed Alfred a promissory note in the sum of $50,000 bearing interest at 4 per cent per annum. The rest of the money would come on or around 9 March. The Boris Morros Music Company, with offices in New York and Hollywood, was now in business, up and operating and ready to start shipping Chekist officers deep into the heart of America.

Whether or not Martha and Zarubin had anything going on in Berlin, once the two had fallen into each other's orbit in New York, they were at it, or back at it, like gangbusters. Since they were both living in the city and had their days usually open, it was easy to get together. The rezidentura had a number of safe flats in Manhattan and apparently he'd take her to them whenever they fancied it. But it wasn't all pleasure. Martha used the occasions to let Zarubin know she and Alfred were having their problems with Morros. He had come to New York the week before to collect the final $50,000 check from Alfred and supposedly teach him something about the music industry. Well, what Alfred got instead was this incredibly superficial conversation that was mainly Morros talking about Morros and how great he was, and his ongoing negotiations with Hoagy Carmichael and Stokowski for their catalogues, and that Morros started getting impatient and was wanting to leave after only 35 minutes or so. When Alfred asked him about why record companies won't focus on quality music instead of popular stuff like 'Chattanooga Choo-Choo', he became very insulting and rude. Martha and Alfred were not happy with him. Morros had no commitment whatsoever to the World Communist Revolution. It was obvious he was there only for the money. Boris Morros was not a comrade by any means, shape or form! This bothered Martha and

Alfred as they'd naturally assumed that on this they'd be working with comrades.

Of course, Boris Morros had complaints of his own:

Vasya, the man calls Chattanooga Choo Choo 'garbage.' No! Let me explain something to you, Vasya, It's wrong! He thinks because he's suddenly part owner of a music company it means he's Paul Whiteman! He doesn't know anything about music! Not the first thing! The man is a complete idiot. Nyekulturny! Tell you something else, Vasya: Chattanooga Choo Choo, that was his song. His, Boris Morros'! Morros picked it out, Morros promoted it. Morros made it into a hit! He, Boris Morros! But this durak Alfred Stern, this idiot ...

24. THE NEW CASE OFFICER

Somewhere in the middle of March 1944, Elizabeta Zarubina came to Alfred Stern's offices and had him place a long-distance call for her to Boris Morros in Los Angeles. When Morros came on, Stern handed the receiver over to her and Zarubina began chatting away with Morros in a very cosy voice, like the two were old pals. After a minute or two, she told him to come back to New York. After that she handed the phone back to Stern to hang up. Boris Morros had only been home a couple of days from his last trip, but rather than protest, he did as he was told. He booked himself aboard the first train he could get and three days later was back in New York, checking into the Sherry Netherlands and waiting for instructions, which would come a little while later.

That evening at the appointed time, Morros began walking, as instructed, up Broadway to 125th Street where he spotted Vasily Zarubin and another man standing together on a street corner. Seeing Morros, Zarubin waved him over and introduced him. 'Boris,' he said, 'this is Jack Soble.' Warily eyeing each other, the two men shook hands. That done, Zarubin motioned the two to walk with him, wordlessly leading them up several blocks to a Chinese restaurant called 'The Far East'. Inside, they were shown to a table and sat down. Looking at Soble from across the table, Morros noticed that while they were walking, Soble had moved much like anyone else, but once he was seated, he seemed to become the very embodiment of negligible: a thin, tired, mournful-looking man, utterly joyless; one of the meek who knows he will never inherit the earth.

At first, the conversation bounced along, like the three were radio actors reading from scripts they'd just been handed. It continued like that when the waiter took their orders and as they waited for their food to arrive. Halfway through their meal, Zarubin informed Morros that, starting now, Soble would be taking over as his case officer. Morros looked at Soble and it was obvious he wasn't particularly pleased at the prospect either.

Zarubin asked Boris Morros to explain the business aspect of Operation Chord to Soble. Morros did so, speaking simply, without any of his customary flair. He soberly explained how the music company would operate and handle the people imported as technicians on short-term contracts fulfilling specialty jobs, vacated for war work, making it appear as uninteresting as possible. Zarubin would occasionally step in with a question or an explanation and Soble would just nod, trying to take it all in. To Boris Morros' relief, Zarubin never brought up any mention of business partnerships or about anyone named Stern. Things between him and the Sterns had not been great and he was happy not to have to discuss them. Once Morros had finished, Zarubin addressed them both, reiterating everything he'd said previously about Operation Chord and how critical it was they pull this thing off and find ways of getting large numbers of their people into America without the enemy knowing anything or being able to keep track of them. He went over what needed to start happening in the next several months, explaining that this would be an excellent opportunity for them to work as a team. Soble and Morros continued silently eyeing the other, each wondering if they would ever trust the man opposite him, deciding probably not.

Eventually Zarubin got up from the table, bid Boris Morros farewell and left. Soble then started to talk, telling Morros what would be expected of him. It was like listening to a corpse. Then Soble started talking about Chord, wanting Morros to remind him of all the points they'd discussed earlier, like he didn't remember them, and it quickly became clear to Morros that the man hadn't a clue about any of it. With Soble, he noticed how everything seemed to register either as an annoyance or a great imposition. Soble went over procedures for communication and future meetings. When he was done, he called for vodka. Then they drank, because they were Russians. The next day Boris Morros took the train back to Los Angeles.

⁂

Sometime later, just before he left, Zarubin had a final meeting with Soble and told him several things he hadn't mentioned previously. One was that Boris Morros had a business partner, a wealthy comrade whom Zarubin had asked to help. I think he's got it all up and running, not something you'll need to worry about, Zarubin assured him. But in case you need to know it, the partner's name is Alfred Stern and he's with us; a fellow countryman. If you ever need to contact him on the phone or anywhere, ask Choudenko to give you the number.

Then Vashya Mikhailovich grinned impishly. Another thing, there may be trouble with this partnership down the road. Zarubin didn't know whether it was still going on, but at one point earlier in the year Boris Morros was having an affair with Stern's wife. Believe me, if you meet her, you will understand. What we have to worry about is whether the old man knows. If there's bad blood between Stern and Morros, it's because of that. But otherwise, I wouldn't worry about it. You'll probably never meet these people. And that was the last time Jack Soble gave the matter any thought.

⁂

It is not known exactly how the Sterns learned the Zarubins were leaving, since none of them are known to have said anything about it afterwards. Zarubin might have let Martha know during one of their assignations or he might have summoned them both and informed them together as a case officer properly should. More likely, though, it was something he left to an underling, since Martha and Alfred Stern were very nearly at the bottom of the hierarchy and the fact that Stern had lent $130,000 to the cause didn't actually change this. Of course, it might also have happened at the same time Elizabeta Zarubina dropped by Stern's office at 30 Rockefeller Plaza asking him to ring Boris Morros for her. It would have been a perfectly good time to inform a very low-ranking fellow-countryman something which, again, officially speaking, was barely any of his concern. On the other hand, Zarubin was someone who rarely told anyone anything he didn't actually have to, and with Martha, being only someone he happened to be sleeping with, it could be reliably assumed he'd leave without telling her a thing.

On the other hand, there is a story, of questionable veracity, which exists about the Zarubin's departure. It was among the many questionable things that made it into the Congressional Record during the height of the Cold War. It says only that, just before leaving, Zarubin asked Alfred Stern if he would take out $5,000 in cash from the bank and give it to him. This Alfred did.

Zarubin was sent home because someone had denounced him to Stalin. The letter had been anonymous and had come from the embassy in Washington. It claimed Zarubin was working for the Japanese – also for the Germans, but mostly for the Japanese. It claimed a lot of other things, some of which, but not all, were crazy. But it alarmed Stalin, like he knew someone, at some level, was moving against him on something. Because of everything they had going on right now in North America, Stalin was determined not to let it spook him further, but the matter needed to be fully investigated. Especially with the war on. Nobody wanted a repeat of the bloodbaths just a few years earlier. Whoever was investigating this was doing it very slowly so as not to cause a panic within the Service. And owing to all the sensitive projects both of them were involved with, there needed to be an orderly handover. Replacements needed to be found. But what was funny was that, of all the strange things Zarubin was being accused of, the oddest was that Elizabeta was the courier who carried the secrets with her to California where a secret radio transmitter was located. The person operating it was one Boris Morros.

Boris Morros came away from meetings with Soble apparently convinced his new boss was too worn out, too confused and clueless to be any kind of obstacle. In defiance of Zarubin's orders, and without telling Alfred Stern anything about it, Morros started a recording subsidiary, ARA, for 'American Recording Artists'. Within a month he was announcing in *Variety* that Hoagy Carmichael had signed to him, along with Phil Harris, Smiley Burnette, Frances Langford and Bob Crosby's Bobcats. While it wasn't exactly a lie, none of it was completely true either. Boris Morros set himself up in a swank new office on Sunset Boulevard with a recording studio somewhere else – he never quite said where. By June 1944, at the same time as American and allied soldiers began coming ashore and liberating France, Boris Morros was announcing the release of the first batch of ARA records, beginning with Hoagy Carmichael's 'Hong Kong Blues', which was about to be featured in the new hit Humphrey Bogart film *To Have and Have Not*. Other songs followed. There was 'Pretty Soon' by Frances Langford, 'See that You're Born in Texas' backed with 'Boogie Woogie Cowboy' by the Cass County Boys. It went on like this for a while. Every week or so, new records came out. Sales seemed to be good. There was 'On the Atchison, Topeka and Santa Fe' by Bob Crosby and his Orchestra, and 'Jumpin' Jiminy' by Skinnay Ennis.

All this came as a surprise to Alfred and Martha. They were not at all happy. Stern telephoned Morros demanding to know what exactly was going on. Morros probably asked him if he'd seen the latest sales figures. 'On the Atchison, Topeka and Santa Fe' was totally knocking it out of the park. And Hoagy? *You know his song is featured in the next Humphrey Bogart, right? But this isn't what we said we'd do! It doesn't matter. Leave it to me on this, okay?* He followed that up with some more assurances and then got off the line.

The months passed. More money went out, records were pressed, released and sold. Never does any money come in, but Boris Morros isn't fazed. Each time Alfred comes off the long-distance line, he feels increasingly like he's been had. They've been taken advantage of, used and forgotten.

⊰᪣⊱

Back in Moscow, after several months, and without breaking too many dishes, the NKVD investigators determined the circumstances concerning the scandalous letter written to Stalin denouncing Vasily

Zarubin as a spy for the Japanese. Their verdict: Zarubin was cleared of all allegations against him. But it should be noted that none of this would have happened if Vasya Mikhailovich hadn't been such a ball-breaker in the first place and driven those two poor officers into the clutches of schizophrenic madness.

Zarubin was no one's idea of a cerebral spymaster. He was a man who thought best on his feet. He went out each day looking to make things happen. Zarubin knocked on doors and talked to people he encountered. He beat the bushes, took notice of what shook out and then decided whether it could be used. He thought on his feet. That's what Zarubin was like and it was what he expected from intelligence officers under him. And if they weren't that way, he made it hell for them. Which largely explains how the whole Dolgov and Mironov situation occurred. It was supposed to be a plum assignment. They were both second secretaries with the embassy. They lived their diplomatic cover, but perhaps a little too effortlessly, at least for Zarubin's taste. They never really grasped that in Zarubin's view, Washington was just another podrezidentura, same as all the others. It wasn't enough that things came to them. They were expected to beat the bushes and they weren't doing this, not to his satisfaction.

The two guys in Washington, Mironov and Dolgov, were, in Zarubin's view, lazy, useless good-for-nothings doing nothing but going to receptions and royally, royally fucking the dog. Put another way, Mironov and Dolgov were thinking, cerebral men; men with desks, educated, polished men who mistakenly equated diplomatic rank with something other than walking garbage. Dolgov and Mironov didn't like him at all. He frightened them and made it impossible for them to enjoy any of the time he was away, which was nearly all the time. They never knew when he'd show up demanding they account for themselves right on the spot.

Though each suffered individually, they must have suffered a great deal together as well. There had been so many shootings recently, they must have constantly worried about their necks. Nothing they ever did earned them so much as a grunt of approval. For Mironov and Dolgov, the strain became unbearable. Sometime in August 1943, they went off the rails together and wrote an anonymous letter to Comrade Stalin denouncing their boss Vasily

Zarubin, his wife and ten other NKVD officers in North America. They were all working for the Japanese and also the Germans. Zarubin was using his wife Elizabeta to carry secret information to someone in Los Angles named Boris Morros, whose job it was to transmit it to the Japanese using a secret radio. They also worked for the Germans, but mostly for the Japanese. The letter got into Comrade Stalin's hands and things suddenly went crazy. An investigation was launched, which was why the Zarubins were brought home, along with, it turned out, a lot of other people. The investigation went on through the spring and early summer of 1944. In a report to Comrade Merkulov, an unidentified officer wrote: 'We have determined that this is a matter of far-fetched and false provocation ... instigated by a former worker of the American station Vasily Dmitrievich Mironov and his accomplice Vasily Georgievich Dolgov, who took advantage of their official positions while working abroad and also blatantly violated the principal rules of konspiratsia and Chekist secrecy.'

It was, however, determined that at least one of the two men, Mironov, had been suffering from schizophrenia. The strain of work, and fear of Zarubin, had simply been too much for them. This sort of thing happened more often than one would think with Chekists not used to working abroad. Both men were reduced in rank and sent to special psychiatric hospitals, at least for a time. Later, when more was known, both were shot. Still, a good many Chekists must have heaved a sigh of relief that the damage caused by the incident was so limited and that hopefully it meant that the time of bloodletting was past.

The investigation went on for six months. In the end, Vasily Zarubin and Elizabeta Zarubina were absolved of any suspicion of wrongdoing. No one was going to shoot them. But, they also weren't being sent back to the Citadel. Although Zarubina's field deployments would continue for a few more years, Zarubin's operational career was over. He got a promotion and, until his retirement years later, he was one of NKVD's foreign intelligence branch's most senior chiefs. Even if it wasn't his time to retire, it was his time to start a garden and begin growing vegetables.

What Comrades Merkulov, Beria and Stalin did not know was that at the same time Mironov and Dolgov had written their unhinged letter to Stalin denouncing Zarubin, they had also sent a very similar one to FBI Director J. Edgar Hoover. It came to the Director's office on 7 August 1943 and at first no one knew what to make of it. The letter was written on a Russian typewriter, addressed to 'Mr. Guver', since Russian does not have an 'H'. Hoover ordered for it to be translated and what the letter claimed was bewildering to say the least. It said Zubilin was really Zarubin, and Zubilina was really Zarubina, and that Zarubin was actually working for the Japanese and using his wife as a courier. She brought the material to Boris Morros in Los Angeles, who transmitted it to Tokyo via a secret radio. When the FBI checked its files, they found they had one on Morros marked 'Internal security' with its mention of a meeting with Zubilin, the Soviet diplomat, who, the day before, they'd recorded with Steve Nelson discussing developments at the Radiation Laboratory. All that was in a different file marked 'Espionage-R' (Russia) and part of their ongoing high-level atomic spies investigation. While there was all anyone would need to link Morros with Soviet espionage, none of it seemed to have anything at all to do with atomic weapons. Zarubin with Steve Nelson did, but Zarubin with Boris Morros did not. And President Roosevelt had made it quite clear to Hoover that unless it directly involved stealing atomic secrets, he and his dogs should turn a blind eye to it. Still, it put Boris Morros in an odd light.

The 'Guver' letter also claimed Zarubin had played a major role in the Katyn Massacre of thousands of Polish army officers, the poorly buried mass graves of which had only recently been uncovered by the Germans, and which was still heavily in the news. In addition, the letter also named the nine NKVD officers working in the US, Canada and Mexico. Looking into it, the names mostly checked out. With the exception of Mexico City, all of them were either vice-consuls, AMTORG, Soviet Purchasing Commission, or the New York-based 'XY line'.

If this is just the tip of the iceberg, gentlemen, what does it say about the iceberg? No point in telling the President. He'll either shut it down or gab it back to the Soviets. But what did it all mean? The idea that Zubilin-Zarubin might be transmitting material to Japan was simply nuts, but everything else did possibly make sense.

The men named in the letter were ones they'd already had their eyes on. So then what was this? Why was someone in the Russian Embassy telling them these things? Who could possibly have written it?

Not knowing what to do with it, Hoover and his people kept very quiet about the letter, telling no one of its existence for a very long time. Morros was kept on the list for surveillance, but for a long time it produced nothing, at least nothing which found its way into his file. As for Boris Morros' file itself, a note was added making oblique reference to the letter, which was highly, highly classified. But then the Boris Morros file went back to the stack and was again, for a time, forgotten.

～❈～

Through the spring and summer, Martha and Alfred did little besides stew and grow steadily angrier as they watched the money disappear. And were they getting anything for it? For God's sake! It was supposed to be an espionage operation, their wartime service to communism. Is Operation 'Chord' ever going to happen? Is this really how the comrades in Moscow Center do things? We're here, trying to serve! Meanwhile, in the world outside Martha and Alfred's quiet little corner of the war, a lot was going on. American, British and Canadian armies had landed in France and had begun liberating Europe. Then there was a massive parachute assault into Holland to get their tanks and troops across the Rhine and then home by Christmas. Only this wasn't a complete success and after that, everything was mostly bogged down, until just before Christmas when there was a winter offensive by the Germans in Belgium. For a while it was successful in pushing back and defeating the American Army, but it ultimately failed. And now the Red Army was gathering on the Vistula, near where Martha had been, gathering up their divisions, tanks and guns, getting ready for that final attack on Berlin. Let it burn, Martha tells their friends. The Russians can render that city into dust!

Blue, abandoned and angry, that's how Martha and Alfred felt; like cast-offs hung out to dry. And still no word from whoever was supposed to be their case officer. Martha and Alfred were fuming. They'd handed over all this money, and they'd done it gladly, because that's why they were there. They were in this struggle. They wanted, more than anything, to be part of something with like-minded comrades. And in the end, all they had been part of was a phony business cover run by that slimeball Boris Morros. And to think they called him 'Comrade!'

On 15 March 1945, Stern received a letter from an unidentified individual who wrote: 'Morros is shrewd but not when it comes to knowing what will go over in music.' The writer said some more bad things and then closed with: 'If you bump into Hoagy Carmichael, ask him how things are going with Boris.'

Reading it, Alfred Stern could only implore the Almighty to cause the case officer to present himself so they could get this all cleared up and finally be of some real service.

꧁✥꧂

Of course, at this point, Soble didn't know about any of it. Morros had said there were no problems and for a couple of months that had been good enough for Soble. One less thing on his plate. Away in Los Angeles, Morros stayed out of Soble's sight and hopefully his mind. Certainly the LA podrezidentura wouldn't have wanted him around. He sent a couple of messages to Soble that told him only as much as to cause him to lose interest. In Show Biz there were all sorts of disappearing acts and Morros knew most of them. You want to shine, you better know how to fade out.

As for the Sterns, Soble hadn't given them a moment's thought. He didn't think he needed to. Then one day, Choudenko asked him if Alfred Stern and his wife were his agents, and Soble, remembering his last chat with Zarubin, told Choudenko they were. You need to get in touch with them, Choudenko said. They're really unhappy about something. Soble asked if Choudenko had a number for them. Choudenko said he did and wrote something down. Then he told him that when he called to say he wanted to 'speak to Sam'. You can say it to either him or his wife. Meet with them and find out what the problem is.

Soble called the Sterns that evening, but before he did, he tried to remember what Zarubin had said about them. Wealthy comrades, fellow-countrymen, a business contract with Morros, cover business, music publishing, partnership agreement, learning the business, repayment. Apparently something had gone very bad. So bad that Stern had gone outside of channels to make his dissatisfaction known. Then Soble remembered something about Morros having an affair with Stern's wife. He called the number. A woman answered. Soble said to her, 'I'd like to speak with Sam,' and the woman answered, 'Oh, yes,' sounding elated, like this was the moment she'd been waiting for. Soble met with them and discovered the Sterns were very nice, though in an odd way, since they were apparently quite rich and not really accustomed to dealing with comrades. But they were very friendly and eager to serve. They invited him to dinner. He brought his wife. It went well. After that, there were more meetings and they even went out a couple of times. Stern was some kind of capitalist businessman and she was a famous book author, bestsellers she said. One of them was even going to be made into a motion picture. The Sterns were comrades, though. They believed and all they wanted was to serve and to do things. And that was where the problem lay. Finally, Soble told Stern he'd talk to Morros and try to straighten it out, which Soble did, or at least tried to do – several long-distance phone calls and an exchange of telegrams which always ended with a feeling of uncertainty and confusion. Whenever Morros told him it would all be taken care of, he doubted it ever would be. And he was right.

In July 1944, Soble ordered Morros to New York, figuring if they got him face to face, away from his home turf, getting straight answers from him might not be so difficult. Morros took the train as ordered. When they learned he'd arrived in New York and had checked into his hotel, as usual, they phoned with instructions for a rendezvous. So far, so good. Soble and Stern went to the meeting point and waited for Morros to show up, but Morros never did. Later he passed word back that, on his way there, he realised he was being followed. It wasn't the first time it had happened, he told Soble. Just the other week back in Los Angeles, he was driving with his son when his son noticed a car following them. Soble reported it to Moscow Center. Morros took the train back to Los Angeles without ever meeting them. Soble wasn't sure what to think. Had Morros pulled another one? Soble decided to try a different tack. In August 1944, he and Alfred Stern took the train to Los Angeles and when they got there, they dropped in on Morros in his fancy office and demanded he explain himself.

Which Boris Morros did. He obliged with his best song and dance about the music industry and Hollywood and record-pressing plants and the future of vinyl. He pulled out all the stops and whatever he said apparently worked. Stern and Soble took the train back to New York, confident an understanding had been reached.

What neither of them realised was that the FBI had observed them.

25. LIFE AFTER WARTIME

Somehow the FBI identified Alfred Stern as one of the two men seen meeting with Morros. Sure enough, outside Stern's office there was now a plaque for the Boris Morros Music Company. They decided they needed to find out more. One night in October 1944, agents broke into Stern's office and photographed some of his papers.[1] From this they learned Stern had entered into a business partnership with Morros and had given him $130,000.[2] It was decided a little more needed to be known about Stern. The routine task of assembling a precis on him fell on one John G. Johnson, Special Agent at the New York office.

The FBI already had a file on Stern dating back to the late 1930s, but being a typical 'Internal Security – C' file, there wasn't much to it, just a few sheets of paper detailing who he was and who he associated with; maybe some odd newspaper clippings. But a glance at it told Johnson where to look for more. They had fatter files on notable people, groups and circles of friends. It was just a question of knowing where to look. Stern was just one of the thousands of left-wing types they opened files on each year. Few had done anything; they'd just crossed a threshold. Stern had run for Congress on the communist-affiliated American Labor Party ticket along with his close friend Vito Marcantonio, the left-wing lawyer, activist and now Congressman representing East Harlem. That was probably enough right there. According to the file, Stern was also friends with other well-known communists and communist sympathisers, among them Albert C. Kahn, Max Yergen and George Seldes. Stern had given money to or lent his name to any of dozens of 'Committees For' and 'Leagues Against'. For Special Agent Johnson, all this was fortunate, as the Bureau maintained extensive files on those people and groups. Giving these files a combing through, he was not surprised to find Alfred Stern was all over them. Special Agent Johnson learned how Stern had served several times as city housing commissioner and had been a special advisor on housing issues to different big-city mayors and governors. From informants they learned Alfred Stern had once gone into Nazi Germany back before the war, carrying in money for different Jewish organisations, and how he'd once driven Pierre Cot, the radical French activist and, as they already suspected, OGPU agent, into Texas, across the Mexican border without the Feds finding out until now.

The rest of Stern's life – his birth, education, wartime service, employment, marriages, divorce, remarriage – was all pulled from public records, along with a peppering of occasional information from unnamed 'confidential informants'. Of his current wife, Martha Stern, nee Dodd, the report noted that she was the daughter of a former American Ambassador. It mentioned her earlier, short-lived, marriage, her uncompleted degree and brief employment as assistant books editor at the *Chicago Tribune*. Of Martha's time in Germany and the two bestselling books she'd subsequently written about it, the report said almost nothing. This was a routine report on an individual, against whom nothing was even alleged, something the FBI did all the time. It gave no conclusion and made no recommendations. Even so, anyone reading it would immediately know Alfred Stern was a commie fish swimming around in a commie sea, full of other left-wing and communist fish. However, there wasn't anything about him that actually smelled Russian; no apparent connection with Moscow, which was the only thing they were interested in at that moment. Special Agent Johnson submitted his report on 4 January 1945. Seven copies were printed. A few might have been read. Mostly, it just went into files, including Stern's. For the time being, the file on Alfred Kaufman Stern was still rated only 'Internal Security – C'. Alfred Kaufman Stern was not anyone of interest. That his wife wasn't either went without saying.

The 'entente cordiale' between Boris Morros and the Sterns didn't last long. Money started leaving the account at a fearsome rate and Morros either wouldn't explain why or his explanations wouldn't hold water. By January 1945, Alfred Stern went directly to Stepan Apresan, the new rezident, to whom he and Martha had once been socially introduced. Apresan listened to Stern's words and then he wrote to Moscow about it. When Moscow wrote back telling him to get it taken care of, he took the matter to 'the Professor', Stepan Choudenko, who then went to Jack Soble and told him he needed to fix it. Listening to Choudenko's words, Soble realised he was being granted more than a little freedom of action, which was good since Alfred Stern had let Soble know there'd be something in it for him if he got it settled favorably.

In early February 1945, Jack Soble took the train to Los Angeles, remaining there for ten days.[3] What he did during most of that time is not known. He probably stayed in a hotel he'd randomly picked, since, as an 'illegal', he did not have the option of bunking at the vice consul's, which was probably what the visiting 'legals' usually did. Four days after he arrived, Alfred Stern showed up. According to the report, 'On the fourth day of his stay, he [Soble] was joined there by Alfred, who had decided on his own initiative to see the business in which he had invested money.'[4]

The report indicates they went to see Boris Morros at his office. It does not say whether they came with appointments or just dropped in. Also not known is whether they brought muscle to the meeting. The podrezidentura could have lent some, if Soble had wanted. Soble did have the freedom, and might have thought some 'presence' might help things. By now Soble was quite aware how effectively Morros could put up flak when he needed to. Soble was determined to have the matter settled. Soble's report only indicates that Boris Morros was cooperative, though at one point it admits there was a great deal of shouting. According to the report, the three talked for a while, then Stern and Soble demanded Morros take them to the recording studio, which had already cost Stern so much money. Having little choice in the matter, Boris Morros drove with them to a mostly empty building in an industrial part of South Los Angeles. Alfred Stern was expecting to find a recording studio, but it turned out to be something else.

Interestingly, the address Morros brought them to, 5810 South Normandie Avenue, would, years later, figure significantly within the annals of popular American recorded music. It was the site of the record-pressing plant from which, in the 1960s, 70s and 80s, the notorious, legendary Bihari brothers spewed out millions of cheap pop and rhythm-and-blues records, aimed squarely at the most mainstream and urban audiences. But all that was still more than a dozen years away. At the moment that Boris Morros was unlocking the door and leading them inside, 5810 South Normandie Avenue was not supposed to be a record factory or anything resembling one. According to the building occupancy records from that time, it was still supposed to be a vacant former mattress factory.

The building itself wasn't large, but inside much of it was empty. At one end, in a corner, were record-pressing machines. From Soble's report it is unclear if any of the machines ran or if perhaps some did and there was some production taking place. Either way, it was in bad shape and a lot would have to be done to get it up to scratch, which would cost a lot of money. Morros insisted they were sitting on a gold mine.[5]

Morros admitted that buying all this had used up Stern's funds, along with $62,000 of Morros' own money. They were so close. They just needed more. 'The foundation of this business is the record factory. Unfortunately, it is far from a real factory, despite the vast expenditure,' Soble writes.

> The thing itself – the record factory – is a major point of contention and the focus of heated arguments between Alfred and Boris. The problem is that Alfred contends (in front of Boris) that the original idea had been to publish sheet music, not to build a record factory. Boris does not deny this, but he says that this decision had been changed the eve of Vasily Mikhailovich's [Zarubin's] departure, and it had been decided to build a record factory. Boris argues that this was a very sensible decision, because the popularization of any song, dance tune, and so forth, is currently achieved through records, not sheet music.[6]

Jack Soble and Alfred listened as Boris Morros went on and on about all the money that was going to rain down on them once long-playing records went on the market. And when will that happen? How much longer can this war go on? Soble was dumbfounded. Stern was incredulous. *What about communism? What about the struggle? What about bringing those agents up from Buenos Aires?* Morros was equally incredulous. *What about it?*

It isn't known how nasty things between Borris Morros and Alfred Stern became. For a while Morros and Stern screamed at each other. Describing it in his book, Morros admitted something about himself: 'I have never pretended to be an even-tempered man. During that stormy week I called Stern every foul name I could think of in all the languages I know – and I know profanity as it is spluttered around the world. Stern, the Harvard man, just sat there and took it in with the uncomprehending look of a hurt child.'

It must have been nasty, but eventually everyone calmed down. Reflecting on it in the report's preface, the writer, presumably Choudenko, admitted that it happened, but stressed that when it was over, everything was still on track. 'As a whole, the inspection went smoothly,' he wrote. 'Except for one conversation, in the course of which Boris swore at Alfred using vulgar and obscene language.'[7]

But the reality was that the situation was dire. 'The money is almost gone,' Soble wrote in his report. 'The financial statement shows that a couple of months ago the money given by Alfred – $130,000 – was already gone. Morros had put in $62,000 of his own as well. Of the sum total of $192,000, $6,500 are left in the bank in NY. Boris proposes an "immediate additional investment" of $150,000. This sum should be invested by home, rather than Alfred (the latter cannot be expected to do this, since Alfred accuses Boris of squandering money and of complete incompetence at managing it).'[8]

But far worse than that, Morros had forgotten that the purpose of the company was providing cover for an espionage operation. Soble ended his report by requesting permission to dissolve the Boris Morros Music Company. Moscow Center's permission came shortly afterwards. Soble gave the order and Comrade Boris Morros did as he was told and wrote Comrade Alfred Stern a check for $100,000, settling and ending all business ties between them. Officially, Stern and Morros wished each other well and moved on to other opportunities. Alfred showed Soble his gratitude by slipping him $4,000 in cash.

Chord got forgotten, along with all the other ideas that never got off the ground. On a trip back to Russia a couple of years later, Jack Soble had a brief reunion with Zarubin, who let Soble know he had much bigger regrets from that particular tour of duty.

As for Boris Morros, he remained on the NKVD's books. Oddly, Moscow Center's opinion of him remained stellar for another decade, likely buoyed by Lavrenty Beria's fond, mistaken memories of their time together 'stealing horses' in Baku. For this reason, perhaps, Moscow Center's wisemen felt it politic to forgive Morros' artistically driven, poor decision making. Morros remained in the sunlight for several more years. Soble, a survivor who knew about human frailties and foolishness first-hand, was inclined to go along with Moscow.

As for the Boris Morros Music Company and its subsidiary ARA, without Alfred Stern's money, it soon began falling apart. Records continued coming throughout 1945, but aside from one from Hoagy Carmichael, the rest were just odds and ends by relative unknowns. Morros let his son Richard take it over once he got out of the army. He sold the presidency to someone named Mark Leff, who, a year later, sold it to someone else. In 1947, Hoagy Carmichael, ARA's only real star, left and signed on to Decca Records. It ceased operations after that. Over the years, though, records[9] have very occasionally come out on a label calling itself 'ARA'. Why this has kept happening is not known, though it likely isn't to make money. Nevertheless, ARA is remembered and to this day enjoys a cherished place in the history of American recorded music as the Hollywood record company that operated as a business cover for a Soviet spy ring.

❧

In early 1945, Martha's novel, *Sowing the Wind,* finally came out. The publisher, Harcourt, Brace and Company, released the book in early January, then, as now, an unmistakable indicator of low expectations of the book's performance. The reviews were polite and sales poor. Everyone agreed, clearly, it was horrible timing. After all, this was 1945: America had been at war for three years, and at the moment, no one gave a damn about moral dilemmas enveloping a playboy Luftwaffe ace in pre-war Berlin. The book's dismal reception must have stung Martha deeply. The book had taken a couple of years out of her. She wasn't sure when she might be ready to try writing again.

The ending of the war in Europe left Martha feeling out of sorts. Unlike nearly everyone else alive, Martha Dodd had managed to get through the entire Second World War without ever actually doing anything. She'd wanted to, but now it was too late. It was over. This must have riled Martha no end, especially since, in her own mind at least, she'd committed herself, body and soul, to the fight against fascism years before everyone else. She came here ready to go. Never had it been her intention to stay out of the war; it had just turned out that way. Martha had answered the call seven years earlier, ready and willing to serve, for the 'Cause of the Worker all over the World'. Call it Comintern, call it Stalin, or just Moscow, Martha answered the call; she stood ready, standing by, awaiting orders! But the orders never came, not unless you counted 'Chord', which she was starting not to.

Where had she gone wrong? She'd offered Moscow everything: no games, no conditions, no playing hard-to-get. She'd even recruited her husband, her brother, and her best friend Jane. All she'd done in the entire war was talent-spot and wait for them to order her to do something. Meanwhile, the whole world had changed. Everything she'd known in Berlin was all gone now, bombed to bits. She saw the pictures of it in magazines and in the newsreels. Berlin, *her* Berlin, all of it gone, everyone killed. Maybe not everyone, maybe 90 per cent. So were probably 90 per cent of those men she'd slept with. But she'd never really thought about them very much in the first place.

By now, she had pretty much figured out that her lover Boris Vinogradov had probably been shot. She'd had a drink a while back with a reporter she knew who was just back from Moscow. He didn't know anything in particular, he just knew that they ended up shooting a lot of their best people. You had to expect it was that. They didn't need a reason. Martha still thought about Boris a lot. For years she'd dreamed of introducing Alfred to Boris, but now she knew beyond anything that it would never happen.

Martha also realised how, all around her, women she knew were suddenly pregnant and having babies. It jarred her too. Martha had never cared for children, but suddenly she wanted one. In July

Martha and Alfred became adoptive parents of a newborn baby boy whom they named Robert. The baby's mother was a young woman who'd gotten pregnant by a man who wanted to marry her, but at that moment couldn't for some reason. Though she could neither read nor write, she was presented with papers to sign, which meant, they said, she could get her baby back when she was able to provide. A few months later, when the young woman and her husband, the baby's father, tried getting him back they learned it said nothing of the sort, only that she was giving up her baby forever without any rights. As much as they begged to get their child back, they found they had no legal recourse. They began a long, fruitless battle which, in the end, yielded only the names of their child's adoptive parents.

But motherliness never came to Martha. She tried, but after a couple of months gave up, later admitting sheepishly to friends that succumbing to *that* urge had been a mistake. Alfred's feelings about it are not known. He already had a son and daughter from his previous marriage and was not, apparently, close to either. Was it possible he longed for a second chance at being a father, or in the end, had he just given in to Martha like he usually did? No one knows. They kept Bobby rather than trying to give him back, but mostly he was left in the care of nurses and nannies. Martha went back to whatever she'd been doing.

At that moment in time Martha didn't feel much enthusiasm for writing. What she wanted to be was a spy. It seemed to her that she was supposed to be spying on somebody or something. Even though the 'big war' was over, the real one, the one that mattered, the one she and Alfred and the others had signed on to, was still ongoing and, in fact, was entering into a new phase. Martha was sure of it. It would be a whole new war and it was going to need operatives. None of these had been picked out yet, so there was no reason she and Alfred couldn't still get deployed. Or just herself, if that's what they wanted. She needed to make them want to use her. Discussing it with Alfred, they agreed the best way to ensure they were not overlooked was to get themselves right in front of the local big Soviet wheels.

Jack Soble understood what the Sterns wanted, but there really wasn't much he could do for them. That kind of thing was up to Choudenko or whoever was above him. They were the ones who assigned people to things, certainly not Soble. As it was, Zarubin had dumped too much onto his plate. There were too many people he needed to maintain contact with.

The Sterns and Sobles continued occasionally going out. The Sterns had them over for dinner and a couple of times Martha and Myra went out to movie matinees together. Alfred got Soble to let him tag along on some of his 'contact runs', including several to Boston, where he met Soble's brother Robert and others, getting to know them in the process. Other times Alfred accompanied Mikhail Chaliapin on his run and acted as his dogsbody. Stern's idea was to make himself indispensable.

Sometime during the autumn of 1945, at Alfred's insistence, Soble brought him to meet Stepan Choudenko. They met on the corner of 74th and Central Park West. There were brief introductions, after which they followed Stern to where his car was parked. They all got in and Alfred drove them up to Ridgefield. As she had done previously, Martha probably met them at the front door and welcomed them in. They likely made it really nice. They talked about all sorts of things. Stern, of course, talked a lot about business. He explained about investment and how he always had his eye out for possible partners to cooperate with on ventures. He then went on about different industries and where he thought the opportunities were going to be. Choudenko listened to him and kept thinking how so much of what this man was talking about were things that had never once crossed Choudenko's mind.

At some point during their get-together, Stern talked up his ideas about constructing business cover. Choudenko listened to him politely while not being able to disguise his own bafflement. Choudenko made the requisite short, agreeable sounds as he waited for the subject to change again. Then Stern asked Choudenko if he could recommend other companies in which he could invest his money and which the Soviets could then, *ahem*, use for their own *intelligence* purposes. Choudenko listened to the question and promised Alfred Stern he'd keep it in mind and let him know. The meeting wrapped up soon afterwards. Martha acted very friendly and they told him he should think about bringing up his whole gang from the consulate there for the day. Hey, use the pool. Open bar. We can have a cookout! Choudenko thought it was a great idea. They'd do this again soon!

That summer, the war against Japan ended, when, one after another, two Japanese cities were obliterated by two atomic bombs dropped from American bombers. On the same day that this happened, Soviet Russia declared war on Japan and invaded Japanese-held Manchuria. A few days after that, the Japanese surrendered.

The war was over because of the atomic bomb, something Martha and certainly no one she knew had ever heard of before. She wondered if Zarubin had known about it while he was here. Had the Americans kept the secret from them or had it been something they knew about? Zarubin had certainly never said anything about it. Never once had he or anyone else ever suggested Martha keep her ear to the ground about something like this. Why hadn't he trusted them?

26. FUN WITH JANE AND GEORGE

Normally Jane Foster was an avid letter writer, but once she began her OSS training at a hastily converted country club outside Washington, she disappeared and Martha and Alfred stopped hearing from her for a long time. They assumed whatever she was doing was hush-hush, so she was being kept incommunicado. But her real reason for not writing, it turned out, was that she couldn't stand knowing her letters were being read and censored before ever reaching the eyes of her intended reader.

But now, almost as soon as the war ended, letters from Jane began appearing in their mailbox. It turned out she was in the Netherlands East Indies, her old pre-war stomping ground, only now it was calling itself Indonesia.

As far as Jane's personal life went, it was crazier than ever. Since she'd seen them last, Jane had gotten married, then divorced, then remarried to the same man. Now she was wondering if that had been a mistake. Highly amused, Martha and Alfred wrote back telling her she should come stay with them once she was stateside. Alfred even suggested he could line her up with a lawyer if she wanted an annulment.

Jane was one of the few women Martha ever got that close to. Martha had plenty of social friends she'd spend time with, but none of them had the wit or the spunk to keep up with her like Jane did. Jane was educated, witty, worldly as hell, hard-drinking and not overly monogamist. She was an artist, whose art heavily reflected the world she was in and a lot of it reflected her time in the Netherlands

East Indies. She was also an intellectual and a communist. Her time in the Netherlands East Indies resulted in her hatred of the Dutch, both as colonisers and, truth be told, as people.

For most of the two years Jane spent overseas she was in Ceylon, sleeping in tents and living a rough, rear-echelon lifestyle that was long on boredom yet not without its pleasures. There were always plenty of men around, and a lot of impromptu parties and drinking and screwing around. Jane's gang of OSS gals included the future famous Julia Child, future well-known writers, academics and the wife of a prominent future CIA man. But at the time most were just looking for some fun to relieve the boredom. Her husband, George Zlatovsky, a sergeant working in counter-intelligence for the US Army, was serving in Europe. Like Jane, he was a communist and not overly monogamous.

Much of Jane's work had involved disinformation campaigns, including writing comic books in Malay aimed at degrading enemy morale and encouraging different indigenous groups to rise up against the Japanese. Then, during the summer of 1945, Jane was flown to Burma to help organise native groups. At the time, she and everyone else assumed the war would go on easily for another year or two. But then the US dropped atomic bombs on Hiroshima and Nagasaki, and a couple of days later the war was over.

Suddenly a potentially dangerous situation was developing in the Netherlands East Indies. The native population had risen up in dozens of anti-Japanese militias. The Japanese Army was still in control, and while they had made it clear they had no interest in fighting anyone, to some degree it was out of their hands. The Indonesian militias weren't interested in fighting them either, but what they were adamant and willing to fight about was their insistence that the Dutch, their hated former colonial masters, not return. They declared independence. Militias appeared, some communist, some tribal, some armed with weapons given to them months earlier by the Americans and British. Some Japanese army units, unsure of what they should be doing, handed over their weapons to the militias. There were sporadic gun battles, including one where a senior British officer was killed. Worried about what it might portend, the Allied high command told the OSS to send in a team to find out and report back. A team of area experts sent in included Jane.

On the ground in the newly declared Indonesian Republic, Jane Foster saw a lot of things, talked to a lot of people and asked a lot of questions. She interviewed Indonesian independence leader Sukarno about what he thought of Allied intervention and he told her they'd welcome the British coming in for a while to stabilise things as long as it meant the Dutch would not come back. But he warned, if the Dutch did return there would be a very nasty war. Sensing that Jane was possessed of a strong anti-colonial streak, Sukarno urged her to stress this point to the Allied leadership. Jane promised she would.

Jane and her team went back and reported their findings. She was then asked to write up a longer, more in-depth study on the situation. Since she was slated for separation, they told her she could write it up during the trip home and hand it in when she arrived in Washington. Jane did exactly that. She took her time and wrote what she thought was a very reflective report on the problems and challenges the post-colonial Java, Sumatra and the whole Malayan archipelago presented. When she offered her report, she watched it get stamped 'Top Secret'. With a sinking heart, Jane realised her expert assessments would never be read, at least not by the people who actually needed to know about the situation in Indonesia. She was glad she'd kept some copies for herself.

Jane left Washington, went to New York and spent the next several weeks living and partying with Alfred and Martha. They threw a Christmas party and introduced Jane to Soble. Morros might also have been at that party and been introduced to her as well. Later, she gave Soble a copy of her Indonesia report. And with that, Jane Foster was back on Moscow Center's books. She'd been given the codename 'Slang' right before going into the OSS.[1] Then George Zlatovsky, Jane's husband, showed up. A communist and Spanish Civil War veteran, he'd spent his war in the European theater and had fought in the Battle of the Bulge. He was also just as hard-drinking and crazy as Jane. Neither could decide whether they loved or hated each other, so they did plenty of both. She was wild and impetuous and from money. He was not. At some point Soble recruited him. Moscow Center approved and gave him the codename 'Rector'. Not long after, the US Army Counter-Intelligence Corps sent Zlatovsky to Austria, fast becoming a hotbed of spies from both sides. Soon Jane joined him there and began working at a US-run radio station aimed at displaced persons from countries liberated by the Soviets. Both of them were soon sending back reports.

Not surprisingly, their love of drinking, partying and screwing around on each other made the Zlatovskys quite effective at gathering the kind of information Moscow Center wanted. They learned who US counter-intelligence had in its pocket and who they were looking at. Moscow had a winner on its hands and credit was going out to Jack Soble for finding it.

Roosevelt's orders to Hoover regarding Soviet espionage were quite specific in the way only unwritten orders can be. Unless it directly involved the Manhattan Project, Hoover and his men were to go easy on whatever Soviet espionage they came across. FDR's thinking had been that any problems which might arise would get settled via his personal relationship with Stalin. Apparently it never occurred to him that his personal charm might not work on everyone or that the days of his life might be numbered the same as everyone else ever born of woman.

The degree to which Hoover and the FBI had actually followed Roosevelt's directive remains a matter of dispute. While it's easy to argue that Hoover ignored FDR's orders and did as he pleased, some argue that his investigations were often hit or miss, representational or just downright lazy. As it was, Hoover's men had their hands full trying to keep the Manhattan Project's secrets secure. In the latter regard, they considered themselves successful, but regarding the former, they were aware the Russians were robbing them blind.

When it came to dealing with Stalin, FDR had always believed the relationship between the two leaders would solve any serious problems which might develop between them. The new American president, Harry Truman, had no such faith. Meeting Stalin at Potsdam convinced him that the Russian leader was one very tough customer who was neither overflowing with goodwill nor likely to ever get talked into anything. Later, when shown the extent of Soviet espionage, he gave Hoover much freer rein over how he went after spies.

Hoover's boys went back to the Zubilin case. Re-examining the 'Mr. Guver' letter, they tried to extract fact from all its batshit craziness and figure out what part Boris Morros might actually be playing. They knew Zubilin had been a Third Secretary at the Soviet Embassy in Washington for over two years without anyone from the State Department ever meeting him. What had he been doing those two years besides that meeting with Steve Nelson in Oakland in 1943 about the experiments at the Radiation Laboratory and then the one he had the next day with Morros in Hollywood? They really needed to find out.

Also utterly puzzling was the 'Guver' letter's claim that Zubilin's wife had been running at least as many networks as he had, even aside from the assertation that she was sending it to both the Japanese and Germans, and that the one transmitting it to the enemy was Morros, of all people. Even if everything else it said was true, this had to be completely nuts! There was no way Morros could be running a radio station. He might have looked and acted like a big shot, but at the end of the day, Boris Morros was really just another man on the make in Los Angeles. So then if that was true, and it definitely was, why was he meeting with Zubilin only one day after Zubilin had learned we were about to start building an atomic bomb?

Was it possible the two events were unrelated, other than being two stops on a circuit Zubilin travelled? The local FBI office knew Morros was someone continually attending events and ingratiating himself with whatever Russian government luminary happened to be passing through. But they also knew Morros had family still living there, so none of it was surprising. The question must have come up about that visit from Alfred Stern and that other man whom they hadn't identified. Why had Stern entered into a very short-lived business partnership with him? They still didn't know. By now, their investigation of Stern had closed and he was judged of no interest to them. Still, the FBI put a pin in it, in case it came up again. There was always a possibility it might.

❧

Then, just a month after the war ended, two events took place which changed everything and marked the beginning of a new epoch soon to be called 'The Cold War'. The first involved Igor Gouzenko, a cypher clerk at the Soviet Legation in Ottawa, Canada. He worked for Colonel Nikolai Zabotin, the Soviet military attaché, encrypting and decoding radio messages between Zabotin and GRU head-quarters in Moscow. For Zabotin and Vitaly Pavlov, his NKVD counterpart (and a Zarubin protégé), Ottawa was a very quiet, but highly productive gold mine with all kinds of good stuff continually coming in. Gouzenko liked Canada. Even though he had little direct contact with Canadians, he liked them, thought they were good and that he'd prefer staying there than going back to Russia. It wasn't long after the war ended that he was told he and his family would soon be heading home.

On 5 September 1945, Gouzenko made his move. He went to his office at the embassy and removed over a hundred pages of communications from files, secreting them all over his clothing and person. Then he walked out of the building and for several days wandered the streets of the Canadian capital, unable to find anybody to defect to. It is an epic story told excellently elsewhere. Gouzenko and his family were given secret asylum by the RCMP, which originally tried to have nothing to do with him. Eventually, though, after he showed them the documents and explained what they meant, they began to understand. Soviet spying and theft of atomic secrets and weapons technology was at staggering levels, not just in Canada, but also the US and Britain. A few days later, Canadian Prime Minister Mackenzie King flew to Washington to discuss the matter with Truman, noting that, according to the documents Gouzenko had smuggled out, an assistant to Secretary of State Edward Stettinius named Alger Hiss seemed to be directly implicated. Soon after, King sailed to London where he raised the matter of arresting Alan Nunn May, a British scientist working at the Chalk River natural atomic reactor, whose apparent espionage for the Soviets included providing them with uranium isotope samples obtained from that reactor as well as from the one which the Manhattan Project had constructed in Chicago. It was their first inkling that the Russians had successfully put their people inside the project. A silent alarm went off which only a few people could hear.

The second event occurred a few weeks later, in October, when Elizabeth Bentley, a Vassar-educated woman the same age as Martha, walked into the FBI's New York office, again offering detailed information about Soviet espionage. They thought at first she might be deranged, as she'd been drinking heavily, but once Bentley started talking, they realised she knew a great deal about the spy networks. She had, in fact, been single-handedly running 'the Sound', Moscow Center's name for a vast constellation of highly productive American networks, ever since the death of her lover and boss, Yakob Golos, two years earlier.

The 'Sound' networks were unlike anything else. Golos had started building them back in the 1930s using people recruited via CPUSA's secret apparatus. Its core were people working for the US government. His networks were vast and organised according to Golos' own whim, far outside the rules of *konspiritsia*. While Golos knew the names of the people in them, it seemed no one else did, including Moscow Center, something they couldn't stand. According to Bentley, Golos told her that they had all joined on the understanding that they were serving Comintern and the World Communist Revolution, not Moscow. Golos told her he wasn't sure how eager they'd be to continue if they learned otherwise. For years, she and Golos had fought to keep his spy apparatus out of Moscow's hands. It was theirs, it was Comintern, it was American, and not necessarily Russian. It was something Zarubin and the others didn't grasp, but then Russians don't always grasp that not everything is theirs to take. Golos, having once been Ukrainian, knew this.

For years, Comintern had hung on as a fiction, a fig leaf for people who needed to believe they were serving something other than Moscow and Josef Stalin. In 1943, on Stalin's order, it stopped being even that. Comintern was once its own nation, with its own leadership, governance, intelligence and counter-intelligence organisations with networks that went all over the world, across oceans through its networks of seamen. Some comrades continued clinging to that, including Golos. He remained a fervent communist to his death, but by then he'd also grown to hate Russians. It was something he'd passed on to Elizabeth Bentley. Bentley provided the FBI with a dizzying amount of information. Her 115-page statement caused the FBI's investigations to be widened to include the people she had identified.

It turned out that what Bentley told them dovetailed nicely with what another defector had revealed to them a year earlier.

Viktor Kravchenko had been a senior supervisor at the Soviet Purchasing Commission's massive complex of offices on 16th Street in Washington, DC. It employed hundreds of Russians: industry experts, purchasing agents, translators, typists, administrators, book-keepers, drivers and, of course, dozens of secret police. Kravchenko's defection hadn't been something the US government had relished, initially viewing it more as an annoyance than a valuable windfall. Stalin had wanted Kravchenko back so much that he even enlisted FDR's former Ambassador to Russia Joseph E. Davies to plead on his behalf with the President. But much as FDR craved harmonious relations with Stalin, he granted political asylum to Kravchenko. Hoover had him pumped for information, but until Bentley sang, none of it was of much use to the FBI Director.

But now, a frightening picture was beginning to emerge showing the sheer immensity of Soviet espionage throughout North America. The Russians had stolen everything they could get their hands on: anything that involved radar, electronics, metallurgy and chemistry. They had also wormed their way into the Manhattan Project. Suddenly it was imperative for Hoover to find out what they'd stolen and who'd been helping them.

The FBI determined that, since before the war, the Soviet Union had four different intelligence organisations[2] operating in the US, each with its own mission and all of them, apparently, utilising personnel supplied to them by the American Communist Party's 'secret apparatus'. How extensive was this? If what Elizabeth Bentley had told them was true, then apparently it was very extensive.

Needing to determine the level to which the CPUSA's secret apparatus was supporting Soviet espionage activities, the FBI launched its 'COMRAP' (for Communist Apparatus) Investigation. One of the first things it examined was the CINRAD (FBI acronym for Communists in Radiation Laboratory) Investigation two years earlier and the night that the FBI's wiretap recorded the meeting between Steve Nelson and Zarubin about what Nelson had been hearing out of the Radiation Laboratory in Berkley. Steve Nelson, old-time Comintern labour organiser, helped run their Shanghai headquarters before coming home. He had secret apparatus written all over him. And during the meeting, he'd insisted Zarubin first listen to what he had to say on the way things were being organised.

Only after hearing a litany of labour-management complaints did he go on about the experiments at the laboratory. It was all the proof anyone needed that they were working together, hand in glove.

Elizabeth Bentley was another product of the secret apparatus. They'd spotted her, gotten acquainted, saw she was highly educated, energetic and organised, also unemployed and frustrated. Perfect. She was spirited away from the party and sent into secret work. How many more were there like her? Dozens? Hundreds? Thousands? Then there were all the people she was naming. Most were nobodies working in different departments, passing on reports and memos, but some weren't. Some were special assistants and deputies to department heads. They needed to be checked out.

Then of course there was the question of how much they'd stolen from Los Alamos. If there was a spy at Chalk River, was there one in Oak Ridge? Or any of those dozen other places? It would be wise to assume there were. Were they being supported by the secret apparatus? The FBI took the names Elizabeth Bentley had given them and began digging. It took them in many different directions. They started finding other people and making connections. Among the many names that kept coming up was Alfred Stern and his wife, the well-known author Martha Dodd.

❧

Gouzenko and Bentley's defections had a particularly stifling effect at street level. Things on the ground froze; operations stopped. People in the process of recruitment were left high and dry as their would-be handlers either went to ground or were ordered back to Russia. Since neither defection got mentioned in the news, no one had any idea what was the cause of it. It had taken Moscow Center a couple of days to figure out what had happened with Bentley, but there was absolutely no idea what the story was with Gouzenko. The Canadian government kept insisting it didn't know anything; neither did the Americans. Both insisted they were looking for Gouzenko at their Soviet ally's request and would let them know once they knew something. Meanwhile, Soviet agents and infiltrators continued their activities with no sense of anyone being on to them. For erstwhile spies like Martha, Alfred and Martha's brother Bill, the prospects of ever getting deployed were now only that much more unlikely. Still, contact with the Sterns continued. Occasionally, Martha was asked to write up summaries about various public figures. She did as was required and also continued sending in names of potential recruits. Occasionally, they'd get taken up on their long-standing offer to serve as a summer resort for the consulate staff and their children. Alfred used one such occasion to confront Choudenko and demand he tell them why they were otherwise being avoided. All he got back was a sheepish grin.

The Sterns' friendship with the Sobles by now was on the fade. Much as the Sterns tried to endear themselves with gifts and dinner dates, neither Jack nor Myra cared. Alfred might have been an educated, cultured and committed gentleman, but he was also an overbearing know-it-all with a frank opinion on nearly everything. Then there was his swagger. The way he carried himself seemed to announce to the world that he was a rich cuckold. It was funny at first, but like everything else about Alfred Stern, it grew tiresome. But then, so did his wife, Martha. They could tell she was a hellcat. Brazen, she'd taken Myra to a safe flat one time when they'd needed to wait out a rainstorm before a matinee, and while they were she let her know she knew the locations of several others in Manhattan. Why would she have had any business even being in one? None, not unless it was to screw Yasha Mikhailovich. The Sobles weren't stupid. They remembered what had been said to Jack that last time about Martha having an affair with Boris Morros. No, they were pretty sure it hadn't been him. Hellcats don't unleash themselves on guys like that. That was not her taste, not by a longshot. There were no stranger fellow-countrymen than the Sterns. Strange and annoying and not even worth being treated to a very expensive lunch.

When it came to that, Jack Soble much preferred Ester Rand, one of Zubilin's most promising agents-in-development. Rand was young and vivacious, but neither demanding nor so wearyingly promiscuous. For the price of an expensive lunch, she would merrily ply him with all the latest gossip from a dozen different Jewish organisations and their galaxy of players. Who was favoring the Socialist Workers Party and who went for the Trotskyites, and their feelings toward Stalin. Sometimes she'd even bring along her friend Alice Martin, who was also very interesting and knew lots of things about people in Washington. Alice Martin was married, her husband in the military, and she wrote for a left-wing paper. Yasha Mikhailovich had said the Martins were 'good people, and coming more and more into our direction', and that they'd soon be ripe for recruitment. It was one of the things on Jack Soble's to-do list he hadn't quite gotten around to.

Then there were Stern's different business ventures. He and Jack's brother, Robert, and another fellow-countryman had set up something called the 'Inter-American Pharmaceutical Corporation', a business partnership for importing and exporting medicines and drugs between North and South America, which Soble suspected was really an initiative by Stern to create another operation 'Chord'. Luckily it hadn't worked out. In the end, it sold and shipped a single load of war-surplus penicillin to Mexico before internal squabbles caused them to end it. Apparently, Stern's personality was the main reason his brother and the other partner quit.

It bothered Soble the way the boundary lines kept getting crossed. That was not how *konspiritsia* worked. Alfred and Robert were brothers, but they represented two entirely separate networks. Soble had heard American fellow-countrymen tended to ignore network boundaries like this, but he knew they'd been put there for a reason. If something were to go wrong, and one had to expect that in this business, there was no telling what might get exposed in the process. But American comrades, for all their noble intentions, were completely incapable of adhering to even the most basic rules of *konspiritsia*.

27. A BRISTLE BRUSH
FACTORY IN FRANCE

On 17 February 1947, Jack and Myra Soble took the Oath of Allegiance and became naturalised American citizens. A few days later, Jack Soble applied for a passport. The reason he gave on his application was to inspect and buy a bristle brush factory in Verberie, Oise, France. He was also planning to visit family and friends in Austria.

Moscow Center decided Jack Soble should come to Europe and run the Zlatovskys for them. It would be a major promotion and completely uncharacteristic for an officer whose life was spent completely in the field, far away from all the internal politics. But in Moscow Center's eyes, Jack deserved it. With Jane Foster and George Zlatovsky he had struck gold. They were apparently getting their hands on top-notch counter-intelligence material. That she was OSS and he was army intelligence called for special handling. They decided it would be prudent that their case officer could also be at least partly American and previous experience working with them was also a big plus. Jack Soble would move to Europe at least part of the year and be their case officer. To financially support the operation, Moscow Center found a bristle brush factory in northern France up for sale and told Soble that he and his cousin Boris, who was in the boar bristle trade in Canada, should come and check it out. If they liked it, they would buy it for them and they could start operating it, with Jack Soble using it as cover. The distance between there and Salzburg, Austria, didn't trouble them. He was in the bristle trade and could go anywhere there were pigs and everyone would accept him; no one would ever question him being there. That kept everything very simple. Soble would divide his time between there and America. During the six-month period that he was away, the American networks would be run by his trusted subordinate Boris Morros.

Suddenly Jack Soble felt the dread deep in his gut. Boris Morros was going to be a problem. He'd never told anyone, but in the two years since the whole 'Chords' debacle, things with him had gone bad. He only contacted Soble when he wanted to float one of his schemes and see if he could get Moscow Center to give him money for something. Since Soble wouldn't play around with his ideas, Morros got testy. He'd often hang up on Soble, then purposely screw up the rendezvous and fallbacks when he was in town. But instead of reporting it, Soble ended up putting little things occasionally in his reporting, lightly suggesting Boris Morros had also been present, had lent a hand and was a good comrade. Soble did this because it was easier than confronting Morros, but also because something had happened which caused him to wonder if those bullshit stories Morros had told of being old 'friends of the rain' with Beria back in Baku in the old days might actually be true. It made Soble afraid.

The 'Chords' mess was finally wrapped up, and the whole thing had left Soble so irritated at Morros' behavior that he wrote Moscow Center requesting to have Boris Morros deactivated as an agent. He said Morros was unreliable and refused to adhere to the security protocols. It was a completely routine request. As he expected, a little while later he was informed his request was approved and permission was granted to deactivate Agent Frost, which was Morros' codename. But then, suddenly, the permission got rescinded with no explanation given. Soble wondered how it was even possible and realised the order must have come from very high up. But how high up? Soble mostly left Morros alone after that and decided it was better to make up little harmless pieces of praise than doing something to anger an enemy. And now Soble would have to get Boris Morros to actually do a job. He was going to run the networks. Not like it was impossible, but it did mean getting out and travelling around and having meetings with the different agents and also the people who weren't quite agents yet, ones like Ester Rand and Alice Martin and her husband in the army and that couple who were doctors at the veteran's hospital near the nuclear site. All of them required contact and handling: dinner and drinking and talking politics. Yasha Mikhailovich had found them all during his travels and had said they were good possible agent material. Morros had to meet with all of them and cultivate them or they'd end up getting written off. He'd have to do that, plus everything else. Could he? Could Boris Morros perform? He had to. Both their necks were on the line. Soble needed to have a very serious talk with him.

✲

Just before Soble left, he did meet with Boris Morros and he made it very clear this time there'd be no fucking around. He'd be gone for six months and while he was away, Boris Morros had to run the networks. Soble was serious, but Boris, characteristically, acted blasé about the situation. He yawned back to Soble that he was too busy to run around playing cowboys and Indians just because some idiots back in Moscow wanted to talk to Soble about this and that. That was when Jack Soble pulled out all the stops. He told Boris to straighten up and fly right. He delivered it in such a way that Boris couldn't fail to get the full impact of what he was saying. Your neck is on the line, Boris. For once Soble's message seemed to stick with Morros. Realising Soble wasn't kidding around, he gulped and told Soble he would see to the networks while he was gone; that he could count on Boris Morros. See that you do, said Soble coldly, ending the meeting sooner than he should have. Knowing for once he'd left Boris Morros completely off balance felt very good to Jack Soble.

✲

Arriving In France, Jack Soble met up with his cousin Boris, who had been running his own boar bristle import-export business from Quebec. Together, they visited the bristle factory, checked it out and decided it was good. They sent the word to Moscow Center, arrangements were made, papers were signed and the factory was theirs. They spent the spring and summer getting the factory up and operating. Both of them went on bristle-buying trips. One of Jack's runs took him to Austria where he spent several days visiting with the Zlatovskys.

It must have amused Jack Soble that he was being credited with their success. If credit was due anywhere, it was with Martha and Alfred. After all, they were their friends, not Soble's and he barely knew them. He had met Jane at the Sterns' 1945 Christmas party, when she'd just come back from Indonesia, and then a few days later at a bar where she handed him a copy of her Indonesian report. As for George Zlatovsky, Soble had only met him that one time at Stern's after a party, and at the time Zlatovsky had been too hungover to talk much. Now he was their handler. He'd guessed that being a close friend of Martha Stern's, she was probably also wild and crazy. He didn't see why George Zlatovsky would be any different.

They weren't. He met up with them in Salzburg. They seemed somewhat bewildered that it was him, but when he informed them he would herewith be their case officer, they accepted it readily enough. Once Soble saw them in operation, he realised how good they were. It was as if they owned the place. He worked for the United Nations Relief and Rehabilitation Administration (UNRRA), which was dealing with refugees and emigres, but he was really doing counter-intelligence for the US Army. Jane worked at a radio station also operated for different refugee and emigre groups. They spent a lot of time working with the army's 430th CIC detachment, based at Camp Truscott outside Salzburg. It sounded like George and Jane had something going on with half the organisation. As a result, the 430th was hemorrhaging documents, intel and, more importantly, counter-intel. The 430th seemed to be doing a lot of things its members were eager to talk about. There was all the stuff going on against the Soviets, but the 430th was also finding common cause with some of the Nazis who had managed to avoid getting arrested and stuck behind the wire. Some of them knew where the Commies were and would help uncover them for a ticket out. So the 430th had taken over the ratlines from the SS and were now sending people to Argentina and Spain. They didn't mind talking to George and Jane about it.

At one point Soble asked them if they were still married, and the two just laughed and told him it was a good question and that maybe they'd have an answer for him next week. They'd married and divorced several times and they weren't done yet. George and Jane laughed and loved, drank and fought, screwed around and screwed around some more, and fought and made up again, and in the process had brought in all these other people who were telling them things and giving them reports, and it showed no sign of slowing down. Soble finished up his visit, wrote his report and returned to the bristle factory. Moscow wrote back that they'd let him know when they wanted him to come, and until then, carry on as before.

His summons finally came during autumn. Jack took a series of trains, first to Paris, where someone name Kusnetsov gave him a thick wad of American dollars and directed him to Prague, where a man named Ivanov met him in a park by the main station and handed him a sheet of paper bearing his photo, but with a name he didn't recognise and the rank of Lt Colonel. In Moscow he was put up in a two-room suite at the Hotel Metropole, one of the city's best hotels.

Nearly every day for several weeks Soble attended debriefings where different groups of people asked him questions. He was asked to explain everything he had done since being activated in 1942: buying the cafeteria, whose idea it had been to get the money from the Imperial Bank of Canada, where his brother Robert had been when all that was going on. They wanted him to tell them about the networks, the agents, people in the rezidentura and what exactly his dealings with them had been at different points in time. They wanted him to tell them about the technicians and the couriers, the women who did the typing, Sylvia Doxie Callan and all her nervous breakdowns, the man who worked for Northrop Aircraft company, Choudenko, Stepan Apresian (the Soviet Vice-Consul in New York) and their crew. Mostly, though, it was different people asking him the same questions over and over.

He kept being asked his thoughts on the Gouzenko defection. How bad was it? Bad, he told them, and without mentioning their names described how Alexander Elias and Aja Anschilewitz, two Canadian agents he'd met up with, had both been worried out of their minds and wanting to know what they should do. Soble assumed things since then had settled down somewhat, but of course he didn't know because he hadn't seen them. He added how they'd watched one of their comrade's houses get raided by the RCMP, which they said had something to do with it. Mainly, though, they wanted to know what to do. They all listened gravely to what Soble told them and nodded back. Some mumbled that perhaps things are overextended. So much requires correction, reinforcement. It would be terrible to lose Ottawa. Yes. Over and over.

But what they really wanted to know about was his boss from 1942 to 1944. Vasily Mikhailovich, whose last name, he now learned, was not Zubilin but Zarubin. Soble learned this even though his name in any form was nearly always left unspoken. Still, they wanted to know everything he could tell them. Some, however, were more intent on determining, as precisely as possible, what the limits were to Soble's knowledge of his boss' activities. It took Soble a while before he realised what they were trying to find out about was the atomic stuff. Had Zarubin been running atomic spies? Until now it hadn't occurred to Soble that anything they'd carried or any of the clandestine meetings Zarubin had had with any Americans might have had anything to do with those bombs. Those two bombs had levelled whole Japanese cities and killed hundreds of thousands of people. Our spying had something to do with ... *that*?

The interrogators quickly came to the conclusion that Soble's ignorance on the matter was vast, and that was good. The fact that Zarubin had kept Soble in the dark reflected well on Zarubin and Zarubin's wife. The fact that Soble could demonstrate his own ignorance so well meant he wasn't someone they'd need to worry about, which was also good. It seemed much of what Vasily Zarubin and his wife learned of in America had made them potentially very dangerous.

They wanted to know everything Soble did with Zarubin during the almost two years he'd worked under him. Mostly Soble said he couldn't remember, but then they started charting it all out, week after week, and going over very precise details. Soble's memory was actually voluminous; he just didn't want them being aware of it. Grudgingly, he'd give little things up here and there, but mostly he kept it contained. As furious as he'd been at Zubilin/Zarubin/Vasily Mikhailovich for screwing up everything, something told him a great many juries were weighing him right now, so he buried his anger and was very careful about how he 'remembered' things.

Inevitably, the discussion came around to 'Chord'. For two long years, Jack Soble had dreamed of the day he'd be asked to tell the full story about that whole stupid disaster and would get to point fingers where fingers needed pointing: at Vasily Mikhailovich. Now it appeared they wanted to hear it, many different people, many different sides and factions, all with their knives out, so they could finally settle accounts with each other. Soble realised he would have to be very careful so as not to displease anyone, because enemies were the last thing he needed.

Soble concocted an acceptable story about how it hadn't been Vasily's fault any more than it had been Morros', and he told it, over and over, to different groups of listeners. Why had Chord gone so wrong? On whom should blame be laid? Should it be Stern? Was it Zarubin? Or was it 'John Frost', their name for Boris Morros?

If it had actually been up to Soble, he would have told everyone that the one to blame was, of course, Vasily Mikhailovich. Zarubin had been the one in charge. He should have seen right from the off that Stern and Morros were oil and water and could never work together, but he didn't because he chose to approach a business problem not with an open mind, as he should have done, but instead with a Chekist's characteristic deep disdain of money and for anyone tied up in it.

Anyone else would have seen that putting the two together would be problematic. Zarubin hadn't because in his mind all businessmen were exactly the same. Of course, Soble wasn't going to tell them that. Instead he said something about Stern and Boris being highly individualistic persons, which would have required Zarubin's own hands-on control. Soble said he was sure it would have worked had he been there to run it. It was a lie, but one they could all be forced to accept. What about John Frost? Should he be accorded blame?

Well, of course he should. Boris Morros had sold everyone a bill of goods, knowing full well he was going to change the whole game the moment he had Stern's $180,000 in his pocket. Boris Morros was a liar and a crook, and a scoundrel of the worst sort. He deserved every bit of blame that could be placed at his door, and in a just world, he would have been taken out and shot!

But, of course, he couldn't tell them that either. The last thing he needed was to get on the wrong side of Beria's friends, who were sure to see an attack on Boris Morros as an attack on them. So instead Jack Soble praised Boris as a canny Hollywood businessman, a man like themselves, who shot from the hip and could operate on intuition. He instinctively understood that a successful music company didn't need to record music themselves; they just needed to have the masters – and there are all kinds of ways to get masters. Boris Morros figured that out. He knows it and I know it and now you all know it, and you know who doesn't know it? Nobody in Hollywood, and no one in the American music recording industry.

Which meant the fall guy could only be one Alfred Kaufmann Stern, Wall Street financier, would-be plutocrat, dilettante communist, Jew and non-Russian. Was it, they would ask, because Alfred Stern was ultimately timid about going the distance to make the company a successful enterprise? Why wouldn't he do that?

Why? Soble wanted to shout out, but didn't. Why? Because Boris Morros, that rat bastard, that utter shit, had taken him for such a ride, spending Stern's money like it was actually *his*! And Zarubin set it all up so it would happen. Why else would he do it? Why else would he say Morros was bedding Alfred Stern's wife, when in all probability, the man who was doing it was Vasily Mikhailovich himself!

But Soble didn't. Instead he nodded a bit sadly and again and again told them yes, Stern was too timid, but then he'd say only that John Frost had taken risks and some aspects of the market turned out more volatile than anyone had expected. If only Alfred Stern had possessed the intestinal fortitude to double his bet, do whatever it took to get ahead of the market and bet on vinyl, by now we would all be rich and a certain record factory in west Los Angeles would be operating a cover for critical espionage operations in southern California. Again, if circumstances had allowed Comrade Zarubin to remain in America, the outcome might have been very different.

But who was the heavy in this lesson? Yes, it was Alfred Stern, Soble told them all. This wasn't even remotely true, but it was the only safe answer Soble could give, so he kept giving it. He also noticed that almost every time he said anything at all supportive of Zarubin, there was a little tremor of tension shooting among those gathered. Silent, invisible, exploding fireworks. But unless it was posed within questions directed at Soble, no one said anything about Zarubin. It seemed he was on everyone's minds, but nobody's lips. What did this mean?

⸙

They made Soble do a lot of drinking, which he wasn't used to, but he did his best. Though he knew better than to ask, there seemed to be a lot going on inside the walls at Moscow Center. During the drinking sessions things would be whispered into his ear, a different sort of fragment. Not everyone running foreign intelligence, at least not everyone in the illegal side, were Beria's men, but he was sticking them in. Beria owned everything, but had it laid out in little fiefdoms and suzerains. Soble didn't know any of it, though to everyone else, knowing it all, it was a matter of life and death. It had been a number of years since anything graver than a few people here and there being taken out and shot occurred. You could never tell when another purge might start; Beria was a bloodthirsty sod. Soble didn't think there was anybody there out for him. Why would there be? Soble was a nobody in the bristle trade. He preferred it that way. If they'd wanted to kill him, they'd have done it by now.

⸙

The telephone was ringing. Boris Morros picked it up. Speaking on the other end was someone who identified himself as a special agent with the FBI Los Angeles Field Office and could Mr Morros please come downtown and answer a few questions?

Boris Morros told them he'd be right down.

The reason Boris Morros' phone rang was because FBI Director Hoover had lately noticed the COMRAP investigation wasn't moving. Hoping to jolt it back to life, he wrote to the handful of field offices involved and instructed them to revisit whatever unfollowed-up leads they might have to see if anything worthwhile might have been overlooked. The only real thing the Los Angeles Field Office had was Boris Morros. After reviewing his file, they decided there was a chance he might still have something to tell them about Zubilin.

246

On the morning of 14 July 1947 they phoned his home and invited him in for a chat.

❧

It isn't known how Boris Morros was met when he came to the large federal building's entrance that morning. Was a special agent there waiting for him, to shepherd him through the lobby and hallways, or did he have to find his own way up to the FBI's Los Angeles Field Office? Either way, he was brought into a small room where at least one special agent was waiting. Morros introduced himself; so did everyone else. Morros got pointed to a chair. They showed him pictures of him with Zubilin and asked if he recognised him. Morros said he did. He was Vasily Zubilin, an official with the Soviet Embassy. Then they showed him photos they'd taken of Morros with two men. Could he identify them? Yes, he could. One was Alfred Stern, whom Zubilin had forced on Morros as a business partner. What about the other one? Finger tapping the photographs: Can you tell us his name? With a touch of smugness, Morros told the agents the man was Jack Soble. Great, and who is Jack Soble? Boris Morros told them he was the one who had replaced Zubilin. The two FBI men tried very hard not to look at each other. Then they asked him if he could tell them more about it. Boris Morros couldn't have gotten very far before the FBI men knew they'd struck gold.

The agents probably asked Morros if he would excuse them for just a moment. Once they were out of the room with the door shut behind them, they would whisper to each other that Hoover needed to be informed immediately and that a stenographer should be brought in. One would take off down the corridor while the other went back in and continued the conversation. A minute later the stenographer entered the room, followed by another. In a nearby office typists had set up and began typing the notes. From the transcripts, briefs were written up and then teletyped to Hoover, sometimes several times an hour.

But had they struck gold? It appeared they had. In a memo written 21 July 1947, just days after completing their initial interrogations, D. M. Ladd, Assistant Director for Domestic Intelligence, elatedly wrote Hoover that in his opinion, 'Information provided by Morros was of paramount significance,' and that his 'apparent willingness to cooperate may constitute the most significant development in the Bureau's coverage of Soviet espionage since the breaking of the "Corby" and "Gregory" cases more than eighteen months ago'. Ladd added that they'd now also found evidence from previous investigations which appeared to corroborate some of what Morros had said. 'The prior FBI investigation had shown Morros and Soble were in contact with each other between 1944 and 1945.' Ladd wrote Hoover, adding that, while it was unlikely they'd ever prove it, they had good reason to think Jack Soble might also be a mysterious someone previously mentioned in the Gregory case as 'unidentified Jack', whom the informant Elizabeth Bentley claimed was her superior.

Things were finally starting to come their way now. What they kept asking themselves was what could they do with this network without the Russians finding out? Some even suggested that if Soble were truly the non-entity Morros kept saying he was, was there any way their boy could be made to outshine Soble, replacing him and worming his way further into Moscow Center's heart? This seemed a possibility.

Surprisingly, Hoover did not share in their elation. If anything, the find left the Director chastened. Boris Morros was an accident. He had dropped onto their laps and the wonderful gold seam he represented was something that had just been sitting there for years in plain view, only nobody bothered to explore it, not even his own people. It irked him no end. To Hoover, Ladd's suggestion that the 'Jack' in this case might also be the 'Unidentified Jack' in another didn't bolster the find's value. All it told Hoover was that communist subversive infiltration was more pervasive than he'd imagined. The Commies were everywhere and had them outclassed, numerically and qualitatively. They had not grown lazy. They had infiltrated the fabric of American society. *We are in deep trouble.*

How many more were there? And it was his fault. He'd let the Bureau grow lax during the war and now this was their reward. In response to the Ladd memo, Hoover wrote: 'An angle giving me great concern is that we had some of these clues for some time and closed them out and only recently reviewed the case and re-opened it with these startling developments. How many other like situations exist right in our own files is what concerns me.'

Would it really be possible to take someone like Morros and feed him back to the Soviets? Could they take advantage of this situation and turn the spy ring around and use it to feed Moscow poisoned garbage? Would Hoover like that?

Hoover would, but Hoover also had a feeling that what Morros had said about all those communist spies might prove even more useful at home in the fight against communists, socialists, progressives, liberals, Jews, negroes and their disgusting America-hating ilk. Though he never told it to Ladd or anyone else, it would be the real motivation behind the FBI investigation known to history as MOCASE, or the 'Morros-Case', something which, even now, the FBI remains sensitive about.

28. SOBLE GOES
TO MEET ZARUBIN

One morning Jack Soble was sitting, half-dressed, in his hotel room waiting to hear if he'd be needed that day, when he got a call from the front desk telling him someone was there for him and that he should come down right away. Soble finished dressing, put on his coat and hat and went downstairs, wondering who it might be this time. They rarely told him ahead of time what he'd be doing on any given day. He might find himself being debriefed by one or several people. It would usually last until some preordained moment and then just stop. They wouldn't wind up what they were talking about to a logical conclusion; they'd just stop at whatever the last sentence was, close their notebooks, and not continue the discussion for sometimes days or even weeks, at which point he was expected to continue exactly where he'd left off. Sometimes there was never a second meeting. Jack Soble knew better than to fight it or try to out-think them.

The elevator brought him down to the lobby where he found a man in a bad suit who was going to take him someplace. Soble recognised him right away; he'd been Zarubin's driver back in America. He introduced himself as Prokhorov and told Soble that 'the old man wanted to talk'. They followed him outside to a parked automobile. They drove across Moscow and pulled up outside an apartment building. Inside was Zarubin, very happy to see him. Though no one else was there, it was obviously his home. They talked about things back in America: politics, baseball, how the networks were holding up. He wanted to know about Ester Rand and the Martins. Soble told him about his last meeting with the Martins and how badly it had gone. He'd assumed they were already a lot further along in the recruitment process. At this Zarubin smiled and gave a 'no use crying over spilt milk' shrug and that was that. They talked about other things for a while and then he told Soble something he'd already guessed: he'd fallen from favor with Moscow Center. Hearing this admission, Soble nodded sympathetically, but he knew better than to ask for details.

The discussion came around to Boris Morros. What did Soble think of the whole matter? Soble told him what a mess the whole business had been. Hearing how Morros had gone his own, new direction the moment Stern's money was in his pocket caused Zarubin to give a sad look, almost a smile of disappointment. He'd really expected better. Soble started talking about the record factory, but Zarubin waved his hands. He'd heard enough. This wasn't a post-mortem.

The conversation moved to the Sterns – Alfred and Martha. He grinned. Has Alfred Stern figured it out yet? Even the littlest bit? Probably not. Martha! He shook his head. Soble tried to feel amused. He told Zarubin how he'd tried to deactivate Morros two years earlier. How he'd pled his case and gotten permission, only to have it all rescinded a couple of days later. What was going on? Zarubin uttered nothing but his silence said everything: *Beria.*

So all that stuff about himself and Morros was true? Zarubin nodded. Apparently they worked together and Beria had a warm spot in his heart for Morros, something he didn't have for Zarubin, for some reason. Soble wondered if that had been the cause of his problems. Probably not. If that was the case, he'd simply have been liquidated. This had to be something else. *Best never to seek a god's favor.* Best when what happens in the Field stays in the Field. Soble nodded. He didn't need to be told such things.

So, Jack, what do you think of our friend in Hollywood? Talk to me. Good question, thought Soble. What indeed did he think of him? What can anyone say about Boris Morros without running the risk of liquidation? Only one thing. 'Boris Morros likes money,' Soble began. Zarubin appreciated his understatement, but he pressed him further. 'Do you trust him?' 'Do I trust him? Sure, I trust him. I trust him to be Boris Morros.' 'But do you trust him as a comrade?' 'Boris likes money,' Soble repeated.

'Do you think he could be a traitor?'

Soble was dumbfounded. To even say that!

'Do you?'

Jack told him he did.

'Why?'

Soble didn't know what to say. He just wanted to go home. He told Zarubin he trusted him because he trusted him and that Boris Morros was a comrade. Zarubin weighed Jack Soble's words, adding them to his scales for calculation. He told Soble that he'd received a letter from Martha, which he'd gotten via someone at the embassy in Washington, saying she thought Morros might be a double-agent. What did Soble think of that? Soble thought about it and then told Zarubin he supposed Martha had too much imagination. He didn't think he was a double-agent. Zarubin smiled and told him he didn't think so either.

After that Prokhorov drove Soble back. The days of debriefings continued. He'd find himself thinking about Boris Morros and wondered if there could be any truth to what Martha had alleged. He decided there couldn't be. The woman was a harridan, a scarlet woman, a royal pain in the neck. That Soble had made her husband out to be the heavy in all that Chord business was wrong, because he was the closest thing there was to an innocent, injured party. But God Almighty, he was an unbearable putz! Soble just hoped Boris Morros was following orders, doing his job and running the network. Because if he wasn't, there would be hell to pay.

Meanwhile, at FBI Headquarters in Washington, Hoover ordered the field offices to prepare reports on Jack and Myra Soble, Alfred and Martha Stern, plus another person associated with MOCASE whose name remains hidden to this day. Hoover then met with the Special Agent in charge of the New York Field Office, who'd flown down to brief the Director. They discussed Jack Soble and, since Morros had claimed he was Zubilin's replacement, tried to figure how he might fit in with the New York rezidentura, whom they'd had their eyes on for some time now. After that, the subject turned to Martha and Alfred Stern and how important it was to find out what it was they had going on with the Russians. As for Morros, they agreed he was probably telling the truth about some things but lying his head off about others. Even so, they thought Morros showed promise and that he might be used against the Soviets: to infiltrate the Soviet Secret Service, even to the point of possibly becoming their much-dreamed of 'Man in the Kremlin'. Hoover ordered discreet inquiries be made, along with surveillances so they could be certain Morros wouldn't double-cross them.

After that, Hoover went to Attorney General Tom C. Clark for authorisation to conduct surveillance on his list of purported Soviet spies. At the top of the list was Jack Soble, his wife Myra, followed by Alfred Stern, the millionaire financier, and his wife, the noted author Martha Dodd. The rest of the list included Jane Foster and her husband, George Zlatovsky, somewhere with the military in Austria; Leigh Melament, Zarubin's New York assistant; and all those others mentioned by Morros – a Miss Ester Rand, a Mrs Alice Martin, Ilya Wolston, Floyd C. Cleveland, and a handful of others that he didn't know much of anything about. Martha's brother Bill was also added to the list, even though Morros hadn't mentioned him.

On Hoover's orders, FBI Special Agent Aubrey S. Brent put together a preliminary report using available information on what they had gathered about Jack Soble. There wasn't much, and since nearly everything they discovered came from their naturalisation paperwork and his passport application, none of the information was more than a few months old. Up until then he'd been invisible. Jack Soble had been born Abromas Sobolevicius on 15 May 1903 in Vilkaviskis, Lithuania. He, his wife Myra and son Larry had entered the US in San Francisco less than two months before Pearl Harbor. At the time he noted his profession as 'boar bristle trade'. Currently, they resided in Apartment 1-L at 630 170th Street in Manhattan and owned and ran the S&V Cafeteria, a run-down place on Broadway and 74th. Just as Morros had told them, Jack Soble was away in France where, according to his passport application, he had gone to buy and run a boar bristle brush factory. Myra had stayed behind, running the business and raising their young son.

Hoping to find out more, the FBI put a cover on the Sobles' mail deliveries and a tap on their telephone and then sat back to see what came in. They yielded nothing. The Sobles didn't receive anything besides junk mail and Mrs Soble almost never used her phone. When it did ring and she answered it, which she didn't always do, she never said much. A couple of times someone did call asking about Jack, to which she said she didn't know, maybe in another month, before hanging up. Their bank records, when they got hold of them, didn't reveal much either. Reporting back to Hoover, the agents advised that it was unlikely they'd find out anything more before Soble returned.

⁓❦⁓

The Sterns were a somewhat different story, though in the end, the results were about the same. They were high-profile people with lots of money, a good deal of which they contributed to many different causes. They also had plenty of upper-crust friends and acquaintances, nearly all of whom were either communists, communist sympathisers, socialists, fellow travellers and the like. Hoover was ready for them.

Attorney General Clark had handed Hoover and Ladd a renewable one-year court order authorising visual and technical surveillance on the Sterns. Hoover immediately placed mail covers on their apartment, country home and at Alfred's office. Any letters coming to them were pulled out during the sorting and handed to a special agent, who'd open them using special techniques, log them, copy them, and re-insert them into their original envelopes before handing them back to the postman to deliver. This created a jurisdictional bottleneck, since the local post office handling the Sterns' mail was over the line in Connecticut, making it a task which could be carried out only by a special agent from the New Haven office. It probably took a while before a work-around could be thought up.

Tapping the Sterns' telephones proved an easier task, which was fortunate since both Martha and Alfred spent time on the phone. Rather than having to sneak in and place physical taps on their telephones, as they did in the past, the agents now listened in from the local telephone exchanges. Later, their authorisation was widened to allow microphones to be placed inside their walls. They had also started using a vacant, boarded-up house adjacent to one end of the Sterns' property, giving them a view of the Sterns outside at their patio, pool and tennis courts. In the city, sometimes they followed them around on the streets or in cars. Informants were also found: a doorman, already of the opinion the Sterns and their friends were a bunch of communists, readily agreed to keep an eye on their comings and goings. At their country house, they enlisted two local black teenage girls who had recently been hired. They wanted to get Ralph Scott, the Sterns' butler and handyman, to talk to them, but apparently he wouldn't. The FBI's note said that they should see if they could learn anything through Scott's brother who lived in Philadelphia at Lakewood-3-2801. Whether the lead was ever followed up is not known. What they had in place was good enough for the moment. The FBI's surveillance of Alfred and Martha Stern had begun.

❧

During that first month, the Sterns sent out and received plenty of mail, much of it in support of myriad left-wing causes and groups. They also spent time on the phone. At first what the FBI found out about them wasn't that surprising. They were rich commies who actively supported a variety of different liberal-leftist causes, just like all their rich, commie friends. Nearly everyone they rubbed shoulders with, the FBI already had files on. On the phone, Mrs Stern was a pro. She was always careful about what she said. She knew how to avoid mentioning specifics and didn't name names she didn't have to, seeming natural as she did it. The husband was not careful. He dropped names, said where he was going, where he'd been and what he thought about this and that. As they'd begun to suspect, Alfred was a sap. He might have been an investment genius, but he was an overbearing idiot. If anyone was the brains of the outfit, it had to be Martha.

But it turned out, for all that seemed to be going on with the Sterns, there wasn't much actually happening, certainly nothing you could take to the Attorney General. Alfred and Martha's social swirl might have entirely consisted of wealthy, socially prominent communists, sympathisers and assorted pro-Moscow types, but that wasn't the same as smuggling atomic secrets or conspiring to assassinate a Trotskyite. It wasn't even against the law. Moscow Center didn't have its thumbprint on any of it, at least not that they could see – yet. They wondered why that was. They'd expected to have something solid and indictable after a month of surveillance, but instead what they had couldn't even be considered chickenfeed.

Could this be because Jack Soble was still away in Europe somewhere and as a result the entire North American spy apparatus had decided to go on vacation? Soble was sold to them as Zubilin's replacement. They'd assumed that meant Soble had to be a spymaster equal to his mysterious predecessor. Maybe all he was was just a new case officer? Time would tell about that. And what about the others besides the Sterns, like Jane Foster and her husband? What about Floyd Cleveland, Mark Zborowsky, Ester Rand and all the others whom Morros professed only fragmentary knowledge about? Were they a coherent spy network or just a completely random hodge-podge of persons? In the end, July to August had been a bad first month. But they still had eleven months to make their case. Certainly something would come through by then.

There was one curious thing about the Sterns that needed to be mentioned, though, not that it was anything that could necessarily be considered 'espionage-related'. In the last year, Alfred and Martha had, in a short period of time, become extremely close friends with former Vice President Henry Wallace and his wife, Ilo. Wallace had recently bought a 115-acre farm and moved into the area following his firing by President Harry Truman from the post of Commerce Secretary after he'd given some speeches criticising the President for his increasingly hostile policies towards the Soviet Union. The Sterns had apparently already been acquainted in some capacity with Wallace and had reintroduced themselves when they'd moved in. The four hit it off and were now spending an almost inordinate amount of their free time together. On any given summer evening they might drop by the other's home for drinks, tennis, a swim in the pool, maybe dinner, and endless talk of politics and solving the world's problems, often into the wee hours.

It didn't need mentioning that Henry Wallace would certainly have been President at that moment had the leadership of the Democratic Party not conspired to have him replaced at the convention by Harry Truman, whom everyone at the time had considered a 'safe' non-entity senator from Missouri. But now, Truman was President and Wallace was in the political wilderness. Of course, it also went without saying that Wallace remained a very popular political figure and would likely be many people's choice were he to decide to run in the upcoming 1948 elections. Everyone assumed he would. The only question in their minds was whether Wallace would run as a Democrat or as an independent.

Neither Hoover, Ladd nor the FBI men watching then knew whether or not they should be concerned.

29. THE WORLD
ACCORDING TO ILO

Ilo Wallace couldn't have been anyone's idea of a Democratic Party politician's wife. She didn't like small talk or rubbing elbows or the endless rough and tumble of left-wing American politics, being neither left-wing, liberal, nor even Democratic. Ilo was from Iowa, where she and Henry and everyone she knew had always been staunchly Republican. Of course, all that had ended in the 1920s, after Warren Harding's and the subsequent other two Republican presidents' categorical refusal to enact any policy or price supports put a good many Iowa farmers out of business. For a while they supported Progressive candidates like Bob LaFollette, but they had never been Democrats, not even when out campaigning for Roosevelt in 1932. Party loyalty hadn't been something Roosevelt required. Besides, he'd come to Wallace not just for his support, but for his ideas. He hadn't required it when making Henry his Secretary of Agriculture, possibly the most powerful job in Washington after FDR himself. But then, as anyone would tell you, in Iowa and everywhere else nobody understood agriculture and the problems facing farmers better than her husband, Henry Wallace.

The only reason she and Henry were Democrats was because back in 1936, FDR had been forced to bow to Party pressure and made him join. They didn't like that Henry was Secretary of Agriculture three whole years and still an independent. FDR had allowed Henry an almost free hand running things and not just agricultural policy, but also rural electrification, farm loans and so much else. With all that, it didn't seem too great a price to pay, so they went along and officially became Democrats.

This unfortunately meant the Wallaces were now required to participate in Democratic Party rallies and dinners. It was all right for Henry since he loved giving speeches and talking with people about issues and politics. But Ilo didn't. She also didn't care much for Jews and when it came to black people, she expressly did not want to have to talk with them or allow them to get close enough to touch her, or her clothing. This was not good, considering Henry Wallace, her husband, was the undeclared leader not just of the Democratic Party's liberal left-wing, but also all the liberal, progressive and left-wing groups outside of the Democratic Party, including the communists, which, taken together now, two years after FDR's passing, constituted an extremely large and important voting bloc. Which was why so many people thought Henry Wallace had a good shot at becoming the next President of the United States.

People were angry at how quickly Truman had ditched the New Deal and begun squaring off against the different unions. They didn't like Truman's foot-dragging on civil rights issues or his hostility towards the Russians. Unlike Truman, Wallace still proudly carried the New Deal banner, high for all the world to see. Ilo's reservations about all this was something Wallace's inner circle were adamant to keep contained. The solution was obvious: do not drag her into any political events and maintain a *cordon-sanitaire* around the area they resided – South Salem, Lewisboro, Ridgefield and environs.

Back in Manhattan, Wallace's days were spent in the fray: writing articles from his editor's desk at *The New Republic* that everyone read and commented on, travelling around the country giving speeches before thousands, endlessly meeting with different people and organisations, having strategy sessions, keeping the undeclared coalition together. But afterwards, he went home to Farvue Farm, where he was just another ordinary rich guy with a 115-acre plot of land. It was a fine solution and everyone was happy, at least up to a point. Much as Ilo liked knowing her husband's minions were not going to show up uninvited, and she would not have to attend functions, she wasn't stupid. She had no intention of letting a swarm of left-wing crazies have free rein with her Henry. She needed to know what was going on among the backrooms. She needed to know who was coming on strong and who was trying to nudge him, and in what direction. Who was using him? Where were the obvious alliances? Who was commie? That was key. She did not want her husband getting caught up in some communist-led conspiracy. She knew they were out there. There were the obvious ones and there were the more clandestine ones. What Ilo needed desperately was someone she could trust, who would serve as her eyes and ears. Luckily for Ilo, Martha and Alfred, their new best friends, were just that.

Ilo had never been someone who made friends easily or quickly. She was also sixty-two and had lived within a certain level of society far too long to trust anyone just popping in out of the blue, seeking friendship. Thirty-three years of being married to the most brilliant, successful man around had only made her hyper-aware of all the people that came out of the woodwork, constantly worming their way to Henry. New friendships were not something she regarded with anything but extreme wariness. Better no friends than friends you couldn't trust. She had constructed a world where strangers didn't just breeze in offering companionship. But with Martha and Alfred, it appears this was exactly what happened.

But then, they hadn't exactly come completely from out of the blue. Martha and Alfred were people they were already nominally acquainted with, at least Henry was. He'd met Alfred once in 1944 with Boris Morros. He was aware of Stern's role as an activist-donor and his connection to Vito Marcantonio and the American Labor Party crowd. As for Martha, they'd met ten years earlier at some function where she was accompanying her father. They got into some deep conversation and had kept in touch since. In 1945, Martha's novel *Sowing the Wind* and Henry's book *Sixty Million Jobs* both came out at roughly the same time, and they did a friendly copy-swap. A year later, Wallace and Truman had a high-profile parting of ways over Wallace's vocal disagreement with the President over what Wallace considered his stance towards Russia, causing the Wallaces to decamp from Washington.

But instead of going back to Des Moines, they relocated to New York. Henry assumed editorship of *The New Republic* and bought the 115-acre farm up on the Connecticut border which, as fate would have it, was just up the road from the country home of Alfred and Martha Stern.

About the time they arrived, Henry received a letter from Martha and Alfred welcoming them to the neighborhood, telling him how greatly they admired and respected him. But then Martha followed it up with a letter to Ilo, repeating what she'd said to Wallace, but now directing her admiration towards Ilo and letting her know it was she, and not her husband, whose friendship Martha was seeking.[1] Ilo was bowled over. Martha Dodd Stern, the world-renowned, glamorous, terribly witty journalist, author and witness to some amazing recent history, wanting to be ... *girlfriends!*

Ilo had spent her entire adult life being the blocker, the hazard, the thing doing its best to get in the way and intercept whoever it was trying to cozy up to Henry, whether it was a man, a woman or a task force or committee. Ilo had always been the obstacle, never the object. She had never been in anyone's sights, not until now. Now, a glamorous, exciting woman, easily twenty years her junior, was expressing her admiration and desire to be her friend.

It appears Ilo found herself beguiled, almost in spite of herself, by Martha's offer. Did Ilo make any women friends, real ones, during her dozen-odd years in Washington? Quite possibly not. No one goes to Washington to make friends. Besides, the whole time they were there, their official residence was a hotel. Now, finally, they were back in the country, even if it was Westchester County, with a 115-acre farm, big enough that Henry could run all the plant-hybrid and animal-breeding experiments he could dream up without any of those political chancers showing up and bothering them. And now it turned out Alfred and Martha Stern were living nearby with a nice little spread of their own, plus a pool and tennis courts, which was good since, as it happened, Ilo and Henry were both crazy for the game. They also loved talking politics, business, science and housing policy and solving the world's problems over drinks. They started getting together and within a very short time it was like they'd all known each other for years.

Ilo felt safe with the Sterns. She knew she could trust them. From the beginning, they made it clear to Ilo their loyalty was with them. For Ilo, what clinched it was how devotedly Martha had taken care of her sick son that autumn – for more than a month while she herself had come down with something. Ilo would often drop by and watch her give him penicillin shots, then holding him, comforting him, even though she could just as easily have left it to his nurses. She had to admit that for all Martha's kittenish, hard-drinking ways, she was the right sort; someone Ilo knew she could trust, come hell or high water!

30. A LITTLE WEEKEND BASH

On 27 August 1947, while reading through the Sterns' outgoing mail, the FBI's New Haven Field Office learned[1] Alfred and Martha were throwing a bash that weekend. The guest list included Paul Robeson, Lilian Hellman, Frederick Field, Paul Trilling, Leopold Stokowski and Margaret Bourke-White; all the usual top-drawer luminaries of the Left. Also coming was Ignace Zolotowski and Miodrag Markovic, the Yugoslav Consul General whom the FBI presumed was also a Soviet spy. The New Haven Field Office duly informed the New York City Field Office, which immediately tried to find someone to infiltrate it, but they were not successful. Luckily they had planted microphones inside just two weeks before. Also, since it was a clear and balmy summer evening, much of the party took place outdoors, around the Sterns' pool and patio, which allowed the FBI to easily observe it from their numerous hidden vantage points. They learned the party's purpose had been to spur discussion among influential left-wingers about Wallace running as a third-party candidate. They also learned Martha had successfully prevailed on Ilo Wallace to sit at a table with Paul Robeson, though Robeson had to agree beforehand not to touch or talk to her.

A third-party candidacy? Hoover had to have been scratching his head in complete bewilderment. It didn't make any sense! If what he was seeing were Moscow Center's fingerprints, why would they be doing this? Hoover had no doubt the Soviets were planning to conquer America and turn it communist, but then how could getting Wallace to run on a third-party ticket be part of that plan?

The NKVD had to know third-party candidates didn't have a prayer of winning.

The FBI had had its eye on Wallace for years, both because of his increasingly leftward political leaning as well as his standing as a high government official. Their clippings files of articles about him and texts of speeches he gave were extensive. By now they also knew who among his people they could go to and pump for information. What they were hearing was that Martha Dodd Stern and her idiot, millionaire husband Alfred had come out of nowhere that spring and propelled themselves into Wallace's innermost circle. Alfred was suddenly one of Wallace's closest advisors, something that left many miffed. Martha had gotten herself onto his speechwriting team. Though she seemed to fit in nicely there, something she'd done earlier that year still had some people fuming.

That spring, when Wallace's people decided he'd go on an extensive tour of Europe and the Middle East, Martha immediately elbowed her way in and put herself in charge of making arrangements for the French leg, since she claimed she knew all the most important left-wing and moderate French politicians. In reality, Martha knew Pierre Cot, currently a member of French Parliament and a Zarubin-recruit, and some others she knew through her brother. Not knowing this, they let her help. They impressed to Martha that the hosting delegation needed to represent broad-based political groups and voices. Martha nodded and told them not to worry. She then wrote to Cot, who assembled a delegation of thinly disguised communist front groups to meet and talk with Wallace. When this meeting happened the French press immediately noticed and the ones that weren't communist howled. The American correspondents picked up on it and the editorial cartoonists had a field day drawing up Wallace like he was a fool.

Among those still angry was C. B. 'Beanie' Baldwin, Wallace's longtime top deputy. Like his boss, Baldwin had grown increasingly leftward. Beyond the New Deal, he had no love for the Democrats, but communism was farther than he was willing to go. Whatever warmth he might have felt toward 'Uncle Joe' Stalin and Russia during the war had cooled. For a long time he had been quite cordial with Alfred, but now that rope of geniality had begun to fray. Beanie and Alfred both advocated for a third-party run, though it turned out for entirely different reasons. Beanie Baldwin thought establishing a progressive third party was something America needed and that if enough people united behind it, there would no longer need to be any compromising with the Democrat bigots, bankers and bosses. Alfred, Martha and the other 'not-communists' saw a third party as the best way for the communists to control the whole leftist bloc.

All through the summer, Baldwin, Stern and the others worked to convince Wallace to do a third-party run. Wallace, not being sure what he should do, remained aloof and continued to speak vaguely as if he intended to remain with the Democrats. The main reason for this was that one of Wallace's closest friends, Frank Kingdon, a prominent radio commentator and liberal activist, thought otherwise. A longtime advocate of third parties, Kingdon had recently changed his mind and now believed Wallace needed to stick with the Democrats. Wallace didn't know what to do. He'd listened to Kingdon and to Beany Baldwin, Alfred Stern and others. Kingdon had told him he could either run as a third party, or as Democrat, in which case he would be defeated by Truman and end up having to support him in the November election. The only real question was going to be how much of Wallace's progressive agenda could he bring to the table alongside the bigots, bankers and bosses? Wallace probably knew Kingdon was right and could also guess the next point he was about to make. The communists were not getting to the table. The United States was not going to become friendlier with the Soviets. Wallace didn't know what to do. He didn't like communists, but he didn't think he should abandon them and the thought of having to sit at the same table as those other people disgusted him. Was it even worth it? Wallace didn't know.

On 24 September 1947, the FBI was alarmed to learn Martha and Alfred had become the latest targets for popular, red-baiting columnist Westbrook Pegler's invective. In that and the next day's *New York Journal American*, Pegler used the recent publication of a book full of colorful, often fanciful tales of New Deal Washington. He mentioned one about an ambassador FDR had appointed 'by accident': Martha's late father, William E. Dodd. According to the tale, FDR had wanted Walter E. Dodd, a professor at Yale, but the name FDR's flunky pulled out of the telephone directory was the Dodd chairing the History Department at the University of Chicago. Since FDR knew neither man personally, the mistake went through unnoticed, until it was a done deal. After that, Pegler began referring to Dodd as 'Wrong Dodd', 'Phonebook Dodd' or simply the 'Stupid Envoy' who'd prematurely fouled up relations with Hitler, all to the benefit of the Soviet Union. But it turned out that the real reason Pegler had brought it up was to direct his venom at Martha, along with Alfred and her brother Bill. When it came to the Phonebook Dodd's offspring, Pegler told his readers, 'the fruit didn't fall far from the tree'. He described how Martha, Alfred and Bill were the supporting angels for all these different leftist-commie-pinko organisations and causes. It led Pegler to venture that by sending Dodd to Berlin, FDR had really sent someone who was in fact a 'Soviet ambassador'.

Hoover wondered how Martha had suddenly become a target. He knew how Pegler operated; he was doing this at someone's behest. Whose? Had it been fed to him by someone on the House Un-American Activities Committee (HUAC)? They'd better not be thinking about subpoenaing the Sterns and forcing them to testify in front of their headline-hungry committee. The last thing Hoover wanted was for the Sterns to get spooked. Getting HUAC to back off was just about impossible. These guys were permanently facing re-election. It wouldn't matter that the Bureau had spent months or years working on the case only to have it blown. Another fear crossed Hoover's mind. Could the information HUAC was feeding Pegler come to them from someone in the Bureau? This thought frightened Hoover more than anything.

One afternoon, following a long day of debriefing, Jack Soble returned to his hotel and found Zarubin and Prokhorov waiting for him in the lobby with wrapped packages of food and jugs of wine. They all went up to Soble's room and had a party. They ate and drank and sang songs and talked endlessly about America and laughed at the stories they told each other about the crazy things they'd done. But then after a while Zarubin got a little morose. Things weren't good. They had their knives out for him, he told Soble, with great bitterness. But then Zarubin smiled and said he'd show them. He asked Soble that when he got back to New York, he should find Lucy Booker and greet her for him. Give her some money, tell her who it's from. Do this for me. Soble promised he would. As for the others, Morros, the Sterns, he said nothing. Then he grew sullen again and told Soble that his son had TB and that he probably contracted it while they were living in Greenwich Village. After that Zarubin got very drunk. But before he passed out, he admitted to Soble that he was not in good standing with the Soviets. Who knew what was going to happen, so this would probably be the last time they'd see each other. After that, he was out. Soble helped Prokhorov put him to bed. For a while they stood and looked at him. 'It's not fair what's happening to him,' said Prokhorov sadly. 'This is the man who stole the atom bomb.' Eventually Prokhorov dozed off in a stuffed chair. Soble did the same in another. When morning came, Soble's phone rang to summon him for another day's meetings. Zarubin was still sound asleep in the bed, while Prokhorov half-dozed in his chair. When Soble returned that evening, there was no sign they'd ever been there. He never saw either again.

⁕

According to a report from Special Agent John R. Murphy of the New York City Field Office, on 10 October 1947, Alfred and Martha Stern met again with Zolotowski and discussed Palestine and biological warfare. Murphy reported that four days later Stern met with Wallace advisor Lou Frank, who mentioned the Zolotowski visit and said that 'the material was good and that he would use it in the Baltimore speech'. The next week Wallace told the crowd America's nuclear monopoly was meaningless since biological warfare was every bit as deadly as an atomic bomb, but that it was within the competence of most small, half-developed nations to manufacture biological weapons.

Ilo Wallace admitted to Martha that she didn't know what to make of Martha's friends Zolotowski and Markovic. Were these men communist? Martha assured her they were not. They simply considered Wallace a 'great man' and they looked to him for leadership.

Ilo listened to what her friend had to say and she accepted it as the truth.[2]

The FBI never had any doubt Zolotowski and Markovic were spies of some sort; it went without saying. Were they working for Moscow Center? Probably not. Were they part of any of the networks? Probably not. Were they worth following full time? No, intermittently, maybe, if only to get an idea of who they were meeting with. Besides, even if you could nail them for something, the worst that could happen is they'd get sent home and replaced with someone not as easy to spot.

When the investigation of Martha and Alfred began in July, top among the priorities was finding good confidential informants. Hoover had a feeling that this particular case might end up in a courtroom, which meant the evidence they came up with needed to be legally admissible. This initially proved difficult. It wasn't that there weren't people who knew them that they could make talk, it was that none of them knew Alfred or Martha that well and they needed them to be close enough that their evidence would be legally admissible. What they were getting off Boris Morros probably wouldn't stand up in a courtroom. The man was simply too much of a liar.

Martha proved a much more difficult target than they'd initially imagined. During the war years, she ran a literary salon out of her lush, Upper West Side apartment. The artistic and literary elite of the day flocked there. The Sterns, needless to say, put on a good spread and it was not unknown for some to get lucky with Martha, the hostess, who definitely had it! As for Alfred, although he was generally regarded as a tendentious bore, the scale of his political activity and patronage demanded he be listened to. The Sterns were well regarded socially within New York's left-wing elite and got around a good deal. Martha knew a lot of people, but not closely. She ran at a velocity few people could match for very long. There were a number of women she was friendly with but not really any 'girlfriends'. There were indications that Martha might be into women, but nothing definitive was ever said about it.[3] With guys it was different. Most never got anywhere. The ones who did, she'd be friends or lovers with for a while and then move on. With some, there was a cordiality which sometimes endured, sometimes not. Whatever the case, it wasn't something Martha ever talked about and she expected her lovers to do the same. Either way, the FBI wasn't getting much.

With Alfred, many men claimed they knew him on the basis of a business luncheon. They didn't have to know him very well to say he had a certain acumen when it came to business investments. They could also mention his interest in liberal politics and the American Labor Party and public housing issues. They could also say he was a know-it-all, but, as the FBI investigators quickly learned, you could reach that conclusion without having to know him all that well:

> It would not appear from preceding information that inform-
> ant T-17 was a close personal friend of Mr. Stern's ... In
> December 16, 1946 Stern wrote a letter to the above inform-
> ant regarding purely business matters, addressed in a formal
> tone ... Reply of informant to Stern dated Dec. 17 1946,
> enclosing a copy of Stern's investment portfolio, stated, 'It
> was nice to renew your acquaintance,' and was also in formal
> tones.

Not having friends to inform on him, Alfred Stern instead had private bankers, and the flash of an FBI badge was all it took to get them talking. Both described Stern as an extremely demanding know-it-all who required them to do a lot for him: travel tickets, hotel reservations, letters of introduction, arranging meetings, foreign banking privileges, tax advice. They did it all happily and with the greatest efficiency and discretion because Alfred Stern's investments made money and that made money for them in turn. Stern's business interests were diverse, ranging from housing construction, small factories, pharmaceuticals, chemicals, vinyl, business opportunities in South America, the music business. They'd discuss import-export, trade finance and other things. Politics? Left-wing politics? Russia? Not really, but they did recall him continually running finances for different left-wing and progressive groups, but there was nothing really to any of it. Money came in and out, most only for a couple of months. Really? Nothing to it! During the ten years Stern banked at Chase, his account had been handled almost exclusively by one Dusan Tripp, who kept extensive notes of his every dealing with

Stern, including his involvement with Boris Morros. This from January 1944:

> I was Mr. Stern's guest for luncheon today. We discussed his new connection with Mr. Boris Morros, with whom he expects to start a music publishing enterprise, later on may do some moving picture productions.
>
> Feb. 11 1944 notation by Mr. C. B. Lundquist indicating writer had been invited by Stern to attend showing of Boris Morros' production of 'Tales of Manhattan' at 20th Century Fox Studios. Also present were Mrs. Stern, Mr. Morros and representatives from Lehman Brothers and Loomis Sayles.

Tripp journal entry, 26 October 1944:

> I called on Stern, who is now a partner in the Boris Morros Music Corporation, Hollywood, California. They have a subsidiary called American Recording Artists, manufacturers of music records. He asked me to obtain an introduction to the production manager at Celanese Corp. of America in order to discuss a certain new process they have for manufacturing records ... Stern will see Mr. William Lester in this connection.
>
> On May 8, 1945, Tripp of Chase advised Stern had invited him to lunch and told him he had severed his connection with the Boris Morros M. C. and had sold his stock interest to Morros and that he had no further interest in that company.

Asked about the import-export pharmaceutical businesses, Tripp explained that Stern was very interested in trade with Latin America, and had investments with companies in Cuba and Mexico and was very interested in that market. Inter-American Pharmaceutical Corporation and Trade Development Corporation had both been set up to buy and sell pharmaceutical products for the global export market, though the initial emphasis would be on Latin America.

Inter-American hadn't worked out. They'd worked one deal, there had been problems with delivery, followed by disagreements over profit distributions. It was dissolved after that. Tripp had the names of the two partners for the first: Dr Irving V. Sollins and Dr Robert Soblen. The special agents already knew Robert Soblen was Jack Soble's brother, but who was Sollins? Hoover ordered his agents to find out.

❦

Interestingly, in Moscow, Jack Soble was being asked the same questions. Who is Irving Sollins? Soble shrugged. All he knew was that Sollins was someone in Washington that Stern and his brother Robert knew. They didn't like his answer. But is he a fellow-countryman? Soble assumed he was but didn't know. Why? The problem was they suspected Sollins was part of 'the Sound': a vast Washington, DC-based network operated by the secretive Yakov Golos. It if was true, then all three comrades were members of three completely separate networks and for them to be associating with each other was a flagrant violation of the rules of 'konspiritsia'. The interrogator fumed. The American comrades were always doing this? Why? At this point, Soble might have answered 'Because they're Americans. Americans like to take the initiative and do things on their own and associate with whomever they please, rules of konspiritsia be damned.'

❦

It couldn't have taken the FBI very long to learn that Dr Irving Sollins was a medical doctor living and working just outside Washington in Bethesda. His short-lived business partnership with Stern and Soblen was just one of a number of ventures he was involved in, none particularly lucrative. A year earlier he'd worked for UNRRA, which ended when he was fired for buying and selling pharmaceuticals from agency stockpiles as they were being declared surplus. Apparently Sollins and Stern became acquainted through the growing friendship networks which permeated Washington's then vast left-wing community. Did the FBI need to look deeper into Sollins? It was decided they did.

31. SOMEPLACE NICE FOR LUNCH

Myra Soble had also been reading Westbrook Pegler's columns in the newspaper. Her English not being that good, she had to wrestle with Pegler's trademark breezy patter, his nicknames and coded words in order to figure out what he was saying about Martha and what its meaning might be. She remembered Zubilin once telling them that Martha's father had been *nomenklatura*, did something with Hitler for FDR who'd sent him and family, which included Martha, to Berlin. But then there was this thing about phonebooks which she did not understand at all. *Bad Dodd? Stupid Envoy?* Myra probably got a nasty laugh out of that, though mostly Myra Soble was worried. To her, Martha only meant problems that didn't need to exist. As a spy, Myra saw it all very simply; she was from the shadows, and so was Jack, his brother, their cousins in Quebec and now France, and for all she knew, everybody else involved in the global boar bristle trade. They all believed in conducting their business without being noticed. It was the same as being invisible. That's how they liked it. They recoiled at working around anyone drawn to the spotlight and attracting attention. And attracting attention was something that came naturally to that *kurva* Martha Dodd Stern!

What was it about America that drew rich people to communism like flies to shit? Myra so hoped Moscow would let them drop the Sterns as agents. Maybe they'd say yes and that'd be it with those people. That would be wonderful! Why did Moscow think so highly of them? Zubilin told them she'd been some kind of operational hero in

Berlin before the war, but Myra couldn't imagine what spectacular operational things she might have done, unless it involved being a whore.

One day there was a knock on Myra Soble's door. She opened it to find a prosperous-looking Boris Morros smiling in the hallway. He'd just arrived from Los Angeles, he explained, and was inviting her and little Larry out 'someplace nice' for lunch. This wasn't something Myra normally ever did, but this time she accepted. Boris was, after all, a comrade and she was bored out of her mind, so why not? As he promised, the restaurant was nice. Boris was very good with Larry and had him laughing, and all the while he regaled her with stories about all the different movie stars he knew. All in all, it was very pleasant. Inevitably he asked when Jack might return. She told him she didn't know. Boris nodded and didn't ask any more questions or say anything business-related until the end. As he was helping Myra and little Larry into a cab, he told her to let Jack know everything with everybody was good. She took that to mean the networks. She nodded and they said goodbye.

A few days later the FBI listeners overheard Alfred Stern phoning Myra, telling her he'd be giving a speech that evening at an elementary school near her. He suggested she come, and that perhaps afterwards they could meet for a drink. They heard her telling Alfred she'd 'see about it'. When he gave the speech, the FBI had some of its people in attendance, but Myra never showed up.

One day, not long after his final drunken get-together with Zarubin and Prokhorov, Jack Soble found himself brought before Pyotr Fedotov, Moscow Center's head of foreign intelligence, who informed him that his time in Moscow was almost over and that he'd soon be free to travel back to France, though he should not travel back to America for at least another month. Soble nodded, knowing better than to ask the reason. Then Fedotov asked what he thought of Boris Morros. Before he could assemble a version of the story he told everyone else, Fedotov grinned and said, 'He likes money, doesn't he?' Soble grinned back and assured him those rumors were all true. Fedotov then told Soble about Morros' latest scheme. 'He thinks he can ride us,' Fedotov said. 'When you get back I want you to tell him we find his ideas very interesting and quite possibly something we'd be willing to invest in, but it will require additional study on our part. Suggest that he continues to keep us informed so that we know about developments in this area so we can move quickly should the time come. Can you do that?' Soble assured him he could. 'Good,' said Fedotov. 'We also think Boris Morros is a good comrade. He just needs to be kept motivated.'

The discussion turned to the Sterns. Fedotov observed that Soble wasn't using them at all and asked if there was a problem. Soble answered that there wasn't much they could use them for anymore. He described how Alfred Stern appeared to be trying to set up businesses Moscow Center could use for fronts. Fedotov seemed to take that information without reaction. What about Martha? Soble explained how she'd published another book and that they'd adopted a boy who was now two. Soble acknowledged her willingness to help out any way she could, but there simply wasn't anything. Fedotov then mentioned how the Sterns had complained about him to Choudenko. Soble nodded. They had complained to him about Choudenko as well. But again, neither he nor Choudenko had any work for them. Fedotov then mentioned how Martha had gone to Comrade Sorokin at the embassy in Washington, offering to serve in any capacity. If he can find any use for them, he's welcome to them, Soble answered. Then Fedotov asked if Soble was aware that the Sterns had of late become quite friendly with the former American vice president Henry Wallace. Was Soble aware of this? Yes, Soble answered, the Sterns had informed him of this. Didn't Soble think this presented a worthwhile opportunity? Soble shrugged. He didn't know. She says he is considering running for president next year. Soble didn't say or do anything. Well, didn't Soble think it might be important? Soble shrugged. How do Americans feel about Harry Truman? Soble answered that nobody was crazy about him. He's not Roosevelt? No, he's not Roosevelt. Do Americans miss Roosevelt? Yes, but missing someone is not going to bring them back. But doesn't Wallace remind people of Roosevelt? Soble answered that it didn't mean they'd vote for him in an election. It would be very good for us if they did. Perhaps, but they won't, was Soble's answer. But are you sure? Soble wasn't sure. Mrs Stern said she and her husband were going to pursue the Wallace candidacy. Would you be willing to keep an eye on it? Jack Soble told him that what was going to happen would happen and that any involvement by the Soviets in any form would be of no benefit and much possible risk if anything went wrong. He could have added that anything Alfred Stern was involved in ran a high possibility of something going wrong, but he didn't. Even so, Fedotov seemed to get his point. For a long moment Fedotov didn't say anything, but then he mumbled something about Martha once being one of the great spies in her day. It was too bad her talents got squandered like they did. The next day Soble boarded a train to Paris.

✦

Jack Soble returned to New York sometime in November. He summoned Boris Morros who, to Soble's surprise, arrived without any of his usual difficulties, claiming he had to come anyway for business. Morros arrived looking happy and prosperous, just as Myra had described his earlier visit. He also wasn't alone. He now had a personal assistant, a tall, good-looking young man, obviously a gentile, named Bob Burton. Morros explained that Bob was the son of a friend and he had agreed to take him under his wing and teach him the entertainment business for the grand sum of $50 a week. Things were going exceedingly well business-wise, he told Jack. He'd pulled off a number of nice deals and, at the moment, was sitting pretty.

Soble briefed Morros on his meetings in Moscow. Things had changed there, he explained. Soviet intelligence had reorganised again. He also told Morros that Vyacheslav Molotov had taken a personal interest in him and had asked why Morros wasn't being used more effectively. He didn't mention the report Martha had sent to Zarubin denouncing Morros as a double-agent. Instead he listened approvingly while Morros listed everything he'd accomplished running the networks while Soble was away. It was good. He let Morros know he'd be taking more responsibility for the networks, since Soble would be selling the S&V Cafe during the next year or so and focusing more on operations abroad.

Following the meeting, Morros contacted his FBI handlers, who, while happy the meeting had gone well, did not like the idea of Soble setting up permanently in France, since that meant his case would get taken over by the CIA. As for the Sterns, they wondered why Soble hadn't made any effort to contact them.

On 22 November 1947, a periodic FBI progress report relating to the MOCASE investigation indicated their search for information on the Sterns brought them to Albany, New York, for records from the State Board of Dental Examiners on one James A. Kickering. About all they learned was that Kickering was originally from Florida and had graduated from the Howard University School of Dentistry in 1925. They also sought information on Dr Milla Wolkind, also a dentist and 'possibly the mother of Beatrice Halpern van Tassel', the wife of Alfred J. van Tassel, President of the Trade Development Corporation, a company established by Alfred Stern.

Special agents also learned that van Tassel had only recently moved to New York City with his family from Alexandria, Virginia. With this information a request to obtain records went to the Virginia State Motor Vehicle Bureau. Once they started digging into his Washington, DC connection they found his name listed among people in contact with Nathan Gregory Silvermaster, who headed up one of the most elusive Washington-based Soviet spy rings.

The investigation of Irving Sollins was also yielding some results. They learned that in 1928 he had travelled to the Soviet Union on a false passport and that sometime afterwards he'd gotten a valid one which he'd also used to travel to Russia. Sometime after that, the Department of State received a complaint from the father of Sollins' former wife that 'Sollins is a great friend of "Spy Jacobson"', a reference to David Werner Jacobson, an American citizen convicted as a Soviet agent in Finland in 1934. After that, Sollins' passport was revoked. It had never been reissued and Sollins had apparently not travelled abroad since then.[1] They also learned that over the years he had used a number of aliases: Samuel Bronstein, Samuel Broun, Sam Brown. The investigation continued.

At some point Special Agent J. Harold Glasscock began looking for Harris A. Rohtman, Sollins' former father-in-law, to see if he might elucidate on his old accusations against Sollins, only to find that the none of the Bureau's New York indices showed any references to anyone named 'Rohtman'. The Credit Bureau of Greater

New York was also 'searched against Rohtman's name with negative results'.

> 45 West 43th St, the address which we previously reported as Rohtman's residence in 1936 is exclusively a business building. Louis Goldstein, Superintendent at the building since 1919, advises that Harris Rohtman formerly operated a business known as 'Classic Embroidery,' on the 11th floor of the building. In 1940 the business was moved to an unknown address and the business associate thought to have been Rohtman's son-in-law came to the building sometime after Classic Embroidery had moved therefrom and advised Goldstein that Rohtman had died. Goldstein could not recall anything further about Classic Embroidery or about the Rohtman family.[2]

Sometime after that the FBI found out from an informant that Irving Sollins had been a contact for a Dr Josef Brumlik, a Czechoslovak citizen attached to UNRRA as well as the Czechoslovak Economic Service. He had been associated with the Czechoslovak Consulate since 1941 and during that period had travelled to Mexico where he had dealings with the Czechoslovak Consulate. Brumlik had trained at Charles University in Prague and his brother was still there and 'believed leaning to the left'. Then the informant mentioned that Brumlik had met with Arne Laurin, a 'suspected Czech [Nazi] agent', and a top guy in Czech intelligence.

It went on like this for a long time. It always seemed like they might have found a smoking gun, but it was never good enough. Both Sollins and van Tassel had many left-wing dealings in Washington. The fact that they were acquaintances with people linked to Soviet spy rings just wasn't enough. Eventually both were dropped as subjects of interest from the MOCASE investigation for more promising ones.

Prior to the autumn of 1947, Martha and Alfred had been very careful about not aligning themselves with any of the factions fighting over Wallace, keeping clear of the endless machinations. Being the

Wallaces' personal friends, they didn't have to pass muster with anyone. Everyone knew they were left-wing and progressive. Alfred was close friends with Vito Marcantonio and his American Labor Party, but clearly everyone took it for granted neither were communists. Around Henry and Ilo, Martha and Alfred were the picture of moderation. They could objectively recognise the reasons for a third-party candidacy while at the same time seeing how remaining with the Democrats was the best way to force change.

Unlike everyone else in Wallace's camp, Martha and Alfred's loyalty lay directly with the Wallaces and not with any group. They were their friends, their confidants and advisors. Martha and Alfred didn't have to vie for Wallace's ear. Anytime he needed advice or a sounding board, he came to them. They were so close that rather than needing to exert any influence in a political direction, Martha and Alfred instead seemed to tack with him. It went on like that throughout the spring and summer of 1947. But then, sometime during the autumn, Martha and Alfred stopped tacking and began privately urging Wallace to make a third-party run. By the end of November he had made up his mind.

On 2 December, Wallace held an informal meeting at Jo Davidson's studio, where he announced his decision to run to a select group of his friends. Frank Kingdon had been purposefully left out, which created some problems, since besides being a leading supporter, he was also PCA co-chair, alongside Davidson. When Kingdon heard the news, he did not believe Wallace had gone behind his back. On 4 December, they decided to hold a second meeting at Davidson's and invited Kingdon in the hope of convincing him to continue supporting Wallace.

While they were waiting for Kingdon to arrive, Wallace rang them up and told them he couldn't come. He then dictated a letter to Kingdon over the phone. When Kingdon arrived, it was handed to him. What it said Kingdon didn't like, and he let everyone know it. He accused Beanie Baldwin of writing the letter, not Wallace. When Baldwin denied it, Kingdon called him a liar. Immediately everyone began arguing with him. Kingdon left angry, shaken and deeply offended. In a phone call to a friend, which the FBI duly intercepted, he said that 'it felt like eighteen people had mauled him and put him on the carpet and called him a leper and had, you know, gone to town on him'.[3]

Wallace realised he had committed a massive error and was now on the verge of losing Kingdon entirely. Hoping to repair things between them, the next day, he asked Kingdon to come to Farvue Farm so the two of them could talk honestly. Kingdon agreed to come, but when he arrived, he found Wallace wasn't alone. Martha and Alfred were also there, along with Leonard Goldsmith, of the Civil Rights Congress, a communist front group, which was part of the Progressive Citizens of America. Seeing them there, Kingdon likely felt he'd walked into another ambush.

There's no way of knowing exactly what was said, but from the fragmentary accounts it's easy to guess how it went down. Wallace apparently began by telling him he intended to run against Truman, not as a Democrat, but as an independent. Kingdon said he was making a big mistake and that the only way he could ever be successful would be if he had a 'Gideon's Army', and from what he was seeing, Wallace plainly didn't have one. He'd been haemorrhaging supporters ever since his bungled European tour.

Kingdon likely then told Wallace his organisation had too many groups controlled by communists. The best he could hope to accomplish was to bring his progressive coalition into the Democratic Party and by doing so, influence it into becoming more liberal, less beholden to the bigots, bosses and bankers currently running the party. He could do this, but it would mean separating from the communists. That was it. Kingdon had been in the political game a long time and this was how it was done. He repeated what he'd told Wallace previously: a third-party run would be futile. Wallace would lose, and he and progressive Americans would have nothing at all to show for it. To this, Wallace likely replied that while he didn't agree with the communists on a great number of things, they were a legal organisation and represented a lot of good people who'd fought hard for human rights and equality when nobody else would. Now they were as entitled to sit at the table as anyone else. He would not abandon them.

At some point Martha, Alfred and Goldsmith stepped in and took over Wallace's side of the argument. Kingdon's anger began to cool. The discussions carried on throughout the evening. Probably Alfred and Goldsmith had the sense to hang back and let Martha do most of the talking, coming in only when needed. It may have been Martha's finest hour. She reasoned with Kingdon, probably pointing out that he'd been the one to tell everyone the fundamental problem with the American political system was its dependence on a two-party system and that up to now there had been numerous attempts to break the pattern, but none of the parties ever had the pull necessary to challenge this system. Right now they had this pull, she probably told him. Slowly Kingdon started coming around. Martha probably said he was wrong about the communists being so pervasive. They weren't, she insisted. It was all red scare tactics devised by the American fascists to divide and conquer. Kingdon began to relent. After Wallace went to bed Martha and Alfred invited Kingdon over to their house to continue the discussion. The evening continued until around 2am, when they drove out to a nearby roadhouse-inn which stayed open, to get something to eat. At around 7am they all called it a morning and went to bed. Later that day, Wallace and Martha had a telephone conversation which was monitored by the FBI.[4] Wallace told Martha, 'It was very fortunate that you, Alfred and Goldsmith were there to soften him up a little, because he certainly seemed to appreciate it.'

But the grand reconciliation turned out to be only a brief truce. Even though Kingdon accepted Wallace's decision and even supported it, the people who'd attacked Kingdon that night at Jo Davidson's studio never stopped being hostile. Kingdon realised Wallace's broad-based coalition was a sham and that the bulk of PCA's membership were communists hiding inside innocuous-sounding front groups. After Kingdon learned this included Martha and Alfred, he wrote to her to let her know he knew. Later Martha mentioned the letter to Wallace, describing it as 'written in a frenzied tone, marked by a pattern of redbaiting'. On 29 December 1947, Henry Wallace formally announced his decision to run for President. Within a week Kingdon resigned from his co-chairmanship of the PCA and walked away from the Wallace camp, never to return.

32. INFORMANTS

By early autumn 1947, the FBI had put together a stable of confidential informants. On a report, twenty informants, numbered T-1 to T-20, were listed, their names and any identifying characteristics removed.[1] They seemed to fall into two categories: people connected to the spy network which Zarubin had set up and handed off to Soble, who handed it off to Boris Morros, who then handed it to the FBI; or social acquaintances of the Sterns, strewn over different far left-wing and communist groups. 'Confidential Informant T-1' was close to Soble, and had apparently also worked with Zarubin himself.[2]

According to T-1, Zarubin (then referred to as 'Zubilin') recounted an incident in which he and someone named 'Studenko' (later identified as Choudenko) drove out to visit the Sterns in their country house and that during the visit, Studenko's conduct with Stern had been exceedingly vulgar. More significantly, Zarubin had claimed that the 'stated reason for the disagreement between Stern and Morros was that Morros had immoral relations with Stern's wife. Informant further advised Soble had high regard for Martha Stern, but realises she is a sex maniac.'[3]

One unnumbered informant stated Soble had told him he'd been dodging Alfred Stern's attempts to contact him, something which was confirmed by Confidential Informant T-6, who added that Myra Soble had declined to furnish him with any information. Later, the same, or another, unnumbered informant reported that the Sterns had invited Myra to their farms, but that she declined and went instead to Atlantic City.

Confidential Informant T-8 had been present on 14 August 1947, when Martha and Alfred discussed having 'Nicky' (Zolotowski) carry the letter for them to someone in Paris. Thanks to the receipt of this information, FBI men were present in the lobby of the Barbizon Park Hotel to witness Alfred Stern handing off the letter to Zolotowski. T-8 also stated that the person it was to be delivered to was Pierre Cot and not Jack Soble, something subsequently confirmed by Confidential Informant T-7. Confidential Informant T-4 confirmed that Henry Wallace's disastrous reception in France had been arranged by Pierre Cot at Martha's behest. T-10 knew Sylvia Crane, back when she was Sylvia Katz.

It was also T-7 who reported to the FBI that Martha had contacted Harry Freeman, the American assistant manager of the New York bureau of TASS, the Soviet news agency, and that they spoke to each other 'in very cautious terms'. This confirmed something the FBI already knew. On 26 January 1948, they monitored a conversation between Martha and Harry Freeman. He told Martha that 'his friend whom she'd met previously was now in New York and would be willing to meet her'. They set up a meeting for the following evening at the Mayan Restaurant on West 51st Street at 7pm. They were also listening later that evening when Alfred got home and Martha passed him a note about it, which he then absent-mindedly, and much to her consternation, read aloud. From listening to Martha cutting her husband a new one, they surmised the upcoming meeting was probably an important one.

Four special agents were in place around the Mayan Restaurant dining room when Martha came in alone at 7.05 the following evening. She was seated alone at a table. Then Harry Freeman arrived with another man and went to the bar. Alfred arrived and met the two men at the bar. They had a drink together, after which Freeman left. Alfred then led the man to Martha's table and the three had dinner together. At around 9pm they left the restaurant and took a taxi, which brought them to the apartment building where Miodrag Markovic, the Yugoslavian Consul General, lived. The man at first protested and refused to go in, but after considerable persuasion, relented. The three went in and stayed until around 1am, when they left together. They walked several blocks to the 8th Avenue subway station and boarded a subway train. The Sterns got off at 72nd Street, while the individual stayed aboard. At 42nd Street he disembarked and made his way to the surface, checking to see if he was being followed. The man was later identified as Valentin Arkhipovich Sorokin, Second Secretary of the Soviet Embassy in Washington, DC. The FBI men learned he had checked into the Lincoln Hotel on the 25th and was observed checking out on 20 January.

Hoover ordered background information on Sorokin, but all they had was the biographical information the Soviet government had furnished. Supposedly he was born in Leningrad in 1904, joined the Ministry of Foreign Affairs in 1934, attended the Leningrad Economic Institute in 1935, all of which, experience had taught them, was likely as not wholly made up. But after digging through State Department lists of Russian technical experts allowed in under the secret visa program (which George Messersmith and George Kennan had helped run in Berlin) they found that in 1932, a Russian metallurgical engineer with the same name had been let in to work at the Arthur G. McKee Company in Cleveland, helping design a steel mill to be built in Magnitogorsk. Could they be the same person? Of course the bigger question was what Martha and Alfred were doing talking to him. From the way they'd all been acting, it was pretty clear Sorokin wasn't their case officer. But then, if he wasn't, who was? What was going on?

What was going on, it turned out, was that Martha and Alfred had arranged this meeting with Sorokin in order to plead Moscow's help in the Wallace presidential campaign. The KGB files of that period, examined by Western researchers in the 1990s, makes mention of meetings between a Moscow Center officer and the Sterns. The Valentin Sorokin mentioned in the FBI files, who may or may not have worked in Cleveland in 1932, was in fact someone named Snegerev. He had previously met Martha earlier that month at a party attended by many well-known leftist writers. Martha had complained to him about Earl Browder, the former CPUSA president, whom Martha and other hard-liners believed was dangerously deviating from the correct course and was now verging on revisionism. She entreated him to report her belief Moscow should break with Browder. Sometime after that, Martha asked their mutual contact Harry Freeman to arrange another meeting, which was the one they had observed at the Mayan Restaurant and afterwards. Sorokin/Snegerev had gone to the meeting only after clearing it with 'Vladimir', his boss, who suggested he 'determine Martha's attitudes and possible usefulness as a talent spotter', but not anything more than that. One of the things Vladimir suggested was to see what they could tell him about Michael Straight and *The New Republic*.

Instead, Snegerev got pitched. Martha and Alfred told him of their involvement in the Wallace campaign, how they'd become close friends and confidants to Wallace and his wife, and how they'd guided him into a markedly pro-Moscow posture along with a stated commitment to ending America's nuclear monopoly. They'd accomplished all this; what they needed now was Moscow's support and guidance. Snegerev listened to them as they made their plea, a smile frozen on his face. He knew he had a problem. After finishing their meal and paying the bill, Martha and Alfred suggested getting a drink somewhere else. Probably more out of politeness than anything else, Snegerev agreed and got in a cab with them. When the cab let them out in front of an apartment building and not a nightspot as he'd expected, he balked. Who was this person they were going to see? The Yugoslav Consul General? Snegerev was alarmed. Lines were being crossed! *Konspiritsia!, my friends, Konspiritsia! There are rules, protocols for this and this is not how these things are done!* Even so, Martha somehow talked him into it and he went inside.

The three spent several hours meeting with Miodrag Markovic, who presumably added his bit, detailing his own meetings with Wallace about ending the arms-building craziness that was going on between America and Russia. Perhaps listening to them made Snegerev recall the intrepid Chekists from his own distant past; that earlier golden age: ready to fight the good fight against fascists, capitalists and reactionaries! How they and other American communists are all … *ready for action, Sir!* But looking at them, with all their earnest, mindless eagerness, Snegerev mainly saw a tall, bare, splintery wooden post waiting for him, and behind it, a bullet-splattered wall. He'd been warned about the American comrades, always seeing possibilities where none existed, at least none that involved coming out of alive. He kept smiling and waited for the meeting to end.

Discussing it together afterwards, Martha and Alfred had their doubts. They were already certain they were being observed and couldn't be 100 per cent sure Sorokin wasn't really an FBI plant. But even if he wasn't, they worried he might be a 'Kravchenko', gathering material in advance of his defection. Snegerev, besides having his own misgivings, quickly learned Moscow Center harboured its own great discontent with Martha and Alfred. Over the years they'd repeatedly directed them to take a low-key approach to espionage, to not be so obvious about their communism and support for the Soviet Union. It would have been far better if they'd made the whole world believe they were Republicans.

On 11 February 1948, Assistant FBI Director Richard Ladd, in compliance with Justice Department requirements, submitted to Hoover a completed questionnaire entitled *Annual Justification for Continuation of Technical or Microphone Surveillance of Alfred Kaufman Stern and his wife Martha Dodd Stern*.

When asked to detail specific valuable information obtained since previous report, it only said that the surveillance 'furnishes information referring to subjects' social and business contacts'. The only example it cited was an 8 November 1947 telephone call with a Mildred Wolford of Ridgefield concerning the Sterns' plans about giving up their New York apartment to live permanently in the country home in Connecticut, adding 'informant is in a position to furnish additional information if the subjects meet with other subjects in Mocase or any other individuals'.

It went on to say that 'information received indicated that he is in direct communication with Zubilin at the present time, the latter being in Europe. Stern may be operating a network of intelligence agents in this country. He is a close associate of Henry A. Wallace and very active in communication with the PCA. It is recommended that this surveillance be continued.'

The Special Agent Commanding added his remarks: 'In view of the importance of this case and the nature of the information ascertained, it is believed this informant should be continued.' It was followed by remarks 'Added at the Seat of Government: The subject is a principal subject of the Mocase investigation, having been associated with Vassily Zubilin and Boris Morros and Jack Soble in intelligence activity during 1943, 1944, and 1945. Information received indicates that he is in direct communication with Zubilin at the present time, the latter being in Europe. Stern may be operating a network of intelligence agents in this country. He is a close associate of Henry A. Wallace and very active in communication with the PCA. The installation is considered very secure and is operated at small cost … It is recommended this surveillance by continued.'[4]

Hoover gave it his approval and the surveillance continued for another year.

In late February 1948, there was a communist-led coup d'état in Czechoslovakia. It had been neither unexpected nor wholly bloodless. Even so, the world was shocked, especially when Jan Masaryk, the pro-Western foreign minister, died after being pushed out of a narrow bathroom window. The new communist regime officially ruled his death a suicide, hoping no one in the West knew that throwing people out of windows, or 'defenestration', was a time-honoured Czech method of regime change. For many American leftists, it was yet another reason to further distance themselves from Moscow. It would have been an excellent opportunity for Wallace to do the same, but his team of 'not-communist' speech writers (which included Martha) chose another course. In a speech they furnished him with,[5] Wallace told the crowd that what the communists actually did was move against a 'rightist plot' personally instigated by the American Ambassador against the Benes–Masaryk regime. It was such a ridiculous lie, voters wondered if Wallace had lost his marbles.

In March 1948, Alfred Stern and a group of partners attempted to buy *PM Magazine* from its owner, Marshall Field, who had put it up for sale. But once Field realised their aim was to turn it into a pro-Wallace vehicle, he refused to sell. For a while they tried to find a 'shell' buyer, but failed.

That March, the FBI also listened in on a telephone conversation between Martha and Carl Sandburg. She called to get him to speak out in support of Henry Wallace. Sandburg refused. The conversation became nasty and before hanging up, Martha accused her former lover of being a 'revisionist'. It was the last time they spoke.

On 18 March, Snegerev had another meeting with Martha and Alfred, this time in the lobby of the Commodore Hotel. Snegerev, having survived this far in a diplomatic-spy apparatus, evidently knew the wisdom and value in not taking the initiative on anything.

He did the safest thing he could think of: he nodded attentively as they described everything going on within the Wallace campaign and made sympathetic noises to their rantings about Truman's warmongering and refusal to share atomic energy secrets with the world. He promised to pass along their requests to serve the communist revolution any way they could. In the end, he said he'd be back in touch and left.

In April 1948, the Sterns' friend Ignace Zolotowski returned to Poland, his tour of duty completed. At around the same time Henry Wallace resigned from his post as editor of *The New Republic*. Relations between him and Michael Straight had been festering ever since France. Straight made numerous attempts to alert him to the number of communists inside his camp, but Wallace refused to acknowledge their presence. Straight had been drifting rightward for some time. By April, the simmering disagreement between Straight and Wallace over the Soviet Union finally came to a head. Wallace resigned to focus entirely on his presidential campaign. Not long after, *The New Republic* and Michael Straight declared their support for Harry Truman and its opposition to Stalin and Soviet expansionism.

By now, Wallace recognised he had no chance of winning the election and that the best he could hope for was to force Truman to alter his rightward stance and make room for the progressives whom Wallace intended to bring into the Democratic tent. For Wallace, peace was the pre-eminent issue. Unless Truman committed to peaceful coexistence with Russia, he would keep his followers away from the Democratic Party. But Truman wouldn't budge. After that Henry Wallace announced he was launching a new political party, which would be called the Progressive Party.

On 1 May 1948, Confidential Informant T-3 reported that Alfred Stern had invited socialist philosopher Corliss Lamont to a meeting to be held at Lillian Hellman's on 5 May to discuss the possibility of buying *PM*. Lamont reported he was interested in donating to the Wallace campaign, but not in donating towards the purchase of the magazine. T-3 also reported that a 'Mr. Masters',[6] one of their building neighbours, had phoned to invite Martha and Alfred downstairs for a drink. Martha urged Alfred to go, but could not go herself 'as she was having a group of 35 PCA women to her house the day for a meeting'.

On 4 May 1948, Informant T-6 reported visiting with Martha and Alfred at their apartment for dinner. There the informant was introduced to Cedric Belfrage and to Jimmy Aaronson, the editor of *The Front Page*, the Newspaper Guild's in-house bulletin. They had just returned from a meeting with Lillian Hellman and dropped a number of names, including Louise Bransten, the very wealthy San Francisco leftist doyenne, whom the FBI was certain they could connect both to Martha's former lover Bruce Minton and Kheifitz, the head of the San Francisco rezidentura. T-6 reported that at about the same time that Jimmy and Cedric left, four women from the 'Women for Wallace' campaign arrived to help Martha address envelopes. The informant understood they were all communists. The women departed just before dinner was served. Sitting down, Alfred asked, 'Are you still in the Party?' During the dinner Alfred said, 'Henry Wallace has been a great boon for the Communist Party and had he not come to the front, it would have been necessary to use Senator Claude Pepper instead.' Stern added that 'The Party does not expect Wallace to remain on the Communist Party "bandwagon", but believes he will stay at least until the November elections.' 'Informant believes that Alfred considers himself to be Wallace's top advisor,' the report said and noted, 'Alfred does not get along with Beanie Baldwin and is disgusted because Wallace has no philosophy and is following Baldwin's advice in setting up a platform.'[7] Later, they told the informant they were 'being watched all the time'.

On 12 May 1948, Informant T-3 advised that Martha had informed them that 'she intended to walk the picket line in front of the Greek Consulate in support of the American Council for a Democratic Greece'. Thus alerted, a number of FBI special agents observed Martha Dodd Stern marching in the picket line at approximately 5pm. A subsequent FBI report noted, 'She was observed to be carrying a picket sign and shouting "Stop the fascist murders in Greece". Motion pictures of this picket line were taken and are being made part of the exhibits in this case.' The report also mentioned that the marchers represented a number of different groups, including Congress of American Women, the Civil Rights Congress, Veterans of the Abraham Lincoln Brigade, the American Labor Party, the Furriers Union, the International Workers Order, the National Maritime Union, and American Youth for Democracy.[8]

On 8 July 1948, someone calling himself 'Mr. Michael' visited the Sterns in their country home. The FBI men recognised him as Valentin Sorokin from the Soviet Embassy in Washington. Despite the house being bugged, the FBI apparently did not learn the reason for Sorokin's visit. But according to the brief report Sorokin/Snegerev filed afterwards, the Sterns wanted to know if Moscow 'had anything' for them. Apparently it did not. At one point Alfred raised concerns their telephone was being tapped. They discussed at length the situation within the Wallace campaign and the third-party movement. They complained of 'adverse influence' coming from Lillian Hellman and her connections to the Catholic Church and Bishop Sheen. They spoke of a 'fashionable preoccupation of the Catholic leadership with psycho-analysis'. But then, they noted, the same was true with so many of their well-heeled comrades. 'Communists go to them as they would go to priests for Confession, in order to reduce stress,' he reported them telling him, adding that Communist Party chief Browder had told him the same thing.[9]

The Progressive Party held its convention in Philadelphia between 23 and 25 July, the same city where the Democrats and Republican had held theirs. Among those covering it was Martha's brother Bill, reporting for *The Dispatcher*, an unabashedly leftist newspaper put out by the Longshoremen's Union in San Francisco. While the union was sending a number of its delegates to the convention, sending Bill, or anyone, to cover it had been considered more than it was willing to shell out for. After being informed of this, he wrote Martha and she apparently came up with the necessary funds for him to attend. Bill was in high form in his convention coverage. In an article entitled 'Choice of Wallace or War', he wrote how Wallace 'showed how the high ideals and achievements of the New Deal under Franklin Roosevelt had been betrayed by Harry S Truman. He sketched the unnecessary and dangerous foreign affairs crises provoked by the bipartisan madness of the moneychangers who rule the roost in Washington.'[10]

The Dispatcher was Bill's final stab at journalism. He had been on the skids for years. After getting fired from his foreign broadcasting job at the FCC, the only company who would hire him was the Soviet news agency TASS, and they fired him after learning about his previously being an NKVD operative. Soviet intelligence groups had strict rules about poaching from each other's patch. He got handed his walking papers by his American boss, Harry Freeman, who was sincerely very, very sorry. After finally getting hired by *The Dispatcher*, Bill moved with his wife and their two children to San Francisco, rented a house in Mill Valley and he commuted to work in the city. They'd hoped to make a fresh start, but by now Bill's alcoholism had worsened. After a few months his wife left him, taking their two children back to Oregon, where she'd grown up, and filed for divorce.

The FBI hadn't had much luck penetrating the Stern household. They'd hoped the two local black teenage girls might prove useful inside sources, but the cook kept them on short leashes and as a result, neither ever got close to Martha or Alfred. The one they really wanted talking to them was Ralph Scott, the family's majordomo, but his staunch loyalty to the Sterns was a brick wall to the FBI men.

On 3 August, *The New York World Herald Telegram* carried an article naming Mrs Alfred Stern, daughter of the late US Ambassador, as a 'Financial Angel' supporting communist undertakings. On 16 August, a column in *The New York Daily News* stated that 'Martha Dodd, daughter of the one-time envoy to Germany, has invaded journalism by helping edit a weekly newspaper with national circulation', a supposed reference to the *National Guardian*, which her husband and his friends had recently established.

Somewhere around this time, Martha had another meeting with Snegerev in which she informed him she'd become one of Henry Wallace's speechwriters. She suggested the Soviet Embassy supply her with drafts for speeches or at least with the basic tenet which could be developed or mentioned in Wallace's speeches. Please, she said, we need guidance from Moscow on this. Snegerev went back and informed Moscow Center. A few days later a reply came. 'Using Liza [Martha] for contact or work with Wallace is highly inadvisable,' it said.[11] But before Snegerev could get back to them, Alfred Stern sent him a request which he duly transmitted to Moscow. 'Alfred requesting a speech by Comrade Vyshinsky recalling "Joint Struggle" by USSR and US against fascist Germany. We need this right now!' The request was apparently ignored.

A few days before the November elections, Alfred Stern travelled to Chicago to give a speech in support of Wallace and the Progressive

Party. It was held in the auditorium of the Chicago Institute of Psychopathic Analysis, which he had supported for years. Stern's speech incensed a member who loudly denounced him, saying his talk was nothing more than communism and that it was evident that the Progressive Party was in the hands of communists. After that, he, or someone else in the audience, loudly proclaimed that if war ever broke out between the US and Russia, he was going to volunteer to fight against Russia.

In the end, Truman roundly beat Dewey, and Wallace didn't even get two million votes. Four years earlier he'd been the most important political figure in America. But he'd let the communists run his campaign; he delivered the speeches they wrote him. The old supporters, the labourers and the farmers and the blacks, all fled and voted for Truman, which was probably why Truman beat Dewey so handily. For Wallace it was a humiliation. But Wallace, proud and aloof, wouldn't show it. As for Martha and Alfred, a couple of days after the election, they boarded a passenger liner bound for Guatemala, with plenty of stops. They'd promised themselves the trip for a long time. However, Martha was so seasick, they got off in Cuba and ended up staying there for a month.

In February Alfred and Henry drove together to Chicago for a Progressive Party conference. It was a mess. They'd come together to try to figure out what had gone so wrong and what the course should be for the future. But there was disagreement and finger pointing over everything. They tried not to make it about communists and Soviet Russia, but that didn't work. The Progressive Party fractured. Stern and Wallace drove back. A few weeks later, Wallace resigned from the Progressive Party.

The friendship between Henry and Ilo Wallace and Martha and Alfred lasted a while after that. They had dinners together and swimming and tennis throughout the spring and summer. What mortally wounded their relationship came later that season. A large group of communists living in Peekskill, New York, were having their annual summer cookout in one of the town's parks when a group of anti-communists attacked them with bottles and rocks. It turned into a melee and the police were called in. It was mostly the picnickers whom the police then attacked, with dozens subsequently beaten and arrested.

There was an uproar in the press, but it didn't last long. The leftists gathered voices to protest. Truman, of course, wouldn't say anything, Eleanor Roosevelt did. Martha begged Wallace to add his voice; to protest, to say something. But he wouldn't. Wallace was afraid he was being set up. Infuriated, Martha called him a revisionist and a 'fascist enabler', before walking out of a dinner. They stopped seeing each other after that.

Eventually Wallace did his turnaround. He denounced the Soviet Union for its tyranny and threat to peace and freedom. He denounced communists in America. When the Korean peninsula erupted in war, Wallace publicly supported Truman's decision for American military intervention as necessary for fighting communism. It made Wallace look like less of a fool, but the damage done had been irreparable.

To the tens of thousands of Americans trying to get clear of their own leftist political pasts, it had been infuriating to hear Wallace proclaiming publicly that he didn't know who was a communist, that he wasn't certain he'd ever actually met one, and sounding like he was saying it in all honesty. It was too much. Many joined the closer-to-right-of-center organisations like Americans for Democratic Action.

Wallace stepped away from politics and went back to developing hybrid plants and animals. He continued to be highly successful at this. It is said that nearly all the eggs consumed by people in the world today are from chickens developed by Henry Wallace. He and Ilo stayed close. They didn't hear from the Sterns again until almost ten years later when they were sending him their greetings from Moscow. He sent the letter on to J. Edgar Hoover.

33. A TURN FOR THE WORSE

Back home in America, Soble observed Wallace's defeat without feeling anything. He was aware Martha and Alfred were involved in his campaign and had sought Moscow Center's help. He had to shake his head at their stupidity. Why hadn't they been able to figure out Moscow wanted nothing to do with Wallace? They'd seen him in action during his Siberia visit and concluded he was an idiot. Several months later, after seeing him getting doinked out of the vice-presidency, they concluded he was also a loser who'd never be President, dismissing him from any further consideration. If Martha and Alfred thought wasting their time and money on him was going to make Moscow Center want to give them assignments, well, those two fools could believe anything they wanted. It wasn't Soble's problem. He just wished Alfred would take the hint and quit phoning.

❦

December 1948, Alger Hiss is indicted for perjury. Five days later, Lawrence Duggan commits suicide following an FBI interrogation. A week later the FBI identifies Judith Coplon, a secretary working in the Department of Justice's Foreign Agents Registration Section, as a Soviet spy. Moscow Center halts most of its espionage efforts in North America.

In late February 1949, Jack Soble returned to New York, settling into a new apartment arranged by Boris Morros. He informed Boris that Beria had agreed in principle to Morros' proposed $350,000 TV project. It was what, 70 years later, Morros' biographer would call 'the first of many dubious promises'.

On 1 March 1949, the FBI special agent for New York submitted another Justification for Continuation of Technical or Microphone Surveillance on Alfred and Martha Stern to Hoover. It once again stated it was necessary for building their case against known Soviet spies. Though it again cited few examples where the surveillance had provided any critical information, Hoover approved it and submitted it to the Justice Department as the law required.

On 2 March 1949, Soble finally agreed to meet with Alfred Stern. Stern once again asked for an assignment, anything, for him and Martha, only to be given a vague non-answer. Afterward he disgustedly described the meeting as 'the same old merry-go-round'. Shortly after that, Moscow Center officially dropped Alfred and Martha as assets.

Martha had another meeting with Snegerev, who connected them to a man named 'Kostrov' who tasked them with writing assessments of different public figures. Martha and Alfred did it for a while, until they concluded it was just 'busy work'.[1]

On 29 August 1949, US Air Force monitoring aircraft detected radiation emanating from around Semipalatinsk. What it meant was clear: the Russians had detonated a nuclear device with a radiation signature identical to that of the bomb dropped on Nagasaki four years earlier. They had stolen the American bomb design and now had their own. The search for the atomic spies in America took on a fever pitch. So did the general anti-communist paranoia raging across America.

Meanwhile, *Venona*, the US Army's Signal Intelligence Service's secret project to decrypt coded Soviet Embassy cable traffic, was beginning to yield some results. It pointed to a German-born British physicist named Klaus Fuchs. In January 1950, Fuchs was arrested. He talked, which led to the arrests of Harry Gold, David Greenglass and Julius and Ethel Rosenberg. Harry Gold and David Greenglass both talked, but Julius and Ethel Rosenberg would not. Fuchs, Gold and Greenglass all served lengthy prison sentences. Julius and Ethel Rosenberg both died in the electric chair in early 1953.

Initially the FBI had been reticent about poking into Foreign Service circles for information about Martha. But once they did, they found Katherine Hollister Smith, the astute and highly opiniated wife of former military attaché Captain Truman Smith, who was happy to share her memories and summary judgements about Martha and her family. She and Truman had been old Germany hands long before taking the Berlin post in 1935. He had been assigned to Munich for several years following the armistice. Both spoke German and knew the country well. Many of their old military friends were now in leadership positions in the Wehrmacht, the Luftwaffe and government. Putzi Hanfstaengl was an old pal and, being an inveterate gossip, had told them plenty.

In Katherine Hollister Smith's opinion, Martha's father, the Ambassador, was an idiot who should have stayed hidden behind the plow. His wife acted like a shellshock victim; the son was drunk and probably a spy too, for the Russians! Wasn't that what losers like that usually did? And Martha? That young 'woman' was a whore. 'She was one of the ones Putzi Hanfstaengl had as his mistress! Listen, I love Putzi, but come on. The man was a hound! Then of course Udet and Goering and all those others. Didn't someone say Blomberg, the chief of staff? He never said anything to her about it? None of them had ever said anything to her about it, except for Putzi but there was a lot of sniggering going on for a couple of years.'

On 15 January 1951 the Special Agent in charge of the MOCASE investigation wrote a memo considering whether Martha and Alfred could be charged under Section 20 of the Internal Security Act. In March 1952, the FBI began considering the possibility of submitting the MOCASE investigation to the Justice Department for possible prosecution. But then they decided to hold off for a few more years.

With no possibility left of ever going back into spying, Martha and Alfred turned to other pursuits. Alfred focused on public housing issues and his investments. Martha decided the time had come to write another novel. As a writer, Martha was neither fast nor prolific. Though she had written *Through Embassy Eyes* and *Ambassador Dodd's Diary* in an uncharacteristic flurry, she dawdled over writing her first novel, *Sowing the Wind*. As a result it came out as the war was ending and popular interest in pre-war Nazi Germany was at its lowest. Even though it had garnered good reviews, sales were disappointing. She promised herself she'd try again, but for all her ongoing political activism, she didn't find anything in it that captured her imagination enough to want to write a 'serious' novel about it. That changed after she started reading about how at the University of California at Berkley there had been a major conflict between the faculty and the Board of Regents after the board instituted loyalty oaths for its faculty. One psychology professor, Ernest C. Tolman, had led the battle against it, arguing that it went against the spirit of free speech and open inquiry necessary for higher education. In January 1952, Martha and Alfred travelled to San Francisco and Oakland to interview Tolman and talk to other oath resisters. The FBI was following them. To their shock, on the train ride back Martha ran into J. Robert Oppenheimer, whom she knew socially. Apparently he didn't hand her any secrets.

While inspired by Professor Tolman, *The Searching Light's* protagonist, John Minot, was a thinly disguised version of Martha's father, William E. Dodd. Like him, Minot was a university professor and a farmer, finding his happiness living simply and apart from all the university's politics and rivalries. Yet he gets drawn into the loyalty oath conflict on a matter of principle. He stands up to the regents when they present a modified version of the oath, urging his colleagues to reject it as well. Though this leads to Minot's dismissal, it sparks the other faculty members to stand up and fight the regents. For most of 1952 and 1953, Martha focused on the book, often writing late into the night. When she finished writing it, she sent it to a number of publishers, but none were interested.

On 18 October 1952, Bill Dodd died of stomach cancer. His death had not come quickly and his treatment had been expensive and painful. Having little money of their own, his wife, Katherine Hubbard Dodd, had been forced to ask Martha for assistance. Alfred had grudgingly paid for his care only after making his soon-to-be widow promise she would sell Bill's securities to reimburse him. She did not like Martha and Alfred and they did not like her. In Martha's eyes, her brother had always gone for the wrong kind of girls, ones with no political sense. Once he died, things came apart between them. Katherine didn't want the obituary Martha had written put in any of the Bay Area newspapers. She told Martha she could do whatever she wanted on the East Coast. So Martha spoke of her brother as a heroic, 'pre-mature anti-fascist', recounting all his efforts to resist the government's tyranny and bullying the same way he fought the Nazis and fascists in Europe and Asia. Bill's widow didn't need Martha to tell her what her husband was. Bill wasn't a bad guy, just a loser, a drunk and a slob, unable to step clear from his father's shadow, and whatever it was he'd had going with his sister had to have been messed up. But he'd always meant well. The notice she'd posted hadn't said much beyond the bare facts. He'd managed to stick with *The Dispatcher* for several years through to 1949, but then the International Ladies Garment Workers Union got thrown out of the Congress of Industrial Organizations for being too commie. After that, the union went into its own inner struggles and he lost his job. Things turned around a little when he was hired by the University of California at Berkley to teach a history course as an adjunct, but before he could get going he was embroiled in the matter of having to take a loyalty oath. Bill wouldn't and was dropped before he could even start. After that, he worked for a while selling books at Macy's department store before the cancer had made work impossible.

Bill's body was cremated and his ashes sent to join his parents in the family plot at the Rock Creek Cemetery in Washington, DC – a city none of them had lived in for very long – ensconced for eternity among its great and good.

34. DOWN MEXICO WAY

On 28 June 1953, an item appeared in 'Lyon's Den', a column in the *New York Post*, in which Leonard Lyon mentioned 'that the daughter of a US Ambassador would soon be subpoenaed by the McCarthy Committee'. For Martha and Alfred, it was all the warning they needed. Alfred bought two station wagons which they loaded up with their most important possessions. Then, after making some decoy phone calls indicating they were about to go on a vacation to Maine, they drove off a day or two later, Alfred driving one car, Ralph Scott driving the other, without the FBI surveillance teams noticing anything. A few days later, the FBI's man in Mexico City sent back a photograph from a local newspaper showing the Sterns in Cuernavaca. For all the manpower the FBI used to keep them under surveillance, Martha and Alfred had flown the coop, right under their noses.

In Mexico life was good. There was already a thriving community of artists, writers and other political exiles there, which had been steadily growing ever since the witch hunt began. Plenty of Martha and Alfred's friends and comrades were already there. Dalton Trumbo was present, along with other screenwriters including Howard Biberman, Albert Maltz and Lion Feuchtwanger. Journalist and film critic Cedric Belfrage was there as well, having been accused of being a Soviet spy. The Sterns first rented a house, but then, when they learned of a vacant lot a few houses away from Diego Rivera and his wife Frida Kahlo's house, they bought it, engaged an architect and had a villa built.

Escaping like they did put the FBI in a pickle. The Sterns hadn't broken any laws coming to Mexico and they were free to go any-where they wanted that didn't require a passport. As it was, they'd been having a difficult enough time building their case while keeping their eye on them and legally tapping their phones. While it was also possible to do the same things there, none of it would be legally admissible, which wasn't going to help their case against them. The FBI had already encountered this problem when they seized Alfred Stern's business records as they were about to be loaded aboard a Mexico-bound aircraft at Idlewild Airport in New York. They found plenty in Stern's records they could trace to the Boris Morros Music Company. It might have even been enough to make a case against him, except that since the seizure hadn't been legal, they couldn't.

The Sterns' screenwriter friends were still getting work, writing under assumed names and taking lower fees, but since the cost of living there was so much lower, it evened out. Of course, most exiles didn't have it so lush. They were a lot further down the economic ladder. Some had been academics, but most were ordinary guys who'd lost their jobs after coming under suspicion and suddenly found themselves facing criminal prosecution. They fled, with their families, and often with only the clothes on their backs. Once in Mexico, they were forced to make do with what they could get.

Science-fiction writer Crawford Kilian remembers how, as a child, he'd had to make the sudden 'midnight escape' to Mexico with his parents. In addition to being a communist, his father had been an electronics technician working at a television station in New York City when the call came to flee. The drive took several days and until they arrived, he was under the impression they were going to California. Once they got there, they were tapped out financially. Luckily, Mexico's first television studio was being set up and his father was hired, but at only a fraction of his salary in the States. His mother also found a job at Cuernavaca's English-language school. Even so, the family remained dirt poor – not that it prevented them from having one or two servants.

Even with the poverty, Kilian's memories of their exile seem mostly pleasant. There was a large empty lot where on most Saturday mornings, all the American kids would show up to play softball, after which one of the richer parents would feed them all sandwiches for lunch, and it went on like this for a couple years. He remembered the Sterns. They had a big place and had people over all the time. Martha was a show-off. The first breasts he ever saw were Martha's. He spotted them once when she was sunbathing without her top. Even as a kid, he'd heard stories about Martha's affairs, but then she wasn't the only one having them. Everyone, it seemed, was playing musical beds. 'They were all a rather horny lot,' he observed. He thought Alfred Stern also seemed like he was having a good time himself. Once he handed Bob a book and told him to have some fun. It turned out to be Rabelais' ribald tales.

Kilian vividly remembers Bobby Stern as part of the group of boys who hung around together. He seemed nice enough, but at the same time distant and insular, as if so much noise was going on inside his head that communicating with other kids was next to impossible. Looking back on it years later, with the benefit of hindsight, Kilian guessed Bobby was suffering from something. Even so, Bobby's life in Mexico was happier than back in Ridgefield.

But as nice as life seemed, one worry nagged the Sterns. Once, several years earlier, Morton Sobell, one of the exiles, was kidnapped by off-duty federales who stuck him in the trunk of a car and drove to the Texas border, where they handed him over to the FBI. He was then put on trial and found guilty of espionage, receiving a lengthy prison sentence. What if the FBI chose to do the same with them?

⁂

After unsuccessfully shopping her manuscript for *The Searching Light* to major New York publishers, Citadel Press agreed to take it on after Alfred agreed to buy $4,000 worth of copies in advance of the printing. It was published on 1 January 1955, and even though it carried the endorsement of Albert Einstein, sales were few beyond those which Alfred had previously paid for.

According to KGB files shown to Western researchers in the early 1990s, on 26 January 1956, 'Louis' (Alfred Stern) paid a visit to the Soviet Embassy in Mexico City. He met with 'Ostap', one of the Moscow Center rezidents, and presented them with a letter to Ilya Ehrenburg, written by his wife 'Liza' (Martha), dealing with her book. On 14 May they had another meeting where Alfred was asked to fill them in on their recent activities, the situation among the American communists and other leftist political exiles. Ostap needed to find out if they should start cultivating Martha again. Moscow recommended it 'should be done in a way that she doesn't think you know something about her previous work with us. This is necessary,' it continued, 'because we aren't sure that Liza and Louis don't have some unpleasant memories of their previous time with us'. Ostap's next message home was that the Sterns were fearful of extradition to the US and had made a request through someone named 'Skipper' to find out through the Russian Ambassador 'whether a move to the USSR might be possible. If not the USSR, then the GDR, China, or Czechoslovakia.' Ostap added that the Sterns were financially secure with a million dollars in Mexico which they planned to transfer to Switzerland. He ended the communication with 'No American Passports'.

In January 1957, US Attorney General Thomas Gilchrist impanelled a grand jury and brought in Boris Morros to testify. The FBI had serious concerns about how Morros would handle himself. They were aware that in the past, he had not been honest with them. Once he had told his handlers about meeting Jane Foster in Paris that previous November, when they knew for a fact she was in the US. There had been other instances as well. They worried that the grand jury would see through Morros's lies, in which case the entire MOCASE investigation would crash and lots of traitors would walk free without ever being charged. But they needn't have worried. Boris Morros had the grand jury eating out of his hand and the criminal case went forward.

On 25 January 1957, at 6am, a team of FBI and NYPD officers kicked in the door of Jack and Myra Soble's apartment and arrested them. They were devastated to learn their accuser was Boris Morros, their dear friend and comrade. At the same time the other members of the 'Jack Soble Spy Ring' were also being arrested, though this was apparently an act of theater since, as the available records suggest, most of them had already been turned.

As the handcuffs were being put on him, Jack Soble swore he would beat the rap by proving Boris Morros was a liar. But his bravado didn't last long. Within a few days, both Jack and Myra were cooperating. Jack Soble roundly cursed Morros, but bit by bit told them what they wanted to know about being a Soviet spy in America. They had plenty to say about Martha and her husband, none of it very nice. It was easy to tell how much they regretted ever meeting them. In their trials, they both pled guilty and accepted their seven- and fifteen-year sentences without much comment. Both were freed a year or two early and had their American citizenship restored before they died many years later.

Within a week of the Sobles' arrests, Martha and Alfred were visited by a consular official from the American Embassy who served them with subpoenas to appear before a grand jury of the Southern District of New York on 14 March. The Sterns immediately hired William O'Dwyer, brother of New York City Mayor Paul O'Dwyer, who petitioned the court to quash it because they hadn't made provisions for the Sterns to travel from Mexico to New York. New subpoenas were issued and delivered to the Sterns, along with several hundred dollars to pay for travel expenses. Again, the Sterns never showed, and in June 1957, they were found guilty of contempt of court and fined $25,000 each.

The FBI began secretly working with their Mexican counterparts in the federal police to stage a nighttime raid on the Sterns' villa. The plan was to capture them and then ship them up to El Paso as they had done with Morton Sobell seven years earlier. Even though their cooperation was coming from the highest levels of the Mexican government with secrecy all around, it nevertheless reached the ears of certain parties within the government which were sympathetic to the Sterns and what they'd been fighting for.

On 1 July 1957, the Justice Department began preparing a three-count indictment against the Sterns. On 12 July, Moscow sent Ostap a cable reading, 'Message from Prague: Friends prepared to grant asylum.' Eight days later, the three Sterns, carrying Paraguayan passports, made it out as the Escomillas (a family consisting of a husband, wife and twelve-year-old son), and boarded a KLM airliner in Mexico which took them first to Montreal and then to Amsterdam, and on to Prague, where they were welcomed as heroes.

35. PRAGUE

At Prague airport, there were people waiting to greet them. Newsreel cameras filmed the Sterns being handed bouquets of flowers, standing before microphones, denouncing American racist imperialism, and praising the wonderful Czechoslovak people for their dedication to freedom of expression. Then they were filmed waving to the well-wishers as they stepped into limousines before being taken away to their new lives in a part of Prague most Praguers never got to, and there escape from memory.

Among the first things Alfred did upon arriving was to go to the Narodni Banka, open a special account and deposit a large amount of hard currency into it. From there, everything was easy. Residency documents, *Prukazy* and permits were secured almost painlessly. They were also offered a very nice residence in a very nice part of Prague, on very friendly terms, and they were about to buy it when abruptly, for some reason, they suddenly weren't so sure about it. Something made them wonder if Prague really should be their first choice. Maybe they should look elsewhere. Perhaps Moscow might be nicer.

They went to the Russian Embassy, explained who they were and what they wanted. On 5 August, someone in Prague named Peshekhonov reported to Moscow that the Sterns wished to 'settle in Moscow before September since they have to put their son in school', adding that 'if Moscow wasn't possible, they might consider China and would only remain in Czechoslovakia as a last resort'. The Sterns expected permission would be given immediately, but

Moscow wasn't so sure it wanted someone like Martha living among them.

The Sterns were handed over to Col. Mikhail Korneev, an NKVD officer. Korneev talked with them over several days to understand the situation and see what could be worked out. He apparently suggested other places besides Moscow as possibilities. On 17 August 1957, he wrote that the Sterns 'categorically refused to live in East Germany, that they have lots of money and they can't comprehend why they weren't being let into the USSR. They don't understand why there is no resolution regarding their case.'[1]

In the memo, Peshekhonov mentioned the Sterns were offering their villa in Cuernavaca along with a houseful of museum-quality paintings. Moscow wasn't interested. They'd been warned already. It would be a mistake to create the impression of being in the Sterns' debt for anything.[2] They also knew that behind Alfred Stern's offer was the sudden worsening of his relations with Morton Halperin, the man he'd more or less handed the villa over to in a fit of generosity. An old comrade, Halperin was a well-regarded writer, fallen on tough times. Something which had just happened caused Stern to change his mind. Now he wanted Halperin gone, out of the house. They could have the property if they'd just force him to leave. The Mexico City rezidentura didn't want to go near it. They remembered Halperin from his wartime days as OSS's man in Mexico City.[3] He'd always shared stuff with them and they weren't going to turn on him now at the behest of some rich American just because he once did some work for them.

Moscow Center recommended to the Czechs that the Sterns remain in Czechoslovakia and be kept from travelling abroad to anywhere west besides Switzerland until they received Czech citizenship. It would, however, be allowable for them to visit the socialist countries without restriction. Korneev reported that the Sterns 'felt a desire to live in China as the climate is the same as in Mexico'. On 19 August, an inquiry was sent to Beijing. In a memorandum dated 22 August, Korneev mentioned that 'Martha is afraid for her son whose real mother lives in Chicago … A few years ago they went to court with this woman who was demanding that her son be returned. The court took the Sterns' side. The Sterns believe the trial was instigated by "John" [Morros].'[4]

Another thing Alfred Stern let Korneev know about were certain financial irregularities committed by Soble while he was their case officer:

> Alfred tells us how 'Czech'[Soble] would periodically take money from him, supposedly needed for our work. In doing so he would refer to a request we had supposedly made, Alfred would give him $3–4,000 USD at a time. Alfred wonders how 'Czech' could have squandered this money.

On 28 August 1957, the KGB petitioned the Communist Party Central Committee to allow the Sterns to settle in China. On 31 August, a reply came from Beijing that 'the PRC [People's Republic of China] is opposed, since they don't know who the Sterns are or anything about them. The PRC does not like the idea of the Sterns communicating with foreign countries while they're there.' The KGB man added: 'The situation in Shanghai is very complicated.'[5]

In early September 1957, the Sterns travelled to Moscow, checking into the newly opened Hotel Ukrainia,[6] a towering, 'Stalinist empire' style luxury hotel, to make their entrance into what they hoped to be their new city. The Russians hadn't decided whether they wanted to give them citizenship, but they were happy to host them, present them with bouquets of flowers and extol them as heroes, before taking them around to visit with mega-popular Soviet writer Ilya Ehrenberg as Martha had requested. Ehrenberg took them to the Aragvi, a Georgian restaurant known for its quality service, unaffordable prices and the fact that it was off-limits to all but the country's cultural and political elite. There, Martha wrote she was delighted by the open-hearted Russians.[7] Later, they were taken to Tolstoy's home, which had been turned into a museum. By coincidence, a few days later, an American journalist also happened to visit it and noticed Martha's signature and comments in the guestbook, which made the papers around the world. Martha, herself playing the journalist card, asked if she could meet and interview Guy Burgess and Donald Maclean, the recently defected former members of the Cambridge Spy Ring. She was turned down without explanation. Sometime after that they were told their request for Soviet citizenship as well as residency had been declined. Not long after that, sometime in late September, Vakrushev, the deputy department head of the Committee for Cultural Relations, reported that Martha and Alfred had informed them that they had decided to return to Czechoslovakia as permanent residents. It was reported that Stern had been offered 'an interesting job in the export-import field'.

⊱✣⊰

Martha, Alfred and Bobby returned to Prague, accepted the friendly offer of a nice residential property, and began living out the remainder of their lives. Initially there were some problems getting the kind of furniture they wanted, but they got that solved. They had money and, under communism, money could get them anything. But while the communist system could be breathtakingly flexible in certain matters, at the same time there were aspects of the law which were unbending to the point of being draconian. Under communism, everyone who was not old or disabled had to have jobs. This included foreign residents not under diplomatic protection. Alfred, because of his known expertise in public housing matters, was given an advisory position in the Ministry of Housing Construction. Being the daughter of a famous diplomat, Martha was hired by the Foreign Ministry to instruct young, proletarian wives of junior Czechoslovak foreign service officers on the intricacies of table manners and etiquette. But neither job worked out. Alfred's expertise turned out to be precarious. People in the ministry followed through on one of his suggestions and it turned out to be a very expensive mistake. As for Martha, it soon became clear that she knew very little about etiquette and her table manners were abysmal.

⊱✣⊰

Martha and Alfred did have one friend, Jiri Hajek, a high-ranking government official whom they'd been 'assigned'. He was the deputy foreign minister and a good fellow who spoke perfect English. Until recently, he had been at the UN in New York, so associating with them wasn't particularly risky for him. He'd take them around occasionally, invite them to openings and receptions – depending on who they were feting – and introduce them to important people who spoke English. He was also there to take their calls and knew how to get things done. He was even gracious the time they called him when their plumbing was clogged.

Bobby was put into a Czech school which included some foreign students. Among them was Mary Wheeler, from Prague's tiny American exile community. Looking back after nearly 70 years, she remembers that all the girls in their class thought Bobby Stern was cute and they all joked about wanting him for their boyfriend. But Bobby never really fit in. Even after he got a handle on speaking Czech, something his parents never achieved, he remained a lonely little boy, remote and difficult to engage with.

The Sterns made repeated attempts to get to know and become friendly with different English-speaking Czech artists and writers in Prague, but they didn't get anywhere. Hajek might introduce them and there'd be a conversation, but it would never go beyond that. Any attempt to get to know an artist or writer was met with a blank wall. Nobody voluntarily wanted anything to do with them. There were reasons everyone shied away. Czechoslovakia was just then beginning to de-Stalinize. The show trials were over, amnesties were starting to be declared for certain classes of political prisoners, but otherwise things were still extremely harsh. People were hoping it might be the start of a period of quiet, so the last thing anyone wanted at a time like that was to be associated with any American of any kind.

It turned out Mary Wheeler's father, George Wheeler, US Army Major-turned-defector, was the group's de facto leader. No one knew exactly how many there were; probably never more than twenty. A few were academics or worked for international organisations. There were some other families besides the Wheelers. There were the Chapmans, now the 'Čapeks' – Abe and Bella and their two girls Ann and Laura, who were there because CPUSA had ordered them to flee so they wouldn't get subpoenaed. So they went, the four of them. And now they were stuck in Prague, working crap jobs for crap pay. There were the Wards, who'd previously been living in Vienna while the father was studying music under the GI Bill, only to find themselves in the middle of a bungled spy-gambit and forced to defect against their own will.

There were people in transit; Americans that had been living elsewhere in the East who'd show up, stay for a month or two then move on to Poznan or Sofia or Beijing. Others were just lost souls who'd drifted in like dust and stayed. They weren't the kind of people anyone would ever get close to.

This wasn't Mexico. There was no crowd of kids for Bobby to kick about with or Saturday morning softball games or drop-of-a-hat get-togethers. They might manage a picnic together in the summer in one of the city's many parks with no one holding their breath over who might show up. There wasn't much joy in the exiles' hearts. The Sterns made some effort to get to know the others. It wasn't that it didn't pan out. There was some success getting to know the others, but not much follow-up or reciprocation They were as much stand-offish as dispirited and uneasy. Part of the problem was simply that the Sterns were hard currency, while everyone else was paid in korun. The disparity was just too much. Still, people passed through and if it was someone they knew, or who knew someone they knew, there'd be gatherings and the Sterns would be invited just like everyone else. Sometimes the Wheelers would invite them to the symphony or to an opera and they'd go. Prague had a few jazz clubs, but the music played was really glorified Dixieland and not anything they were interested in, and neither Martha nor Alfred really cared that much for classical music.

Martha couldn't see much beauty in Prague. On a very basic level, she and Alfred didn't care for it. It's hard to guess what it was that turned them off. Could it have been that as staunch Stalinists, being made to live in a communist state undergoing de-Stalinization was bothering them? Was Prague too politically oppressive for them, or not oppressive enough? To anyone who's ever spent time in Prague, it's a baffling thought. Even in the harshest of times, Prague was outwardly a charming city, chock full of nice places to go to while away afternoons and evenings. Its coffee houses, pubs and watering holes are legendary, but these were never really to Martha's tastes. Martha and Alfred never had a pub or coffee house to call their own, to kill a few hours in reading a book or newspaper, and where being by yourself wasn't an issue. If this was something they'd wanted, they could have had their own favorite dozen.

In Prague there were a couple of hotel bars where English-speaking foreigners sometimes gathered to talk in hushed voices over drinks under low lights. Everyone knew they were being watched, so it almost didn't matter. On odd nights something not quite like the old stammtisch might serendipitously come to life at the Hotel Evropa on Wenceslas Square, where foreign journalists usually met up, being around the corner from the CSTK press agency. Martha would prowl there sometimes, so the story went, looking for reporters to talk to and perhaps more. If she also went to other places, it isn't remembered.

With so many friends all living somewhere far away, Martha's avidness as a letter-writer didn't seem to flag. She wrote many letters and stayed in touch with as many of her friends as she could. On rare occasions, old friends made it to Prague. When they did, Martha and Alfred did all they could to show them a good time, but visits didn't happen very often.

In 1958, Martha and Alfred visited China. They stayed in Beijing, saw the sights, met high officials, travelled, and then spent time with the local American community, which was larger and livelier than Prague's. Its spiritual godfather was W. E. B. Du Bois, the black nationalist statesman. Du Bois introduced them to Sidney Rittenberg, a former US Army sergeant and Chinese linguist who'd stayed behind after the war and joined the Chinese Communist Party. He was one of only a few foreigners friendly with Zhou Enlai, Lin Biao, Chu Teh, and even, to a lesser extent, Mao Zedong himself. Stalin apparently hadn't liked this and at Stalin's urging, Rittenberg had spent the next five years in a prison cell, only to be taken out and rehabilitated two years after Stalin's death. Now Sidney Rittenberg was back in the Chinese Communist Party Central Committee with no hard feelings. He remembered Martha very pleasantly. They had lunch together a number of times and he thought her a witty conversationalist. On one occasion, Martha asked if he thought the Chinese could build an atomic bomb.[8] He prefaced it by telling her he didn't know anything about the matter, but if the Chinese could construct so many incredibly intricate sculptures, they could probably figure it out.

They'd gone in search of 'Young Revolutions' but whatever China was, it wasn't one. Based on what she saw and heard in interviews, Martha wrote a number of lengthy feature articles which all showed up in the international left-wing press. If she got paid for any of it, it couldn't have been much.

Martha Dodd really wanted to write about what she'd witnessed in Berlin but had left out of her book. In particular she wanted to write about her two martyred best friends Mildred and Arvid von Harnack. There were monuments to them in East Berlin, but in the West, no one had heard of them. They had operated one entire wing of the 'Red Orchestra', probably the war's most important spy network, and had inflicted serious damage against Hitler and the fascists. They'd also all been caught, tried, found guilty and beheaded.

Martha remembered the last time she and Mildred said goodbye to each other, one day in late autumn in 1937. They both knew that would be it. They had coffee together and they kept the conversation light, and the whole time they looked each other squarely in the eye. There would be no letters. Whatever Mildred was going to do, she didn't want any letters coming in from America. When the moment came, they smiled, said goodbye, then turned and walked away. Almost ten years passed before Martha learned what they'd done and how they'd died. In 1959, Martha and Alfred visited Germany, went to East Berlin and saw the memorials which the communist government had installed for them. It saddened Martha that people knew about Mildred and Arvid in the East but not in the West.

Martha kept trying to write about Mildred but found it difficult. She'd get a few pages in and quit. During that time, she made repeated stabs at it. There was nothing driving her writing and she blamed this on being in Prague.

After five years of trying to make the best of it, the Sterns decided they'd had enough. Someone suggested Cuba might just be the Young Revolution they'd been hoping to find. Word was Castro, Guevara and that crowd were achieving some amazing things, that Cuba was the place to be, and that you could have a pretty nice time there. Maybe it was time to say *adios* to Prague.

They explained it to Dr Myslyl, the young lawyer Jiri Hajek had recently introduced them to. They'd been colleagues back in New York; now he was home and smart at a lot of things. He'd told them the best way around the jobs requirement was setting up a company, say import-export, which the communists allowed under certain circumstances. He could set something up for them, and if they did that, they could then hire servants as employees.

Now Dr Myslyl listened to them talk about Cuba. He nodded and told them it was a fine idea, but advised them not to sell anything. Keep the property. It was one of the few in Prague where the title was absolutely not disputable. They needed to not sell it. It would be a terrible idea. *Just go to Cuba. Come back whenever you feel like it, because you will. Everything will be fine.* So they did. They went to Cuba and for about five years life was great.

⌘

Cuba was everything they had dreamed of. Fidel Castro seemed to possess all the promise they'd once seen in Stalin and the Soviet Union, and best of all, it was taking place here in the Americas! Life was joyful and good. The Havana Libre Hotel, where they lived, was a spectacular place, having been built only a few years earlier as the Havana Hilton. Martha and Alfred moved into the penthouse and life once again was a great big party. They had been visiting Cuba for years, but what they were seeing now was different. The revolution had changed them. For the first time they wore their defiance and pride openly, which made them even more joyful than before. In their minds, they'd been in a war of sorts with the *Yanqui*, who tried to walk over them, like they'd been doing for years. But the Cubans had shown them! As far as they were concerned they had won that war, and this made the Sterns and other American comrades that much more welcome.

In Havana, hot winds blew and music seemed to be playing everywhere, late into the evening. The beaches were all open, and so were some of the biggest nightclubs – under new management, of course. From what Martha and Alfred could see, everyone was happy. Martha and Alfred seemed to fit in perfectly. Both already spoke pretty good Spanish and both enjoyed the company of all these vibrant, fun people arriving from all over the world.

One such colourful personality Martha and Alfred probably spent time with in Havana was Robert F. Williams, a black militant who, though not particularly left-wing, had fled to Cuba after he and a group of black war veterans ambushed a group of Klansmen en route to a lynching. In Havana, Williams became a soul music DJ whose program *Radio Free Dixie* was blasted over the airwaves daily via Radio Havana's international broadcasting arm. Williams' propaganda value was hard to argue with. The Sterns also got to know Abdallah Schleifer, the Arab Nationalist theoretician; Comrade Ly Van Sau, the Vietcong representative; Meng Cheang Eng, with the Khmer Rouge; and others representing different groups.

Martha and Alfred had only been in Havana a few months when President Kennedy was assassinated in Dallas. That put a big freeze on life there while everyone waited to see how it would turn out for Cuba. Sure enough, Lee Harvey Oswald, the man they said killed him, had been connected with something in New Orleans called 'Fair Play for Cuba', which, once word got around, told everyone it had to be CIA and nothing else unless you wanted to include the Mob. Everyone there knew the CIA and the Mob both had it in for Cuba, and everyone agreed that was why he'd been killed. As for Martha and Alfred, JFK wasn't someone they held in high esteem. Truth be told he was just as bad a warmonger as Eisenhower. 1964 started out pretty tense and only became more tense with the American military intervention in the Dominican Republic. But eventually that battle ended and America's imperial focus shifted to Vietnam and Southeast Asia. With that, things calmed down and the good times in Cuba carried on.

Initially, their son Bobby remained behind in Prague, since he was still in school. He'd been left in the care of a guardian and the housekeeper. By now Bobby was a teenager attending high school. Once he was finished, he was expected to do his two years' military service before going on to university. Alfred and Martha both thought he should study medicine, but that didn't happen. By now it was also becoming obvious their son was having 'problems', and not necessarily disciplinary; something else. Bobby Stern was a nice boy and was always well behaved and polite in school, as elsewhere. There was just something wrong, obviously wrong, with him. Even though he was intelligent, sometimes he just wouldn't, couldn't learn. The Sterns flew back to deal with it. Dr Myslyl had told them that having their son diagnosed by a Czech child psychologist might not be a good idea. On things like this, he told them, their attitudes tended to reflect political exigencies and it would be better to have

Bobby examined and treated in Vienna, where the doctors had a more enlightened approach to similar cases. He could arrange to get them an exit visa for that without any trouble. The doctors in Vienna examined Bobby and declared that he suffered from schizophrenia.

Bobby told his parents he thought Prague and the Czechs were too stressful for him. He wanted to go back to Mexico. Was there any way he could do that? There was. They still owned the villa and some other properties in Cuernavaca and Mexico City proper. Ralph Scott was still there, watching over things for them. They decided to find a place for him to live and have Ralph Scott act as his companion and guardian. This seemed to work out well. Besides, Mexico City was a direct flight to and from Havana. Seeing each other would be a lot easier this way.

It was now the mid-1960s. Life in Cuba was still good. Old comrades and people they'd known from the Wallace campaign days kept showing up. It was mainly a question of catching a direct flight to Havana from Mexico City or Montreal, something that could be accomplished in a matter of hours. The Sterns' lawyer, Victor Rabinowitz officially had the Cuban government as a client, and he flew down frequently, as did their other lawyer, Leonard Boudin, along with lots of other people. There was a young Socialist Workers Party activist there named Fred Jerome whose father they'd known back in the day. Fred covered Cuba for the *National Guardian*, the paper Stern helped bankroll years earlier. He quickly became a second son to them.

Slowly, things began to change for the worse. People weren't always pleasant and the Cuban authorities had started to tighten up on foreign residents. More and more of the old crew of colourful characters were being hustled out or leaving of their own accords, while fewer and fewer new people came in and stayed. Martha and Alfred felt the cold shoulder from people who'd once been friends. People were now less willing to see them as fellow communists and comrades. The Sterns decided to return to Prague.

36. SIX MONTHS OF REVISIONIST DEBAUCHERY

In February 1968, Martha Dodd and Alfred Stern left Havana, boarding a Moscow-bound Aeroflot TU-114 fast turboprop airliner. It was the fastest propeller-driven commercial aircraft in the world, as fast as any jet airliner. It was showing the world just how excellent a Russian aircraft could be. Revolutionary people celebrate the triumph of Soviet industry.

They were looking forward to seeing Moscow again. But what they saw there, the shoddiness, the hypocrisy and corruption, broke their hearts and disgusted them. It seemed ordinary Russians' pride, their dignity and fundamental socialist decency had turned to shit. At least that was how Martha saw it. Russians were horrible to them. Wherever they went, once anyone realised they were foreigners, they were all over them, scamming them, begging them for American dollars, British pounds, Deutschmarks, anything. And the officials, clerks and everybody else were also intent on cheating them out of their money. It was as if the Russians had all given up on socialism. But if that wasn't bad enough, when they got to Prague, they quickly found something completely different was going on there as well.

Major political changes had been happening in Czechoslovakia while the Sterns romped in Cuba. A certain limited relaxation was beginning to take place under Alexandr Dubcek. Now, as long as people basically behaved themselves, they could express themselves and speak their minds, which they started doing. As the winter melted away, with the first blush of the new season came a blossoming of social and political renewal among the Czechs and Slovaks. Soon, the Western press were calling it 'the Prague Spring'. When Alfred and Martha Stern stepped off the plane at Prague's Ruzyne airport, it had barely started and they probably didn't even notice it at first. But in the days and weeks that followed, this tidal change very quickly became apparent. At first they were horrified.

On the streets of Prague, the Czechs and Slovaks openly embraced everything about the West – the Beatles, blue jeans and rock and roll music – and by doing so, had turned their backs on socialism and their brothers in the East. This disgusted the Sterns and broke their communist hearts all over again. They considered 'socialism with a human face' as 'double-speak', because in their eyes, socialism already had a human face. But what was happening here wasn't socialism at all, but the worst kind of revisionism. It was money-grubbing, capitalist and imperialist and fascist to boot. Everybody acting free and thinking only of themselves, acting and talking like ... hippies!

Worst of all, in Martha's eyes, was the way the Czechs were now acting about the Russians. Earlier, the Czechs had made a big show of deep affection towards them; their Russian brothers, their friends, their liberators! Now, suddenly, it was obvious all of it was a great big lie. Now the Czechs couldn't even pretend they liked the Russians a tiny bit. And after all the Russians had done for them!

All over Prague, on the streets and in its many squares and public places, it seemed a festival was going on. People were celebrating the spring and renewal of life and of freedom. At first, Martha and Alfred hated it, hated everything about it: the cheap coarseness of it, its betrayal of everything they had fought for, and for so long, and how quickly they had just dropped the flag at the first flash of Western baubles. In one letter Martha referred to it as 'six months of revisionist debauchery'.

But as the Spring went on their revulsion withered. They started going downtown and saw how festive everyone was. It finally occurred to them that once they got past the Prague Spring's flash and gaudiness, all anyone was asking for was to live honestly and to have peace in the world. Their demands were reasonable, even in a Stalinist society. It was something the 'Dictatorship of the Proletariat' was supposed to allow and provide for. They thought about what they saw in Moscow and they started to realise the whole thing had been bad and unworkable from the very beginning. It was now a matter of making the best with what they had without turning to the West. They still thought it was important not to do that.

Of course the Russians were closely monitoring everything and what they saw alarmed them. This was too radical. If Czechoslovakia kept doing this, the rest of the Bloc might establish debaucheries of their own. It needed to be stopped.

On 21 August 1968, at 7am, the Sterns' telephone started ringing. It was Bobby calling from Mexico City, asking if they were alright. Martha and Alfred were puzzled. They were fine. Why wouldn't they be? Bobby told them he'd heard on the news that the Russian Army had invaded. It was the first they had heard of it!

Though they couldn't see anything when they went to their windows, upon opening them they could hear the rumbling of tank treads on Plzenska Street a few blocks down. People were out, moving back and forth. Then they heard the shooting and smelled the smoke coming up from across the river. The Prague Spring was being crushed.

On the streets of Prague and elsewhere, Czechs and Slovaks were telling the Russian, Bulgarian and Polish invaders that they weren't saving them from anything, that they were not welcome and should go home and leave them be. Some started fighting back, attacking the tanks first with signs and pleading, then with fists, rocks and Molotov cocktails. At some point the Russians started shooting.

The experiment of 'socialism with a human face' ended the way the pessimists predicted. It was destroyed. For a while there was nothing and life slowly returned to something approaching normality. The Sterns had retreated into their wealth and privilege. Jiri Hajek was out of the government, and aside from Dr Myslyl, they no longer had any connections. They had become non-persons. Martha's letters from the period don't indicate how much, if any, of the Soviet invasion they might have personally witnessed, but it is clear that it affected them greatly. Their God had completely failed them.

Smarting from a sense of betrayal, Martha and Alfred became, very quietly, dedicated supporters of the Czech dissidents. This came through Rita Klimova, a disgraced economist, fallen-away Stalinist, and one of Martha's very few Czech acquaintances. She understood better than anyone Martha's feelings of betrayal. Rita Klimova's parents had been communists and as soon as Hitler moved into Czechoslovakia, they fled to the US and she spent the war years in New York City. English wasn't her first language, but the sheer abrasiveness of her Bronx accent, coupled with her own natural brashness, made most people assume Rita Klimova was a working-class New York Jew. Up until sometime in the1960s, she had been a Stalinist economist and popular media pundit. She was also the daughter, wife and daughter-in-law of prominent Stalinist economists, all of whom, it seemed, had had their 'road to Damascus' moments at around the same time. For them, the key to a nice, fulfilling, respected life had been a question of accepting the lie, and repeating it, with all the other reasonable people who agreed it wasn't too much to ask – only it was. Rita Klimova could no longer say it and neither could her father, her husband and father-in-law. They all lost their posts at universities and the economic institutes. Suddenly she was scrambling to scrape together a living doing Czech–English translations. Which, apparently, was how Martha came to be in Rita's orbit.

An apostate, cast out from academia and communist respectability and needing to survive, Rita Klimova turned half-feral, half hunter-gatherer, relentlessly foraging between a half-dozen different Czech publishing houses, mostly being paid a pittance for work the salaried staff didn't want to do. Martha at that point had been doing rewrites for a publisher that produced titles in English. For a while they'd work together on different projects, hoping they might generate enough money. Martha, of course, didn't need the money, but welcomed the social exposure. Ultimately it didn't work out enough for Klimova to make it more than an occasional thing, though the two remained friendly enough that she would breeze by or invite Martha out somewhere. Martha learned that in Rita's endless darting from place to place she was connecting into the Czech dissident underground. She knew them all. She was even a close friend of a surrealist playwright named Vaclav Havel. At a time when betrayal was becoming all too commonplace, they trusted her because they knew Rita Klimova was beyond rehabilitation. She kept her association with Martha secret since there was no point in it; she was someone people were, at best, only very dimly aware of. Under this cloak, Martha Dodd Stern slowly became their secret benefactor.

In 1970, Martha and Alfred made another trip to Cuba. Perhaps they hoped it might provide some respite from the grey, authoritarian gloominess which had taken over Czechoslovakia. Though they did get to spend time with Bobby, who flew in from Mexico with Ralph Scott and whatever Cuban and American comrades were still around or able to fly in, the Marxist regime there coupled with the obvious harshness of life was enough to convince them it was bad. Rabinowitz dropped in, being an official paid legal representative of the Cuban government. Since he was also the Sterns' lawyer, Alfred and Martha let him know they'd had enough and wanted to go home. They asked him if some kind of deal could be worked out.

Shortly after the Sterns returned to Prague, one of Moscow Center's people reported that 'the Sterns informed the Central Committee of the CPCS of their intention to leave the CSSR'. It noted 'negative changes in their views' and 'contacts with right-wing elements expelled from the KPCM'. In ruminating over this news, one Moscow Center official mused:

> The information that the Sterns may possess about the activities of Soviet intelligence is outdated and mostly known to the Adversary from the testimony of the traitor 'John' (Boris Morros).
>
> If we receive an official inquiry from the relevant agencies of the CSSR regarding the Sterns, we deem it possible to respond that there are no objections on our part to their moving to the West.

At around the same time, Rabinowitz wrote the Sterns saying he'd made some inquiries within the Justice Department and their reaction was that unless they submitted themselves to a comprehensive interrogation, there could be no deal. The Nixon Administration had no sympathy for their plight. As far as they were concerned, they were traitors who had made their beds and could now lie in them.

At around the same time, George Wheeler informed Alfred and Martha that they were going home. Sometime in 1972, he and his wife went to the US Embassy and applied for passports, something they had attempted unsuccessfully more than once in the past, but this time they got them. Martha and Alfred did not ask what they'd had to tell them in order to get them. Instead they congratulated them and wished them happy lives and not to forget to write.

The Wheelers flew back to Washington State, where George Wheeler bounced between a number of teaching jobs until one stuck. He also joined with brother Donald who had become a dairy farmer in Oak Harbor, Washington, after inexplicably losing his university post during the McCarthy witch-hunt. What he never knew was that he was one of the first people identified as a Soviet agent from the wartime Venona decrypts. They determined that the member of the Soviet spy network, known as the 'Sound', called 'Iskra' was Donald Wheeler, a US Treasury Department official. Rather than risk giving away that they were deciphering the Soviet diplomatic cable traffic, it was decided against arresting him and charging him with espionage and treason. Instead somebody whispered something that made him come under general suspicion and that way he was fired from the university where he was teaching. Rather than fight it, Donald Wheeler became a successful dairy farmer. He invited George Wheeler into the business, which George accepted, and for the rest of their lives everything was good. As for Wheeler's four children, all but one stayed in Prague. For them and others of their invisible class, the Iron Curtain hadn't been their problem. Their parents might have had their passports taken away, but theirs weren't. Prague was home.

In 1975, Martha and Alfred were severely injured when the limousine they were being driven in was hit by a carful of drunken medical students. All the young people were killed and Martha and Alfred ended up spending more than a month in hospital before they were allowed to go home. Neither fully recovered. As the years passed, their health worsened. Alfred developed cancerous skin lesions while Martha had digestive problems.

Martha and Alfred's last years together were lonely ones. Once the Wheelers left, that was it for the Americans. Everyone they knew was now gone. People still came through, but this was becoming increasingly infrequent. Friends from Cuba came after some begging. Rabinowitz visited once, so did some others, but mostly their friends' letters stopped arriving because they'd died. Fred Jerome visited once, but mainly his presence felt more constant since he'd agreed to act as their buying agent, sending things they couldn't get their hands on in Prague: Tums, Bisodol mints, Alka-Seltzer, men's socks and panties that properly fit, toothbrushes with pink, hard rubber spikes on the other end, cocktail napkins decorated with signs of the zodiac. Year after year, Jerome did this, until it finally became too much. In the end he felt used and unappreciated and he let them know he couldn't do it for them anymore. After that he drifted away.

During the years the Sterns had lived in Cuba, Martha and Alfred felt like they were still part of things. Plenty of American leftists kept coming through, with fresh news from America and messages from old friends and comrades, more than a few of whom had risen up in the world. Jacob Javitz was now a senator; others had positions in universities, research institutes and non-profits. They'd gotten on with their lives but still remembered their exiled friends. Martha and Alfred felt like they were still in the swing of things. But in Prague there was none of that.

For a long time the 'negotiations' with the Justice Department didn't go anywhere. While there was a Republic administration running things there didn't seem to be any interest in moving forward. This might have been because of their lawyers. Rabinowitz and Boudin were attorneys for left-wingers. They did it more out of conviction than greed, but at the same time, their business model required the better-heeled clients providing them with a revenue stream which the poorer ones could not. Resolving the Sterns' case in a timely manner was not really in their interest, as much as both men might have considered Alfred and Martha their personal friends.

What ultimately broke the logjam was Martha's friend Sylvia Crane who got her friend Don Edwards, the Democratic Congressman from California, to look into the matter. The 1976 elections had recently taken place and with Jimmy Carter, a Democrat, in the White House, they found a not unsympathetic reception. Edwards went between the White House and Justice Department. The more he looked into it, the more he realised that there was no good reason to leave the case unresolved. Much as the FBI might howl at the injustice of letting Soviet spies go free, the fact was, their case against the Sterns had always been slim and by now, with both Boris Morros and Jack Soble dead and Myra Soble unlikely to deliver anything on the witness stand other than hearsay, there was no reason not to let the Sterns come in from the cold. Finally, Edwards secured a deal from the Justice Department.

Sometime during the spring of 1979, Alfred and Martha met with a small group of Justice Department and FBI officials at a beachfront hotel in Slovenia. For several days, the Sterns were put through day-long question-and-answer sessions. A lot of the questions had to do with Zarubin. They also wanted to know about Martha's time in Berlin, but mostly if it was true that she knew him there. They wanted their version of Jack Soble, Robert Soblen, Susan B. Anthony, Jane Foster, George Zlatovsky, Henry Collins, Irving V. Sollins and others, many of whom were names they honestly hadn't heard of before. They wanted to hear what they had to say about Boris Morros. Getting them to talk about him ultimately didn't take much urging, though they were spitting angry the whole time. Boris Morros! May his soul eternally rot in hell!

It's fair to assume Martha and Alfred were asked a lot of questions about the Wallace campaign. Who had given them that stuff about biological warfare? As for the campaign staff and the matter of who was and wasn't a commie, were the FBI even interested at this point? It was 1979 and whatever secrets CPUSA thought it had had probably already long before revealed themselves to the FBI. Hoover had died several years earlier and by now the aftertaste of the witch-hunts was still present and couldn't have tasted too good. There's a fair chance the interrogators didn't delve too far into that. What the FBI were not particularly interested in hearing anything about were Mildred Fish, Arvid von Harnack or Boris Vinogradov, though Martha insisted otherwise. In the end, Martha and Alfred answered enough of their questions that the DOJ and FBI were satisfied. They left the hotel and returned to Washington. A few days later, it was announced that the Office of the Attorney for the Southern District of New York had agreed to quash its 1957 indictment against Alfred Stern and Martha Dodd Stern. Justice had prevailed!

When word got out, scattered one-, two- and three-person celebrations took place all over New York, Washington, DC, and California. The news of it made a good number of papers in America as well as across the world. But it was not a big story. In the end, as

McCarthy-era *cause célèbres* went, Martha and Alfred Stern were in the minor league. The fact he was a 'pink millionaire' and she was an ambassador's daughter might have added some poignancy to it, but not enough to attract much attention. While popular interest in the McCarthy era was starting to grow now that it was safely 30 years in the past, what still pricked most Americans' sense of injustice was the rotten treatment meted out to Alger Hiss and to a lesser extent Hollywood screenwriters Dalton Trumbo and his crowd. Martha and Alfred hadn't really come to the fore until after the whole thing with McCarthy had peaked and everyone had started wanting to put it all behind them. Martha and Alfred were also problematic since they carried equally the taint of espionage with persecution. It was, perhaps, why their story had never captured any sustained public interest. *Man on a String*, the 1959 movie based on Morros' book, hadn't exactly brought in the crowds. Still, a lot of people stuck by them and were glad that the government had finally seen to reason. Finally, the Sterns could come home. Only it turned out there was a catch.

When the US Attorney's Office dropped the three-count indictment against the Sterns, it left intact the $25,000 fine which it had levied against them for failing to appear in court. That amount had compounded and grown many times in the twenty years since. Add to that all the taxes Alfred Stern hadn't paid. Any way it got sliced would be a pretty penny. In the end, what it meant for Alfred and Martha Dodd Stern was that they couldn't go home to America, but they could go anywhere else. So instead they flew to London a number of times during the 1980s. They enjoyed it as much as their poor health allowed. They did some shopping and went out to dinner and saw shows. However, nice as it was, they found London tiring and extremely expensive. They saw a number of doctors on a great many health issues. They discussed finding some nice assisted-living situation, but concluded that the money they had wouldn't last very long if they did. They returned to Prague and lived as best they could. They'd spend a couple of weeks in the summer on the seaside in Yugoslavia, and some years Bobby would come with Ralph Scott, his guardian. Bobby held down a job as an assistant mechanic at a garage in Mexico City.

After Jane Foster and her husband deployed to Austria in 1946, Martha and Alfred never heard from them again. Even though they fully understood that the rules of *konspiritsia* forbade further contact, as time passed, Martha and Alfred felt increasingly put out by their friends' failure to write. When they learned they'd been indicted at the same time on the same charges as themselves by the same grand jury, but had dodged arrest and extradition simply by moving to France, they began to suspect the Zlatovskys might actually have secretly cut a deal with the Feds. In the late 1970s, they heard Jane was writing a memoir, and wondered long and hard what Jane might say about them. Shortly after Jane died in 1979, her book, *An UnAmerican Lady*, came out in the UK. What little it said about Martha and Alfred wasn't particularly kind, portraying them as shallow dilettantes. Martha and Alfred delighted that the book sold few copies and mostly only in Britain.

In 1983, Philip Metcalf, a young historian with whom Martha had corresponded, published a book called *1933*, about Berlin during the first two years of Hitler's rule. Both Martha and her father featured prominently, along with Diels, Roehm, Goering, Schleifer and Blomberg. It hit the bestseller lists and with its success came more inquiries and requests for interviews. Academics, scholars and journalists wrote with questions, seeking interviews, wanting clarification. It started off with questions about William E. Dodd, her father. Since she'd edited his diary and decided what went in and stayed out, she was the reigning authority on him. For years, she'd answered them and talked to his would-be biographers and decided whether or not to grant access to his papers. But then they wanted to ask Martha about herself – about her experiences in Germany and later. As for all the other McCarthy/witch-hunt stuff, what did Martha have to say? Just a few years earlier Martha might have launched into her fiery polemics. She would have proclaimed again and again, loudly, their innocence, and repeated for the umpteenth time that they weren't, and never had been communists or Russian spies.

But it seemed too many of the questions they were asking were personal. She could tell they were really hoping to get her to dish the dirt and tell the world who she'd had sex with. The very question was so … impertinent! In Martha's estimation there was nothing lower than someone who'd 'kiss and tell'. Whatever she'd thought of Thomas Wolfe was one thing, but when she'd heard the things he'd said about her to Max Perkins and others, after that, in her opinion, Wolfe was garbage. Now, Martha was tired of it all. She had run out of things to say. She often thought about writing another book. Every other year or so, she'd make a stab at it and then quit.

A couple of times a year, they might invite Czech people they knew over for dinner. People came, mainly because they knew Martha and Alfred had '*Tuzex bony*'[1] and could be talked into selling them some once dinner was over, while they were having a last drink before taking their leave. Most were people Hajek had introduced them to back before the Russian invasion and the period after that of 'normalisation' had ended their brilliant careers and turned them into 'non-persons'. Hajek was one of them. Sometimes their lawyer, Dr Myslyl, would also attend, though more out of niceness than anything else, since he could get all the bony he needed himself. The dinner conversations were anything but brilliant – speaking in English, as demanded by the hosts, had become a struggle for their guests, so it was stilted. The Sterns felt like old dogs no longer able to perform old tricks. They were dreadful evenings for everyone involved.

Alfred Stern died from cancer on 26 June 1986. His passing was noted in the *New York Times* and elsewhere in the Western press. The memorial get-together held at Corliss Lamont's house was well-attended by the old friends and comrades whom death had not already taken. Alfred's work as a liberal activist, public housing proponent and passionate supporter of countless left-wing causes was remembered and celebrated. That he'd spent so much of his life in exile because of his refusal to give in to the fascist McCarthyites was also noted and much reflected upon. As for those ancient allegations about spying for the Soviets, well, just as they'd known all along, it had all been lies. The fact that the charges against him and Martha had been dropped proved it. They talked about Alfred's widow Martha, and how she was still there in Prague, resolute and defiant. All of them agreed that a way needed to be found to bring her back so she could at least die at home, but that would have to be a battle for another day.

Alfred's death left Martha more alone and disconsolate than ever. In the letters she wrote to her remaining friends, Martha spoke of the terrible emptiness that made each day largely indistinguishable from the one before or the one following. Except for the occasional, brief visit from Dr Myslyl or Rita Klimova, Martha's sole connection to the world was Lilinka Sperlova, her longtime, English-speaking secretary. It went on like this for a year or two, then Sperlova announced she needed to retire. They notified the Labour Ministry, but no replacement could be found. In the end, Dr Myslyl told Martha he would post an advert in the *Mlada Fronta Dnes* classifieds and that he'd bring her whatever replies came in, but that she would have to take it from there, though he would write up the employment contract for whoever she decided to hire.

The advert was posted and ran for a week, but only one person responded. According to her CV, Dora Slaba had worked at Radio Prague's British Section until 1968, and after that at the Czech Academy of Sciences doing something dismal involving the translation of scientific papers into English. Myslyl guessed she'd been part of that crew which had kept broadcasting during the Soviet Invasion. They'd had their one day of glory and had been made to pay for it every day since. Yes, that was how they dealt with anyone brave or stupid enough to stick their heads up. Political unreliability could be a terrible thing; not that Stanislav Myslyl had any experience with it personally. All he knew was that 1968 was already a long time ago and nineteen years spent in Purgatory was long enough. His guess was that by now, the StB no longer gave much of a damn about anything, let alone where this woman worked. He gave the CV and letter to Martha who, after looking at it, decided to give her a call and invite her over for tea to discuss the position.

37. THE PINK LADY

Technically speaking, Dora Slaba wasn't Czech. Czech wasn't even her first language; it was her third. Dora was a Sudeten Jew and her first language was German. She was only five when the Nazis marched into the Sudetenland and her family fled to England. Once in London, they all switched to English, and for the next eight years she did everything she could to make herself as British as possible. They could have stayed and should have, but somewhere in the course of it, Dora's mother turned socialist, and after the communist takeover of Czechoslovakia, she declared that they needed to return and 'be part of the Revolution'.

Needless to say, going back was a mistake. None of them could speak Czech and because they spoke German, the Czechs automatically disliked and distrusted them. Being Jewish seemed only to make it worse. They were German Jews and the fact that they'd spent the war in England put them with the capitalists. But then when they tried to leave and return to England, they found they couldn't. It wasn't allowed. So they went to Prague, found a flat, got jobs, learned to speak Czech and settled into what they surmised would be the rest of their lives.

Dora picked up Czech quickly, but it was her English that was her fortune. She started doing voice work for Radio Prague before she even left high school, and she was working there as part of her curriculum by the time she was attending Charles University. After that, she was a full-time announcer and producer. Throughout the 1950s and most of the 1960s, Dora and her colleagues lived lives of relative privilege. All they had to do was keep their heads down, say what they were supposed to say in front of the microphone and not ask any questions that they weren't supposed to ask. When the Prague Spring came with its lessening of restrictions, she took it all in without comment or reaction. Unlike most Czechs, Dora knew enough about Russia to know they wouldn't take it for long.

It came early one morning in August 1968. Dora heard the airplanes flying overhead, landing troops and light tanks before dawn at Ruzyne airport. At the same time, thousands of tanks and hundreds of thousands of Russian, Bulgarian and East German troops were streaming in across the borders, fully believing they were liberating Czechoslovakia from the clutches of the capitalists and revisionists. Dora turned on the radio and, to her surprise, heard her colleagues broadcasting to their fellow citizens the outrage that was happening, telling them to stand up to the invaders. After twenty years of keeping her head down, Dora knew what she had to do. She kissed her husband and daughter goodbye, left their apartment in Zizkov, and made her way downtown, past the crowds of people surrounding the Russian tanks that were already on Wenceslas Square, to the studios of Radio Prague, where she spent the next three days broadcasting in English and German, telling the world exactly what was happening. For some reason, the Russians, whose tanks were standing right outside, did not know their location. By the time they did, Dora and several others had moved to a hidden remote broadcasting facility in the country. That lasted another day. When they eventually got word that the Russians had located them and were on their way, Dora and her colleagues drove off in a Skoda that wasn't theirs, abandoning it at an open crossing point on the West German border. Two days later, Dora was back in London after twenty years.

But it didn't work out. It was not the London she'd known from the war. Jobs were hard to come by. The Czech emigres already there regarded her with suspicion – worse, as an interloper intent on stealing their 'rice bowls'. The British weren't much better. She couldn't get voice work because her accent wasn't right. One day, sitting by herself in Hyde Park, she was approached by two men she guessed were StB. They told her that if she returned she could have her old job back. She decided to do it. A few days later, she was back behind the microphone at Radio Prague. After one week, she was informed her position had been cancelled and was told to report to the Labor Ministry for reassignment. For the next fifteen years she toiled in a sub-basement at the Czech Academy of Sciences translating scholarly articles into English. Then one day in 1987, while scouring the classified pages of *Mlada Fronta Dnes* in search of Jeffrey Archer novels, she saw an advert for an English-language secretary that promised good pay and congenial working conditions. She'd never seen a 'help wanted' advert in a newspaper before for anything, let alone for an English-language secretary. It wasn't how things worked under communism. Still, she decided to apply for it. Shortly after, she got a call from what sounded like a very old lady with a southern American accent inviting her to come to her house to discuss the job over tea.

The first thing Dora noticed that first day walking up to her house from the nearby tram stop was that there were no cars parked on either side of the street, except for a single white Lada sedan with the motor running and two men sitting inside it smoking Sparta cigarettes and eyeing her suspiciously as she approached. Without a doubt, they were StB gorillas. The logical question to ask after that would have been: what were they doing there? But Dora didn't ask herself that question. Living under communism taught you not to ask even obvious questions like that. The housekeeper opened the door and let Dora in. She took her coat and bag, and from her rude manner Dora immediately knew the woman already regarded her as her enemy. She led Dora down a hallway to a staircase going to the upper floors. She stopped, turned to Dora and, like a castle tour guide, dramatically extended her hand, pointing to the top of the stairs, where there stood a very old lady wearing a pink pantsuit. Their eyes met, and on cue the pink lady began regally descending the stairs, like a showgirl, her left hand stylishly upraised while her right hand did all the work, furiously clutching and releasing her grip on the banister rail as she made each step. Watching her, Dora felt the pink pantsuit was reminiscent of episodes of *Columbo*, where the women wearing them were inevitably rich old ladies, who, for reasons that soon would be revealed, had just murdered their husband, their lover or their lover's girlfriend.

The woman introduced herself to Dora: 'Martha Dodd Stern. How do you do?' She offered Dora a bony hand to shake. She was a tiny woman, Dora realised, and her blue eyes, though rheumy, still seemed ablaze with fire. They went to the living room. Dora sat on the couch while the old lady lowered herself into a stuffed chair. The housekeeper brought in a tray with a teapot, cups and saucers, teaspoons, bowls of sugar, lemon and milk and a plate of sugar biscuits, set them out of the coffee table, poured each a cup of tea and then withdrew.

The old lady waited until the housekeeper was halfway down the hall before she began speaking. Over tea, she explained to Dora that she was an author and had been a journalist for years; a globe-trotting journalist, she noted, who had filed countless stories from all over the world. She asked Dora to tell her about herself. She seemed to find it amusing that Dora was a Jew from the Sudetenland and that she'd spent the war in London. She asked about her time with Radio Prague and how she'd liked being a journalist. Dora had never considered herself a journalist, but she told her what she thought she wanted to hear. The old lady nodded. Dora guessed that she was now going to ask about 1968 and the Soviet tanks, but she didn't.

The old lady explained that she and her husband had settled in Prague a long time ago. He had died two years earlier and she still maintained a great deal of correspondence and was working on another book, so she needed a secretary. It would be very easy work.

The salary she offered was more than twice what the Academy paid. She also said she'd take Dora along on her spring shopping trip to London. She even agreed to have it written into Dora's employment contract. What could Dora say but yes?

❧

At first, it was like a dream. Dora would show up each morning at eight, but the old lady rarely got up before ten. During that time, Dora would get coffee in the kitchen, chat with the cook and housekeeper, then go to her office, which had once been Mrs Stern's writing room. She'd go over the previous day's correspondence, finish up whatever hadn't been completed and prepare it for her signature and mailing. Mrs Stern would come downstairs after having breakfast in her room. They'd go over the letters that were going out, and put them in the envelopes and give them to Honza, the driver, who would take them down to the central post office, since they were all international. By then, a new batch of letters would arrive and Dora would help her sort them. Often Dora would read them aloud to her, other times Mrs Stern would read them herself using a magnifying glass.

Sometimes she'd insist on writing her response immediately, other times she'd give the letters a dismissive wave and mutter something about responding 'some other time'. Sometimes the old lady would just want to talk. Even at her advanced age – Dora guessed she had to be at least 80 – she could be extremely witty and even risqué. She liked telling stories and as a journalist had apparently lived and reported from all over the world. Her tales were often very interesting and she had a knack for telling them.

But sometimes, right in the middle of one, just as it started getting interesting, she'd suddenly clam up and refuse to say anything more, no matter how much Dora might beseech her. Once, when Dora tried coaxing her to continue, the old lady, to Dora's surprise, suddenly snapped at her very angrily. Dora backed away and never pushed her after that.

Neither the cook nor the housekeeper could speak English, and though they'd act very friendly to her, it was clear to Dora that they regarded her as a threat. Dora guessed they were robbing the old lady blind. Though she ate like a bird, the household grocery budget could have fed a large extended family. Also, Dora couldn't help noticing that books and some of the many small art objects kept disappearing. Figuring that her loyalties rightfully lay with her employer and not with them, she once brought the matter up with the old lady, only to have her give a sad, knowing shrug and mutter something about 'the devil you know'.

As for the driver, Honza, he was something else entirely. From what Dora gathered, Honza, in his earlier life, had been an 'adventurer' who'd worked all over the world, though he didn't talk about it. He spoke a smattering of languages, including English, after a fashion. Somehow, Honza seemed to regard Dora as an implicit partner in crime. Back when Mr Stern had been alive, Honza regularly made trips to the German border where there were shops selling all sorts of goods that couldn't be had, even in the Tuzex stores. He'd use the occasion to buy goods for himself and apparently his friends, at presumably a healthy mark-up. But now that Stern was dead, he was having a hard time coming up with a pretext for a border run. Neither the cook nor housekeeper could think up anything they thought the '*stara pani*' might want or need, but Dora could. Once, remembering her own time in England, she mentioned how much she liked the very tart orange marmalade. To Honza, the suggestion could have come from heaven itself. Mrs Stern, he declared, must have some English orange marmalade! Very early the following morning, long before the *stara pani* woke, Honza drove the Sterns' Mercedes to the German border to buy her some, along with whatever else he had in mind.

That afternoon, when he came back to show his appreciation, he offered Dora a carton of Camel cigarettes. Dora refused them, which Honza took with his customary good humor. Later on, when she was back in her office, Dora heard voices in the back yard. She peeked out of the window and saw Honza standing by the garage wall, shooting the breeze and smoking cigarettes with one of the StB men, like the two of them were old buddies. She noticed the StB man was holding the same carton of Camels Honza had offered her an hour earlier.

⚜

Without fail, every Tuesday, two things arrived in the mail. One was the Sunday *New York Times*, the other was a copy of *People* magazine. Neither one Dora was allowed to touch. The *People* magazine was Mrs Stern's and eagerly awaited; the *New York Times* had apparently been for her husband, since she seemed to have no interest in it whatsoever. However, Dora was forbidden to touch it because it now went to the old lady's friend, Rita Klimova and 'The Resistance'. Rita Klimova usually came by for it on Wednesday mornings while the old lady was still asleep. Most times the housekeeper gave it to her, but sometimes it fell on Dora to bring it out to her when she'd buzz at the front gate. For some reason she hated Dora and always gave her a dirty look, either then or whenever she came over to visit with the old lady. Dora presumed it was because she thought Dora was an StB plant, which was understandable, though Dora could not imagine why the old lady would rate any StB plants at all. But then again, she had no idea what the old lady was even doing in

Prague, since she couldn't speak Czech and seemed to have no love for Prague or for Czechoslovakia in the first place.

As time wore on, the old lady's facade fell away, and she stopped being so solicitous and collegial to Dora and instead became a whining, miserable and endlessly needy old lady who looked upon her more as a nursemaid and companion than as a secretary.

Certainly, she was being paid well for it, but as the months passed, Dora would find herself wondering if any amount of money would be enough to make putting up with her worthwhile. The old lady was bored; she had nothing to do. Initially, she'd talked about writing another book, but she never wanted to sit down and write it or even start dictating it. She'd start and almost immediately lose interest. Several times, she'd get a call from someone, presumably Klimova, telling her that the American Embassy would be holding a reception for somebody or something and she'd order Dora to get on the phone and have them put her and Dora on the guest list.

Dora spent several hours on the phone talking to different embassy secretaries, reminding them that Mrs Stern had been the daughter of an American ambassador and asking them, please, please, to include her on the list for the reception and to send out an invitation. For some reason they didn't seem to want to, and one even said they were surprised she would even want to attend. Dora had no idea what they meant when they said that, and she told herself that she would ask the old lady what all this 'I think you know full well' business they kept throwing back at Dora could have meant. But then finally they relented and asked if the address they had for Mrs Stern was the correct one.

When the engraved invitation did finally arrive in the mail, the old lady then demanded Dora accompany her. Dora didn't want to. She didn't want the trouble that might come with it. But in the end she and the old lady both dressed up in their fanciest evening dresses. Honza drove to the American Embassy in the detestable Mercedes, and for the next two hours Dora tried to stand as invisibly as she could while the once-famous author and daughter of some long-dead ambassador made the rounds, introducing herself to everyone and talking like this was and had always been her milieu. Dora Slaba looked on and what came to her mind was that Martha was a nobody acting like a somebody.

Eventually, the reception ended and she and Martha exited the building. Honza picked them up and for the fifteen or so minutes it took to bring them back to the house, the old lady seemed ebullient and nourished. The white Lada was parked where it always was and for the first time Dora wondered if it was always the same two gorillas or if there were many. As the limousine was about to drive away, Dora pushed the door open, bid them goodnight and began walking down past the Lada to the tram stop, hoping she wouldn't have to wait long for the next one to Zizkov.

The kicker came a few months later, in March 1989, when another call came in, presumably again from Klimova, telling the old lady that there'd be a demonstration that afternoon in the plazas next to the Rudolfinum by Staromak. She immediately got it into her head that Dora should attend, to witness and assess and then report back on how it went, as if the old lady might have an investment in it somehow. She insisted Honza drive her down in the limo. He would park it and wait there while she attended. He'd drive her back afterwards, and she and Mrs Stern would have tea together and Dora could tell her all about it.

Of course, it didn't work out that way. Once they got there, Honza refused to stay with the car, insisting on accompanying Dora to the demonstration. He seemed even more chipper than usual, which only made Dora feel certain something terrible was about to happen. It did.

The demonstration looked the same as all the other ones Dora had studiously avoided over the years: men with long hair and beards grown ridiculously as sign of protest, people angry at having had to live their lives in stupidity, all because the Communists and Moscow owned them. If only General Patton had ignored his orders from Ike and come in anyway, it might all have been different. But he didn't and it was what it was. And the organisers, Klimova, Havel, Dienstbier, all standing together, waiting to begin addressing the assembled groups of people, waiting for the signal to suddenly congeal into a crowd.

Suddenly, Honza grabbed Dora's wrist, saying, 'Hey, there's some friends of mine. Come on over, I'll introduce you!' It was the gorillas from the white Lada; a dozen of them, all smiling and saying, 'Hi Dora,' 'Good to see you, Dora,' 'How's the girl?' Somehow, as far as they were concerned, she was one of them. She wondered what the old lady knew about any of it. She certainly never acted as if she was aware of them parked outside her house day in and day out. Was it deliberate, like she was with the cook and housekeeper's endless thefts? And was this demonstration all being paid for and put on by her? Was that the deal? Did the gorillas know this? Would it make any difference to them if they did? By rights, Martha Stern should have seemed mysterious, but there was something about her personality and awful neediness which seemed to totally negate it.

Dora started to leave, but one of the gorillas grunted at her, 'Not yet!' and so Dora stayed put. A minute later one of the organisers stepped in front of the microphone and began to speak. The gorilla nodded at Dora and she started to walk away. Just as she was stepping out of the crowd, the tussle started. She just walked up and down some side streets for twenty minutes before circling back around to where the limo was parked. Honza was already there, smoking a Sparta and smiling. Neither said anything on the drive back. A few weeks after that Dora and the old lady got into an argument over her promised trip to London. She quit after that.

38. ON THE GOOD SHIP LOLLYPOP

Rita Klimova, it turned out, was very good at keeping secrets. Unbeknown to Martha, Rita had another American friend in Prague. Her name was Harriet Mackova, she was from Georgia, married to a Czech Baptist preacher, and had been introduced to her by someone at the embassy. They knew about Rita's dissident activities, and with things already beginning to heat up, they had no idea at all what might happen if this time it went the distance. If it did, and something told them it might, Klimova or someone from her group were likely to be the ones in charge. If that was the case it was a good idea to have her already talking with the 'right sort of Americans', which Harriet most definitely was.

Harriet was a Republican, a Baptist; an exceedingly blunt, highly judgemental person who hated Communists with a venom, but also didn't care for flakes, hippies, liberals, leftists or rock musicians. This, in their minds, was a good thing, because Rita's chief partner in crime was Vaclav Havel, and he was pretty much all of the above.

They also knew that Havel was friends with the dissident rock musician Michal Kocab, who happened to be married to, of all things, an American woman named Marsha, and this was something they happened to be very worried about. In communist Czechoslovakia, having an American wife was very nearly a mathematical impossibility, as exotic as being married to a Martian; something which really was not supposed to happen, only it had. Marsha Kocab was, by all appearances, an utterly guileless, big-eyed hippie girl from

Wilmington, North Carolina; a modern dancer blown into Prague ten years earlier on some magical zephyr, and who, from what they could gather, walked between raindrops. No one at the US Embassy had any idea what her game was, though they knew with utter certainty she had to be playing one, and not knowing what it was scared them.

The anti-communist resistance in Czechoslovakia was driven and fueled by rock and roll, and the spooks at the Embassy understood that rock and roll meant freedom and magic, and ultimately ... America! But nice as it seemed, in their minds and that of the Reagan administration back in Washington, this was not exactly the way they would prefer it. It would be one thing if the America the Czech dissidents loved was the America of Norman Rockwell and Donny and Marie, but theirs was the rancid, discordant America of Frank Zappa and Lou Reed, not the one they wished to promote. And who was behind this? The adventuress Marsha!

In their extreme innocence, Czechoslovakia's rock and rollers considered Marsha Kocab a sort of living Statue of Liberty. As such, she was exerting an astounding and immeasurable influence upon things. Now the Embassy was hearing that Vaclav Havel, whose spoken English was nearly indecipherable, was using Marsha as his interpreter in interviews and as a go-between with different NGOs. They feared Havel and the others might get 'funny ideas' from this woman, which was why they had decided to get Harriet introduced to Klimova, talking to her and getting her to pass along certain understandings about politics and freedom and, of course, business and free enterprise, just to balance it all out. They had to understand this was not the Dawning of the Age of Aquarius.

The US Embassy had no idea Rita Klimova knew Martha Dodd. Harriet didn't know it either, since she'd never even heard of Martha Dodd. Of course, if she had, she'd have told Rita Klimova exactly what she thought of that 'traitor whore'! Marsha had also never heard of Martha, but if she had, her judgement likely would not have been so harsh.

The Embassy had taken it on faith that Harriet would never be friends with Marsha Kocab, because of all the things Marsha was that Harriet could not possibly countenance. In reality, Marsha and Harriet were best friends. Marsha wasn't bothered by Harriet's extreme judgementalism. She and Harriet had each other's backs. It had been that way for 10 years and would continue so until Harriet's death, 32 years later.

The year was 1989. Some 21 years had passed since the Prague Spring and the subsequent 'Intervention of the Fraternal Nations', with their thousands of tanks. Charter 77 had been more than 10 years ago. The intervening years had taken their toll on the heroes of 1968. They were all growing old. They'd lost. They'd known it for years. Except now another one was starting to brew. It was Vaclav Havel, and Jiri Dienstbier and rock star Michal Kocab and Rita Klimova and all the others, and as the weeks and months passed, Dora Slaba and a lot of other Praguers found themselves wondering if maybe this time those idiot dissidents might actually pull it off. The demonstrations kept popping up with the StB goons always there to tamp them down. But then they'd pop up again, and whatever petty brutalities the goons inflicted on the protestors simply wasn't enough to deter them.

Then they started hearing about the pro-democracy demonstrations going on at Tiananmen Square in Beijing. The state-controlled Czech media didn't say much about it, but what got through told the people that hundreds of thousands of Chinese had risen up and demonstrated until the Chinese communists sent in the tanks to crush them. It made Czechs wonder what they'd do under similar circumstances. Then summer came and, as was always the case, they turned their minds to other things.

In July and August, as always happened, everyone in Czechoslovakia that could, got in their Skodas and Ladas and drove down through Austria and into Yugoslavia for a couple of weeks in the sun and on the beach in Croatia. But what happened instead was that thousands of East Germans began showing up in Prague in their Trabants and then going to the West German Embassy asking for entry visas. More than a thousand swarmed into the inner courtyards, thousands more flooded into Mala Strana and across the bridge to Staromak, the Old Town. No one knew how to cope with it, certainly not the police or the people's militia, all of whom turned back. There were more and more demonstrations taking place, and they could barely deal with them besides grabbing a few demonstrators to stomp, kick and arrest. It went on throughout the summer and into the autumn.

On 17 November, another demonstration took place near Namesti Republiky, just outside Old Town. It was bigger than usual and the police were ready. This time they brought in the People's Militia, with clubs, thick acrylic shields and riot gear. They started beating the demonstrators, thinking it would make them flee like it always did. But this time the reaction was completely different. People rose up and the demonstrations grew exponentially. Soon there were half a million people crowded onto Wenceslas Square, holding house keys, rattling them as a way of letting the communist rulers know it was time to leave.

The US Embassy tried to stay on top of it all, but it wasn't easy. They knew people who knew Havel, and they'd try to find out things from them or other people who knew other people. It was a good thing they'd introduced Harriet to Klimova, because the two of them got together fairly often for chats, and whenever she'd hear anything interesting Harriet would let it get back to them. Harriet also knew something about Havel and the others, but not so directly. Her husband had that connection to some of the other Protestant church leaders, including the father of Michal Kocab. It was only then that the embassy found out about Harriet's connection to Marsha Kocab. Harriet might have been sharp-tongued and strongly opinionated, but as a pastor's wife, she knew how to exercise discretion and confidentiality. A couple of days into it, when it had started to become clear that the revolution wasn't going to stop and the police and militias were starting to give up, the people knew there was no turning back. Harriet came by Marsha's flat with an invitation in her hand from the US Embassy. They were inviting Marsha and her husband over to dinner at the ambassador's residence. After nearly a decade of being a leper, the American Ambassador Shirley Temple Black and her staff wanted to meet with them to get their take on what was happening. So Marsha and Michal went.

It was made to look like a reception, but it felt decidedly impromptu. A long table was set up with platters of cheese and pickles, sliced roast beef, ham and open-faced sandwiches and desserts. All around Marsha were people she'd known for years, all gathered in one spot, gravely conferring with each other and with the Americans. More than once, she and Michal were corralled by people she assumed were senior embassy staff who were hammering them with questions. What did they think? What was going to happen next? Did anyone know?

In one corner of the large room Marsha spotted Rita Klimova talking in her harsh Bronx English with some people, one of whom was a very old lady that Marsha didn't think she'd ever seen around. Who was she? Was she with the embassy? She didn't think so. Unlike everyone else, including the embassy staff, she was dressed fancily, like it was the much-awaited social event of the year and not something which had been thrown together over a couple hours.

At the end of it, Ambassador Shirley Temple Black concluded the train had indeed left the station. She was correct. A couple of days later, the communists gave up. A new government was installed. Suddenly, Czechoslovakia declared itself a free and democratic nation. Havel became president and Michal became a minister in the new government. Over the next ten years Kocab featured in nearly every government that was formed.

For a while Marsha wondered who the elderly American woman might have been who was with Klimova. She asked Harriet if she knew. Harriet didn't, but said she'd ask Rita. She never got the chance. Havel named Rita Klimova as his Ambassador to Washington and flew off soon afterwards for America. She did visit with Harriet just before she left, but with all they had to talk about in a very short amount of time, Harriet forgot to ask about the old lady at the embassy.

It isn't known if Rita Klimova ever managed to say goodbye to Martha or even get together with her after the revolution. She had been its benefactor for years, but once it was done, she was promptly forgotten.

❦

During the summer of 1990, an unprecedented number of Americans visited Prague. It was not yet set up for the enormous tourist trade. Many of the foreign visitors were young people: Americans, British, Canadians, Belgians, Finns, French, Australians. Many of them, who'd come with backpacks, decided it beat whatever was back home and decided to stay. Others followed. Some stayed for years, setting up businesses, hanging out in cafes during the day, getting drunk and clubbing at night. Most eventually went home, but some are still there.

For Martha Dodd, the impact of the change from communist rule to democracy on her life was close to non-existent. The only thing that really changed was that one day the white Lada with the StB goons stopped showing up. That was it. Martha's own freedom of movement and expression were as they had always been. The household continued running as it always did. The cook, the housekeeper and Honza all continued to squeeze the old lady for whatever they could without attracting attention. She ultimately found someone to replace Dora, who spoke English 'after a fashion'. Martha's lawyer, Dr Myslyl, came by and told her he didn't see any problems that Martha needed to worry about. So Martha didn't. By now she was beyond that.

Under communism there had always been a tiny trickle of journalists and historians journeying to Prague hoping to interview her. Now, with the Wall down, more called. They'd write, then phone, saying they were downtown, could they come by for a chat? Others just showed up at the door and took their shot. She always shook her head and said no. She was too old, too tired, too many aches and pains. No, she didn't have anything to say about the Velvet Revolution. Goodbye.

For Czechs and Slovaks, and especially for Praguers, the spring and summer of 1990 was a crazy, wonderful time. There was an air of exuberance they would never know again. After living for decades under the Soviet shadow, suddenly the Cold War was over and the Eastern Bloc of socialist nations overnight ceased to exist. Czechs might be atheists, but they still believe in magic, and the magic was everywhere they looked. But, of course, the problem with magic is that it can't make all bad things disappear, and there were some very unpleasant realities lurking which at that moment people preferred not to think about. Democratic rule still wasn't quite a done deal. The Wall may have come down, but the communist police state wasn't going to dismantle itself overnight. In the end, the StB disbanded and the communist leadership withdrew to their villas, more than a few of which were there in Martha's Prague 5 neighborhood. But there were also still half a million Soviet troops stationed in bases within their borders, and as far as they were concerned, no one had said anything about them leaving. That wouldn't come for more than a year, but when it did, Michal Kocab, Marsha's long-haired, rock star husband, led the Czech government's negotiating team.

39. A DEATH IN PRAGUE 5

Martha Dodd died in Prague one day in early August 1990. CSTK, the still communist-run Czecho-Slovakian press agency, made the announcement. It noted she was 82, had been in poor health and had been living in exile in Prague ever since 1957, when she and her husband and son fled the United States during the height of the McCarthy era. It noted that she had once been a bestselling author as well as a journalist and was the daughter of the American Ambassador to Nazi Germany during the 1930s. She was predeceased by her husband, Alfred, who had died of cancer in 1986 and was survived by Robert Stern, an adopted son, currently residing in Mexico City.

What the CSTK brief didn't mention was that her death was the result of a burglary. Her house had been broken into several nights earlier and the thieves had left her tied up. By the time the servants found her the next morning and called an ambulance, she was too far gone and never recovered.

In Czechoslovakia, the reaction to the news of her passing was, at best, bewilderment, since almost no one recalled ever hearing about her. The only time she'd ever been mentioned was on her arrival in 1957. That she had been the daughter of an American ambassador and was witness to many fateful events in Berlin during the Nazi years also didn't stir anyone. Czechoslovakia had its own painful and ugly experience dealing with Hitler and the Nazis, so someone else's wasn't likely to provoke any great interest. That Martha and her husband had come to Prague at the invitation of the communists told them all they needed to know about the dead woman. Some people pick their sides, everyone else has their side picked for them. As for what the Czechs thought about the McCarthy era in America, they only knew the smidgen the communists had taught them, which meant they believed the exact opposite. It wasn't about liberals being oppressed, it was about communist spies trying to do to America what they did to the Czechs. Besides, the Czechs knew all about betrayal. People probably didn't bother wondering what her story was. She had cast her lot with them and she could rot in hell.

Mainly her existence there in Prague, unseen among the population, was just another oddity which Prague, a city with a mind of its own, seems intent on keeping hidden among its collections. It had been that way since the time of the alchemists and the mad Habsburg Emperor Rudolf II, whose collection of oddities became the stuff of legend.

Gene Deitch, the American cartoonist and animator, remembered hearing the news of Martha's death from his wife Zdenka and feeling more relief than anything else. In the very short time they'd known them, Martha and her husband had both proven themselves excruciating, uncultured bores. He never figured out what their story was, but then, like everyone else living under communism, he'd made a point of not trying to. Marsha and Harriet both remember hearing about it on television and then asking each other if either had ever heard of her. Neither had, and they thought that was strange. Later, Harriet found out the dead lady had been a friend of Rita Klimova, and she wondered why she had never mentioned it to her. But the next time she saw Rita, she forgot to ask. There were too many, more important things to talk about.

Dora Slaba remembered seeing it in the newspaper and then on the news. It did not surprise her, nor did it particularly sadden her. She'd had her life. Now it was over and the fact that no one would miss her was not Dora's problem. And with that, Dora mostly put it out of her mind. But then, several months later, she ran into Honza on the street in Zizkov. He asked if she'd heard about the old lady. Dora said she had. Too bad, he said. She was a nice old woman. Dora said nothing. She didn't particularly feel like holding a memorial service.

Then Honza leaned in and asked Dora if she wanted to know what *really* happened. Dora stared hollow-eyed as Honza started telling her how 'the guys', meaning of course the StB goons parked out front all those years, were suddenly all out of jobs and had no money coming in. Well, someone had put it into their minds that the old lady had gold stashed among all her riches.

So, they broke in. Honza was in his quarters and didn't hear anything. But they came into her room and demanded she tell them where the gold was. When she told them she didn't have any they tied her up and left her on the floor, stealing whatever they thought was worth grabbing before leaving. The housekeeper found her when she came in the next morning. She called the police and an ambulance. The old lady was taken to the Motol hospital, since that was where they treated foreigners and it was nearby. She died a day or two later. The police checked it out, but couldn't find anything. And guess who inherited the house and more besides? Dr Myslyl. It all went to him.[1] Nice, huh? Dora said goodbye to Honza and walked on.

So that was what happened. It bothered Dora to think of the terror which the old lady would have experienced that night. She thought about her and tried to see if she could muster up any sadness for her, but she couldn't. Instead, she remembered her own thoughts that time, seeing her at the embassy reception, trying so hard to be the Belle of the Ball; a nobody trying to be a somebody!

POSTSCRIPT

Prague is a city of ghosts. As a modern Westerner, you might insist ghosts aren't real. Just don't waste your time trying to argue the point with Praguers. Though nearly all Praguers are atheists, they'll curtly inform you that, whether you believe in them or not, they're there just the same. Most of Prague's ghosts are, of course, without names, but there are a great many with. That so many reside there is not really a mystery, at least not to Praguers. They know that, while everyone born must inevitably die, it isn't ordained that every soul will find eternal rest. Some stay behind, unable or unwilling to depart. And Prague, the crowning jewel of Central Europe, almost entirely undamaged by the previous century's ravages, offers countless familiar places for its ghosts to find refuge. And why shouldn't they remain there? Prague has always been a self-contained universe. It's likely that more than a few of Prague's dead stay because it never occurred to them their eternal reward could be anywhere else. In the rest of the world, all this may be a matter of wild-eyed conjecture, but in Prague it is accepted as fact by even the most rational and atheistic.

Since Prague's rediscovery by the West in the 1990s, its ghosts have become a cottage industry, along with Franz Kafka, Rabbi Loew, Tycho de Brache and the great alchemists Edward Kelley and John Dee. Walking tours are offered most days on any of these subjects. The ghost tours are usually the best because they go all over the old city, allowing a great many ghosts to be visited over the course of an easy two-hour stroll.

They're all silly stories, of course; silly, bloody and salacious, just the way Praguers like them, and nearly always without a single drop of deeper meaning. But there are a few tales that are different, because they're sad. There is one in particular that stands out, not just because it's sad but because it is also of our modern world. It is the 'Old Indian of the Na Frantisku Embankment'. The story goes he came to Prague with a Wild West show, got sick and was left behind. When he recovered, he found himself stranded in a place where he knew no one and everyone tended to view him as savage and not quite human. He wandered the streets for a while before dying. That his ghost is seen on the Na Frantisku Embankment suggests he'd lived rough on the riverbank, where even now, drunks and tramps spend their days. It is said he can sometimes be seen there on the embankment at the moment the sun sets, begging the Great Spirit to return him to the American West so he can finally sleep in his own land, among his own people. But unless someone, somehow, finds his bones, or perhaps a piece of his clothing, and brings them back to America, his poor ghost is doomed to wander Prague for eternity.

Any day now, Prague magic will exert itself and stories will surely begin filtering down from around Klamovka in Smichov of an apparition of an old lady in a pink pantsuit, clamouring passers-by for copies of *People* magazine, or pink rubber-tipped toothbrushes or Tums or Bisodol mints, or panties that fit. Just as celebrity fades, so sometimes does obscurity. Prague is, after all, a city of ghosts and eternity is a very long time. It's a sure bet that any day now Martha's restless spirit will reveal itself.

ACKNOWLEDGEMENTS

After spending years in what seemed an endless journey, piecing together and parsing Martha Dodd's very strange life, here I am, suddenly, at the end. After all this, the task of acknowledging all who've helped me should be a happy one, yet somehow it's mostly melancholy, I feel, knowing so many of them have already gone on to the 'next place'.

Firstly, I want to thank Dora Slaba, who first mentioned Martha to me over Big Macs back in 1992. She died shortly after we reconnected and I got her to tell me her story about Martha. Being American, I'd felt obliged to promise Dora I'd 'make her a movie star'. I guess we'll just have to see about that. I also want to thank Martha's attorney, Stanislav Myslyl, for sharing some of his memories of Martha and Alfred. Last I heard, he's in his nineties and still with us. I hope he continues to do so. I'm grateful to Sydney Rittenberg for recounting his memories of lunching with Martha and of her time socialising among the American exile community in Beijing. I also want to thank Gene Deitch, the last of the great postwar American animators and one of the tiny, disparate handful of Americans who lived in Cold War Prague, for telling me about his brief acquaintance with Martha and Alfred and how amply it had justified his wife Zdenka's stern admonition to 'never, ever, under any conditions, talk to anybody who speaks English!' Fair winds to them both.

Thanks to presidential historian Robert Dallek for recounting his years of scholarly correspondence with Martha regarding her father, and how he crashed and burned while attempting a drop-in visit on Martha during the 1980s. Also to Shareen Blair Brysac for talking to me at length about Martha and her friendship with Mildred Fish von Harnack. Thanks also to Rebecca Donner, who, like Brysac, wrote an excellent biography of Mildred. She shared some useful insights into Mildred's unique method for smuggling microfilm to a Treasury Department agent.

I want to thank Canadian science-fiction author Crawford Kilian for sharing his childhood memories of Martha, Alfred and their son during their Mexican exile. Thanks also to Nancy Hodes and Ann Kimmage for their memories of growing up in exile in 1950s Prague, and later to Beijing. I want to thank Georgiana Shobris for passing down what her mother had once told her about being at a dinner which Martha also attended. I want to thank Czech economist Oldrich Kyn for his insights into the character of Rita Klimova and of post-revolutionary Czech politics. Rest in peace, Oldrich.

A big, big vote of thanks to Marsha Kocab and Harriet Mackova, who were, apparently, the only Americans living in Prague during the 1980s who actually talked to each other and had each other's backs. Neither had heard of Martha while she was alive, but afterwards were a bit surprised at her close proximity and secret role in the Velvet Revolution. I am especially grateful to Harriet for telling me all about her 'state-sponsored' friendship with Rita Klimova. Sadly, Harriet passed in 2021. May her memory be a blessing.

When it comes to practising and writing history, it very quickly becomes apparent that all any of us can hope to be is but another honest link in the endless chain of written human memory. One way or another, our work inevitably rests on those preceding us. Martha Dodd scholarship, such as it exists outside secret police archives, originates with the research of the late Douglas Wheeler of the University of New Hampshire, who passed it on to his student, John F. Fox, who wrote the definitive doctoral dissertation about Martha, before becoming the Chief Historian of the Federal Bureau of Investigation. I am not the only beneficiary of his work. By now, there is a good number of people like myself who have read and parsed it for information and corroboration. I thank both of them for extending their generosity and collegiality to someone whose own connection to academe is best left unexamined.

I'd be remiss if I didn't thank retired FBI counter-intel guy Robert Baker, who after spending his career on the Soviet target, went and wrote a cracking bio of Vasily Zarubin. Baker is a great guy, who not only gave me lots of insight into counterintelligence, but also showed me the art of not getting snookered by everything you read in an intel file. Anytime, dude!

Though I've never met or corresponded with any of them, I am nevertheless deeply in debt to a number of writers whose works formed the bedrock of my research. The most obvious is Erik Larson, whose bestselling book *In the Garden of Beasts* masterfully tells the story of Martha and her father, Ambassador William E. Dodd, during their nearly five years in Berlin during the 1930s. But there is also the 'Holy Trinity' of American Communism and early Cold War Soviet espionage research: John Earl Haynes, Harvey Klehr and Alexander Vassiliev. Without them, there wouldn't be much of anything to work from.

I'd like to thank the people running the Manuscript Division of the Library of Congress for keeping the papers of both Martha Dodd and her father William E. Dodd. I'd also like to thank the University of Delaware Library's collections department for putting the papers and letters of George Messersmith online and available to anyone wanting to read them. One doesn't need to traipse too far about the interweb or in recently written history to see how much they are being used.

To Alan Levy, Diana Reynolds, Rob Urban, Jiri Kominek and Colonel Josef Fucik, Prague colleagues with whom many horses were stolen, all now in the ranks of Prague's ghosts. Wait up for me. I'll be with you shortly.

Speaking of Prague, I'd like to thank Sallie Lynch, Andrea Snyder Edney, Jan Stojaspal, Mark Baker, Eva Munkova, Michael Jetton and particularly my research mate Thea Favalaro for sharing her expertise on American exiles living in Communist Czechoslovakia and points East. In London, I'd like to thank my agent Andrew Lownie and my editor at Icon Books, Ellen Conlon, for all their efforts bringing my book to life. And in Dallas, my gratitude goes to Dee Hill, Mark Bartos, Glenn Holman, Jimbo Wallace, Fanny Kerwich Doyle, Alex Mena and Susan Owens, the legendary Angel of East Dallas. Also thanks to Jerome Weeks and Tim Rogers, but especially to Will Clarke, Dallas' Literary Surrealist Supreme and, for many years, my Saturday morning writing-and-coffee mate. Then there are all the others. You all know who you are. Thanks. This includes you, Pete Capelotti!

And to my dear wife Katerina and our daughter Kathleen, I thank most of all.

ENDNOTES

Chapter 1

1. In *Ambassador Dodd's Diary*, Dodd writes: 'From June 13 on, I was pestered every hour of the day by newspaper people and photographers. All kinds of stories and pictures, silly and otherwise, appeared in newspapers all over the country. I never dreamed of such publicity.'
2. Dodd, *Embassy Eyes*, p. 10.
3. Ibid., p. 16.
4. Ibid., p. 5.
5. Writing to Stimson, Sackett said, 'The impression I got of Hitler is that of a fanatical crusader. He has a certain forcefulness and intensity which gives him a power of leadership among those classes that do not weigh out his pourings. His methods are those of an opportunist. While talking vigorously to me, he never looked me in the eye.' Sackett to Stimson, Personal, 9 December 1941, 862.50/723.
6. Burke writes: 'Hitler did not impress Sackett. The magical quality of his personality, which captured so many admirers, escaped the American Ambassador.' *Sackett and the Collapse*, P.185.
7. See Letter to George Gordon, 6 July 1933, Box 40, W.E. Dodd Papers.
8. Messermith, 'Some Observations on the appointment of William E. Dodd as Ambassador to Berlin,' Unpublished memoir, Messersmith Papers.
9. Ibid.
10. Ibid.

11. Dodd, *Embassy Eyes*, p. 20.
12. Ibid.
13. Fromm, Bella, *Blood and Banquets*, p.120.
14. Dodd, *Embassy Eyes*, p.21.

Chapter 2
1. The Spartacists were a group of Communist and radical left activists who led an uprising against the moderate Social Democrat government of Friedrich Ebert in January 1919. While it made some initial gains, it was soon crushed by the army assisted by right-wing militias. It's two leaders Karl Liebknecht and Rosa Luxemburg were both murdered after being taken prisoner.
2. Comintern, or Communist International, was an international organisation dedicated to spreading the World Communist Revolution. Supposedly it was independent of Moscow, and to a certain degree it was, while at the same time it acted as a foreign intelligence arm of the Communist Party Central Committee,
3. Enver Pasha was an Ottoman Turkish military leader, War Minister, and an original leader of the Young Turk Revolution. By 1919, following the collapse of the Ottoman Empire he had fled to Berlin. After meeting Radek, he would serve as General von Seeckt's secret envoy to Moscow.
4. Baker, *Rezident*, pp. 5,6.
5. Literally, *Society for Industrial Demand*.
6. Baker, p. 7.
7. Hilger, *Incompatible Allies*, p.46. Dallin, p.82.
8. Baker, p.16.
9. Dallin, pp. 84–86.
10. Costello & Tsarev, *Deadly Illusions*, pp. 63–64.
11. Dallin, p.78.
12. Not all network members were caught. Dallin points out that many German Communists had already escaped using false identities and passports; p.119. In *The Rise and Fall of the Third Reich*, Shirer writes: 'Goering's police raided the Karl Liebknecht Haus, the Communist headquarters in Berlin. It had been abandoned some weeks before by the Communist leaders, a number of whom had already gone underground or quietly slipped off to Russia.' p.191.
13. Baker, p.20.

14. Soviet People's Commissar for Foreign Affairs, Maxim Litvinov reportedly told Hitler, 'We don't care if you shoot your German Communists.' Hilger – Meyer, p.252.
15. Dallin, p.119.
16. Ibid., p.122.
17. Dallin notes that American Communist Party chief Earl Browder had served as CPUSA's liaison with Soviet Intelligence. *Soviet Espionage*, p.87.
18. When Kitty Harris first came to Berlin, she enrolled as a language student.
19. Both Browder's sister, Margaret, and his wife, Kitty Harris, served as a couriers between Berlin and Paris. Another courier for the Berlin network was Sergei Basov, a Russian-born seaman with an American passport. Baker, *Rezident*.
20. See *Communist Party Clandestine organization and Activity Secret Apparatus 1954–1956*; CIA document. CIA-RDP78-00915. This report examines the activities of 'Secret Apparatus' units inside Communist Party organizations worldwide. For a good explanation of the Secret Apparatus' work in the US, see *Red Conspirator: J. Peters and the American Communist Underground*, by Thomas Sakmyster, University of Illinois Press; Champaign, 2011.
21. See: *Some observations on the Appointment of Dr William Dodd as Ambassador to Berlin*. George S. Messersmith Papers, U Del Archives.
22. Dodd, *Through Embassy Eyes*; p. 23.
23. Ibid., p.107.

Chapter 3
1. *Stammtisch* is a large table usually reserved for locals.
2. Reynolds would later become one of America's most famous war correspondents, covering the 1940 Battle of France, the London Blitz, the North African campaign and the liberation of Europe. After the war he wrote more than a dozen books on a wide variety of topics, including bank robber Willie Sutton, the Custer Massacre, different WWII battles and historical personalities. Quentin Reynolds died in 1966 and has largely been forgotten.
3. 'the other man pays', p.110. Reynolds, Quentin, *By Quentin Reynolds*, 1963 New York, McGraw-Hill.

4. *Embassy Eyes*, p.25.
5. Reynolds, p.108; Reynolds does not identify the ousted reporter, other than he'd been hired 'from the UP' and was someone they didn't actually know, so they hadn't been able to 'go to bat for him'.
6. *Embassy Eyes*, P.28.
7. According to Erik Larson, the reason everyone was waving and cheering was actually that they saw the car's licence plate, and seeing that it was from Berlin and with a low number (being a diplomatic plate) surmised the vehicle's occupants were high-ranking Nazi officials.
8. In *By Quentin Reynolds* (pp.118–21), Reynolds places it at shortly before midnight, which doesn't sound likely, considering everything that was to follow.
9. Ibid, p.121.
10. Ibid.
11. *...two six-foot storm troopers, half supporting, half dragging a human figure. I could not tell at first if it was a man or a woman.* Quentin Reynolds, p. 121–22.
12. *Embassy Eyes*, p.29.
13. Ibid, p.29–30.
14. Ibid, p.29.
15. 'It was in fact a puny office, understaffed and underfinanced, barely capable of dealing with a German Communist Party that in 1930 claimed 250,000 adherents in 4,000 political cells.' *The Gestapo*, Rupert Butler, p. 21.
16. 'Diels is really a decent man who ... insisted that order could not be brought about unless S.A. men were punished in the same way as others.' Letter from Messersmith to William Phillips, 27 April 1934 Messersmith Papers.
17. *Some Observations on the Appointment of Dr William Dodd as Ambassador to Berlin.* George S. Messersmith Papers, U Del Library Archives.
18. FBI Report on Alfred K. Stern Case, 2 July 1957, NY100-65568.
19. Description of Messersmith's discovery about Martha being Udet's mistress can be found in an essay he wrote for his never-completed memoir; MSS0109 1957-00, Messersmith Papers, U Del Library Archives.
20. Ibid.

Chapter 4

1. Gisevius, Hans Berndt, *To The Bitter End*, pp. 41–2.
2. Ibid. p.40.
3. Der *Stahlhelm–Bund der Frontsoldaten*: a league of ex-servicemen serving as a paramilitary. Stahlhelm was heavily right-wing, but leaned more towards the Monarchist, German National People's Party. After the Nazi seizure of power, it tried staying independent of the Nazis, but was ultimately merged into the SA.
4. Butler, Rupert, *The Gestapo*, p.21.
5. At that time the individual German states were staunchly independent, particularly when it came to the police.
6. *Embassy Eyes*, pp.52–57.
7. Ibid, p.52.
8. Ibid, p.53.
9. Ibid. p.53.
10. Ibid, p.53
11. Ibid, p.54.
12. Ibid., p.49.
13. Ibid, p.49. Martha was probably referring to Carl Boemer, who was in the Propaganda Ministry's Foreign Section.
14. Ibid., p.47.
15. Joachim von Ribbentrop, the future Foreign Minister, spoke excellent English, but was not, at this point, part of Hitler's inner circle.
16. Hanfstaengl's mother was a Sedgewick, among the most distinguished 'old line' American families.
17. GSM letter to J. Pierrepoint Moffat, Chief of Western European Division, US Dept of State, June 13, 1934.
18. 'She had a brief affair with Putzi.' Conradi, Peter. *Hitler's Piano Player*, 2006. p.122.
19. Martha met him at a formal dinner, *Behind Embassy Eyes*, p.41.
20. I rather enjoyed being treated, Ibid., p. 41
21. Poncet was universally regarded as the best-informed foreign diplomat in Berlin.

Chapter 6

1. As we shall see, Rabinovich later went on from Berlin to New York, where he worked under cover of being a representative

of the Soviet Red Cross. Following America's entry into WWII, he moved his operation to Washington, DC, and the safe house he operated just across the district line in Bethesda is a popular spot among local fans of Cold War espionage.

2. Louis Budenz, *This is My Story*, New York and London, Whittlesey House, 1947, pp. 254–55,

3. The story of Golos and 'Johnny' comes from Russian spy historian Teodor Cladkov's *Nash Chelovek v N'yu Yorke Sud 'ba Rezidenta* (Our Man in New York, The Fate of a Resident) Moscow 2007. The details it provides match reasonably well with the FBI's 1949 investigation into the passport scandal, See FBI HQ 100-340473, NYO letter to FBIHQ, 25 April 1949.

4. Ibid.

5. Wilder letter to Martha, Box 63, W.E. Dodd papers, Library of Congress.

6. Shirer, Rise and Fall, p.121.

7. telephone in the bedroom: Metcalf, *1933*.

8. Packebusch, an architect, had been in the SA from 1926–31, during which time he'd been on Stennes' staff. He joined the SS in 1931 with membership no. 18038.

9. didn't want to be seen in the city or among crowds: *Embassy Eyes*, p. 134.

10. should not antagonise the Nazis by being seen with him: Ibid, p. 134

11. that she was "playing with fire", Ibid, p.136

Chapter 7

1. At an SA barracks on 10 Hedemannstrasse, *Terrorism in the 20th Century: A Narrative*, Nash, Jay Robert, p.108.

2. using whips, iron bars and rubber truncheons: Ibid.

3. before Fleitmann realised the Gestapo meant business: Ibid.

4. The von Clemm family were founders of what would become Citibank. Karl von Clemm and his brother Werner were then involved in international barter and swaps involving Mexican and American oil imports and finished German industrial goods. In a few more years, both brothers would find themselves in US federal prisons, having been caught smuggling bonds and

German diamonds into the US inside the false bottom of a Bud-weiser beer crate. Both would admit to spying for the Abwehr.

5. In conjunction with the Nuremburg War Crimes trials, NARA Modern Military Branch Diels Interrogation, 18 October 1946.

6. While Messersmith makes many references to his constructive and friendly working relationship with Diels, he makes no mention of this episode. However, when discussing arrangements to get former Chancellor Bruning out of Germany, Messersmith does allude to conjuring up a passport for him. *'Even now, I do not believe it is advisable to set forth what these arrangements were, but it was not long thereafter that Dr Bruning passed safely over the German border into Holland one night.'* MSS0109 1969-00; GSM Archives. make reference on at least one occasion to providing an American passport with a high-ranking German official needing to escape Nazi Germany.

7. All of it had been Himmler and Heydrich's fault, he told Diels.

8. Goering had stood idly by, the whole time.

9. rather amusing to watch the Nazi leaders spying on each other, Fromm, *Blood and Banquets.*

10. the sinister face, lovely lipped and gaunt Diels, Letter to Thornton Wilder, 14 December 1933.

Chapter 8

1. *One might think the Germans believed in Jesus.* Dodd, William E.; Ambassador Dodd's Diary; entry for Dec 25, 1933.

2. Like a frightened rabbit; *Embassy Eyes*, p,133.

3. *possible friction between Hitler and Goebbels on one side and Goering on the other*; Ibid, January 3, 1934.

4. *'Diels, you can't sit on both sides of the fence.'* Diels, Lucifer Ante Portas; p. 379.

5. *'The SA is the pace maker in all this filth'*, Ibid.

6. *He detailed how Roehm had been conspiring*; Bullock, Allen, *Hitler: A Study in Tyranny*, 1962, p.295.

7. *'You understand what the Fuhrer wants?'* Padfield, Peter, Himmler, p.141.

8. in a shut-down tire factory in Stettin, Philip Metcalf, 1933.

9. We are no man-hating organization, Ibid.

10. a rather pathetic, passive-looking creature, Embassy Eyes, p. 134.

11. Ibid, p.134.
12. Ibid, p.135.
13. MSS0109-1957-00 Messersmith Papers, UDel Archives.
14. only with a great deal of difficulty, Ibid.
15. the more reasonable element in the party. Ibid.
16. but he is a good friend of our country, Ibid.
17. Himmler would pass the position on to Reinhardt Heydrich, who held the post until his assassination by Czechoslovak commandoes in 1942.
18. Diels was too decent for the political police, Letter to Philips, April 1934 Messersmith Papers.

Chapter 9
1. KGB Archives, Vasiiev White Notebook #2 45: File 14449, Vol. 1 'Liza', Excerpt from letter to 'Arkhip' from C, dated 28.3.34.
2. One possible explanation might be that, having visited France several years earlier, following her graduation from high School, Martha detested Paris and the French in general, even though Armand Berard, a Frenchman, was one of her lovers at the time.
3. KGB Archives, Vasiiev White Notebook #2 45: File 14449, Vol. 1 'Liza', Excerpt from letter to 'Arkhip' from C.
4. Baker, Robert K. *REZIDENT: The Espionage Odyssey of Soviet General Vasily Zarubin*. 2019 self-published.
5. US Department of State passport application # 78318, in the name of Edward Joseph Herbert: in FBI Washington Field Office letter to Director FBI (FBIHQ) dated December 5, 1947, entitled Vasili Mikhailovich Zubilin, was (with Aliases) Elizaveta Yurevnia Zubilin, was, INTERNAL SECURITY – R (Russia) (FBI File Number 100-3407 73).
6. Solow, Herbert. Stalin's American Passport Mill. *The American Mercury*, July 1939, pp 302–09.
   see also FBI HQ 100-340473, NYO Letter to FBI HQ dated April 25, 1949. 1 (Jimmy Sullivan Investigation).
7. Baker, REZIDENT.
8. Ibid.
9. Having a foreign birth certificate made out to a false name on a fake Czechoslovak passport would later prove to be an unending problem for him as he grew up and came of age in Moscow.

10. Baker, REZIDENT p. 134. Taken from Stavinsky, pp. 132–37, 149–53, 179–80.
11. F.30594 v.1 'Nikolay' to C. 1934 'On Morros.' Yellow Notebook #3 Text. Vassiliev Papers.

Chapter 11

1. Creelman, Eileen. 'Picture Plays and Players: Boris Morros, Paramount's Musical Director, Talks of Russia, Music and Caviar'. *New York Sun*, June 21, 1938.
2. Morros, Boris, *My Ten Years as a Counterspy*, Dell Paperbacks, New York, 1959, p. 11.
3. Gill, Jonathan, *Hollywood Double Agent: The True Tale of Boris Morros, Film Producer turned Cold War Spy*. Abrams Press, New York, 2020. p. 3.
4. Morros, p. 11.
5. Ibid, p.12.
6. Gill, p. 6.
7. Morros, p. 12.
8. Gill. p. 13.
9. Ibid, p. 12–13.
10. Ibid, p. 17.
11. Ibid, p. 24.
12. Ibid, p. 24.
13. Ibid. p. 25
14. Morros, p. 21.

Chapter 13

1. Not coincidentally, Americans booking Russian vacation tours did it through World Tourists Inc., an AMTORG subsidiary run by Yakub Golos, who was also responsible for creating American identities and acquiring US passports for Moscow Center operatives.
2. Dodd, *Embassy Eyes*, pp 24–25.
3. While none of Martha's letters to Boris are known to exist, his responses to them are included among her papers at the Library of Congress, and from his responses, much can be inferred about her letters' contents.
4. Weinstein and Vassiliev, *The Haunted Wood*, p. 51.

5. Cipher cable from 'Alexander' dated 3.3.37. White Notebook #2 - 49, p. 34 p. 35 p. 36 p. 37 p. 38.
6. Dodd, Embassy Eyes, p. 202.
7. Dodd, Embassy Eyes, pp 186–88.

Chapter 14
1. Currently called *Vladikavkaz*, capital of Russian Ossetian Republic.
2. Dodd, *Embassy Eyes*, pp 202–03.

Chapter 15
1. Boris to Martha, 11 July 1934, Box 10, Martha Dodd Papers, LOC.
2. Boris to Martha 5 August 1934, Box 10, Martha Dodd Papers, LOC.
3. Boris to Martha, 5 August 1934, Box 10, Martha Dodd Papers, LOC.
4. Carpozi, p.37.
5. Baker, p.212.

Chapter 16
1. 'Alexander' to Moscow Center 29 Oct 1934. Vassiliev White Notebook #2-45 pp. 13–17. File 1449 Vol. 1 'Liza'.
2. Rexford G. Tugwell was also Assistant Secretary of Agriculture under Henry Wallace.
3. Letter, Martha Dodd to Agnes Knickerbocker, 16 July 1969.

Chapter 17
1. Missing was Thornton Wilder, her long-time literary mentor, who was gay.
2. Donald, David Herbert, *Look Homeward; A Life of Thomas Wolfe*, NY, 1987. p.322–23.
3. Ledig-Rowohlt, *Thomas Wolfe in Berlin*. American Scholar, Spring, 1953, p. 186.
4. Fox writes: 'As Elizabeth Nowell compiled Wolfe's correspondence she found a number of letters concerning Martha that described her relationship with Wolfe in embarrassing language. Martha demanded that these letters be redacted as "they can have no serious import in the study of his life and letters

and knowing Tom's recklessness and inaccuracy they might very well be of a slanderous quality regarding my life, both politically and morally."' Nowell saw to it that the letters were 'sealed and in the safe'. Fox, p. 103.

5. Ibid.
6. BV letter to Moscow Center, 5 June 1935.
7. Sergei M. Kudryavtsev was a classic Moscow Center field man with journalistic cover. Stints in Ottawa, Ankara and all over South America. He happened to be in Havana during Castro's takeover in Cuba. Though Moscow had supported Castro, they actually knew very little about him or his group, and when they unexpectedly overthrew Batista, having no idea what to do next, they appointed Kudryavtsev Ambassador to Havana. Unschooled in diplomacy, Kudryavtsev approached the task like the spy he was. Within a year, Castro had him thrown out of Cuba in a minor diplomatic kerfuffle.
8. From a 16 Jan. 1936 letter from "Rudolf" to Moscow Center.
9. Emir's' report on meeting with 'L' on 16 January 1936.
10. Ibid.

Chapter 18

1. Memorandum on M. D. (apparently 1936) White Notebook #2 46.
2. Memorandum on M. D. (apparently 1936) White Notebook #2 46, p.25.
3. In the report, it's written down as 'P. Hirard', though this could be the result of misspelling by either Bukhartsev, a transcriber in Moscow, or by Vassiliev, the Western researcher allowed access by the KGB in 1991.
4. Letter, 'Rudolf' to Moscow Center, Sept 1936, White Notebook #2, 46, p. 18–25.
5. Letter, 'Rudolf' to Moscow Center, 29 October 1936, White Notebook #2 47, 31.
6. Letter from Martha to Vinogradov, 25 October 1936, White Notebook #2 47, p. 27
7. Letter from Martha to Vinogradov, 29 January 1937. White Notebook #2 48 p. 31, 33.
8. Prince Jan Adrezej Sapieha-Rozansky (1910–89).

9. Earl Browder, head of Communist Party USA, also a talent spotter and agent handler working directly for Moscow Center.
10. Letter from 'Alexander' dated 9 March 1937.
11. White Notebook #2 50, p. 39, 40, 41.
12. Ibid.
13. Strangely, Dodd seems to have left out the fact that on 29 July, after sailing out of Baltimore, the ship ran aground somewhere in Chesapeake Bay, enroute to Norfolk, where it remained for as much as a week and was considered so damaged, it was sold off to another company. Whether this odd omission should be attributed to Dodd himself, or Martha and Bill Jr, who edited it for publication, cannot be determined.
14. Apparently FDR was aware that Dodd's reports were now all handwritten, since he no longer trusted any of the embassy stenographers. George Messersmith, one of the few who could decipher them, had just returned to Washington, DC following his promotion as US Minister to Austria to Assistant Secretary of State. He indicated in his unpublished memoir that reading these handwritten reports made him realise Dodd's once-sharp mind was falling apart.
15. 'Alexander' to C, 5.11.37.
16. Alexander to C 12.11.37, White Notebook #2 53 pp. 50–52
17. 1947/48 reminiscence about Mildred. Martha Dodd Papers, LOC.

Chapter 19

1. Earl Browder was described as the CPUSA 'liaison' with NKVD.
2. Browder's niece Helen Lowry would later marry Iskhak Ahkmerov and, following the end of his American deployment, settle in Russia with him.
3. 13 April 1938, message from Gennady to Moscow Center, BLACK NOTEBOOK p.23.
4. Message, 25 May 1938, Nikolay (NY) to Moscow Center, found in both Black Notebook and White Notebook #2.
5. Letter, Martha Johns Dodd to William Dodd Jr, 29 November 1937, W. E. Dodd Papers, LOC.
6. 29 June 1938 Letter, Nikolay (NY) to Moscow Center, Black Notebook. p. 45 : 'Igor' contacted 'Liza' on 15.VI. Liza's first

question to Igor was, 'What happened to Vinogradov? Was he arrested?' Igor replied that Vinogradov works in Moscow, and that he was surprised at Liza's question. To this, Liza said that she had asked that question because she had not heard anything from Vinogradov in over a year. Vinogradov had promised to marry her as soon as he obtained permission in Moscow, and naturally, she had been waiting to hear from him. Now she wants to know what she should do about her domestic life – should she wait for Vinogradov or get married? She decided for herself that it was useless to wait for Vinogradov; she came to this decision following a conversation several months ago with the embassy counselor Umansky, who, it seems, had told her frankly that, first of all, he didn't know what had happened to Vinogradov, and second of all, he does not think that he would be able to marry her. She has a fiance at present; she wants to know what she should do – could she send an inquiry to Vinogradov by telegraph? If Vinogradov reaffirms his promise, she will wait for him and turn down her fiance. Her fiance – Adolf Stern, 40 years old, a Jew, a man of independent means, who had helped the Communist party with money when he was in Germany a couple of years ago. A liberal; at present, he has received an offer to work at the New York Housing Commission. She does not think her marriage would get in the way of her work with us, although she is not altogether sure what she should do.'

7. Boris' letter of April 29, 1938, Box 10, W. E. Dodd papers. LOC.
8. Letter, Martha Dodd to Boris Vinogradov, 9 July 1938. White Notebook #2, p. 70.

Chapter 20

1. Letter, NY to Moscow Center, 1 December, 1938, Black Notebook p.256.
2. Undated statement, White Notebook #2 p. 54.
3. Ibid.
4. Message, NY – Moscow C. 2.05.1939, Black Notebook, p.267.
5. Clipping from Baltimore Sun, 12/2/1938, Martha Dodd Papers, LOC.

6. Message, NY – Moscow Center, 2 March 1939, Black Notebook, p.169.
7. Message NY to Moscow Center, 13 December 1939, Black Notebook. p. 452.
8. Ibid.

Chapter 21

1. FBI HQ, File 100-340473 NY Office Letter to FBI HQ, 7 November 1948.
2. FBIHQ File 100-340473, letter to Washington Field Office, 22 November 1948.
3. Message from 'Liza' dated 26.12.41, re contacts, White Notebook #2 58 p. 118.
4. Boris Morros, My *Ten Years as a Counterspy*, pp.40–41.
5. Whitebook #1, Moscow Center to Maxim, 'On "Liza"', 24 June 1942 p. 176–77.
6. Message from Liza, 11-03-42 White Notebook #2, p. 59.

Chapter 22

1. During subsequent FBI investigations, Jane was often identified by informants as Martha's 'only friend'.
2. Yellow Notebook #3, 4.4.42 Memo on c/t from NY.
3. White Notebook #1, C. to Maxim 24.06.42, p. 176.
4. Ibid.
5. Ibid.
6. Morros, p.50. Morros puts the date of his father's arrival at 20 January 1943.
7. Morros, p.53.

Chapter 23

1. Morros, p. 58.
2. Ibid.
3. All this is Morros' version, of which there are many. None of which are exactly the same. Zarubin's version of these events is somewhat different. Writing about it from Moscow, eight months later, he describes driving up to Connecticut with Morros, but with Gennady, one of his deputies, doing the driving. At Ridgefield, which he mistakenly calls 'Richfield', he calls Stern

from the Western Union office. Stern shows up, but instead of leaving his automobile parked at the Western Union office, he and Morros get into Stern's car and leave their car there with Gennady watching over it.

4. In Boris Morros' book he indicates Zubilin introduced Alfred Stern to him as 'my good friend Alfred Stern'. In his FBI interrogations, he indicates otherwise.

5. Morros, p. 62.

Chapter 25

1. FBI Report, NY Field Office, 27 Oct.1944. 1 00-203583.
2. The 4 January 1945 report attributes the information to 'a confidential informant', not burglary.
3. '*Peter (Soble) was in Hollywood for ten days*,' someone, possibly Choudenko, wrote in the report to Moscow Center.
4. Vassiliez Yellow Notebook #3, 17, Report NY to Center dated 19 March 1945.
5. In his book, Morros writes: Boris Morros, of course, remembered it differently. 'By this time I had three shifts working in our little plant. There were turning out thirty thousand platters a day. They had to. Our "Nobody's home on the Range" was headed for the hit class.'
6. Yellow Notebook #3 P. 101.
7. Ibid.
8. Ibid. p. 103.
9. Unknown Artist, *The Mighty Pipe Organ*, ST6, ARA Records, Album 6.

Chapter 26

1. Janes's 'gift to Soble apparently marked the star of her career as a Soviet Agent'. Fox p. 224.
2. NKVD, Intelligence Dept of the Red Army, Intelligence Dept. of the Red Navy, and Political Section of the All Union Communist Party of Bolsheviks.

Chapter 29

1. FBI Report, New Haven FO 2/8/1950, 100-57453-423., cited in Fox, p. 255.

Chapter 30

1. In his doctoral dissertation, future FBI Chief Historian John Fox surmises the information probably came from a letter opened by the FBI's New Haven Field Office.
2. FBI letter, Director to SAC Gleason 9/22/1947, New York #100-57453-65.
3. The single reference the author has seen about Martha having sex with other womn is inside an FBI file. The woman in question was a concert pianist, connected to Boris Morros, ten years dead at the time of the reporting. The woman had been distraught on finding out she wouldn't be used in Morros' upcoming feature film *Carnegie Hall*. Morros brought her around to the Sterns'. She and Martha both got drunk and went for it, according to the confidential informant.

Chapter 31

1. Report 23 September 1948, FBI File NY 100-65568.
2. Ibid.
3. FBI Report 12/6/47 100-57453-160.
4. FBI File 12/6/47: 100-57453-160.

Chapter 32

1. FBI File NY 100-65568, Report of 11 Dec 1947, p. 77.
2. Author's note: There is much to suggest Informant T-1 was Leigh Melament, who had served as Zarubin's primary assistant and 'leg-woman' whenever he was operating in New York. She had been the subject of considerable FBI interest once her identity and address were revealed by Boris Morros, after which her name suddenly stopped being mentioned at all.
3. FBI File NY 100-65568 report of 9-23-48.
4. FBI File New York # 100-57453-212.
5. Wallace's chief speechwriter was Lew Frank Jr, a former 'peace mobiliser' whose tune conveniently changed once Hitler attacked Russia.
6. Likely Dexter Masters, the writer and pioneer anti-nuclear activist, who had also introduced them to Jane Foster.
7. FBI File 100-65568, p. 139.
8. FBI File 100-65568, p. 818.

9. White Notebook #2, p. 70: Meeting 8-7-48, Summerhouse in Lewisboro, NY.
10. Choice of Wallace or War, *The Dispatcher*. August 6,1948.
11. Vassiliev White Notebook #2 'C to Wash' Moscow center to Washington, 13-06-48. P. 70.

Chapter 33
1. FBI Report 100-57453, Serials 111, 154, 201, 227.

Chapter 35
1. Report by Col Mikhail Korneev, 17 Aug 1957, White Notebook #2, p. 39.
2. Ibid.
3. Ibid.
4. Ibid.
5. Ibid, p. 41.
6. Ibid, p.42.
7. Ibid, p. 41–42,
8. Interview with Sidney Rittenberg, 21 July 2015.

Chapter 36
1. Tuzex was the name of government-owned shops that sold 'luxury' foreign goods for either hard currency or 'bon' hard currency-convertible certificates. It allowed those Czechs with access to foreign currency to spend it on Western goods. Most ordinary Czechs never got to use them.

Chapter 39
1. Dr Myslyl insists this was not the case.